THE TERRITORIES
OF THE
RUSSIAN FEDERATION

THE TERRITORIES OF THE RUSSIAN FEDERATION

FIRST EDITION

EUROPA PUBLICATIONS LIMITED

First Edition 1999

© **Europa Publications Limited 1999**
18 Bedford Square, London, WC1B 3JN, United Kingdom

All rights reserved. No part of this publication may be photocopied, recorded, or otherwise reproduced, stored in a retrieval system or transmitted in any form or by any electronic or mechanical means without the prior permission of the copyright owner.

Australia and New Zealand
James Bennett Library Services, 3 Narabang Way, Belrose, NSW 2085, Australia

Japan
Maruzen Co Ltd, POB 5050, Tokyo International 100-31

ISBN 1-85743-070-0

ISSN 1465-461X

Typeset and imageset by UBL International and printed by Unwin Brothers Limited The Gresham Press, Old Woking, Surrey

(Members of the MPG Information Division)

Bound by MPG Books Limited, Bodmin, Cornwall

(All members of the Martins Printing Group)

Foreword

The first edition of *The Territories of the Russian Federation* aims to present an insight into an aspect of modern Russia that must be grasped if the country as a whole is to be understood. Not only is it often forgotten that Russia is a federal state, but also that it is still actually emerging as a federal state. The balance of power between the centre, represented by modern Russia's capricious tsar, Boris Yeltsin, and the federal subjects is not yet settled. With Yeltsin ailing and, to an extent, discredited by the financial crisis of August 1998, the political manoeuvrings of the regional grand dukes, as they position themselves for the succession to the nation's presidency, have significant ramifications for the development of the country. Likewise, the diverging economic fortunes of the different territories present another challenge to the structures of the state.

All the themes apparent in the Russian Federation as a whole are played out in its 89 constituent parts. Issues such as the balance of power between executive and legislative branches of government or the progress of market reforms are alive in the territories as much as in the national capital, Moscow. The shifting tides of personal politics reveal the same conflicting and concurrent flows, of liberalism and conservatism, of socialism and nationalism, and the attempts to balance the need for powerful supporters and the drift towards corruption.

This book is divided into three parts. Part One is an Introduction, with an authoritative article providing a context for regional politics and a description of the place of the territories in the national economy. There is also a Chronology of Russian history and politics, some invaluable statistics and information on the federal administration. Much of the economic data, the latest available, is for 1995/96, and clearly demonstrates the general trends of the economic situation. That time has only consolidated the differences between the regions is often made clear in the text of the Territorial Surveys. This, Part Two, is the heart of the book, with individual chapters on each of the 89 federal units. The geographical and historical background, the current political situation and an economic outline are reinforced by the names and contact details of the main officials in every territory. Each chapter includes a map of the federal unit, and there are, in addition, five maps covering wider geographical areas. The profusion of names and status revealed here can be confusing, but the Indexes of Part Three provide an alphabetic listing (including alternative or historical names) of the territories and also group them according to their geographical location within the Economic Areas into which Russia is also divided. As a whole, this book aims to furnish a clear and comprehensive introduction to federal Russia's regions, without an understanding of which the world's largest country must remain opaque.

January 1999

Acknowledgements

The editors gratefully acknowledge the co-operation, interest and advice of all who have contributed to this volume. We are also indebted to many organizations within the Russian Federation, such as the territorial administrations that responded to our enquiries, and, particularly to the State Committee of Statistics and the Russian Information Agency—Vesti. The BBC's *Summary of World Broadcasts: Part 1, Former USSR* has been invaluable for regular coverage of the regions. We owe special thanks to Rebecca Bomford and are very grateful to Eugene Fleury, who prepared the maps included in this book.

The authors of the introductory article, Professor Philip Hanson and Dr Michael J. Bradshaw, are both based at the University of Birmingham in the United Kingdom. Their research programme is one of the few in the world devoted to the federal territories of Russia, and some of the fruits of their studies into a number of the regional economies were scheduled for publication later in 1999.

Contents

List of Maps   page *ix*
Abbreviations   *x*

PART ONE
Introduction

The Territories and the Federation: An Economic Perspective
    PHILIP HANSON and MICHAEL J. BRADSHAW   3
Chronology of Russia   15
Statistics   22
The Government of the Russian Federation   29

PART TWO
Territorial Surveys

Autonomous Republics

Adygeya	37	Kareliya	75
Altai	40	Khakasiya	78
Bashkortostan	43	Komi	81
Buryatiya	47	Marii-El	84
Chechnya	50	Mordoviya	87
Chuvashiya	54	North Osetiya (Alaniya)	90
Dagestan	57	Sakha (Yakutiya)	94
Ingushetiya	61	Tatarstan	98
Karbardino-Balkariya	65	Tyva	101
Kalmykiya	68	Udmurtiya	104
Karachayevo-Cherkessiya	72		

Krais (Provinces)

Altai	107	Krasnoyarsk	116
Khabarovsk	110	Maritime (Primorye)	119
Krasnodar	113	Stavropol	123

Oblasts (Regions)

Amur	126	Ivanovo	148
Archangel	129	Kaliningrad	150
Astrakhan	132	Kaluga	153
Belgorod	135	Kamchatka	155
Bryansk	137	Kemerovo	158
Chelyabinsk	139	Kirov (Vyatka)	161
Chita	142	Kostroma	164
Irkutsk	145	Kurgan	166

CONTENTS

Kursk	168	Ryazan	206
Leningrad	170	Sakhalin	208
Lipetsk	172	Samara	211
Magadan	174	Saratov	214
Moscow	176	Smolensk	216
Murmansk	178	Sverdlovsk	218
Nizhnii Novgorod	181	Tambov	221
Novgorod	184	Tomsk	223
Novosibirsk	187	Tula	225
Omsk	190	Tver	228
Orel	193	Tyumen	231
Orenburg	195	Ulyanovsk	234
Penza	197	Vladimir	236
Perm	199	Volgograd	238
Pskov	201	Vologda	241
Rostov	203	Voronezh	243
		Yaroslavl	245

Federal Cities
   Moscow City   248   St Petersburg   251

Autonomous Oblast
   Jewish (Birobidzhan)   254

Autonomous Okrugs (Districts)

Aga-Buryat	256	Koryak	268
Chukchi	258	Nenets	270
Evenk	261	Taimyr (Dolgan-Nenets)	273
Khanty-Mansii	263	Ust-Orda Buryat	275
Komi-Permyak	266	Yamal-Nenets	277

PART THREE

Indexes

Alphabetic List of Territories (including a gazetteer of alternative names)   283
Economic Areas   285

List of Maps

European Russia	34
Asian Russia	35
Krasnoyarsk Krai	279
Archangel Oblast	279
Tyumen Oblast	280

Abbreviations

Acad.	Academician; Academy	Feb.	February
AD	anno domini	Fr	Father
Adm.	Admiral	Fri.	Friday
a/o	avtonomnyi okrug (autonomous okrug)	g	gram(s)
AO	Autonomous Oblast	GDP	gross domestic product
AOk	Autonomous Okrug	Gen.	General
ASSR	Autonomous Soviet Socialist Republic	GNP	gross national product
		Gov.	Governor
Aug.	August	Govt	Government
		GRP	gross regional product
BC	before Christ		
b/d	barrels per day	ha	hectares
Brig.	Brigadier	hl	hectolitre(s)
C	Centigrade	IMF	International Monetary Fund
c.	circa	in (ins)	inch (inches)
Capt.	Captain	Inc, Incorp., Incd	Incorporated
CIS	Commonwealth of Independent States		
cm	centimetre(s)	incl.	including
CMEA	Council for Mutual Economic Assistance	Is	Islands
Co	Company; County	Jan.	January
Col	Colonel	Jr	Junior
Commdr	Commander		
Commr	Commissioner	kg	kilogram(s)
Corpn	Corporation	KGB	Komitet Gosudarstvennoi Bezopasnosti (Committee for State Security)
CP	Communist Party		
CPSU	Communist Party of the Soviet Union		
		km	kilometre(s)
cu	cubic	kW	kilowatt(s)
		kWh	kilowatt hours
Dec.	December		
Dep.	Deputy	lb	pound(s)
Dr	Doctor	Lt, Lieut	Lieutenant
		Ltd	Limited
EBRD	European Bank for Reconstruction and Development	m	metre(s)
EC	European Community	m.	million
EEC	European Economic Community	Maj.	Major
e.g.	exempli gratia (for example)	mm	millimetre(s)
e-mail	electronic mail	MWh	megawatt hour(s)
et al.	et alii (and others)		
etc.	et cetera	n.a.	not available
EU	European Union	nab.	naberezhnaya (embankment, quai)
excl.	excluding	NATO	North Atlantic Treaty Organization
		NMP	net material product
F	Fahrenheit	no.	number
fax	facsimile	Nov.	November

Abbreviations

obl.	oblast (region)	sel.	seleniyi (settlement)
Oct.	October	Sept.	September
OECD	Organisation for Economic Co-operation and Development	sq	square (in measurements)
		SS	Saints
Ok	Okrug (district)	SSR	Soviet Socialist Republic
		St	Saint
p.	page	Supt	Superintendent
p.a.	per annum (yearly)	sv.	svetac (saint)
per.	pereulok (lane, alley)		
pl.	ploshchad (square)	tel.	telephone
PLC	Public Limited Company		
POB	Post Office Box		
pr.	prospekt (avenue)	UK	United Kingdom
Prof.	Professor	ul.	ulitsa (street)
prov.	provulok (lane)	UN	United Nations
		USSR	Union of Soviet Socialist Republics
q.v.	quod vide (to which refer)		
retd	retired	VAT	value added tax
Rev.	Reverend	Ven.	Venerable
RSFSR	Russian Soviet Federative Socialist Republic	viz.	videlicet (namely)
		vol.(s)	volume(s)

PART ONE
Introduction

The Territories and the Federation: An Economic Perspective

PHILIP HANSON and MICHAEL J. BRADSHAW

It is customary in Russia to speak of the Russian Federation as consisting of 89 'federal subjects'. To convey something of the reality of Russia's administrative regions, however, one must begin by emphasizing that these are not 89 units of equal status, nor is there comparable information on all of them. One of them, the Chechen Republic of Ichkeriya (Chechnya), is, *de facto*, a separate state, even though its secession has not been formally conceded by the federal authorities. Of the remaining 88, the 10 autonomous okrugs (AOks) and one autonomous oblast (AO) are, for most purposes, of lesser status than the 20 autonomous republics, 55 oblasts (regions) and krais (provinces) and two federal cities.

Nine of the autonomous okrugs (districts) officially form part of an oblast or krai. The Chukchi AOk (Chukotka), in the far north-east of Russia, facing the US state of Alaska, is an anomaly: it was taken out of Magadan Oblast in July 1992 and left as a free-standing okrug (free-standing, that is, in a purely administrative sense—in every other sense it is collapsing, the population having approximately halved between 1990 and 1998). The inappropriately named Jewish Autonomous Oblast, of which only 4.2% of the population was Jewish (according to the 1989 census), was separated from Khabarovsk Krai in 1991. The main point about most of the 11 'lesser autonomies', as they might be called, is that they are remote, backward and sparsely populated territories of little consequence. Many of the regional statistics available do not cover them separately. We shall, therefore, in this article refer mainly to the 77 territories with the status of autonomous republic, krai, oblast or federal city. These 77 can, generically, be labelled as 'regions'. Inconveniently, however, among the autonomous okrugs there are exceptions which are of great economic consequence. These are two remote, backward and sparsely populated districts which happen to be floating on oceans of petroleum and natural gas: the Khanty-Mansii and Yamal-Nenets AOks in Western Siberia. As might be expected, their local politicians are considerably more assertive than their counterparts in the other lesser autonomies. As a result, the nature of their administrative, electoral and fiscal relations with Tyumen Oblast, of which they form a part, is a matter of continuing dispute and negotiation.

In the remainder of this essay we shall first describe the evolving status of the Russian federal territories and their relations with central government; then review the differences in the economic development levels and production structures they inherited from the Soviet past; next discuss the different economic trajectories which different regions have followed since 1991; then look at the differences in economic conditions among them and their greatly differing investment potential; and, finally, offer some thoughts about the likely longer-term evolution of these enormously different territorial economies.

THE FEDERALIZATION OF RUSSIA

In Soviet times Russia was a nominal federation within a nominal federation which was, in fact, a unitary state. The quaint patchwork of 15 Union Republics (Soviet

Socialist Republics—SSRs), some of them sub-divided into autonomous republics and other administrative territories, was, in fact, managed by the apparatus of the Communist Party of the Soviet Union (CPSU). The Party's officials formed a clear hierarchy, with appointment from above. The territorial divisions were decorative. Part of the decoration consisted in assigning the names of particular national groups to areas historically associated with them. These labels can be grossly misleading. The Jewish AO, as has already been noted, is one such oddity. Located on the Chinese border and containing very few people recorded as Jewish, it was more a message to Soviet Jewry than any sort of homeland. Many other 'ethnic' territories are more in the nature of heritage sites. Thus, Evenks constituted 14.0% of the population of the Evenk AOk, while Khants were 0.9% and Mansi 0.5% of the inhabitants of the Khanty-Mansii AOk. Even at the higher level of republics, Russians are often in the majority in what are nominally ethnic-minority territories: 73.6% in Kareliya (Karelia), 57.7% in Komi, 60.8% in Mordoviya and 58.9% in Udmurtiya, for instance (all 1989 census figures).

In general, this Soviet legacy has been preserved in the existing administrative divisions within the Russian Federation. When the USSR disintegrated into 15 states there was some discussion of a reshaping of Russia's internal administrative boundaries into units consisting of comparable population size, without ethnic labels, but it came to nothing. Similar proposals surface again from time to time, usually from Russian nationalist politicians, but the regional political élites are now well-established in their existing spheres of influence. Change would be difficult. One consequence of this inheritance is that the 77 main territories or regions vary enormously in population—from just over 200,000 in the Republic of Altai in Western Siberia to 8.7m. in Moscow City (1996 figures). They also vary enormously in levels of economic development, a matter that will be dealt with in the next section.

Boundaries within independent Russia may have changed very little since the Soviet era, but the formal status of several territories has, however, been amended since 1991. While Russia was still part of the USSR, Boris Yeltsin (Russian leader since 1990 and President since 1991), notoriously, advised the local leaderships throughout the USSR to 'grab as much sovereignty as you can swallow'. He was then engaged in doing just that for the Russian Federation. The remark no doubt seemed like a good idea at the time. The 1990–91 'parade of sovereignties', however, did not stop at the level of Russia and the other 14 SSRs. Autonomous republics (then known as Autonomous Soviet Socialist Republics—ASSRs) sought to become Union Republics and autonomous okrugs sought to become autonomous republics. At a later stage, in 1992–95, a number of the territorial regions (oblasts and krais) flirted with the idea of declaring themselves to be republics (within Russia), because the powers of republics were, in some ways, greater.

More precisely, it was members of the regions' political élites who initiated such claims. The extent of popular support for autonomist assertiveness varies greatly. In some republics, such as Tatarstan, it is strong, at any rate among ethnic Tatars. In others, a common attitude is that living in an autonomous republic merely means paying more to support a more elaborate and costly government—which is routinely assumed to be corrupt anyway.

There is some evidence, from work by a US political scientist, Daniel Treisman, that in the early years of the post-Soviet Russian state the degree of autonomist assertiveness on the part of republics and autonomous okrugs was strongly influenced by their economic situation. In those territories with the most economic strength local élites tried hardest to extract more powers from the centre in order to make the most of the assets within their borders. Local politicians in weaker territories were less keen to offend the federal authorities in Moscow. Chechnya is, perhaps, the odd one out. Although a poor, mountainous region, its inhabitants had fought Russian invaders throughout much of the 19th century and in the last decade of the 20th century they saw an opportunity to express their feelings once more.

Such jostling for autonomy, or even independence, became possible with the collapse of the Communist monopoly on power. The regional élites were often little changed in personnel (one study in the mid-1990s found that about two-thirds of regional political élites were former members of the Communist-era regional nomenklatura). The chain of command from Moscow, however, had been broken as early as 1988, when Mikhail Gorbachev (the last Soviet leader, 1986–91) introduced the local election of regional leaders, in place of their appointment from above. This opened the way for the local Party chiefs of the old order (or, often, their deputies) to transform their Party positions into post-Communist power.

From the beginning of the post-Communist Russian state, therefore, there has been a shifting struggle over who was to have what powers at what levels. It is a struggle between the regions and the centre, but also a struggle among the regions. It has been further complicated by a struggle between the branches of government, notably the executive and legislative branches. Friction over budgets and other matters is a part of everyday political life in any federation and, indeed, in any state with different levels of government. What has been special in 1990s Russia is that a new state is being constructed. The rules of the political game were still to be established in 1992, and some of them still are. So far as the federal territories and the centre are concerned, the bargaining has been described by some as a process of 'federalization', the making of a real federation from the smallest of bases. There are other Russians of influence, however, who do not even concede that Russia should be a federation, and who argue even now, at the end of the 1990s, for the construction of a unitary state. None the less, it is on the whole federalization that has been occurring, with the centre becoming progressively weaker.

In March 1992, three months after Russia's emergence as an independent state, three federal treaties (sometimes known collectively as the Federation Treaty) were signed between the federal leadership, on the one hand, and, on the other, separately, the republics, krais, oblasts and autonomous okrugs. Two republics refused to sign: Tatarstan on the middle Volga and what was then the Chechen-Ingush ASSR in the North Caucasus. (Later Ingushetiya was hived off as a separate republic and the cities of Moscow and St Petersburg were granted the status of federal units.) These treaties set out three areas of competence: those that were exclusively federal, those that were shared and those that were exclusively sub-federal.

The powers of the federal centre were predictable. They included: defence; weapons production; foreign policy; the adoption, amendment and enforcement of federal laws; the establishment of federal legislative, executive and judicial bodies; the determination of internal boundaries; citizenship issues; the operation of the federal budget, the central bank and the money supply; and energy, transport and communications policies. The list of shared powers was long, and the treaties contained little guidance about just how these powers would be shared. Exclusively sub-national powers were merely whatever was left over. Relations between regional and sub-regional (local) government were left for later legislation and, in many ways, remain legally unclear now. For instance, there are no clear rules governing budgetary relations between regions and municipalities or rural districts.

So far as federal–territorial relations were concerned, the federal treaties of March 1992 left three important unresolved problems: the non-participation of two republics; the large and ill-defined area of shared powers; and language that appeared (although contradicted elsewhere in the text) to give republics more control than other regions over natural resources on their territories. These problems were compounded by two other circumstances. There was very little to guarantee that devolved responsibilities would be backed by devolved tax-raising powers— that is, the powers to set tax rates and tax bases. Moreover, the judicial system, in practice, was unsuited to act as an arbiter between the centre and the regions when there were clashes over the interpretation of these agreements.

The federal treaties were superseded by the new Russian Constitution approved in late 1993. This specified that where the federal treaties disagreed with the Constitution, the latter had priority. Also, the federal Constitution had precedence, in any conflicts, over sub-national constitutions or their equivalent. The new federal Constitution gave the President of the Russian Federation exceptionally strong powers. These were used to ensure that, for the next three years (approximately), regional governors were appointed and subject to dismissal by the President. That, however, did not apply to the republics, where the presidents were, and are, locally elected. It was only in 1996–97 that the executive heads of all the territories became formally answerable to their electorates rather than to the President.

Meanwhile, the Federation negotiated a series of so-called power-sharing treaties with individual territories. This began in February 1994 with Tatarstan, and had extended to more than one-half of the regions by late 1998. At that time the First Deputy Head of the Presidential Administration, Oleg Suysoyuv, spoke publicly of plans to discontinue the practice and, eventually, to reorder federal–territorial relations uniformly. The power-sharing treaties were anomalous, often allowing conflicting provisions in federal and regional constitutions simply to co-exist. A number of the treaties also included special arrangements on the retention of larger-than-normal shares of taxes collected within the borders of the territory concerned. This applied to Bashkortostan, Kareliya, Sakha (Yakutiya) and Tatarstan—all republics and all comparatively strong economically (Sakha, for instance, contained almost all Russia's diamond mining). Finally, these budget deals were, typically, not published.

'Asymmetric federalism' would be a generous description of the network of centre–territory relations which has emerged. There are probably more accurate descriptions. None the less, many observers have concluded that, however shocking the arrangements may seem to constitutional lawyers, they have probably helped as interim measures to hold Russia together. For much of the 1990s the centre has been weak and divided, with the President and parliament often in conflict and successive governments unable to implement key parts of their agendas (notably in tax collection). Consequently, all the territories, not just the favoured, strong republics, have had considerable leeway. In practice, even in 1993–97, regional governors often defied the centre and acted as though they more beholden to local élites than to a President who could, in theory, dismiss them. Thus, Yevgenii Nazdratenko, in the Maritime (Primorye) Krai on the Pacific coast, replaced a

Yeltsin-nominated reformer who did not please the local establishment. He has since run a grossly corrupt regime while defying the centre's efforts to remove him.

Until the 1998 Russian financial crisis four developments had tended to stabilize centre–territorial political relations. The Russian invasion of Chechnya in December 1994, although ill-managed, costly in human life and unsuccessful in its immediate aim, has acted as a deterrent to less determined and less advantageously located secessionists elsewhere. The development of the Federation Council, the upper house of the national parliament, as a body representing the territories, has facilitated accommodation between the centre and the periphery. The eight associations of territories (based on the 11 Economic Areas) had through 1997 begun to emerge as regular channels for informal policy consultation between the central government and representatives of the regions. These associations have no administrative powers, and all contain internal rivalries, but they had begun to supplement the Federation Council as an institutionalized communications channel. Finally, the Constitutional Court was beginning to act somewhat more independently and usefully in rulings over conflicts regarding the distribution of powers.

The financial crisis has undermined some of this progress. It has brought to the fore an underlying problem: the centre's dwindling power to provide economic help to weaker territories and to use economic levers to achieve some consistency in the implementation of economic policy across Russia.

ECONOMIC DIFFERENTIATION

Russian regional inequality in Soviet times is impossible to assess, chiefly because such data as there were on rouble incomes and outputs concealed differences in availability which, in a geographically huge, shortage economy, were probably very large indeed. It was well-known that the biggest cities had priority in the allocation of consumer goods. Many everyday items that were available much of the time in Moscow were completely unobtainable in many lesser cities and small towns. Then, as now, barter and subsistence food production loomed large in rural areas, and were poorly accounted for in statistical reporting.

It is nevertheless clear that in 1992 the new Russian state had inherited an exceptionally uneven array of regional development levels. Backward, rural territories had little in common with the very big cities such as Moscow, St Petersburg, Yekaterinburg, Nizhnii Novgorod and Samara. In 1991 both Dagestan and Tyva, for example, had rural populations of more than 50% of the total, while at the other end of the scale (omitting the far northern districts and cities with regional status) Kemerovo's rural population consisted of only 13% of the total and Samara's 19%. (The Russian average was 26%.) In a country where poverty was concentrated in rural areas, as it was in the USSR, these differences dictated large inequalities in average real incomes across the regions.

Later on in the 1990s, as local food-price controls waned and the measurement of regional inequalities became a little less problematic, it was clear that differences in territorial per-head real personal incomes were very large indeed. They were also getting larger over time. In November 1997 the average money income in Moscow city, divided by the cost of the 'subsistence minimum' basket of goods at local prices, was more than eight times the equivalent measure for Tyva. This is substantially greater than the range from poorest to richest region in the European Union (EU), using the EU's second-tier definition of 'region' (in which the average population size happens to be very close to that for Russian regions—1.9m.).

INTRODUCTION

The Moscow–Tyva difference is probably over-stated by this measure, because uncounted subsistence food production will loom larger in Tyva. Nevertheless, even if one guesses at a 'true' ratio of 6:1, the range is still enormous.

A more comprehensive measure of dispersion among regional average real incomes, the coefficient of variation, shows a clear, rapid increase after 1992. In that year it was 0.31. In late 1997 it was 0.50. This calculation gives a remarkable picture of a Russia where the regions' economic fortunes have been diverging rapidly since the end of Communist rule. It suggests that there is a large and growing capacity for inter-regional discord under the new economic order. Nevertheless, it does not follow that the centre should be trying to reduce the inequalities of the new Russia directly through regional policy. Inter-regional inequalities in real incomes do not, in fact, account for most of the inequality among Russian households. In other words, there are also very large inequalities within most of the territories. A calculation for November 1996 suggests that one standard measure of inequality, the decile ratio (the ratio of the incomes of the wealthiest 10% to those of the poorest 10% of the population), would have been only one-third as large as it actually was if there had been no inequality within regions and the only differences had been between regions. Still, the territories' divergence is a matter of concern. Whether it should be expected to get worse depends, of course, on what influences have been propelling it so far.

THE PROCESSES OF CHANGE AND THE ROLE OF THE CENTRE

So far as a territory's economic fortunes are concerned, the fundamental measure must be how well or how badly its inhabitants live. The real-income measures that can be made for contemporary Russia are full of problems: neither the data on money incomes nor the data on regional price levels are of good quality, and one cannot assume that the defects produce a bias that is uniform across regions. Regions with particularly large informal economies, such as Kaliningrad, are probably doing better than the official figures suggest; casual observation certainly supports this so far as the Baltic oblast is concerned. Still, the regions that are doing particularly well or particularly badly are probably reasonably well identified from the official statistics. To put these differences in perspective, it should be said that post-Communist economic adaptation in Russia as a whole has taken the form of collapse. Measured national income (gross domestic product—GDP) in 1998 was about 55% of the 1989 level. Only one region, Moscow city, has carried all the outward signs of economic success; and even in Moscow large parts of the population have been left behind and the whole surge of business activity in Moscow hit severe difficulties in 1998. However, a small number of other regions have adapted comparatively well; typically, these were territories which began to show real growth in output (gross regional product) in 1997, well above the marginal improvement of 0.8% recorded for Russian GDP as a whole.

Analyses of inter-regional differences in average real incomes suggest that two kinds of territory have fared less badly than the Russian average in the 1990s: those with particularly strong reserves of exploitable petroleum, gas, metals and hydro-power (such as Tyumen Oblast in Western Siberia and Irkutsk Oblast in Eastern Siberia); and a handful of regions that contain emerging commercial and financial 'hubs' (Moscow, Nizhnii Novgorod, St Petersburg, Samara and Sverdlovsk). St Petersburg apart, maritime 'gateway' territories, such as Kaliningrad (on the Baltic), Krasnodar (Black Sea) and the Maritime Krai (Pacific), have fared far less well than might have been expected. The reasons for this are not clear, but each has a traditionalist, even xenophobic, leadership. In addition, the Maritime Krai has suffered for reasons common to the Russian Far East as a whole (on which, more below).

Those regions where economic adaptation has been more uniformly gloomy are, not to put too fine a point upon it, all the rest. They fall into two main categories: the strongly rural and agricultural regions; and what might be called 'typical Russian regions', mainly industrial, but without the particular attributes that have favoured the emerging hub regions. The former have suffered from a lack of farm restructuring and a massive deterioration in agricultural prices relative to all other prices; the latter have been victims of the lack of competitiveness of Russian industry and have failed to develop new activities on any scale. The natural-resource and the hub regions have in common an engagement with the outside world, either as generators of exports to the West or as magnets for foreign business and for trading in imports, or both. Through 1994 the per-head inflow of foreign currency into a region was a statistically significant, positive influence on per-head real incomes. This influence shows up less clearly thereafter, as currency markets within Russia become more integrated, but it probably provides a clue to early adaptation. If so, this is not surprising. The domestic economy was collapsing, but Western demand for Russian energy and materials was growing; also, Russians' appetite for imports was massive, and incomes from the domestic distribution of imports grew fast.

The reasons why these particular hub regions have emerged are harder to determine. Econometric studies suggest that small business, the development of which in Russia has been generally very weak, has grown rather better in regions with large populations and, therefore, large domestic markets, other things being equal. It seems highly plausible that the development of financial and other services, stunted during the Soviet era, and of new lines of economic activity generally, would be easier in very large cities. In these very large communities a wide range of skills and lines of production are available. This must facilitate the recombining of capital and labour resources into new activities, as well as providing a large market for those activities. Demonstrating statistically that this particular factor has made a difference in Russia, if other factors are held constant, has so far proved to be difficult; but, in a looser sense, it might be said to fit the facts.

The advantages of being a hub region look more durable than those of being a natural-resource region. Energy and raw-materials reserves get depleted and their prices fluctuate. The slide in petroleum and natural-gas prices since 1996 has already made a difference to the regional rankings. In addition, it is in petroleum, gas, gold and diamonds that the Russian élites are most determined to maintain control of what they see as the serious earners. In many cases they are concerned simply to make private fortunes out of these assets, regardless of the long-term development of the business. Even where they do seem to be concerned with longer-run development, they have, hitherto, resisted any dilution of their control. The usual Russian stance is that Western money and Western technology are welcome, provided no Western control comes with them. Typically, such resistance is aided and abetted by regional political leaders, who usually have stakes in the major local assets or are 'cronies', friends or associates, of those who do.

One other factor has been of great importance for the territories of Russia's Far North and Far East. This is the erosion of the enormous subsidies to transport, energy and food supplies that had supported their development in the Soviet era. Most of that development would not have occurred in a market economy. Now that a market economy is being established, these regions have experienced exceptionally severe decline. One reaction has been a large out-migration from them during the 1990s.

These, then, are, in very crude summary, the factors that lie behind the sharp divergence of regional fortunes. It is doubtful whether differences in policies among regional leaders have made much difference to the outcomes. The economic structure inherited from the past, including population size and the presence or absence of major conurbations and natural-resource industries, look to be far more important. A few regional leaders, such as Boris Nemtsov in Nizhnii Novgorod (1991–97), have won reputations as serious reformers; but such cases are rare, and even they have worked with the grain of their region's inheritance. Governors who are overtly hostile to foreign business activity and economic restructuring, as in Krasnodar and Maritime Krais, may be capable of making things worse, but even then they are usually at odds with the mayors of their major cities. The latter, like most governors, tend to be pragmatists who see little benefit for themselves and their careers in making special efforts to block change. In Russia today, however, pragmatism on the part of regional leaders is a rather circumscribed virtue. All too often, governors and their deputies are close to the directors of major, and mostly dying, manufacturing enterprises in their regions. They have conspired to support those enterprises by countenancing the accumulation of payment arrears for electricity and taxes, and the substitution of over-valued barter items and promissory notes for money in such tax payments as are made. All of this has contributed to the unfortunate situation into which the Russian economy has descended.

Whether the economic policies of regional leaders are reformist or traditionalist, the centre now has little influence on them. This is, at first sight, paradoxical. After all, the largest tax revenues come from value added tax (VAT) and company profit taxes, for both of which the bases and rates are determined by the centre, with the revenue raised on each administrative territory split (in principle) into predetermined shares to be retained locally and remitted to the centre. The centre then makes transfers in the form of assistance to needy regions (the Fund for Federal Assistance to the Regions—its Russian acronym being FFPR). That would seem to leave many financial levers in the hands of the federal authorities. It is certainly not a set of arrangements that is popular with regional leaders. However, by 1997 regional budget spending (including local budgets, which are financed mainly by their regions) was slightly more than federal spending. The federal budget was in deficit, but so were all regional budgets, except that of Moscow city. Arrears of tax payments were growing, affecting all budgets adversely. The transfers from the centre were equivalent to about 1.5% of GDP, and falling. Moreover, they were being thinly spread across almost all regions. The leverage that the centre could exert on any territory by manipulating the FFPR was slight.

Reform of the transfer system was under discussion. In 1997 and early 1998 there was some consideration by World Bank and Russian government specialists of the possibility of the centre making its budgetary transfers to the regions conditional on their implementing reforms. An important example of such reforms is that of housing finance. Here federal policy was to reduce and retarget housing subsidies so that better-off families would pay cost-recovery charges for heating, light, water and building repairs, and housing subsidies would be concentrated on low-income families. Many Russian cities spend one-half their budgets on housing subsidies that go indiscriminately to all households, to the cost of health and education spending in the process. There was, therefore, a lot to be said for this idea. However, the pressures on the federal budget have meant that the total funding of regional transfers is likely to go on falling. If they are to amount to much in any region, they need to be concentrated on fewer regions. That, however, undermines their general use for leverage on regions' policies. Meanwhile, with the dismissal of Sergei Kiriyenko's Government in August 1998, and his replacement by Yevgenii Primakov as premier, the federal Government ceased to have a reform agenda to implement. At the same time, other channels of federal influence on the regions have narrowed. The centre had formulated a number of strategic development plans for particular regions, but these have simply not been funded. The bulk of large-scale privatization has been carried out; the scope for centre–territorial bargaining over control of that process has, therefore, dwindled. The placement of defence contracts in this or that region is no longer of much significance; there is now little confidence that if the federal government orders a ship, aeroplane or rocket it will pay for it. That leaves the central authorities with their general powers of legislation and some capacity for indirect economic influence (e.g. by raising or lowering import duties on products that compete with the production of a particular region).

Regional politicians still look to the centre and lobby institutions in Moscow, but there seems to be an element of inertia in this. In interviews, regional leaders are apt to complain that the centre is now just a source of trouble. Some regional policy-makers and administrators have openly questioned a system of remittances to the centre and transfers back to the federal territories. There may be little appetite for secession, but there is also little expectation that the central government will do much to stop the widening of the economic differences between the regions. In the long run, one might expect market forces to operate to reduce these differences—people migrating to higher-wage areas and capital migrating to lower-wage, less congested areas. However, this process could be very long term, and it requires a reasonably well-functioning market economy.

INVESTMENT POTENTIAL

Investment in Russia has fallen even faster than output. The country's capital stock has probably been shrinking, although changes in it cannot be measured with any confidence. Not surprisingly, while domestic investment has been collapsing, foreign investment has been small. A surge of foreign investment in 1996–97 was dominated by portfolio debt investment, mainly in government treasury bills (GKOs). Foreign portfolio investment in Russia merely rearranged the liabilities.

Foreign direct investment is of more substantial importance. It should, in principle, have added to production capacity. The cumulative total of such investment during the 1990s, according to Russian official statistics, was about US $14,000m. by the end of 1998, a tiny amount by world standards. It is this foreign direct investment (FDI), establishing or expanding joint ventures and wholly foreign-owned firms, that can flow to different Russian regions. Together with the growth of new small firms, it has probably been the major positive influence for economic recovery in Russia. The regional distribution of FDI reflects the perceived economic potential of activities in each region, allowing for the barriers to foreigners gaining significant control in those activities. In turn, FDI influences regional outcomes: it must usually have beneficial effects on a region's output. In practice, FDI has been heavily concentrated in Moscow city. At the end of 1997, according to Russian official statistics, Moscow contained 51% of all enterprises with foreign participation, accounted for the same percentage of domestic sales by such enterprises in that year and contributed 59% to their foreign-trade turnover. Such a concentration on the capital city is not unusual for FDI in former Communist countries. Some of it is no doubt recorded in Moscow only because head offices of large companies are often based there; insofar as the resource inflow goes through that head office to provincial production, the real concentration of FDI resources on the metropolis will be somewhat less. Still, there are many Russian regions that have received little or no foreign investment. For what the official figures are worth, the 10 leading regions for foreign investment in 1995–97 received almost three-quarters of all inward FDI; of this, around one-half was going into Moscow city and the rest was distributed in small parcels around an array of regions which changed from year to year. Moscow Oblast (located around the city), St Petersburg, Tyumen and Samara feature with some regularity and prominence. It is clear, however, that in a number of second-tier regions a particular investment project in a particular year can push that region, a little fortuitously, into a leading ranking.

Whether this pattern corresponds well to the potential of different Russian territories is not clear. Western investors can be assumed to know what they are doing, but one of the things they are forced to do is to take into account the obstacles placed in their way, often by regional administrations. There are, for instance, a number of natural-resource developments from which, as noted earlier, foreign business has been more or less excluded. Apart from direct investors, a number of research organizations have been evaluating the economies of Russia's territories. These organizations are mainly in Russia itself. Indeed, the compilation of regional ratings is one of the few Russian growth industries. Typically, they consist of rankings of regions by investment potential and/or risk, on the basis of a collection of diverse indicators. Some of the major producers of regional ratings are *Ekspert* magazine, the (unrelated) Expert Institute of the Russian Union of Industrialists and Entrepreneurs, the Federal Fund for the Support of Small Business (sponsoring a study by Irina Tikhomirova), Troika Dialog, and BankAustria (commissioning studies from the Institute for Advanced Studies in Vienna, Austria). Credit Suisse First Boston (CSFB) has produced a rating by credit-worthiness, an assessment more narrowly related to the territory's public finances.

That of CSFB apart, the purposes of these rankings are broadly similar: to assess the business climate, attractiveness for investment and risk levels associated with the various federal subjects. Their methods vary, but all perforce operate with official Russian statistics. The indicators used include a core of measures that are used by almost all of the ratings analysts: gross regional product, population size, per-head incomes (sometimes with adjustment for the still-large differences in regional prices, some without), strength of the regional budget (deficit as a percentage of expenditure, for example), volume of industrial output. Several try to incorporate measures of human capital, such as average years of education of the work-force, or infrastructure indicators, such as the number of telephones per 1,000 inhabitants. The weighting given to different indicators varies and is sometimes far from clear. We have taken three ratings that are very similar in purpose and devised a kind of 'poll of polls'. The three are the ratings of Troika Dialog (August 1997),

BankAustria (1998) and *Ekspert* (1998). They differ little in their selection of the most promising 10 territories; they differ rather more in their rankings within the 10, except that Moscow city comes out first in each of them. Combining the three (and assigning a ranking of 11th in the list in question to any region that is omitted from that particular list but does appear in the others), we get the following ranking of 10 (in descending order): Moscow city; St Petersburg; Tyumen Oblast; Sverdlovsk Oblast; Samara Oblast; Nizhnii Novgorod Oblast; Moscow Oblast; Krasnoyarsk Krai; Tatarstan; and Irkutsk Oblast.

This selection displays the mixture of emerging commercial hubs and natural-resource regions described earlier. They form the minority of Russian territories that have adapted less badly than most to the market, and they correspond fairly well to the rankings by inward FDI.

PROSPECTS

Output in Russia has been falling since 1989, with a brief halt in 1997. The financial crisis of 1998, with debt default and rouble devaluation in August, threatens to prolong that fall to the end of the millennium. The country has hitherto failed to develop a non-Communist social system that works. However, internal peace has been preserved (outside Chechnya), competitive elections are due in 1999–2000 and Russia's federal subjects have gained a considerable degree of self-government. It is true that in one case this self-government has taken the form of an eccentric personal despotism (Kalmykia), and in several other cases, such as the Maritime Krai, there is rule by a clique which persecutes opponents by illegal means. In many, perhaps most, of the territories of the Russian Federation the local regime is not oppressive.

The general economic decline and the sharp divergence in the regions' economic fortunes are the most fundamental problems that face Russia's regions. The impact of the 1998 financial crisis has probably been most severe in those territories that have hitherto been more successful. The natural-resource regions face declining world prices for their staple exports. The commercial hub regions have been especially affected by the turmoil in banks and financial services, and by the steep fall in imports. The evidence about regional impacts of the crisis is not yet clear, but it may well show that these reverses have slightly reduced the huge differences among the territories of the Federation. If so, however, it will have been a levelling down, conferring no benefits.

Most regional leaders reacted to the 1998 crisis in a thoroughly Soviet way. They imposed price controls on foodstuffs and, in many cases, tried to restrict the delivery of food outside their own regional borders. Superficially, this looks like another set-back for the development of a single economic space in the Russian Federation. It seems, however, that this may not, after all, have been the case. Evidence available by the end of 1998 is that controls on prices and the movement of goods have been ineffective. The development of private retailing and wholesaling has, perhaps, gone too far for such controls to endure. Moreover, the crisis may have imposed a more co-operative attitude in some unlikely places. A number of refractory regional leaders, such as Nazdratenko in the Maritime Krai, administer food-deficit regions. After playing for several years with threats of secession or something close to it, in the months after the August crisis Nazdratenko began to make public statements about the need to preserve a single economic space.

INTRODUCTION

In short, the 1998 crisis may have taught some useful lessons, not only to traditionalists in the national government, but to their counterparts at the level of the federal subjects. If Russia is to emerge from the present crisis with reasonable expedition, and eventually to embark on a sustained economic recovery, the regional élites will have to cease not only their futile attempts to micro-manage the economies of their regions with price controls, but also the support of 'crony' banks and companies in the name of 'stability'. Stability secured in this way blocks the growth of new and more productive activities. If the 1998 crisis has brought home the need to allow freer economic adjustment in the territories of the Russian Federation, it may have done some good.

Chronology of Russia

c. **878:** Kievan Rus, the first unified state of the Eastern Slavs, was founded, with Kiev (now in Ukraine) as its capital.

c. **988:** Volodymyr I (Vladimir 'the Great'), ruler of Kievan Rus, converted to Orthodox Christianity.

1237–40: The Russian principalities were invaded and conquered by the Mongol Tatars.

1462–1505: Reign of Ivan III of Muscovy (Moscow), who consolidated the independent Russian domains into a centralized state.

1480: Renunciation of Tatar suzerainty.

1533–84: Reign of Ivan IV ('the Terrible'), who began the eastern expansion of Russian territory.

1547: Ivan IV was crowned 'Tsar of Muscovy and all Russia'.

1552: Subjugation of the Khanate of Kazan.

1556: Subjugation of the Khanate of Astrakhan.

1581: Yermak Timofeyev, an adventurer, led an expedition to Siberia, pioneering Russian expansion beyond the Ural Mountains.

1645: A Russian settlement was established on the Sea of Okhotsk, on the coast of eastern Asia.

1654: Eastern Ukraine came under Russian rule as a result of the Treaty of Pereyaslavl.

1679: Russian pioneers reached the Kamchatka Peninsula and the Pacific Ocean.

1682–1725: Reign of Peter I ('the Great'), who established Russia as a European power, expanded its empire and modernized the civil and military institutions of the state.

1703: St Petersburg, which became the Russian capital, was founded at the mouth of the River Neva.

1721: Peter I, who was declared the 'Tsar of all the Russias', proclaimed the Russian Empire.

1728: The Treaty of Kyakhta with China secured the Russian annexation of Transbaikal.

1762–96: Reign of Catherine II ('the Great'—Princess Sophia of Anhaldt-Zerbst), who expanded the Empire in the south, after wars with the Ottoman Turks, and in the west, by the partition of Poland.

1774: By the Treaty of Kuçuk Kainavci with the Turks Russia gained a port on the Black Sea.

1783: Annexation of the Khanate of Crimea (now in Ukraine).

1801–25: Reign of Alexander I.

1809: Finland became a possession of the Russian Crown.

1812: The French under Napoleon I invaded Russia.

1825: Accession of Nicholas I, despite an unsuccessful coup attempt by a group of young officers known as the 'Decembrists'.

1853–56: The Crimean War was fought, in which the United Kingdom and France aided the Turks against Russia.

INTRODUCTION

1855–81: Reign of Alexander II, who introduced economic and legal reforms.

1859: The conquest of the eastern Caucasus was completed, following the surrender of rebel forces.

1860: Acquisition of provinces on the Sea of Japan from China and the establishment of Vladivostok.

1861: Emancipation of the serfs.

1864: Final defeat of the Circassian peoples and the confirmation of Russian hegemony in the Caucasus.

1867: The North American territory of Alaska was sold to the USA for US $7m.

1875: Acquisition of Sakhalin from Japan in exchange for the Kurile Islands.

1876: Subjugation of the last of the Central Asian khanates.

1881: Accession of Alexander III (upon the assassination of his father), who re-established autocratic principles of government.

1891: Construction of the Trans-Siberian Railway was begun.

1894–1917: Reign of Nicholas II, the last Tsar.

1898: The All-Russian Social Democratic Labour Party (RSDLP), a Marxist party, was founded, five years later splitting into 'Bolsheviks' (led by Lenin—Vladimir Ilych Ulyanov) and 'Mensheviks'.

1905: Russia's defeat in the Russo–Japanese War contributed to unrest which eventually forced the Tsar to introduce limited political reforms, including the holding of elections to a Duma (parliament).

1912: Lenin formally established a separate party for the Bolsheviks.

1914: Russia entered the First World War against Austria-Hungary, Germany and the Ottoman Empire. St Petersburg was renamed Petrograd.

2 March (New Style: 15 March) 1917: Abdication of Tsar Nicholas II after demonstrations and strikes in Petrograd; a Provisional Government took power.

25 October (7 November) 1917: The Bolsheviks overthrew the Provisional Government; the Russian Soviet Federative Socialist Republic (RSFSR or Russian Federation) was proclaimed.

6 January (19 January) 1918: The Constituent Assembly (elected in November 1917) was dissolved by the Bolsheviks, who were now engaged in a civil war against various anti-Communist leaders (the 'Whites').

14 February (Old Style: 1 February) 1918: First day upon which the Gregorian Calender took effect in Russia.

March 1918: Treaty of Brest-Litovsk: the Bolsheviks ceded large areas of western territory to Germany and recognized the independence of Finland and Ukraine. The capital of Russia was moved to Moscow.

10 July 1918: The first Constitution of the RSFSR was adopted by the Fifth All-Russian Congress of Soviets.

18 July 1918: Tsar Nicholas II and his family were murdered in Yekaterinburg (Sverdlovsk 1924–91) by Bolshevik troops.

11 November 1918: The Allied Armistice with Germany (which was denied its gains at Brest-Litovsk) ended the First World War.

March 1921: As the civil war ended, the harsh policy of 'War Communism' was replaced by the New Economic Policy (NEP), which allowed peasants and traders some economic freedom.

April 1922: Stalin (Iosif Vissarionovich Dzhugashvili) was elected General Secretary of the Bolshevik Russian Communist Party (RCP).

30 December 1922: The Union of Soviet Socialist Republics (USSR) was formed at the 10th All-Russian (first All-Union) Congress of Soviets by the RSFSR, Belarus, Transcaucasia, Ukraine and the Central Asian states of Khorezm and Bukhara.

21 January 1924: Death of Lenin; Stalin then consolidated his power.

31 January 1924: The first Constitution of the USSR was ratified. The RCP then became the Communist Party of the Soviet Union (CPSU).

1928: The NEP was abandoned; the forced collectivization of agriculture resulted in widespread famine.

5 December 1936: The second Constitution of the USSR (the 'Stalin' Constitution) was adopted—Kazakhstan was detached from the RSFSR, to become one of the 11 constituent Union Republics of the USSR. The decade was also dominated by a number of ruthless political purges.

1939: Following the Treaty of Non-Aggression with Germany (the Nazi–Soviet Pact), Soviet forces invaded eastern Poland and then Finland (the Baltic states and Bessarabia were annexed the following year).

22 June 1941: Germany invaded the USSR.

February 1943: German forces surrendered at Stalingrad (now Volgograd), marking the first reverse for the German Army. Soviet forces began to regain territory.

1944: In a consolidation of domestic authority, Stalin ordered a number of mass deportations of populations from the North Caucasus and Crimea. Tannu-Tuva (Tyva), a Russian protectorate from 1914, was formally incorporated into the USSR (as part of the RSFSR).

8 May 1945: The Red Army occupied the German capital, Berlin, and Germany subsequently capitulated; most of eastern and central Europe had come under Soviet control.

8 August 1945: The USSR declared war on Japan and occupied Sakhalin and the Kurile Islands.

January 1949: The Council for Mutual Economic Assistance (CMEA or Comecon) was established, as an economic alliance between the USSR and its Eastern European allies.

July 1949: The USSR exploded its first atomic bomb.

5 March 1953: Death of Stalin; he was replaced by a collective leadership.

September 1953: Nikita Khrushchev was elected First Secretary of the Central Committee of the CPSU.

14 May 1955: The Warsaw Treaty of Friendship, Co-operation and Mutual Assistance was signed by the USSR and its Eastern European satellites, establishing a military alliance known as the Warsaw Treaty Organization (or Warsaw Pact).

February 1956: At the 20th Party Congress Khrushchev denounced Stalin in the 'secret speech'.

November 1956: Soviet forces invaded Hungary to overthrow Imre Nagy's reformist Government.

October 1957: The USSR placed the first man-made satellite (Sputnik I) in orbit around the earth.

August 1960: Soviet technicians were recalled from the People's Republic of China, as part of the growing dispute between the two Communist countries.

INTRODUCTION

April 1961: The first manned space flight was undertaken by Maj. Yurii Gagarin on the Vostok I spacecraft.

October 1962: The discovery of Soviet nuclear missiles in Cuba by the USA led to the 'Cuban Missile Crisis'; tension eased when Khrushchev announced the withdrawal of the missiles, following a US blockade of the island.

October 1964: Khrushchev was deposed and replaced as First Secretary of the CPSU by Leonid Brezhnev.

August 1968: Soviet and other Warsaw Pact forces invaded Czechoslovakia to overthrow the reformist Government of Alexander Dubček.

May 1972: The US President, Richard Nixon, visited Moscow, thus marking a relaxation in Soviet–US relations, a process which came to be known as *détente*.

June 1977: Brezhnev became Chairman of the Presidium of the Supreme Soviet (titular head of state).

7 October 1977: The third Constitution of the USSR was adopted.

December 1979: Soviet forces invaded Afghanistan.

10 November 1982: Death of Leonid Brezhnev; Yurii Andropov succeeded him as Party leader.

9 February 1984: Death of Andropov; Konstantin Chernenko succeeded him as General Secretary.

10 March 1985: Death of Chernenko; he was succeeded as General Secretary of the CPSU by Mikhail Gorbachev.

February–March 1986: At the 27th Congress of the CPSU Gorbachev proposed radical economic and political reforms and 'new thinking' in foreign policy; emergence of the policy of *glasnost* (meaning a greater degree of freedom of expression).

26 April 1986: An explosion occurred at a nuclear reactor in Chernobyl (Chornobyl, Ukraine), which resulted in discharges of radioactive material.

July 1986: Soviet troops begin their withdrawal from Afghanistan (completed by February 1989).

October 1986: A summit took place in Reykjavík (Iceland), attended by Gorbachev and the US President, Ronald Reagan, at which the issue of nuclear disarmament was discussed.

January 1987: At a meeting of the CPSU Central Committee Gorbachev proposed plans for the restructuring (*perestroika*) of the economy.

June 1987: At local elections the CPSU nominated more than one candidate in some constituencies.

21 October 1987: Boris Yeltsin, who had been appointed First Secretary of the Moscow City Party Committee in 1985, resigned from the Politburo of the CPSU.

June 1988: A millennium of Christianity in Russia was celebrated with official approval.

6 December 1988: With the pace of domestic reform quickening, in a speech at the UN Gorbachev outlined his 'new thinking' on foreign policy.

25 March 1989: Multi-party elections to the newly established legislature, the Congress of People's Deputies, took place.

4 March 1990: Elections took place to the local and republican legislatures of the Russian Federation; reformists made substantial gains in the larger cities (elections elsewhere in the USSR produced overtly nationalist majorities in the Baltic republics and Moldova).

15 March 1990: The all-Union legislature approved the establishment of the post of President of the USSR and elected Mikhail Gorbachev to that office.

29 May 1990: Boris Yeltsin was elected as Chairman of the Supreme Soviet of the Russian Federation. Ten days later, with a background of increasing restiveness in a number of other Union Republics, the Russian parliament adopted a declaration of sovereignty within the USSR.

3 September 1990: Boris Yeltsin announced a 500-day programme of economic reform.

17 March 1991: In an all-Union referendum on the issue of the future state of the USSR, some 75% of participants approved Gorbachev's concept of a 'renewed federation' (several Union Republics did not participate).

12 June 1991: Yeltsin was elected President of the Russian Federation in direct elections, with Aleksandr Rutskoi, a former general in the Afghan war, as Vice-President. Residents of Leningrad (as it had been known since 1924) voted to change the city's name back to St Petersburg.

1 July 1991: The USSR, together with the other member countries of the Warsaw Pact, signed a protocol which formalized the dissolution of the alliance.

18–21 August 1991: An attempted *coup d'état* was frustrated by popular and institutional opposition, with Yeltsin prominent in the successful campaign to reinstate Gorbachev.

6 September 1991: The newly formed State Council, which comprised the supreme officials of the Union Republics, recognized the independence of Estonia, Latvia and Lithuania.

8 December 1991: The leaders of the Russian Federation, Belarus and Ukraine resolved to form a Commonwealth of Independent States (CIS) to replace the USSR—the so-called Minsk Agreement.

21 December 1991: At a meeting in Almaty (Kazakhstan) the leaders of 11 former Union Republics of the USSR signed a protocol on the formation of the new CIS.

25 December 1991: Mikhail Gorbachev formally resigned as President of the USSR, thereby confirming the effective dissolution of the Union.

2 January 1992: A radical economic reform programme was introduced in Russia.

31 March 1992: President Yeltsin and the leaders of the country's administrative units signed three documents together known as the Federation Treaty; representatives from the Chechen-Ingush ASSR and Tatarstan did not participate.

June 1992: Yeltsin appointed Yegor Gaidar, an economist and supporter of radical market reform, as Acting Prime Minister. Ingushetiya was recognized as a federal republic separate from Chechnya.

December 1992: The Russian legislature rejected Gaidar as Prime Minister; Viktor Chernomyrdin was appointed instead.

25 April 1993: In a referendum organized by President Yeltsin, in order to resolve the increasing conflict between the executive and legislature, 57.4% of the electorate endorsed the President and 70.6% voted in favour of early elections to parliament.

24 July 1993: In an attempt to control inflation in Russia, all rouble notes printed between 1961 and 1992 were withdrawn from circulation and replaced with new ones; this effectively ended the old Soviet 'rouble zone'.

31 August 1993: A majority of territorial leaders approved President Yeltsin's proposal for the establishment of a Federation Council, which convened in mid-September.

21 September 1993: Yeltsin issued a decree On Gradual Constitutional Reform (Decree 1,400), which suspended the powers of the legislature with immediate effect. The defiance of the legislators, and Vice-President Rutskoi, eventually provoked a state of emergency to be declared in Moscow on 3 October.

4 October 1993: The White House, the seat of the legislature, was shelled by government forces and severely damaged by fire; the leaders of the parliamentary revolt surrendered.

12 December 1993: A proposed new Constitution was approved by 58.4% of participating voters in a referendum. On the same day elections to the State Duma, the lower house of a new Federal Assembly (the upper house was provided by the Federation Council) were held.

11 October 1994: The rouble collapsed, losing almost one-quarter of its value against the US dollar.

11 December 1994: Following the collapse of peace negotiations earlier in the month, President Yeltsin ordered the invasion of Chechnya (which had ambitions to secede) by some 40,000 federal ground troops, who met with bitter resistance.

30 July 1995: Opposition to the continuing war in Chechnya prompted a military accord on the gradual disarmament of the Chechen rebels, in return for the partial withdrawal of federal troops from Chechnya; it remained in effect until October.

17 December 1995: At the general election the Communist Party of the Russian Federation (CPRF) achieved the greatest success, winning 22.3% of the votes cast; the radical nationalist Liberal Democratic Party of Russia (LDPR) won 11.2%, Our Home is Russia (a centre-right electoral bloc headed by Chernomyrdin) 10.1% and the liberal Yabloko 6.9%.

16 June 1996: Eleven candidates contested the presidential election; Yeltsin secured the greatest number of votes (35%), followed by the leader of the CPRF, Gennadii Zyuganov (32%); retired Lt-Gen. Aleksandr Lebed won an unexpectedly high level of support, with 15%, and was later appointed to the Government.

3 July 1996: Amid increasing speculation about his health, Boris Yeltsin won the second round of voting in the presidential election with 53.8% of the poll. Yeltsin was inaugurated as the first democratically elected President of post-Soviet Russia on 9 August.

31 August 1996: Lebed, who only survived in government until October, negotiated a cease-fire with the Chechen rebels; the so-called Khasvyurt Accords included postponing resolution of the issue of sovereignty until 2001.

March 1997: An extensive reorganization of the Government largely favoured reformists; Anatolii Chubais was returned to the cabinet as First Deputy Prime Minister and a post was also awarded to Boris Nemtsov, previously Governor of Nizhnii Novgorod Oblast.

3 November 1997: Russia and Japan agreed to aim for a formal peace treaty by 2000, to resolve the territorial dispute over the Kurile Islands and officially end the Second World War.

17 January 1998: A reallocation of cabinet portfolios, at the expense of Chubais (weakened by a scandal involving payments for a book) and Nemtsov, indicated further erosion of reformist influence, to the satisfaction of a critical parliament.

23 March 1998: Chernomyrdin and his Government were dismissed by President Yeltsin.

27 March 1998: Sergei Kiriyenko, a reformist, but hitherto not a prominent minister, was nominated as premier.

24 April 1998: Kiriyenko was confirmed as Prime Minister by the State Duma, having been rejected twice earlier in the month.

17 August 1998: Following an escalating financial crisis, and in a complete reversal of its monetary policies, the Government announced a series of emergency measures which included the effective devaluation of the rouble.

23 August 1998: President Yeltsin dismissed Kiriyenko's administration and reappointed Chernomyrdin premier.

31 August 1998: The State Duma rejected Chernomyrdin as Prime Minister.

7 September 1998: The State Duma, despite President Yeltsin's proposal to cede power to parliament, again overwhelmingly rejected Chernomyrdin's nomination.

11 September 1998: Nominated as a compromise candidate, the foreign minister, Yevgenii Primakov, was confirmed as premier by the State Duma; the same day two conservatives were appointed to key economic posts.

27 October 1998: Primakov visited Austria, to meet with European Union leaders, in place of the President, who was, again, ill.

5 November 1998: The Constitutional Court confirmed that Yeltsin was ineligible to stand for a further term in the presidency (a presidential election was scheduled for 2000 and a general election for 1999).

24 December 1998: In an address to the State Duma, the Prime Minister, Primakov, both stated a commitment to the market reforms and espoused a 'socially orientated' economy.

Statistics

MAJOR DEMOGRAPHIC AND ECONOMIC INDICATORS

	Area ('000 sq km)	Population at 1 Jan. 1996 ('000)	Population density, 1996 (per sq km)	Average annual increase in population, 1991–95 (%)	Life expectancy at birth, 1995
Autonomous Republics					
Adygeya	7.6	450	59.3	0.4	66.99
Altai	92.6	202	2.2	0.5	61.09
Bashkortostan	143.6	4,097	28.5	0.6	66.39
Buryatiya	351.3	1,053	3.0	-0.1	63.43
Chechnya	n.a.	921	n.a.	-8.4	n.a.
Chuvashiya	18.3	1,361	74.4	0.1	66.54
Dagestan	50.3	2,042	39.7	2.0	70.64
Ingushetiya	n.a.	300	n.a.	-31.8	71.34
Kabardino-Balkariya	12.5	790	63.2	0.2	68.69
Kalmykiya	76.1	319	4.2	-0.6	65.42
Karachayevo-Cherkessiya	14.1	436	30.9	0.3	69.81
Kareliya	172.4	785	4.6	-0.5	61.24
Khakasiya	61.9	586	9.5	0.2	62.31
Komi	415.9	1,185	2.9	-1.4	61.71
Marii-El	23.2	766	33.0	0.1	65.40
Mordoviya	26.2	956	36.5	-0.2	67.71
North Osetiya	8.0	663	82.8	-1.2	66.64
Sakha (Yakutiya)	3,103.2	1,023	0.3	-1.6	62.72
Tatarstan	68.0	3,760	55.3	0.4	66.98
Tyva	170.5	309	1.8	0.2	55.72
Udmurtiya	42.1	1,639	38.9	0.0	64.09
Krais					
Altai	169.1	2,690	15.9	0.2	64.55
Khabarovsk	788.6	1,571	2.0	-1.0	63.07
Krasnodar	76.0	5,044	66.4	1.3	65.74
Krasnoyarsk[1]	2,339.7	3,106	1.3	-0.4	62.54
Maritime (Primorye)	165.9	2,255	13.6	-0.6	63.44
Stavropol	66.5	2,667	40.1	1.3	66.97

Gross regional product, 1995 ('000m. roubles)	GRP per head, 1995 ('000 roubles)	Official rate of un- employment, 1995 (%)	Inflation rate, 1995 (%)†	Foreign investment, 1995 (US $'000)	
1,840.5	4,085.4	3.2	166	n.a.	Adygeya
906.1	5,526.8	2.3	90	5	Altai
39,435.9	9,645.8	2.5	126	2,485	Bashkortostan
7,737.3	7,350.0	2.1	135	599	Buryatiya
n.a.	n.a.	n.a.	n.a.	n.a.	Chechnya
7,518.6	5,525.2	8.3	152	889	Chuvashiya
4,148.2	1,992.1	8.3	139	34	Dagestan
562.7	1,940.4	n.a.	n.a.	n.a.	Ingushetiya
2,627.1	3,325.8	3.8	162	2,450	Kabardino-Balkariya
890.2	2,789.9	10.2	150	1,641	Kalmykiya
1,701.7	3,903.0	5.7	134	n.a.	Karachayevo-Cherkessiya
8,065.3	10,245.5	5.9	149	19,498	Kareliya
5,094.0	8,704.7	3.8	188	1,300	Khakasiya
19,395.1	16,250.7	6.5	146	33,812	Komi
3,927.2	5,124.8	5.3	151	75	Marii-El
5,012.0	5,223.4	7.3	125	2,130	Mordoviya
2,329.0	3,526.6	11.3	138	n.a.	North Osetiya
20,334.8	19,756.0	0.9	133	5,255	Sakha (Yakutiya)
37,829.5	10,067.2	1.5	134	160,640	Tatarstan
1,087.9	3,523.0	3.1	156	n.a.	Tyva
12,452.1	7,593.2	9.9	129	6,058	Udmurtiya
14,887.6	5,526.8	3.2	143	28,529	Altai
15,074.1	9,543.0	6.0	118	32,801	Khabarovsk
30,943.4	6,159.0	2.0	138	26,685	Krasnodar
44,098.9	14,173.8	3.4	164	363	Krasnoyarsk[1]
19,290.2	8,519.3	3.3	122	18,828	Maritime (Primorye)
18,171.7	6,835.1	2.0	141	19,558	Stavropol

INTRODUCTION

MAJOR DEMOGRAPHIC AND ECONOMIC INDICATORS (continued)

	Area ('000 sq km)	Population at 1 Jan. 1996 ('000)	Population density, 1996 (per sq km)	Average annual increase in population, 1991–95 (%)	Life expectancy at birth, 1995
Oblasts					
Amur	363.7	1,038	2.9	-0.9	63.68
Archangel[2]	587.4	1,521	2.6	-0.8	63.38
Astrakhan	44.1	1,029	23.3	0.5	66.11
Belgorod	27.1	1,469	54.2	1.1	68.16
Bryansk	34.9	1,480	42.4	0.3	66.57
Chelyabinsk	87.9	3,689	42.0	-0.2	64.61
Chita[3]	431.5	1,295	3.0	-0.6	62.28
Irkutsk[4]	767.9	2,795	3.6	-0.2	61.16
Ivanovo	21.8	1,266	58.1	-0.5	64.33
Kaliningrad	15.1	932	61.7	1.0	64.81
Kaluga	29.9	1,097	36.7	0.4	64.92
Kamchatka[5]	472.3	411	0.9	-3.4	61.57
Kemerovo	95.5	3,063	32.1	-0.3	61.61
Kirov (Vyatka)	120.8	1,634	13.5	-0.3	64.91
Kostroma	60.1	806	13.4	-0.1	64.69
Kurgan	71.0	1,112	15.7	-0.1	65.25
Kursk	29.8	1,347	45.2	0.2	66.37
Leningrad[6]	n.a.	1,676	n.a.	0.0	62.25
Lipetsk	24.1	1,250	51.9	-0.3	66.28
Magadan	461.4	258	0.6	-8.2	61.02
Moscow[7]	n.a.	6,597	n.a.	-0.4	63.98
Murmansk	144.9	1,048	7.2	-2.3	63.77
Nizhnii Novgorod	76.9	3,727	48.5	-0.3	64.47
Novgorod	55.3	743	13.4	-0.3	62.14
Novosibirsk	178.2	2,749	15.4	-0.1	65.37
Omsk	139.7	2,176	15.6	0.1	66.51
Orel	24.7	914	37.0	0.3	65.87
Orenburg	124.0	2,229	18.0	0.6	65.42
Penza	43.2	1,562	36.2	0.1	67.19
Perm[8]	160.6	3,009	18.7	-0.4	63.10
Pskov	55.3	832	15.1	-0.3	62.21
Rostov	100.8	4,425	43.9	0.4	65.51
Ryazan	39.6	1,325	33.5	-0.4	65.07
Sakhalin	87.1	648	7.4	-2.6	55.34
Samara	53.6	3,312	61.8	0.4	65.56
Saratov	100.2	2,739	27.3	0.3	66.14
Smolensk	49.8	1,172	23.5	0.2	65.07
Sverdlovsk	194.8	4,686	24.1	-0.5	63.99
Tambov	34.3	1,310	38.2	0.0	66.02
Tomsk	316.9	1,078	3.4	-0.2	64.22
Tula	25.7	1,815	70.6	-0.4	63.81
Tver	84.1	1,651	19.6	-0.3	63.31
Tyumen[9]	1,435.2	3,170	2.2	0.3	63.96
Ulyanovsk	37.3	1,495	40.1	0.9	66.75
Vladimir	29.0	1,645	56.7	-0.2	65.16
Volgograd	113.9	2,704	23.7	0.6	66.73
Vologda	145.7	1,350	9.3	-0.2	64.26
Voronezh	52.4	2,504	47.8	0.3	67.33
Yaroslavl	36.4	1,451	39.9	-0.4	65.07

Gross regional product, 1995 ('000m. roubles)	GRP per head, 1995 ('000 roubles)	Official rate of un-employment, 1995 (%)	Inflation rate, 1995 (%)†	Foreign investment, 1995 (US $'000)	
8,326.3	8,011.4	6.2	118	883	. . . . Amur
14,263.1	9,336.3	8.0	145	2,723	. . . Archangel[2]
5,746.6	5,597.7	5.2	160	92	. . . Astrakhan
12,585.9	8,598.7	1.1	128	53	. . . Belgorod
7,801.5	5,272.3	5.9	161	3,090	. . . . Bryansk
33,126.8	8,967.3	2.1	106	17,222	. . . Chelyabinsk
10,037.1	7,738.7	3.5	137	124	. . . . Chita[3]
34,301.2	12,251.3	3.5	140	19,790	. . . . Irkutsk[4]
6,442.7	5,070.6	1.5	138	761	. . . . Ivanovo
5,258.2	5,658.2	6.4	142	8,330	. . . Kaliningrad
8,124.4	7,413.4	2.8	157	666	. . . . Kaluga
5,415.2	12,973.7	5.0	139	794	. . . Kamchatka[5]
36,371.7	11,844.8	1.9	134	1,359	. . . Kemerovo
11,753.6	7,168.1	n/a	134	459	. . Kirov (Vyatka)
5,918.2	7,330.8	8.6	145	21	. . . . Kostroma
6,342.5	5,690.9	7.1	146	24	. . . . Kurgan
9,621.0	7,137.8	1.6	151	901	. . . . Kursk
12,507.1	7,466.9	6.0	131	20,264	. . . Leningrad[6]
13,794.7	11,034.9	1.3	156	3,648	. . . . Lipetsk
3,373.7	12,555.7	11.9	100	13,784	. . . . Magadan
47,607.7	7,201.2	2.9	105	205,012	. . . Moscow[7]
14,357.7	13,577.0	6.9	131	3,025	. . . Murmansk
35,172.3	9,420.2	3.1	112	59,837	. Nizhnii Novgorod
4,407.9	5,923.8	4.3	140	10,333	. . . Novgorod
23,025.2	8,377.4	2.2	116	58,445	. . . Novosibirsk
20,762.4	9,532.8	2.6	125	1,528	. . . . Omsk
6,021.2	6,580.5	2.4	139	18,284	. . . . Orel
18,136.1	8,147.4	0.9	145	720	. . . Orenburg
7,475.3	4,779.3	n/a	141	1,167	. . . . Penza
37,081.0	12,291.5	5.1	119	15,752	. . . . Perm[8]
4,618.3	5,538.9	7.2	136	792	. . . . Pskov
26,338.6	5,949.1	1.4	126	99	. . . Rostov
10,428.2	7,847.3	2.0	169	1,357	. . . Ryazan
6,929.0	10,490.5	6.2	139	48,167	. . . Sakhalin
45,031.6	13,611.7	2.1	135	69,693	. . . . Samara
20,425.6	7,456.2	3.8	125	18,044	. . . . Saratov
7,848.2	6,692.4	n/a	142	5,733	. . . Smolensk
58,097.9	12,376.0	3.8	114	8,386	. . . Sverdlovsk
6,547.8	4,987.3	5.6	145	n.a.	. . . . Tambov
12,828.6	11,896.0	4.5	141	44,338	. . . . Tomsk
12,436.9	6,833.1	1.9	125	12,928	. . . . Tula
11,618.3	7,033.7	2.0	127	67,212	. . . . Tver
108,885.1	34,421.4	2.6	123	102,580	. . . Tyumen[9]
10,695.8	7,160.6	3.6	132	260	. . . Ulyanovsk
10,679.3	6,487.6	5.7	140	5,300	. . . Vladimir
19,629.8	7,272.7	1.5	135	17,341	. . Volgograd
19,326.8	14,292.9	3.1	147	20,004	. . . Vologda
16,535.0	6,600.0	2.2	140	23	. . . Voronezh
14,763.1	10,155.5	9.4	133	395	. . . Yaroslavl

25

MAJOR DEMOGRAPHIC AND ECONOMIC INDICATORS (continued)

	Area ('000 sq km)	Population at 1 Jan. 1996 ('000)	Population density, 1996 (per sq km)	Average annual increase in population, 1991–95 (%)	Life expectancy at birth, 1995
Federal Cities					
Moscow City	n.a.	8,664	n.a.	-0.8	64.95
St Petersburg	n.a.	4,801	n.a.	-1.0	66.12
Autonomous Oblast					
Jewish (Birobidzhan)	36.0	210	5.8	-1.3	61.06
Autonomous Okrugs					
Aga-Buryat	19.0	79	4.2	0.0	n.a.
Chukchi	737.7	91	0.1	-11.1	62.64
Evenk	767.6	20	0.03	-5.4	n.a.
Khanty-Mansii	523.1	1,331	2.5	0.5	n.a.
Komi-Permyak	32.9	157	4.8	-0.5	n.a.
Koryak	301.5	33	0.1	-4.1	n.a.
Nenets	176.7	48	0.3	-2.9	n.a.
Taimyr (Dolgan-Nenets)	862.1	47	0.1	-0.3	n.a.
Ust-Orda Buryat	22.4	143	6.4	0.5	n.a.
Yamal-Nenets	750.3	488	0.7	0.5	n.a.
Russian Federation	17,075.4	147,976	8.7	0.0	64.60

[1] Figures for Krasnoyarsk Krai include Evenk and Taimyr AOks.
[2] Figures for Archangel Oblast include Nenets AOk.
[3] Figures for Chita Oblast include Aga-Buryat AOk.
[4] Figures for Irkutsk Oblast include Ust-Orda Buryat AOk.
[5] Figures for Kamchatka Oblast include Koryak AOk.
[6] Figures for Leningrad Oblast exclude St Petersburg.
[7] Figures for Moscow Oblast exclude Moscow city.
[8] Figures for Perm Oblast include Komi-Permyak AOk.
[9] Figures for Tyumen Oblast include Khanty-Mansii and Yamal-Nenets AOks.

Source: mainly Goskomstat, *The Regions of Russia*, 2 vols (in Russian). Moscow, 1998.

Gross regional product, 1995 ('000m. roubles)	GRP per head, 1995 ('000 roubles)	Official rate of un-employment, 1995 (%)	Inflation rate, 1995 (%)†	Foreign investment, 1995 (US $'000)	
144,370.3	16,611.7	0.5	143	1,312,396	. . Moscow City
47,011.6	9,753.6	1.7	125	154,727	. . St Petersburg
1,188.9	5,637.1	3.7	145	n.a.	.Jewish (Birobidzhan)
n.a.	n.a.	n.a.	n.a.	n.a.	. . . Aga-Buryat
1,344.6	14,138.7	5.5	n.a.	n.a.	. . . .Chukchi
n.a.	n.a.	n.a.	n.a.	n.a.	. . . . Evenk
n.a.	n.a.	n.a.	n.a.	n.a.	. . Khanty-Mansii
n.a.	n.a.	n.a.	n.a.	n.a.	. . Komi-Permyak
n.a.	n.a.	9.0	n.a.	n.a.	. . . . Koryak
n.a.	n.a.	n.a.	n.a.	n.a.	. . . . Nenets
n.a.	n.a.	n.a.	n.a.	n.a.	Taimyr (Dolgan-Nenets)
n.a.	n.a.	n.a.	n.a.	n.a.	. Ust-Orda Buryat
n.a.	n.a.	n.a.	n.a.	n.a.	. . Yamal-Nenets
1,630,078.9*	11,003.5*	n.a.	131	2,796,747	. **Russian Federation**

* The Russian Federation figure is for gross domestic product or GDP per head.
† Percentage change in the consumer price index, Dec.–Dec.

INTRODUCTION

RUSSIAN CURRENCY AND EXCHANGE RATES

Monetary Units
100 kopeks = 1 new Russian rouble (rubl or ruble).

Sterling and Dollar Equivalents (31 December 1998)
£1 = 35.85 roubles;
US $1 = 21.55 roubles;
1,000 roubles = £27.89 = $46.40.

Euro Equivalent (8 January 1999)
1,000 roubles =   37.11.

Average Exchange Rates (roubles per US dollar)
1995	4.5592
1996	5.1208
1997	5.7848

On 1 January 1998 the new rouble, equivalent to 1,000 of the former units, was introduced. Figures in this book are expressed in terms of old roubles unless otherwise indicated.

RUSSIAN INFLATION

The average annual increase in consumer prices in the Russian Federation as a whole, according to official figures as of 31 December 1998, was:
1996	21.8%
1997	11.0%
1998	84.4%

In 1995, according to official figures as given for the territories above, the increase in consumer prices was 131%. For the same year the International Monetary Fund cites a figure of 197% (48% in 1996 and 15% in 1997).

The Government of the Russian Federation

(1 January 1999)

According to the Constitution of December 1993, the Russian Federation is a democratic, federative, multi-ethnic republic, in which state power is divided between the executive, the legislature and the judiciary, which are independent of one another. The President of the Russian Federation is Head of State and Commander-in-Chief of the Armed Forces. The President, who wields considerable executive authority, is elected for a term of four years by universal direct suffrage. The President appoints the Chairman (Prime Minister) of the Government, but the cabinet must be approved by the legislature. Supreme legislative power is vested in a bicameral Federal Assembly.

There are 89 members (federal territorial units) of the Russian Federation. The recognized territories consist of 21 autonomous republics, six krais (provinces), 49 oblasts (regions), two cities of federal status, one autonomous oblast and 10 autonomous okrugs (districts). Largely based on the old Soviet divisions, their status as constituent members of the Federation began to be regularized by the so-called Federation Treaty of 31 March 1992. These three documents provided for a union of 20 republics (16 of which had been Autonomous Soviet Socialist Republics—ASSRs under the old regime, and four of which were autonomous oblasts), six krais and one autonomous oblast. The 10 autonomous okrugs remained under the jurisdiction of the krai or oblast within which they were located (a situation which largely continued throughout the 1990s) but, as federal units, were raised to the same status as oblasts and krais. A further republic, Ingushetiya, was acknowledged in June 1992. Moscow and St Petersburg subsequently assumed the status of federal cities.

Under the terms of the 1992 treaties, republics were granted far wider-reaching powers than the other federal units, specifically over the use of natural resources and land. They consequently represent autonomous states within the Russian Federation, as opposed to being merely administrative units of a unitary state. The exact delimitation of powers remained controversial and, often, modified by bilateral treaty between a territory and the central authorities. This process began in 1995 with treaties with seven republics and one oblast, but by the end of 1998 more than one-half of all the territories had signed such agreements. In March 1996 the precise terms of the delimitation of jurisdiction and powers between federal and regional authorities was decreed; no treaty could change the status of a federal unit, threaten the territorial integrity of the Russian Federation or violate the terms of the federal Constitution.

Autonomous republics, autonomous okrugs and the autonomous oblast are ethnically defined, while krais and oblasts are defined on territorial grounds. Each of the federal units is grouped into one of 11 economic areas (see the index of territories by area in Part Three, at the end of the book). These are the Central Economic Area, the Central Chernozem (Black Earth) Economic Area, the Eastern Siberian Economic Area, the Far Eastern (sometimes known as the Pacific) Economic Area, the North Caucasus Economic Area, the North-Western Economic Area, the Northern Economic Area, the Urals Economic Area, the Volga Economic Area, the Volga-Vyatka Economic Area and the Western Siberian Economic Area.

Of the 89 members of the Russian Federation, the 21 republics are each administered by a president and/or prime minister. The remaining federal units are governed by a local administration, the head (governor) of which is the highest official in the territory, and a representative assembly (usually known as a soviet or duma). Governors are able to veto regional legislation, although their vetoes may be overridden by a two-thirds parliamentary majority. The federal legislature, which created the post of governor in August 1991, intended that the official be elected by popular vote. The federal President, Boris Yeltsin, however, secured an agreement that the governors be appointed. In many regions conflict subsequently arose between the executive and legislative bodies, as the presidential appointees encountered much resistance from the Communist-dominated assemblies. In those cases where a vote of 'no confidence' was passed in the governor, elections were permitted. (This occurred in seven oblasts and one krai in December 1992.) Following President Yeltsin's dissolution of the Russian legislature in September 1993, and parliament's violent resistance, it was announced that all heads of local administrations would, henceforth, be appointed and dismissed by presidential decree. In response to increasing pressure, however, this ruling was relaxed in December 1995, when gubernatorial elections were held in one krai and 11 oblasts. Elections had taken place in a further 10 regions by February 1996, with the majority (45 in krais, oblasts and autonomous okrugs; five in autonomous republics) being held between 1 September and 12 January 1997.

Head of State

President of the Russian Federation: BORIS N. YELTSIN (elected President 12 June 1991; re-elected 3 July 1996).

PRESIDENTIAL ADMINISTRATION

Office of the President: 103132 Moscow, The Kremlin; tel. (095) 20-02-66; Head Col-Gen. NIKOLAI BORDIUZHA; First Deputy Head (Regional and Nationalities Policy) OLEG SYUSOYUV.

The Government

Chairman (Prime Minister): YEVGENII M. PRIMAKOV.
First Deputy Chairmen: VADIM GUSTOV, YURII MASLYUKOV.
Deputy Chairmen: VLADIMIR B. BULGAK, VALENTINA MATVIYENKO, GENNADII KULIK.
Minister of Agriculture and Foodstuffs: VIKTOR A. SEMENOV.
Minister of Antimonopoly Policy and Support for Entrepreneurship: GENNADII KHODYREV.
Minister of Commonwealth of Independent States Affairs: BORIS PASTUKHOV.
Minister of Civil Defence, Emergencies and Clean-up Operations: Col-Gen. SERGEI K. SHOIGU.

Minister of Culture: VLADIMIR YEGOROV.
Minister of Defence: Gen. IGOR D. SERGEYEV.
Minister of the Economy: ANDREI SHAPOVLYANTS.
Minister of Finance: MIKHAIL M. ZADORNOV.
Minister of Foreign Affairs: IGOR IVANOV.
Minister of Fuel and Power Industry: SERGEI VLADIMIROVICH GENERALOV.
Minister of General Education and Vocational Training: VLADIMIR FILIPPOV.
Minister of Health: VLADIMIR STARODUBOV.
Minister of Internal Affairs: SERGEI V. STEPASHIN.
Minister of Justice: PAVEL VLADIMIROVICH KRASHENINNIKOV.
Minister of Labour and Social Development: SERGEI KALASHNIKOV.
Minister for Nationalities Policy: RAMAZAN ABDULATIPOV.
Minister of Natural Resources: (vacant).
Minister of Nuclear Energy: YEVGENII ADAMOV.
Minister of Railways: NIKOLAI YE. AKSENENKO.
Minister of Regional Policy: VALERII KIRPICHNIKOV.
Minister of Science and Technology: MIKHAIL KIRPICHNIKOV.
Minister of State Property: FARIT RAFIKOVICH GAZIZULIN.
Minister of Trade: GEORGII GABUNIYA.
Minister of Transport: SERGEI OTTOVICH FRANK.
Head of the Presidential Administration: Col-Gen. NIKOLAI BORDIUZHA.

MINISTRIES

Office of the Government: 103274 Moscow, Krasnopresnenskaya nab. 2; tel. (095) 925-35-81; fax (095) 205-43-30.
Ministry of Agriculture and Foodstuffs: 107139 Moscow, Orlikov per. 1/11; tel. (095) 207-80-00; telex 411258; fax (095) 207-83-62.
Ministry of Antimonopoly Policy and Support for Entrepreneurship: Moscow.
Ministry of Commonwealth of Independent States Affairs: Moscow.
Ministry of Civil Defence, Emergencies and Clean-up Operations: 103012 Moscow, Teatralnyi proyezd 3; tel. (095) 926-39-01; telex 412327; fax (095) 924-19-46.
Ministry of Culture: 103074 Moscow, Kitaigorodskii proyezd 7; tel. (095) 925-11-95; telex 412101; fax (095) 928-17-91.
Ministry of Defence: 103160 Moscow, ul. Myasnitskaya 37; tel. (095) 296-89-00.
Ministry of the Economy: 103025 Moscow, Novyi Arbat 19; tel. (095) 203-58-78; fax (095) 203-74-82.
Ministry of Finance: 103097 Moscow, ul. Ilinka 9; tel. (095) 925-08-89; fax (095) 924-69-89.
Ministry of Foreign Affairs: 121200 Moscow, Smolenskaya-Sennaya pl. 32/34; tel. (095) 244-16-06; fax (095) 244-32-76.
Ministry of Fuel and Power Industry: 103074 Moscow, Kitaigorodskii proyezd 7; tel. (095) 220-55-00; fax (095) 220-56-56.
Ministry of General Education and Vocational Training: 113833 Moscow, ul.

Lyusinovskaya 51; tel. (095) 237-97-63; telex 411082; fax (095) 924-69-89; e-mail root@com.rkenit.msk.su.
Ministry of Health: 101431 Moscow, Rakhmanovskii per. 3; tel. (095) 923-84-06; telex 411407; fax (095) 292-41-53.
Ministry of Internal Affairs: 117049 Moscow, ul. Zhitnaya 19; tel. (095) 239-65-00; fax (095) 293-59-98.
Ministry of Justice: 109830 Moscow, ul. Vorontsovo Pole 4; tel. (095) 206-05-54.
Ministry of Labour and Social Development: 103706 Moscow, Birzhevaya pl. 1; tel. (095) 928-06-83; fax (095) 230-24-07.
Ministry for Nationalities Policy: 121819 Moscow, Trubnikovskii per. 19; tel. (095) 248-83-50; fax (095) 202-44-90.
Ministry of Natural Resources: 123812 Moscow, ul. B. Gruzinskaya 4/6; tel. (095) 254-76-83; fax (095) 254-82-83.
Ministry of Nuclear Energy: 109017 Moscow, ul. B. Ordynka 24/26; tel. (095) 239-49-08; fax (095) 230-24-20.
Ministry of Railways: Moscow, ul. Novobasmannaya 2; tel. (095) 262-10-02; telex 411832.
Ministry of Regional Policy: 121819 Moscow, Trubnikovskii per. 19; tel. (095) 248-83-50; fax (095) 202-44-90.
Ministry of Science and Technology: 103905 Moscow, ul. Tverskaya 11; tel. (095) 229-11-92; telex 411241; fax (095) 230-28-23.
Ministry of State Property: 103685 Moscow, Nikolskii per. 9; tel. (095) 298-76-89; fax (095) 924-67-04.
Ministry of Trade: 113324 Moscow, Ovchinnikovskaya nab. 18/1; tel. (095) 220-13-50; fax (095) 244-39-81.
Ministry of Transport: 101433 Moscow, ul. Sadovaya-Samotechnaya 10; tel. (095) 200-08-03; telex 411476; fax (095) 200-33-56.

The Federal Assembly

The Federal Assembly of the Russian Federation is a bicameral national parliament. Its upper chamber, the Federation Council, comprises 178 members, two appointed from each of the federal units, representing the executive and legislative branches of power in each territory. The lower chamber is the State Duma, with 450 deputies elected for a four-year term (the last general election was held on 17 December 1995).

Chairman of the Federation Council: YEGOR STROYEV (Governor of Orel Oblast); 103426 Moscow, ul. B. Dmitrovka 26; tel. (095) 205-42-50; fax (095) 292-43-05.

Chairman of the State Duma: GENADII N. SELEZNEV; 103265 Moscow, Okhotnyi ryad 1; tel. (095) 292-69-24; fax (095) 292-02-90.

PART TWO
Territorial Surveys

EUROPEAN RUSSIA

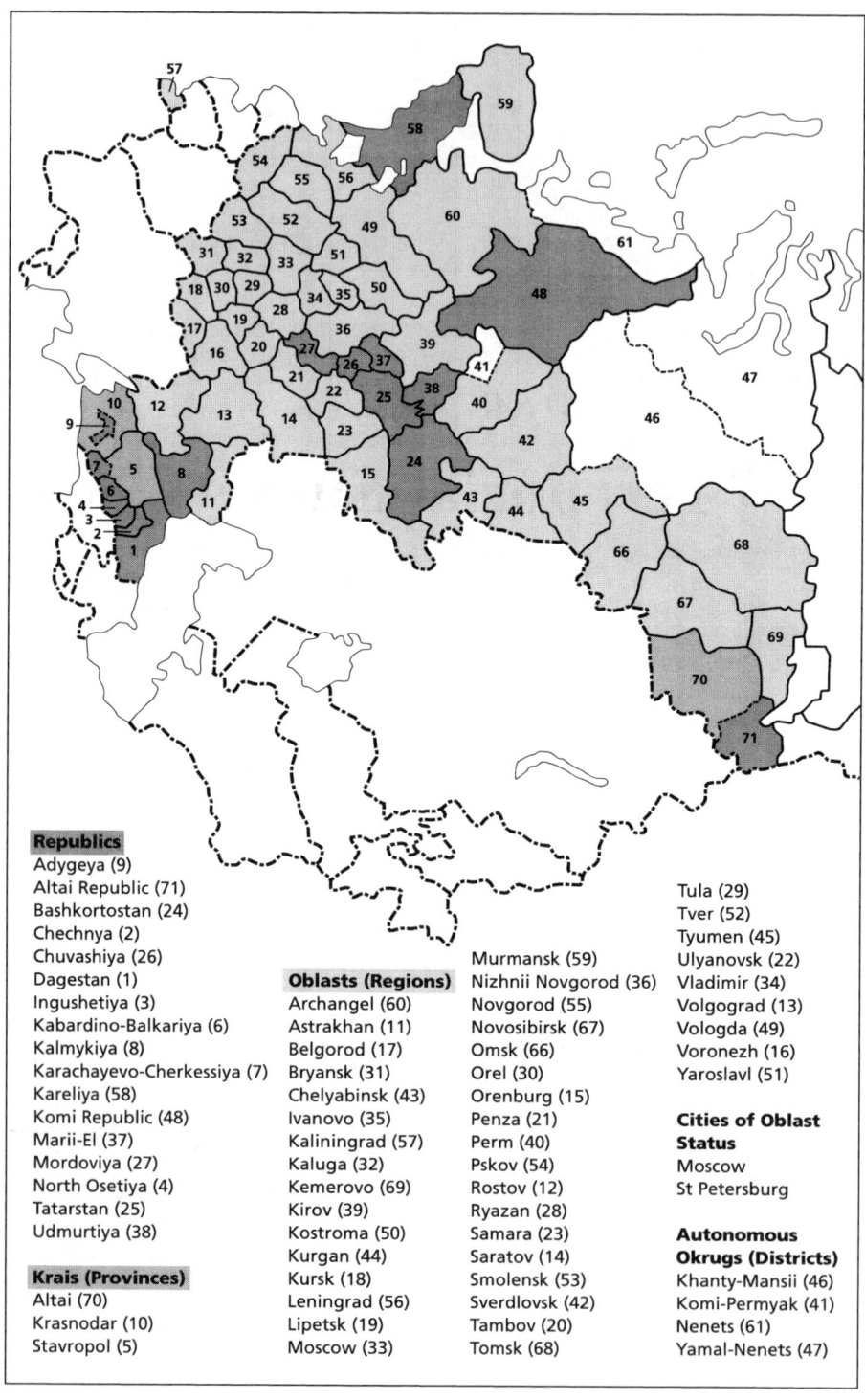

Republics
Adygeya (9)
Altai Republic (71)
Bashkortostan (24)
Chechnya (2)
Chuvashiya (26)
Dagestan (1)
Ingushetiya (3)
Kabardino-Balkariya (6)
Kalmykiya (8)
Karachayevo-Cherkessiya (7)
Kareliya (58)
Komi Republic (48)
Marii-El (37)
Mordoviya (27)
North Osetiya (4)
Tatarstan (25)
Udmurtiya (38)

Krais (Provinces)
Altai (70)
Krasnodar (10)
Stavropol (5)

Oblasts (Regions)
Archangel (60)
Astrakhan (11)
Belgorod (17)
Bryansk (31)
Chelyabinsk (43)
Ivanovo (35)
Kaliningrad (57)
Kaluga (32)
Kemerovo (69)
Kirov (39)
Kostroma (50)
Kurgan (44)
Kursk (18)
Leningrad (56)
Lipetsk (19)
Moscow (33)
Murmansk (59)
Nizhnii Novgorod (36)
Novgorod (55)
Novosibirsk (67)
Omsk (66)
Orel (30)
Orenburg (15)
Penza (21)
Perm (40)
Pskov (54)
Rostov (12)
Ryazan (28)
Samara (23)
Saratov (14)
Smolensk (53)
Sverdlovsk (42)
Tambov (20)
Tomsk (68)
Tula (29)
Tver (52)
Tyumen (45)
Ulyanovsk (22)
Vladimir (34)
Volgograd (13)
Vologda (49)
Voronezh (16)
Yaroslavl (51)

Cities of Oblast Status
Moscow
St Petersburg

Autonomous Okrugs (Districts)
Khanty-Mansii (46)
Komi-Permyak (41)
Nenets (61)
Yamal-Nenets (47)

ASIAN RUSSIA

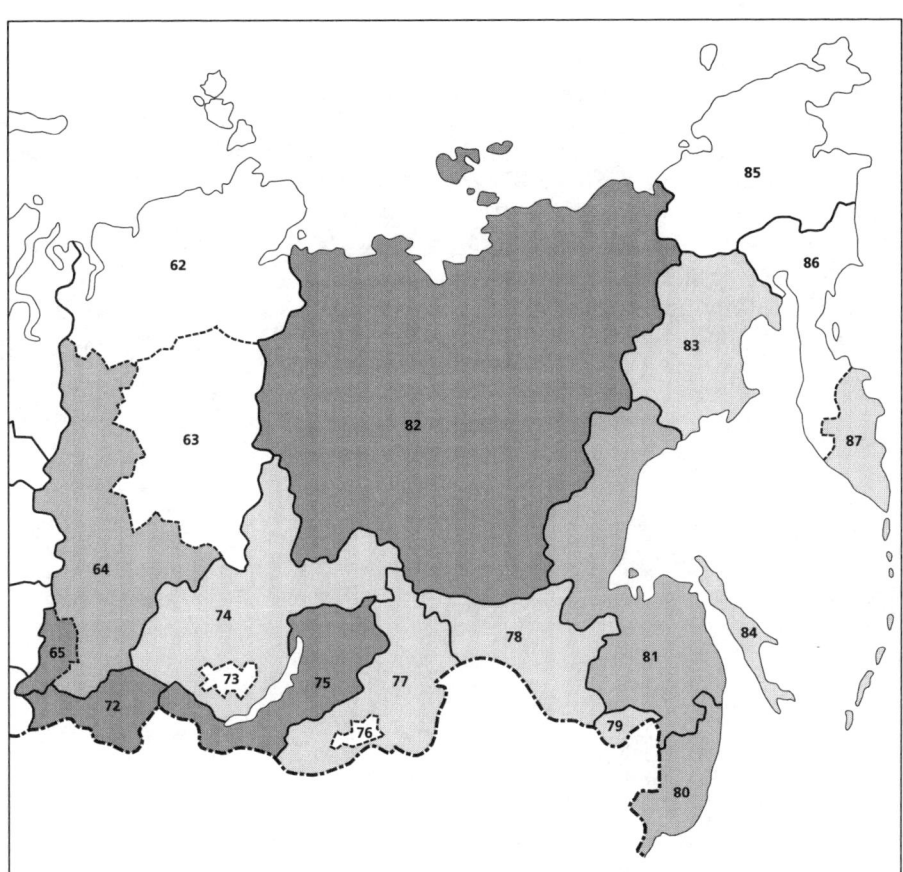

Republics
Buryatiya (75)
Khakasiya (65)
Tyva (72)
Republic of Sakha (82)
(Yakutiya)

Krais (Provinces)
Khabarovsk (81)
Krasnoyarsk (64)
Maritime (Primorye) (80)

Oblasts (Regions)
Amur (78)
Chita (77)
Irkutsk (74)
Kamchatka (87)
Magadan (83)
Sakhalin (84)

Autonomous Oblast
Jewish Autonomous Oblast (79)

Autonomous Okrugs (Districts)
Aga-Buryat (76)
Chukchi (85)
Evenk (63)
Koryak (86)
Taimyr (Dolgan-Nenets) (62)
Ust-Orda Buryat (73)

Notes

The maps distinguish between international borders (dots and dashes), borders between separate federal units (bold unbroken line) and borders of units that are formally part of another territory. Maps of European and Asian Russia are included at the end of Part One. For Krasnoyarsk Krai, Archangel Oblast and Tyumen Oblast, the map at the start of the chapter illustrates the 'core' region only—for the territory as a whole, see the extra maps at the end of Part Two.

On 1 January 1998 a new rouble, equivalent to 1,000 of the former units, was introduced. Any figures cited in this book are expressed in terms of the old rouble, unless otherwise indicated.

AUTONOMOUS REPUBLICS

Adygeya

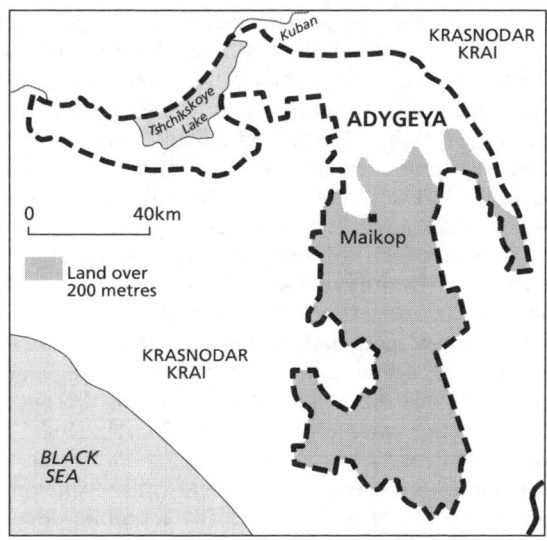

The Republic of Adygeya (Adygheya) is situated in the foothills of the Greater Caucasus, in the basin of the Kuban river. It lies within Krasnodar Krai, of which it forms a part (the city of Krasnodar itself faces territory in north-western Adygeya across the Kuban). The Republic is in the North Caucasus Economic Area. The Black Sea resort of Sochi lies some 40 km (25 miles) to the south of Adygeya, itself land-locked. The territory of the Republic, of which some two-fifths is forested, is characterized by open grassland, fertile soil and numerous rivers. The Republic has an area of 7,600 sq km (2,930 sq miles) and is comprised of seven administrative districts and two cities. At 1 January 1996 it was estimated to have 450,000 inhabitants, of which 53.9% were urban. The population density per sq km in 1996 was 59.3. In 1989, according to the census, of the total republican population some 68% were ethnic Russian and 22% Adyges (otherwise known as Lower Circassians or Kiakhs). Of the Adyge population, an estimated 95% speak the national tongue, Adyge—part of the Abkhazo-Adyge group of Caucasian languages—as their native language, although some 82% are fluent in the official language, Russian. The dominant religion in the Republic, owing to the preponderance of Russian inhabitants, is Orthodox Christianity, but the traditional religion of the Adyges is Islam. The administrative centre of Adygeya is at Maikop, which had a total of 165,500 inhabitants at 1 January 1996. Its other major city is Adygeysk, which had only 12,700 inhabitants.

History

The Adyges were traditionally renowned for their unrivalled horsemanship and marksmanship. They emerged as a distinct ethnic group among the Circassians in the 13th century, when they inhabited much of the area between the Don river and the Caucasus, and the Black Sea and the Stavropol plateau. They were conquered by the Mongol Empire in the 13th century. In the 1550s the Adyges entered into an alliance with the Russian Empire, as protection against the Tatar Khanate of Crimea and against Turkic groups such as the Karachais, the Kumyks and the Nogais, which had retreated into the Caucasus from the Mongol forces of Temujin (Chinghiz or Ghengis Khan). Russian settlers subsequently moved into the Don and Kuban regions causing unrest among the Adyges and other Circassian peoples, many of whom supported the Ottoman Empire against Russia in the Crimean War of 1853–56. The Circassians were finally defeated by the Russians in 1864. Most were forced either to emigrate or to move to the plains which were under Russian control. A Kuban-Black Sea Soviet Republic was established in 1918, but the region was soon occupied by anti-Communist forces ('Whites'). The Adygeya Autonomous Oblast was established on 27 July 1922. From 24 August 1922 until 13 August 1928 it was known as the Adygeya (Circassian) Autonomous Oblast.

Following the emergence of the policy of *glasnost* (openness) in the USSR under Mikhail Gorbachev the Adyge-Khase Movement was formed. This group, which was demanding the formation of a national legislative council or khase, began to raise the issues of nationalism and independence in the Autonomous Oblast. Adygeya officially declared its sovereignty on 28 June 1991 and was recognized as an autonomous republic at the signing of the Federation Treaty in March 1992. Its Constitution was adopted on 10 March 1995. The Communists remained the most popular party (winning 41% of the votes cast in the Republic at the Russian State Duma elections of December), while suspicion of the reformists and the federal Government was widespread. The Republic developed close links with the Republics of Kabardino-Balkariya and Karachayevo-Cherkessiya from the mid-1990s: in May 1998, at the second session of an interparliamentary council, a programme was adopted on the co-ordination of legislative, economic, environmental and legal activities.

Economy

Agriculture is, traditionally, the principal economic activity of Adygeya. In 1995 the territory's gross regional product was 1,840,500m. roubles, or 4,085,400 roubles per head. The territory's major industrial centres are at the cities of Maikop and Kamennomostskii. There are 142 km of railway track on its territory and 1,426 km of roads, of which 1,211 km are paved.

Agricultural production consists mainly of grain, sunflowers, sugar-beet, tobacco and vegetable production, cucurbit (gourds and melons) cultivation and viniculture. The sector employed some 18.5% of the working population in 1995. The fall in overall agricultural production in the Republic slowed during the mid-1990s, although animal husbandry continued to decline. Owing to the growth in prices of resources and fodder and the restriction of credits some 300 farmers ceased activity between 1992 and 1996. The value of agricultural output in 1995 was 775,500m. roubles. There is some extraction of natural gas. In industry, food processing is particularly important, accounting for over one-half of industrial production. Timber processing, mechanical engineering and metal working are also significant. Some 20.7% of the working population were engaged in industry in 1995. Industrial production declined during the early 1990s, but had begun to stabilize by 1995 (when it amounted to a value of 874,000m. roubles). Overall growth in industrial production in 1995 stood at 4.3%, compared to the previous year. In 1995 the trade of the Republic amounted to a value of US $56.6m., of which $48.3m. were imports and $8.3m. exports. Its main trading partners, in terms of exports, were Belarus, France, Kazakhstan, Poland, Turkey and Ukraine. Exports consisted mainly of food products, machine-tools and petroleum and chemical products.

In 1995 the economically active population in Adygeya amounted to 154,200, of whom 4,900 were registered unemployed. The average monthly wage was 241,000 roubles. In 1996 there was a budgetary deficit of 500m. roubles and wage arrears, owing since the previous year, amounted to 53,600m. roubles. There was relatively little foreign investment in the Republic; in 1997 there were just 15 companies operating with foreign funds. At 1 January 1996 there were around 2,200 small businesses registered on its territory.

Directory

President: ASLAN ALIYEVICH DZHARIMOV; respublika Adygeya, 352700 Maikop, ul. Zhukovskaya 22; tel. (87722) 2-19-00; fax (87722) 2-59-58.

Premier: MUKHARBII KHADZHIRETOVICH TKHARKAKHOV; respublika Adygeya, 352700 Maikop, ul. Zhukovskaya 22; tel. (87722) 2-22-22.

Chairman of the Khase (State Council): YEVGENII IVANOVICH SALOV; respublika Adygeya, 352700 Maikop; tel. (87722) 2-19-02.

Permanent Representative of the President of the Russian Federation: PETR PETROVICH MARCHENKO (based in Stavropol Krai).

Permanent Representative in Moscow: PSHIMAF ASKARBIYEVICH SHEVOTSUKOV; tel. (095) 291-00-69.

Head of Maikop City Administration: MIKHAIL NIKOLAYEVICH CHERNICHENKO; respublika Adygeya, 352700 Maikop, ul. Krasnooktyabrskaya 21; tel. (87722) 2-17-08.

Altai
(REPUBLIC OF ALTAI)

The Republic of Altai is situated in the Altai Mountains, in the basin of the Ob river. The Republic forms the eastern part of the Altai Krai and belongs to the Western Siberian Economic Area. It has international borders with Kazakhstan in the south-west, a short border with the People's Republic of China to the south, and with Mongolia to the south-east. Kemerovo Oblast lies to the north, the Republics of Khakasiya and Tyva to the east. The Republic is mountainous (Belukha, at 4,506 m or 14,783 feet, is the highest peak in Siberia) and heavily forested (about one-quarter of its territory). Its major rivers are the Katyn and the Biya and it has one lake, Teletskoye. It contains one of Russia's major national parks, Altai State National Park, covering an area of some 9,000 sq km. The Republic occupies 92,600 sq km (35,750 sq miles) and comprises 10 administrative districts and one city. Its climate is continental, with short summers and long, cold winters. At 1 January 1996 it was estimated to have a population of 202,000 and a population density, therefore, of only 2.2 per sq km. Only 14.2% of its inhabitants resided in urban areas at this time. The census of 1989 put the number of Russians at some 60% of the total and of ethnic Altai at 31%. Some 6.0% of the population were Kazakh, 0.9% Ukrainian and 0.4% German at this time. The Altai people can be divided into two distinct groups: the Northern Altai, or Chernnevye Tatars, consisting of the Tubalars, the Chelkans or Leberdin and the Kumandins; and the Southern Altai, comprising the Altai Kizhi, the Telengit, the Telesy and the Teleut. The language spoken by both groups is from the Turkish branch of the Uralo-Altaic family: that of the Northern Altais is from the Old Uigur group, while the language of the Southern Altais is close to the Kyrgyz language and is part of the Kipchak group. Over 84% of Altais speak one or other language as their native tongue, and some 62% of the Altai population is fluent in Russian. Although the traditional religion of the Altai was animist, many were converted to Christianity, so the dominant religion in the Republic is Russian Orthodoxy. The Republic's administrative centre is at Gorno-Altaisk, which had an estimated population of 48,300 at 1 January 1996.

History

From the 11th century the Altai peoples inhabited Dzungaria (Sungaria—now mainly in the north-west of the People's Republic of China). The region was under Mongol control until 1389, when it was conquered by the Tatar forces of Tamerlane (Tamberlane or Timur 'the Lame'); it subsequently became a Kalmyk confederation. In the first half of the 18th century many Altais moved westwards, invading Kazakh territory and progressing almost as far as the Urals. In 1758, however, most of Dzungaria was incorporated into Xinjiang (Sinkiang), a province of the Chinese Empire. China embarked on a war aimed at exterminating the Altai peoples. Only a few thousand survived, finding refuge in the Altai Mountains. In the 19th century Russia began to assert its control over the region and the Altai territory was finally annexed in 1866. In the early 1900s Burkhanism or White Faith, a strong nationalist religious movement, emerged. The movement was led by Oirot Khan, who claimed to be a descendant of Chinghiz (Genghis) Khan and promised to liberate the Altais from Russian control. However, in February 1918 it was a secular nationalist leader, B. I. Anuchin, who convened a Constituent Congress of the High Altai and demanded the establishment of an Oirot Republic—to include the Altai, the Khakassians and the Tyvans. In partial recognition of such demands, on 1 July 1922 the Soviet Government established an Oirot Autonomous Oblast in Altai Krai. Nationalist feeling remained strong in the region, however, and in 1933 many members of the local Communist Party were purged. On 7 January 1948 the region was renamed the Gorno-Altai Autonomous Oblast, in an effort to suppress nationalist sentiment.

In the late 1980s nationalism re-emerged in response to Mikhail Gorbachev's policy of *glasnost* (openness). As was frequently the case in the last years of the Communist order, such opposition was expressed over issues of local environmental concern and the Soviet Government was forced to abandon plans to construct a hydroelectric dam on the Autonomous Oblast's territory. Renamed Altai, the region became an autonomous republic at the signing of the Russian Federation Treaty in March 1992. It had adopted its State Sovereignty Declaration on 25 October 1990. A resolution adopted on 14 October 1993 provided for the establishment of a State Assembly (El Kurultai), which comprised 27 deputies and represented the highest body of power in the Republic. In mid-1998 an escalating financial crisis in the Republic resulted in a degree of political unrest. Following the blockade by around 1,000 public-sector workers of the State Assembly building, in protest at payment arrears, the legislature adopted an appeal to the federal authorities for urgent financial aid.

Economy

The Republic of Altai is predominantly an agricultural region. Its gross regional product amounted to 906,100m. roubles in 1995, or 5,526,800 roubles per head.

The main industrial centre in the Republic is at its capital, Gorno-Altaisk. Owing to its mountainous terrain it contains just 6,000 km (3,730 miles) of roads, of which 572 km comprise a section of the major Novorossiisk–Biisk–Tashanta highway. In March 1996 the Russian Government allocated some 1,800m. roubles to alleviate the effects in the Republic of the nuclear tests conducted at Semipalatinsk (Kazakhstan) during the Soviet period.

Agriculture in the Republic of Altai, which employed 28.9% of the working population in 1995, consists mainly of livestock breeding (largely horses, deer, sheep and goats, amounting to 81% of agricultural activity), bee-keeping, grain production and hunting. The export of the antlers of Siberian maral and sika deer, primarily to South-East Asia, is an important source of convertible ('hard') currency to the Republic. The territory is also one of Russia's leading cheese producers. The total value of agricultural output in 1995 was 462,600m. roubles. The Republic's mountainous terrain often prevents the easy extraction or transport of minerals, but there are important reserves of manganese, iron, silver, lead and wolfram (tungsten), as well as timber. Stone, lime, salt, sandstone, gold, mercury and non-ferrous metals are also produced. There are food-processing, light, chemical, metal-working and machine-tool industries, as well as factories assembling tractors, automobiles, radios, televisions, engines, boilers and electrical appliances. Industry employed just 9.4% of the working population in 1995, while the value of industrial production amounted to 142,000m. roubles. In the mid-1990s the value of the Republic's exports (approximately one-half of which were antlers) averaged around US $11m. per year, while its imports were equivalent to around $3m.

In 1995 a total of 80,900 of the Republic's inhabitants were economically active, of whom 1,900 were registered unemployed. The average monthly wage in that year was 316,000 roubles. The territory suffered severe financial difficulties during 1998—in July of that year overall arrears in salaries, child benefit and other budgetary payments was estimated to be in excess of 183m. new roubles (i.e. 183,000m. in terms of pre-1998 roubles). At the end of that year the Republic was cited as the territory furthest behind in wage arrears after the Chukchi and Koryak AOks, and the situation provoked industrial action by teachers in January 1999. A budgetary surplus of 3,700m. roubles had been achieved in 1995, although foreign investment in that year amounted to just US $5,000. At 1 January 1996 there were approximately 1,500 small businesses operating in the Republic.

Directory

Chairman of the Government: SEMEN IVANOVICH ZUBAKIN; respublika Altai, 659700 Gorno-Altaisk, ul. Kirova 16; tel. (38822) 27-61; fax (38822) 9-51-21.

Chairman of the El Kurultai (State Assembly): DANIIL IVANOVICH TABAYEV; respublika Altai, 659700 Gorno-Altaisk, ul. E. Palkina 1; tel. (38822) 26-18; fax (38822) 9-51-65.

Permanent Representative of the President of the Russian Federation: VYACHESLAV YEVGENIYEVICH PIUNOV.

Permanent Representative in Moscow: SERGEI KHARISOVICH SHAIKSISLAMOV; tel. (095) 299-41-94.

Head of Gorno-Altaisk City Administration: VIKTOR ALEKSANDROVICH OBLOGIN; respublika Altai, 659700 Gorno-Altaisk, pr. Kommunicheskii 18; tel. (38822) 2-07-31.

Bashkortostan

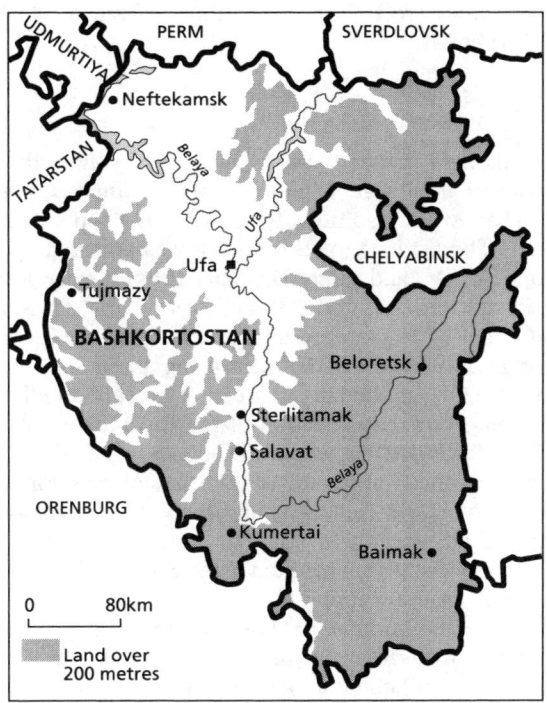

The Republic of Bashkortostan (Bashkiriya) is situated on the slopes of the Southern Urals. It forms part of the Urals Economic Area. Orenburg Oblast lies to the south and south-west of Bashkortostan, the Republics of Tatarstan and Udmurtiya lie to the north and north-west, respectively. There are borders with Perm and Sverdlovsk Oblasts to the north and Chelyabinsk to the east. The international border with Kazakhstan is some 50 km (30 miles) south of the territory. The north of the Republic (more than one-third of its land area) is forested, while the southern part is steppe. Its major rivers are the Ufa and its tributary, the Belaya, which ultimately drain into the Volga. The Republic occupies an area of 143,600 sq km (55,440 sq miles) and comprises 54 administrative districts and 20 cities. At 1 January 1996 Bashkortostan had an estimated population of 4,097,000, some 64.7% of which inhabited urban areas, and a population density of 28.5 per sq km. Most of the Republic's inhabitants are concentrated in the west, which is less mountainous. The most numerous ethnic group was Russian (39% in 1989, according to census figures). Tatars made up more than one-quarter of the population, while Bashkirs only constituted 22%. Of the ethnic Bashkir inhabitants, the census of 1989 showed that some 72% spoke Bashkir as their native tongue. Bashkir is a Kipchak language closely related to that spoken by the Tatars. There are two distinct Bashkir dialects: Kuvakan is spoken in the north of the Republic, while Yurmatin (Yurmatyn) is current in the south. The majority of Bashkirs and Tatars are Sunni Muslims of the Hanafi school, although some Bashkirs, the Nagaibak (Noghaibaq or Nogaibak) were converted to Orthodox Christianity. Ufa, the capital of Bashkortostan, is one of four Muslim muftiates, or spiritual synods in Russia. The Republic's administrative centre is at Ufa, which had an estimated population of 1,096,400 at 1 January 1996. Its other major cities are Beloretsk, Ishimbai, Neftekamsk, Kumertai, Sibai, Sterlitamak and Oktyabrskii.

History

The Bashkirs were thought to have originated as a distinct ethnic group during the 16th century, out of the Tatar, Mongol, Volga, Bulgar, Oguz, Pecheneg and Kipchak peoples. They were traditionally a pastoral people renowned for their bee-keeping abilities. The territory of Bashkiriya was annexed by Russia in 1557, during the reign of Ivan IV, and many Bashkirs subsequently lost their land and wealth and were forced into servitude. Rebellions against Russian control, most notably by Salavat Yulai in 1773, were unsuccessful and the identity and survival of the Bashkir community came under increasing threat. A large migration of ethnic Russians to the region in the late 19th century resulted in their outnumbering the Bashkir population. Formal recognition of the Bashkirs as an ethnic group did not occur until 23 March 1919, when the Bashkir ASSR was created. The Soviet Government remained intolerant of unrest and Bashkir resistance to the collectivization policy of Stalin (Iosif Dzhugashvili) caused many to be relocated to other regions in the USSR. It was this, combined with losses during the civil wars of the revolutionary period, that resulted in the Bashkirs becoming outnumbered by the Tatar population in the Republic.

The Bashkir Autonomous Republic declared its sovereignty on 11 October 1990. On 12 December 1993, the same day that Murtaza Rakhimov was elected to a new post of President, a republican majority voted against acceptance of the Russian Constitution, which was approved in the Federation as a whole. On 24 December the republican Supreme Soviet (State Assembly) adopted a new Constitution which stated that its own laws had supremacy over federal laws. The name of Bashkortostan was adopted. The Republic's constitutional position was regularized and further autonomy granted under a treaty signed on 3 August 1994. By this, the federal authorities granted Bashkortostan, which had one of the strongest sovereignty movements of any of the ethnic republics, greater independence in economic and legislative matters, including that of the right to levy taxes. A further bilateral treaty was signed in 1995. Bashkortostan enjoyed close relations with the Republic of Tatarstan: on 28 August 1997 the Presidents of the two territories signed a treaty on co-operation. Rakhimov even proposed their eventual unification 'under some circumstances'. The Republic's administration was traditionally centralized and conservative but keen to attract foreign investment. A presidential election, held on 14 June 1998, returned the incumbent, Rakhimov, to office. Rakhimov's candidacy was publicly endorsed by the federal President, Boris Yeltsin. No electoral regularities were reported; there had, however, been controversy over the alleged obstruction of opposition candidates prior to the ballot. Rif Kazakkulov, the forestry minister and supporter of the President, was ultimately the only rival candidate in the election and obtained 10% of the votes cast; Rakhimov obtained 73%. In January 1999 the premier, Rim Bakiyev, retired, to be replaced by his first deputy, Rafael Baidevletov, who confirmed the continuation of government policies.

Economy

Bashkortostan's economy is dominated by its fuel-and-energy and agro-industrial complexes. The Republic is one of Russia's key petroleum-producing areas and the centre of its petroleum-refining industry. It produced some 6% of Russia's total petroleum output in 1995 and accounted for around 16% of its petroleum refining. In the same year the territory's gross regional product stood at 39,435,900m. roubles, or 9,645,800 roubles per head. Its major industrial centres are at Ufa (at which the Republic's petroleum refineries are based), Sterlitamak, Salavat and Ishimbai. In 1997 there were 2,908 km of railways on its territory and 24,310 km of roads, of which 20,543 km were paved. Aviakompaniya BAL (Bashkirskiye Avialiniya—Bashkir Air Lines) operates air services between Ufa and major centres within Russia and elsewhere within the Commonwealth of Independent States from the Republic's international airport.

Bashkortostan's agricultural production, the value of which amounted to 7,513,100m. roubles in 1995, ranks among the highest in the Russian Federation. Its main agricultural activities are grain, sugar-beet, sunflower and vegetable production, animal husbandry, poultry farming and bee-keeping. Some 18.9% of the Republic's work-force were employed in agriculture in 1995. As well as its petroleum resources, Bashkortostan contains deposits of natural gas, brown coal, iron ore, copper, gold (with reserves amounting to 32 metric tons in 1997, sufficient for 19 years of production), zinc, aluminium, chromium, salt, manganese, gypsum and limestone. The region's other industries included processing of agricultural and forestry products, mechanical engineering, metal working, metallurgy, production of mining and petroleum-exploration equipment, automobiles, geophysical instruments, cables and electrical equipment and building materials. In 1995 industry employed 27.5% of the Republic's working population. Total industrial output was worth 37,880,000m. roubles in that year. In 1997 the Republic's external trade totalled US $1,000m.: exports exceeded imports by around 400% and largely comprised petroleum products and petrochemical goods.

In 1995 the economically active population in the Republic amounted to 1,747,700, of which 43,100 were unemployed. The average monthly wage at that time was 325,000 roubles. There was a budgetary surplus of 122,200m. roubles in that year. Foreign investment in the Republic in 1995 amounted to US $2.49m. In March 1998 the republican premier, Rim Bakiyev, signed an agreement on a two-year loan arranged by Moscow Narodnyi Bank and HSBC Markets (United Kingdom) to be used in its petrochemicals and hydrocarbons industry. At 1 January 1996 there were 15,700 small businesses registered on the Republic's territory.

Directory

President: MURTAZA GUBAIDULLOVICH RAKHIMOV; respublika Bashkortostan, 450101 Ufa, ul. Tukayeva 46; tel. (3472) 50-24-06; fax (3472) 50-01-75.

Prime Minister: RAFAEL IBRAGIMOVICH BAIDEVLETOV; respublika Bashkortostan, 450101 Ufa, ul. Tukayeva 46; tel. (3472) 50-24-01; fax (3472) 50-57-47.

Chairman of the State Assembly: MIKHAIL ALEKSEYEVICH ZAITSEV; respublika Bashkortostan, 450101 Ufa, ul. Tukayeva 46; tel. (3472) 22-46-50.

Permanent Representative in Moscow: IREK YUMBAYEVICH ABLAYEV; tel. (095) 208-46-62.

Head of Ufa City Administration: FEDUS AGLYAMOVICH YAMALTDINOV; respublika Bashkortostan, 450098 Ufa, pr. Oktyabrya 120; tel. (3472) 31-28-16; fax (3472) 33-18-73.

Buryatiya

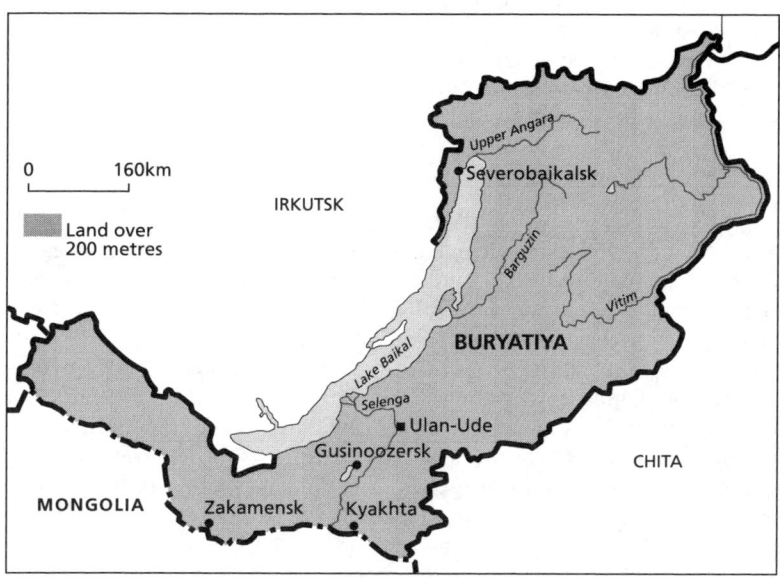

The Republic of Buryatiya is situated in the Eastern Sayan Mountains of southern Siberia and forms part of the Eastern Siberian Economic Area. It lies mainly in the Transbaikal region to the east of Lake Baikal, although it also extends westwards along the international boundary with Mongolia in the south, to create a short border with the Russian federal territory of Tyva in the extreme south-west. Irkutsk Oblast lies to the north and west, and Chita Oblast to the east. Buryatiya's rivers mainly drain into Lake Baikal, the largest being the Selenga, the Barguzin and the upper Angara, but some, such as the Vitim, flow northwards into the Siberian plains. The Republic's one lake, Baikal, forms part of the western border of the Republic. Baikal is the oldest and deepest lake in the world, possessing over 80% of Russia's freshwater resources and 20% of the world's total. Considered holy by the Buryats, until the 1950s it was famed for the purity of its waters and the uniqueness of the ecosystem it sustained. Intensive industrialization along its shores threatened Baikal's environment, and only in the 1990s were serious efforts made to safeguard the lake. Some 70% of Buryatiya's territory, including its low mountains, is forested, while its valleys are open steppe. The Republic's territory covers 351,300 sq km (135,640 sq miles) and comprises a total of 21 administrative districts and six cities. Temperatures in the Republic fall as low as −50°C in winter, which is protracted but sees little snow, and can reach up to 40°C in summer. Buryatiya is sparsely populated: it had an estimated population of 1,053,000 at 1 January 1996 and a population density of 3.0 per sq km. Around 59.6% of the population inhabited urban areas at this time. At the 1989 census some 70% of the inhabitants were ethnic Russians and 24% Buryats. The industrial areas of the Republic are mainly inhabited by ethnic Russians. The Buryats are a native Siberian people of Mongol descent. The majority of those inhabiting the Republic are Transbaikal Buryats, as distinct from the Irkutsk Buryats, who live west of Lake Baikal. The Buryats' native tongue is a Mongol dialect. Some Buryats are Orthodox Christians, but others still practise Lamaism (Tibetan Buddhism), which has been syncretized with the region's traditional animistic shamanism. The Khambo Lama, the spiritual leader of Russia's Buddhists, resides in Buryatiya's capital, Ulan-Ude (Verkhneudinsk), which had an estimated population of 368,100 in January 1996. Other major cities are Gusinoozersk (31,800) and Severobaikalsk (28,300).

History

Buryatiya was regarded as strategically important from the earliest years of the Muscovite Russian state, as it lay on the Mongol border. Russian influence reached the region in the 17th century and Transbaikal was formally incorporated into the Russian Empire by the Treaties of Nerchinsk and Kyakhta in 1689 and 1728, respectively. The latter agreement ended a dispute over the territory between the Russian and the Chinese Manzhou (Manchu) Empires. Many ethnic Russians subsequently settled in the region, often inhabiting land confiscated from the Buryats, many of whom were 'russified'. Other Buryats, however, strove to protect their culture, and there was a resurgence of nationalist feeling in the 19th century. Jamtsarano, a prominent nationalist, following a series of congresses in 1905 demanding Buryat self-government and the use of the Buryat language in schools, led a movement which recognized the affinity of Buryat culture to that of the Mongolians. Russia's fears about the Buryats' growing allegiance to its eastern neighbour were allayed, however, after a formal treaty signed with Japan in 1912 recognized Outer Mongolia (Mongolia) as a Russian sphere of influence. With the dissolution of the Far Eastern Republic (based at Chita), a Buryat-Mongol ASSR was established on 30 May 1923. In the early 1930s, following Stalin's (Iosif Dzhugashvili) policy of collectivization, many Buryats fled the country or were found guilty of treason and executed. In 1937 the Soviet Government considerably reduced the territory of the Republic, transferring the eastern section to Chita Oblast and a westerly region to Irkutsk Oblast. Furthermore, the Buryat language's Mongolian script was replaced with a Cyrillic one. In 1958 the Buryat-Mongol ASSR was renamed the Buryat ASSR amid suspicions of increasing co-operation between the Mongolian People's Republic (Mongolia) and the People's Republic of China.

The territory declared its sovereignty on 10 October 1990, and was renamed the Republic of Buryatiya in 1992. On 30 December a draft constitution was published. It was adopted by the legislature, the Supreme Soviet, on 4 March 1994. The Constitution provided for Buryatiya as a sovereign, democratic, law-governed state within the Russian Federation. It established an executive presidency, a post first held by the then Chairman of the Supreme Soviet, Leonid Potapov, and redesignated the elected legislature as the People's Hural. A bilateral treaty on a division of powers was signed with the Federation Government in 1995. On 21 June 1998 presidential and legislative elections were held in the Republic: Potapov was re-elected President, with 63.25% of the votes cast; a second round of voting for the parliament, following the election of only eight out of 64 deputies, was held on 5 July.

Economy

In 1995 Buryatiya's gross regional product amounted to 7,737,300m. roubles, equivalent to 7,350,000 roubles per head. Its major industrial centre is at Ulan-Ude, which is on the route of the Trans-Siberian Railway.

The Republic's agriculture, which employed around 17.1% of the work-force in 1995, consists mainly of animal husbandry (livestock and fur-animal breeding), grain production and hunting. Total agricultural production in 1995 was worth 1,357,900m. roubles. The Republic is rich in mineral resources, including gold, coal, wolfram (tungsten), molybdenum, brown coal, graphite and apatites. Its main gold-mining enterprise, Buryatzoloto, operates two mines near Lake Baikal. In 1997 the company's largest shareholder was High River Gold, of Canada, which owned a 23% stake. In 1996 its reserves were estimated at 3.2m. troy ounces (almost 100 metric tons). Apart from ore mining and the extraction of minerals, its main industries are mechanical engineering, metal working, timber production and wood-working. The Republic is also a major producer of electrical energy. The industrial sector employed 21.1% of the Republic's work-force in 1995, while its total output in that year was of a value of 4,085,000m. roubles. The service sector with the most potential is tourism, owing to the attractions of Lake Baikal.

The territory's economically active population totalled 420,400 in 1995, of which 8,700 were officially registered as unemployed. The average monthly wage in the Republic was 372,000 roubles. In 1995 there was a budgetary deficit of 6,600m. roubles. Continuing deficits exacerbated the problem of the late payment of wages, a phenomenon common throughout Russia in the 1990s, but increasingly provoking labour unrest (for example, in the education sector in December 1998). Foreign investment in Buryatiya amounted to US $599,000 in that year. At 1 January 1996 there were 5,400 small businesses registered in the Republic.

Directory

President and Chairman of the Government: LEONID VASILIYEVICH POTAPOV; respublika Buryatiya, 670001 Ulan-Ude, ul. Sukhe-Batora 9, Dom Pravitelstva; tel. (3012) 21-51-86; fax (3012) 21-02-51.

Chairman of the People's Hural: MIKHAIL INNOKENTIYEVICH SEMENOV; tel. (3012) 21-51-86; fax (3012) 21-02-51.

Permanent Representative of the President of the Republic in the People's Hural: SERGEI NIKOLAYEVICH BULDAYEV.

Permanent Representative of the President of the Russian Federation: BORIS VASILIYEVICH DANILOV.

Permanent Representative in Moscow: YURII NANZATOVICH TSYBIKOV; tel. (095) 286-30-83.

Head of Ulan-Ude City Administration (Mayor): GENNADII ARKHIPOVICH AYDAYEV; respublika Buryatiya, 670000 Ulan-Ude, ul. Lenina 54; tel. (3012) 21-44-55; fax (3012) 26-32-44.

Chechnya
(CHECHEN REPUBLIC OF ICHKERIYA)

The territory of Chechnya (formerly part of the Chechen-Ingush ASSR) is located on the northern slopes of the Greater Caucasus, on the Russian border with Georgia, which lies to the south. It forms part of the North Caucasus Economic Area. To the east, Chechnya abuts into the Republic of Dagestan. Stavropol Krai lies to the north-west and the Republics of North Osetiya (Ossetia) and Ingushetiya to the west. The exact delimitation of the western boundary remained uncertain at the end of the 1990s, awaiting final agreement between Chechnya and Ingushetiya on the division of the territory of the former Chechen-Ingush ASSR. Chechnya certainly had a short border with North Osetiya to the north of Ingushetiya, while in the mountainous south, between Osetiya and Chechnya proper, there was a strip of disputed territory. The region consists of lowlands along the principal waterway, the River Terek, and around the capital, Dzhokhar Ghala (formerly Groznyi), in the north; mixed fields, pastures and forests in the Chechen plain; and high mountains and glaciers in the south. The former Chechen-Ingush ASSR had an area of some 19,300 sq km (7,450 sq miles), most of which was allotted to the Chechens. At 1 January 1996 the Republic had an estimated population of 921,000, of which just 36.5% inhabited urban areas. The Chechens, who refer to themselves as Nokchi, are closely related to the Ingushetians (both of whom are known collectively as Vainakhs). They are Sunni Muslims, and their language is one of the Nakh dialects of the Caucasian linguistic family. Dzhokhar, founded as Groznyi in 1818, had a population of 405,000 in 1989, but an estimated 182,700 inhabitants in 1995. The Republic's other major towns are Urus-Martan, Gudermes (the oldest town in the territory, founded in the mid-18th century), Shali and Argun.

History

In the 18th century the Russian, Ottoman and Persian (Iranian) Empires fought for control of the Caucasus region. The Chechens, many of whom had been converted to Islam by Sunni missionaries, violently resisted the Russian forces with the uprising of Sheikh Mansur in 1785 and throughout the Caucasian War of 1817–64. Chechnya was finally conquered by Russia in 1858 after the resistance led by Imam Shamil ended. Many Chechens were exiled to the Ottoman Empire in 1865. Subsequently, ethnic Russians began to settle in the lowlands, particularly after petroleum reserves were discovered around Groznyi in 1893. In the Soviet period, upon the dissolution of the Mountain (Gorskaya) People's Republic, a Chechen Autonomous Oblast was established on 30 November 1922; this was merged with the Ingush Autonomous Oblast in 1934. In 1936 the Chechen-Ingush ASSR was created. Continuing rebellions against Soviet rule and some collaboration by the Chechens with the Germans during the Second World War resulted in their mass deportation to Kazakhstan in 1944. The autonomous republic was dissolved. On 9 January 1957 the ASSR was reconstituted, but the Chechens were forced to reclaim much of their territory from Dagestanis who had settled in the area. Furthermore, the territory's Russian inhabitants had seized control of its flourishing petroleum industry, and its mosques, destroyed in 1944, were not restored.

During 1991 an All-National Congress of the Chechen People gradually seized effective power in the Chechen-Ingush ASSR and agreed the division of the territory with Ingush leaders. Exact borders were to be decided by future negotiation, but by far the largest proportion of the territory was to constitute a 'Chechen Republic' (Chechnya). Elections to the presidency of this new polity, which claimed independence from Russia, were held on 27 October, and were won by Gen. Dzhokar Dudayev. The Chechen Republic (Ichkeriya was added to its name by presidential decree on 19 January 1994) under Dudayev, although unrecognized internationally, continued to insist on its independence. In December 1993 the territory refused to participate in the Russian general election and rejected the new federal Constitution. However, Dudayev's policies eventually provoked the Chechen opposition into violent conflict, which first erupted in the capital in August 1994. In early December federal Russian troops entered Chechnya and, by January 1995, had taken control of the city, including the presidential palace. Fierce resistance by Chechen rebels continued throughout the Republic and even, causing increased public disquiet throughout the rest of the Russian Federation, spread to neighbouring regions. In an effort to end the hostilities, the federal President, Boris Yeltsin, signed an accord with the Chechen premier granting the Republic special status, including its own consulate and foreign-trade missions. A peace agreement was not signed, however, until late May 1996, one month after the death of Dudayev in a Russian missile attack. (Dudayev was succeeded by Zelimkhan Yandarbiyev.) The truce immediately showed signs of strain, particularly following the republican parliamentary elections, held simultaneously with the election to the federal presidency. Following Boris Yeltsin's re-election to the Russian presidency, on 9 July, the cease-fire ended with the bombardment of two Chechen villages by federal troops. One month later Chechen rebel forces retaliated with a successful assault on Groznyi, prompting the negotiation of a cease-fire by Lt-Gen. Aleksandr Lebed (newly appointed Secretary of the federal Security Council). This agreement, named the Khasvyurt Accords, was signed in Dagestan on 31 August. At the beginning of September the basic principles of a proposed peace settlement involved a new cease-fire and a moratorium on discussion of Chechnya's sovereign status for five years, until 31 December 2001. An agreement on the withdrawal of the last Russian brigades by January 1997 was signed in late November 1996, signalling the end of a war that had claimed between 60,000 and 100,000 lives. A formal Treaty of Peace and Principles of Relations between the Russian Federation and the Chechen Republic of Ichkeriya was signed on 12 May 1998 and ratified by the Chechen Parliament the following day.

On 1 January 1997 a presidential election was held in the Republic, at which Aslan Maskhadov, former Chechen rebel chief of staff, defeated another rebel leader, Shamil Basayev, by 64.8% of the votes to Basayev's 22.7%. The rivalry, and co-operation, of these two men dominated Chechen politics in the post-Dudayev era. (On 25 March 1998 the republican Parliament officially renamed the capital Dzhokhar, after the late Gen. Dudayev, and changed the territory's name to the Chechen Republic of Ichkeriya.) The main issues to dominate politics were the increasing lawlessness and the islamicization of the Republic.

During 1998 two particularly dramatic incidents drew attention to the disorderly state of Chechen society: Valentin Vlasov, the federal presidential representative in Chechnya, was kidnapped in May 1998 and held for six months; later in the year international attention was focused on the situation in the Republic by the capture and murder of four Western hostages (three British and one New Zealander). With political opposition to Maskhadov led by other former warlords (one, Salman Raduyev, attempted to seize control of government buildings in Dzhokar in May) and organized crime powerful in the territory, violence was constantly imminent. Thus, a state of emergency and curfew was imposed in Dzhokar from 24 June, owing to the rise in crime, and on 23 July Maskhadov himself survived an assassination attempt. At this time some 40 hostages (including five foreigners) were being held in Chechnya. International interest towards the end of the year helped to prompt another campaign against crime and Parliament declared a state of emergency from 16 December. Such efforts were allegedly compromised by political motives. By the end of the year Maskhadov and Basayev no longer vied for political pre-eminence alone. The Chechen President, although still popular, had been challenged by a 'Commanders' Council' (on which Basayev had joined Raduyev and Khunkar-Pasha Israpilov) and his own Vice-President, Vakha Arsanov. The capital of Dzhokar was no longer secure for the Government and Maskhadov was mainly based on the outskirts of the city, in the old military base of Khankala.

The resurgence of Chechen nationalism in the 1990s was accompanied by a renaissance for Islam. Even after the 1996 peace agreements the territory's leadership remained committed to complete independence from Russia, reinforcing this intent with the 1997 decision to introduce Islamic law (*shari'a*—in contravention of federal norms) and religious education in schools. However, religion, while superficially unifying, soon became another factor in the political fragmentation of the Republic. Thus, hostilities between armed groupings in Gudermes in July 1998 resulted in the outlawing of Wahhabis in Chechnya. ('Wahhabis' was a term applied to strict Sunni Muslims, but was, erroneously, interchangeable with 'fundamentalists' and loosely applied to any opposition groups with a religious agenda.) The process of transition to an Islamic state was also a fraught process. In December the Supreme Shari'a Court forced Maskhadov's wife to resign as the head of a charity (because she was a woman holding authority) and make other personnel changes, refrained from deposing the Chechen President himself, but declared the parliamentary speaker dismissed and suspended Parliament itself. Such conflicts over the legitimacy of the very structures of state power were likely to ensure further instability. In January 1999 Maskhadov declared that *shari'a* would be introduced over a three-year period, supervised by an Islamic council or shura. The composition of such a body remained a potent source of dispute, initially between the Government and the Commanders' Council.

Economy

Prior to armed hostilities in the region in 1994–95 Groznyi (now Dzhokhar) was the principal industrial centre in Chechnya. The Republic's agriculture consisted mainly of horticulture, production of grain and sugar-beet and animal husbandry. Its main industrial activities were production of petroleum and petrochemicals, petroleum refining, power engineering, manufacture of machinery and the processing of forestry and agricultural products. Conflict in the 'Great Patriotic War' seriously damaged the economic infrastructure and disrupted both agricultural and industrial activity. A high degree of lawlessness in the latter half of the 1990s impeded tangible reconstruction. By April 1998 around four-fifths of the Republic's population were unemployed. Federal transfers had ensured that in 1995 there was a budgetary surplus of 175,400m. roubles. Such support was promised but less apparent in the late 1990s. There were hopes that Russian finance would be more available during 1999, although the federal Government reported that it had disbursed some 800m. new roubles in aid to Chechnya during 1998. Also, in the middle of that year, the federal authorities had permitted Chechnya to apply to Western governments for assistance, but such sources seemed more unlikely by the end of 1998. Future developments depended on greater stability in the territory, certainly as foreign investment was likely to remain low while kidnapping was habitual. Another asset that could be sabotaged by, or displaced because of, violence was one of Russia's major petroleum pipelines that crossed Chechnya (transit fees from Caspian hydrocarbons could be a major source of revenue in the 21st century).

Directory

President and Chairman of the Council of Ministers: KHALID ('ASLAN') ALIYEVICH MASKHADOV.
Vice-President: VAKHA KHASANOVICH ARSANOV.
Chairman of the Parliament: RUSLAN ALIKHADZHIYEV.
Chairman of the Supreme Shari'a Court: BEKKHAN NUSUKHANOV.
Permanent Representative of the President of the Russian Federation: VALENTIN STEPANOVICH VLASOV.
Representative of the Government of the Russian Federation: GEORGII VASILIYEVICH KURIN.
Plenipotentiary Representative in Moscow: VAKHA SHAMSUDINOVICH KHASANOV; tel. (095) 241-03-59; fax (095) 241-73-80.
Head of Dzhokhar City Administration (Mayor): LECHA BEKMURZIYEVICH DUDAYEV; tel. (8712) 22-01-42.

Chuvashiya

The Chuvash Republic is situated in the north-west of European Russia. It forms part of the Volga-Vyatka Economic Area. It lies on the Eastern European Plain on the middle reaches of the Volga. Ulyanovsk Oblast neighbours it to the south, the Republic of Mordoviya to the south-west, Nizhnii Novgorod Oblast to the west and the Republics of Marii-El and Tatarstan to the north and the east, respectively. The Republic's major rivers are the Volga and the Sura, and one-third of its territory is covered by forest. It occupies 18,300 sq km (7,070 sq miles) and comprises 21 administrative districts and nine cities. The territory measures 190 km (118 miles) from south to north and 160 km from west to east. At 1 January 1996 the Republic had an estimated total population of 1,361,000 and a relatively high population density of 74.4 per sq km. Some 60.6% of the population at this time lived in towns. In contrast to the native peoples in the majority of autonomous republics, the Chuvashs outnumber ethnic Russians in Chuvashiya: in the census of 1989, 67.8% of inhabitants were Chuvash and 26.7% Russians. In addition, 2.7% of the population were Tatars and 1.4% Mordovian. The native tongue of the Republic is Chuvash, which has its origins in the Bulgar group of the Western Hunnic group of Turkic languages and is related to ancient Bulgar and Khazar. It is spoken as a first language by an estimated 76.5% of Chuvashs. The dominant religions in Chuvashiya are Islam and Orthodox Christianity. Chuvashiya's capital is at Cheboksary (Shupashkar—with an estimated population of 461,600 in 1996). Its other major town is Novocheboksarsk, with an estimated 123,500 inhabitants.

History

The Chuvash, traditionally a semi-nomadic people, were conquered by the Mongol-Tatars in the 13th century. Their territory subsequently became part of the dominion of the Golden Horde and many were converted to Islam. From the late 1430s the Chuvash were ruled by the Kazan khanate. In 1551 Chuvashiya became a part of the Russian Empire and Kazan itself was subjugated by Ivan IV in 1552. The Chuvash nation had been formed by the end of the 15th century, with a syncretized culture of Suvar-Bulgar and Finno-Ugric components. In spite of intense Christianization and russification on the part of the Russian state, the Chuvash acquired their own national and cultural identity. The Chuvash capital was founded at Cheboksary in 1551, at the site of a settlement first mentioned in Russian chronicles in 1469. The construction of other towns and forts, intended to encourage migration into the area, followed. The father of Lenin (Vladimir Ulyanov) was of Chuvash descent. After the Revolutions in Russia in 1917 the Chuvash people made vociferous demands for autonomy upon the Soviet Government. A Chuvash Autonomous Oblast was established on 24 June 1920, which was upgraded to the status of an ASSR on 21 April 1925.

Chuvash nationalism re-emerged in the early 1990s: the Chuvash ASSR declared its sovereignty on 27 October 1990. It adopted the name of the Chuvash Republic in March 1992. The territory's conservatism was demonstrated in December 1993, when it voted against acceptance of the federal Constitution, and again in December 1995, when one-third of voters supported the Communist Party. In January 1995 the Chuvash President, Nikolai Fedorov, organized a meeting of republican heads which urged a greater degree of decentralization. In May 1996 the Chuvash Government signed a treaty with the Russian President, Boris Yeltsin, on the delimitation of powers. It granted the Republic greater freedom to determine policy in political, economic and social areas. Elections to the 87-seat State Council were held on 13 July 1998, with further elections for the 23 unfilled seats on 1 November. Compliant voting habits, however, did not mean a passive population—particularly during 1998 the territory experienced a notable volume of litigation, encouraged by the media, over arrears in pension payments and the lack of discounts on utility bills for veterans (in accordance with federal law).

Economy

The Republic's gross regional product in 1995 amounted to 7,518,600m. roubles, equivalent to 5,525,200 roubles per head. Chuvashiya's major industrial centres are at Cheboksary, Novocheboksarsk, Kanash, Alatyr and Shumerlya.

Its agriculture, which employed 20.1% of the work-force in 1995, consists mainly of grain, potato, vegetable, hop, hemp and makhorka-tobacco production, horticulture and animal husbandry. The value of total agricultural output in that year amounted to 2,160,000m. roubles. The Republic contains deposits of peat, sand, limestone and dolomite. Its main industries are mechanical engineering, metal working, electricity generation, production of chemicals, light industry, woodworking, manufacture of building materials and food processing. The industrial sector employed 29.1% of the working population in 1995 and generated 5,322,000m. roubles in income. Chuvashiya's major trading partners are the People's Republic of China, Finland, Germany, Italy, the Netherlands, Poland, Ukraine and the USA.

The economically active population in Chuvashiya amounted to 579,000 in 1995, of which 48,000 were unemployed. The average monthly wage in the territory was 301,000 roubles. There was a budgetary deficit in that year of 21,700m. roubles and the situation did not really improve further into the second half of the 1990s. With increasing media and legal attention to the resulting payment arrears, at the beginning of 1999 the federal authorities announced that Chuvashiya was among the territories that would receive increased assistance for the year ahead. Foreign investment in 1995 was worth US $889,000. At 1 January 1996 there were 5,200 small businesses operating in Chuvashiya.

Directory

President: NIKOLAI VASILIYEVICH FEDOROV; respublika Chuvashiya, 428004 Cheboksary, pl. Respubliki 1, Dom Pravitelstva; tel. (8352) 62-46-87.

Vice-President and Chairman of the Council of Ministers: (vacant); respublika Chuvashiya, 428004 Cheboksary, pl. Respubliki 1, Dom Pravitelstva; tel. (8352) 62-01-71.

Chairman of the State Council (Parliament): LEV PANTELEIMONOVICH KURAKOV; respublika Chuvashiya, 428004 Cheboksary, pl. Respubliki 1, Dom Pravitelstva; tel. (8352) 22-22-72.

Permanent Representative of the President of the Russian Federation: MIKHAIL SERGEYEVICH TIMOFEYEV; respublika Chuvashiya, 428004 Cheboksary, pl. Respubliki 1, Dom Pravitelstva; tel. (8352) 22-00-64.

Permanent Representative in Moscow: GENNADII SEMENOVICH FEDOROV; Moscow, ul. Bolshaya Ordynka 46, korp. 1; tel. (095) 953-21-59

Head of Cheboksary City Administration: ANATOLII ALEKSANDROVICH IGUMNOV; respublika Chuvashiya, 428004 Cheboksary, ul. K. Marksa 36; tel. (8352) 22-35-76.

Dagestan

The Republic of Dagestan (Daghestan) is situated in the North Caucasus on the Caspian Sea. Dagestan forms part of the North Caucasus Economic Area. It has international borders with Azerbaijan to the south and Georgia to the south-west. The Republic of Chechnya and Stavropol Krai lie to the west and the Republic of Kalmykiya to the north. Its largest rivers are the Terek, the Sulak and the Samur. It occupies an area of 50,300 sq km (19,420 sq miles) and measures some 400 km (250 miles) from south to north. Its Caspian Sea coastline, to the east, is 530 km long. The north of the Republic is flat, while in the south are the foothills and peaks of the Greater Caucasus. The Republic's lowest-lying area is the Caspian lowlands, at 28 m (92 feet) below sea level, while its highest peak is over 4,000 m high. Dagestan is made up of 41 administrative districts and 10 cities. The climate in its mountainous areas is continental and dry, while in coastal areas it is subtropical with strong winds. Dagestan is the third-most populated republic of the Russian Federation, with an estimated population of 2,042,000 at 1 January 1996, some 42% of whom inhabited urban areas. Its population density was 39.7 per sq km at this time. In 1989, according to the census, some 27.5% of the population of Dagestan were Avars, 15.6% Dargins, 12.9% Kumyks, 11.3% Lezgis, 5.1% Laks, 1.6% Nogais, 0.8% Rutuls, 0.8% Aguls, 0.3% Tabasarans and 0.3% Tsakhurs, while ethnic Russians formed the fifth-largest nationality, with 9.2%. Dagestan's capital is at Makhachkala, which had an estimated 339,300 inhabitants in 1992. The city lies on the Caspian Sea and is the Republic's main port. Other major cities are Derbent, Khasavyurt, Kaspiisk and Buinaksk.

History

Dagestan formally came under Russian rule in 1723, when the various Muslim khanates on its territory were annexed from Persia (now Iran). The Dagestani peoples were notoriously anti-Russian and conducted a series of rebellions against Russian control, including the Murid Uprising, which lasted from 1828 to 1859. Only then was Russian control established. A Dagestan ASSR was established on 20 January 1920.

The Republic of Dagestan acceded to the Federation Treaty in March 1992 and officially declared its sovereignty in May 1993. The Republic voted against the new Russian Constitution in December and adopted its own on 26 July 1994. Thereafter, Dagestan was seriously affected by the hostilities between the federal Government and rebel groups in Chechnya, most notably in January 1996, when some 2,000 hostages were seized by rebels in the town of Kizlyar, near the Chechen border. Subsequent battles between Chechen groups and Russian federal troops occurred at Pervomaiskoye, north of Kizlyar, resulting in heavy casualties and serious damage to the village. Acts of terrorism and hostage-taking continued throughout the mid-1990s, as in many areas of the North Caucasus (over 100 hostages were reported in the Republic during 1998 alone, with the actual number considered to be probably double that number). Political unrest reached a climax, however, in mid-1998: on 21 May a group of 200–300 fighters belonging to the Union of Russian Muslims (the leader of which, Nadir Khachilayev, was also the head of the ethnic Lak community in Dagestan) occupied a government building in Makhachkala. At the same time around 2,000 demonstrators gathered in the main square of the capital demanding the resignation of the republican Government. A few days later republican forces were involved in armed hostilities with so-called Wahhabis, members of an ascetic Sunni Islamic sect, in the village of Kara-Makhi, Buinaksk district. On 16 August a local supreme body, the Shura (elected the previous day), proclaimed 'a separate Islamic territory' in the village and its neighbours. This move by the Wahhabis added to fears of increasing religious fundamentalism in Dagestan and the North Caucasus generally. Also in August, the spiritual leader of Dagestan's Muslim establishment, Said-Mukhammad-Khadzi Abubakarov, and his brother were killed by a bomb in an attack blamed on Islamic fundamentalists.

On 21 March 1996 the powers of the Dagestani State Council, the supreme executive body, were prolonged for a further two years, in spite of accusations by opposition groups that the ruling Communists were perpetuating their hold on power. When this extra term had elapsed, the republican legislature convened as a Constituent Assembly and, on 26 June 1998, confirmed Magomed Magomedov as the Chairman of the State Council (republican head of state). Late in the year it was agreed to conduct parliamentary elections, for a new People's Assembly, on 7 March 1999 and, at the same time, to have a referendum on whether to institute an executive presidency in Dagestan.

Economy

In 1995 gross regional product in the Republic of Dagestan amounted to 4,148,200m. roubles, or 1,992,000 roubles per head—one of the lowest figures among the federal units. The economic situation in the Republic suffered greatly from the war in Chechnya (November 1994–August 1996), mainly as a result of the transport blockade, the energy shortage and the influx of refugees. The Republic's major industrial centres are at Makhachkala, Derbent, Kaspiisk, Izberbash, Khasavyurt, Kizlyar, Kizilyurt and Buinaksk. There are fishing and trading ports in Makhachkala. It is a major junction for trading routes by rail, land and sea. The major railway line between Rostov-on-Don and Baku (Azerbaijan) runs across the territory, as does the federal Caucasus highway and the petroleum pipeline between Dzhozar (formerly Groznyi) and Baku. There is an airport some 15 km from Makhachkala. In September 1997 the federal Government announced that a new section of the petroleum pipeline from Baku would traverse the southern part of Dagestan, rather than run through Chechnya. The construction of the section was expected to take up to two years.

Owing to its mountainous terrain, Dagestan's economy is largely based on animal husbandry, particularly sheep-breeding. Its agriculture also consists of grain production, viniculture, horticulture and fishing. The agricultural sector employed around 30.9% of the Republic's work-force in 1995 (while just 16.7% worked in industry) and total output in that year amounted to a value of 1,558,700m. roubles. Its main industries are petroleum and natural-gas production, electricity generation, mechanical engineering, metal working, food processing, light industry and handicrafts (especially chiselling and carpet-making). Industrial production in 1995 was worth 1,093,000m. roubles. The Republic's large defence-sector enterprises, such as the Dagdizel Caspian Plant, the Mogomed Gadzhiyev Plant, Aviagregat and the Dagestan Plant of Electrothermal Equipment, were operating below capacity by the mid-1990s. In 1998 all these were thought to be eligible contenders for a contract to manufacture the Gazelle, a light truck produced by GAZ (based in Nizhnii Novgorod).

Dagestan's economically active population comprised 647,000 inhabitants in 1995. Some 53,500 of these were registered unemployed, the remainder earned an average monthly wage of 193,000 roubles. There was a budgetary deficit of 46,600m. roubles. Foreign investment in the territory was minimal (amounting to just US $34,000 in 1995), owing to its proximity to Chechnya and its own incidences of terrorism and unrest during the 1990s. At 1 January 1996 there were 13,600 small businesses registered in the Republic.

Directory

Chairman of the State Council (Head of the Republic): MAGOMED MAGOMEDOVICH MAGOMEDOV; respublika Dagestan, 367005 Makhachkala, pl. Lenina; tel. (8722) 67-30-59.

Chairman of the Government: KHIZRI ISAYEVICH SHIKHSAIDOV; respublika Dagestan, 367005 Makhachkala, pl. Lenina; tel. (8722) 67-19-94.

Chairman of the People's Assembly: MUKHU GIMBATOVICH ALIYEV.

Permanent Representative of the President of the Russian Federation: PETR PETROVICH MARCHENKO (based in Stavropol Krai).

Permanent Representative in Moscow: Gadzhi MAGOMED KADIYEVICH GAMZAYEV; tel. (095) 916-15-36.

Head of Makhachkala City Administration: SAID DZHAPAROVICH AMIROV; respublika Dagestan, 367005 Makhachkala, pl. Lenina; tel. (8722) 67-21-57.

Ingushetiya

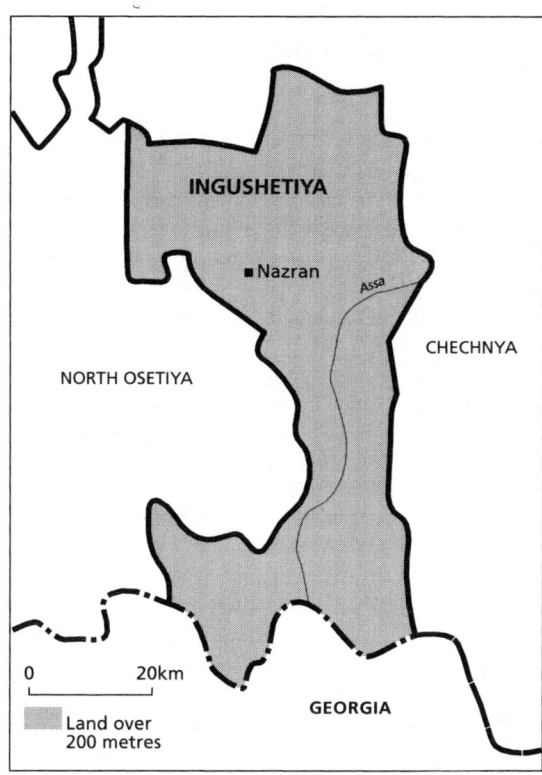

The Republic of Ingushetiya (formerly the Ingush Republic and prior to that part of the Chechen-Ingush ASSR) is situated on the northern slopes of the Greater Caucasus, in the centre of the Northern Caucasus mountain ridge. It forms part of the North Caucasus Economic Area. The Republic of Chechnya borders Ingushetiya on its eastern and northern sides and the Republic of North Osetiya (Ossetia) lies to the west. In the southern mountains there is an international border with Georgia. The Terek, which forms part of the northern border of Ingushetiya, the Assa and the Sunzha are the territory's main rivers. The Republic is extremely mountainous, with some peaks over 3,000 m high. The territory of the Republic occupies about 3,600 sq km (1,400 sq miles) and comprises four administrative districts. The border with Chechnya, however, is not exactly determined, and the Ingushetians are also in dispute with the Osetians. At 1 January 1997 Ingushetiya had an estimated population of 352,000, including some 24,000 displaced persons from the Prigorodnyi raion of North Osetiya and 26,000 refugees from Chechnya. Excluding refugees, the estimated population in 1997 remained at some 301,900. Its population density was, therefore, 97.8 per sq km. The Ingush are a Muslim people closely related to the Chechens (collectively they are known as Vainakhs). They are indigenous to the Caucasus Mountains and have been known historically as Galgai, Lamur, Mountaineers and Kist. Like the Chechen language, their native tongue is a dialect of the Nakh group of the Caucasian language family. Ingushetiya's administrative centre is at Nazran, which had an estimated population of 71,900 at 1 January 1996. There are plans to develop a new capital at Magas (near Nazran), where the presidential residence is already located. Its other principal cities are Malchobek (34,400) and Karabulak (17,500).

History

The Ingush are descended from the western Nakh people whose different reaction to Russian colonization of the Caucasus region in the 1860s distinguished them from their eastern counterparts (subsequently known as the Chechens). The Chechens resisted the invaders violently and were driven into the mountains, while the Ingush reacted more passively and settled on the plains. In spite of this, the Ingush suffered badly under Soviet rule. In 1920 their territory was temporarily integrated into the Mountain (Gorskaya) People's Republic, but became the Ingush Autonomous Oblast on 7 July 1924. In 1934 the region was joined to the Chechen-Ingush Autonomous Oblast, which was upgraded to the status of a Republic in 1936. At this time, many leading Ingush intellectuals were purged and the Ingush literary language was banned. In February 1944 the entire Ingush population (74,000, according to the 1939 census) was deported to Soviet Central Asia, owing to their alleged collaboration with Nazi Germany. Their territory was subsequently handed over to the Osetians. On their return after rehabilitation in 1957 they were forced to purchase their property from Osetian settlers.

Their treatment at the hands of the Government encouraged anti-Russian sentiment among the Ingush and they began to seek more autonomy and independence from their Chechen neighbours. With the ascendancy in the ASSR of the All-National Congress of the Chechen People in 1991, a *de facto* separation was achieved. In June 1992 the Supreme Soviet of the Russian Federation formalized Ingushetiya's separate existence and adopted the law On the Formation of the Ingush Republic within the Russian Federation. The exact borders internal to the old ASSR were not defined, but the Ingush dominated the western territories. In addition, the new Republic claimed the eastern regions of North Osetiya and part of the Osetian capital, Vladikavkaz (formerly Ordzhonikidze). The city had been a shared capital until the 1930s. The raion of Prigorodnyi, with a majority of Ingush inhabitants, was at the centre of the dispute. (A federal law passed in April 1991 established the right for deported peoples to repossess their territory.) Armed hostilities between the two Republics, resulting in the introduction of a state of emergency, began in October 1992 and continued until 1994. Despite a peace agreement, which included provision for the return of refugees, relations remained troubled between the neighbours. Thus, at the beginning of 1999 the Ingushetian leadership condemned North Osetiya for continuing to refuse the return of Ingush refugees to Prigorodnyi, following a border incident on 31 December 1998. This background did not contribute to stability in the Republic, and it too was troubled by incidents of violence and hostage-taking.

On 27 February 1994 simultaneous parliamentary and presidential elections were held in the Republic, as was a referendum on a draft constitution. A total of 97% of the inhabitants of Ingushetiya voted in favour of the document, which thereupon took effect. The population of Ingushetiya remained generally supportive of the regime of Boris Yeltsin, the federal President, but strongly opposed the war in

Chechnya. At the republican presidential election, held on 1 March 1998, Ruslan Aushev was re-elected; his nearest rival was Isa Kostoyev, a member of the federal Prosecutor-General's office. Against a background of continuing extremist violence in the Republic, Aushev, who was sworn in on 14 March, declared his intention to pursue a policy of further stabilization in the Caucasus. His popular mandate, however, also emboldened him in the struggle with the central government—a referendum on the delimitation of powers between the Republic and the Federation was scheduled for 28 February 1999.

Economy

In 1995 gross regional product in the Republic totalled 562,700m. roubles, or just 1,940,400 roubles per head. Essentially agricultural, Ingushetiya was a tax haven during the mid-1990s, and hoped to benefit from the transit of Caspian hydrocarbons from the beginning of the 21st century.

In the early 1990s Ingushetiya's economy was largely agricultural (the sector employed 29.5% of the Republic's work-force in 1995), its primary activity being cattle-breeding. Agricultural production, however, was in a state of serious decline at this time, necessitating certain measures by the republican Government to prevent its collapse. Unprofitable collective farms of the Soviet period were successfully converted into private enterprises and joint-stock companies. By 1 January 1997 there were over 1,000 private farms and 20 joint-stock companies in the Republic. In 1995 the value of its agricultural output was 141,700m. roubles. Ingushetiya's industry, which employs just 11.1% of the working population, consists of chemical production, petroleum refining and light industry. Total industrial production amounted to a value of 63,000m. roubles in 1995. During the mid-1990s the service sector had also made a contribution to the economy: on 1 July 1994 the Republic had become an 'offshore' tax haven (*ofshornaya zona*). This produced substantial benefits to the local economy in terms of registration fees and taxes paid by the companies in the offshore zone. During the period of operation of the tax haven its resources accounted for some 70% of the Republic's capital investments—around 500,000m. roubles. In late 1996, however, it was censured by the International Monetary Fund, which sought to dissuade the republican Government from granting *ad hoc* tax exemptions. A total of 88 enterprises and projects came into being between 1995 and 1996.

In 1995 the average monthly wage in the Republic was just 116,000 roubles. The regional budget showed a deficit of 423,500m. roubles in that year. However, capital investment was high at this time, owing to the operations of the offshore zone. Some of this income was of tangible and sustained benefit to Ingushetiya. Thus, at the end of 1996 the republican President, Aushev, signed an agreement with the president of the major petroleum company, LUKoil, which provided the company with favourable rates of taxation in return for investing some US $5,000m. in a variety of technical and construction projects. LUKoil was also a participant in the construction of the Caspian pipeline running through the territory.

Directory

President: RUSLAN SULTANOVICH AUSHEV; respublika Ingushetiya, 366720 Nazran, pr. I. Bazorkina; tel. (87322) 2-33-07; fax (87322) 334-20-39.

Chairman of the Government (Prime Minister): MAGOMED-BASHIR DARSIGOV; respublika Ingushetiya, 366720 Nazran, pr. I. Bazorkina; tel. (87322) 2-11-26.

Chairman of the People's Assembly: RUSLAN SULTANOVICH PLIYEV; tel. (87322) 2-61-81.

Permanent Representative of the President of the Russian Federation: VLADIMIR AVDASHEVICH KALAMANOV.

Permanent Representative in Moscow: KHAMZAT MAGOMEDOVICH BELKHAROYEV; tel. (095) 912-92-75.

Head of Nazran City Administration: ZAKRE KHASANOVICH SULTYGOV; tel. (87322) 2-53-68.

Kabardino-Balkariya

The Kabardino-Balkar Republic (Kabardino-Balkar ASSR prior to March 1992) is situated on the northern slopes of the Greater Caucasus and on the Kabardin Flatlands. It forms part of the North Caucasus Economic Area. The Republic of North Osetiya (Ossetia) lies to the east and there is an international border with Georgia in the south-west. The rest of the territory's border is with Stavropol Krai, with the Republic of Karachayevo-Cherkessiya to the west. Kabardino-Balkariya's major rivers are the Terek, the Malka and the Baskan. The territory of the Republic occupies an area of 12,500 sq km (4,800 sq miles), of which one-half is mountainous. The highest peak in Europe, twin-peaked Elbrus, at a height of 5,642 m (18,517 feet), is situated in Kabardino-Balkariya. The Republic consists of nine administrative districts and seven cities. At 1 January 1996 the estimated population of the Republic was 790,000 (57.7% of which lived in urban areas) and its population density was 63.2 per sq km, one of the highest in the Russian Federation. Figures from the census of 1989 indicate that at that time some 48.2% of inhabitants were Kabardins, 9.4% were Balkars and 32.0% were Russian. Both the Kabardins and the Balkars are Sunni Muslims. The Kabardins' native language belongs to the Abkhazo-Adyge group of Caucasian languages. The Balkars speak a language closely related to Karachai, part of the Kipchak group of the Turkic branch of the Uralo-Altaic family. Both peoples almost exclusively speak their native tongue as a first language, but many are fluent in the official language, Russian. The capital of the Republic is at Nalchik, which had an estimated population of 237,100 at 1 January 1996. Its other major city, Prokhladnyi, had around 59,500 inhabitants at this time.

History

The Turkic Kabardins, a Muslim people of the North Caucasus, are believed to be descended from the Adyges. They settled on the banks of the Terek river, mixed with the local Alan people, and became a distinct ethnic group in the 15th century. The Kabardins were converted to Islam by the Tatar Khanate of Crimea in the early 16th century, but in 1561 appealed to Tsar Ivan IV for protection against Tatar rule. The Ottoman Turks and the Persians (Iranians) also had interests in the region and in 1739 Kabardiya was established as a neutral state between the Ottoman and Russian Empires. In 1774, however, the region once again became Russian territory under terms of the Treaty of Kuçuk Kainavci. Although the Kabardins were never openly hostile to the Russian authorities, in the 1860s many of them migrated to the Ottoman Empire. The Balkars were pastoral nomads until the mid-18th century when they were forced by threats from marauding tribes to retreat further into the Northern Caucasus Mountains and settle there as farmers and livestock breeders. They were converted to Islam by Crimean Tatars, followed by the Nogais from the Kuban basin, although their faith retained strong elements of their animist traditions. Balkariya came under Russian control in 1827, when it was dominated by the Kabardins. Many ethnic Russians migrated to the region during the 19th century. In 1921 Balkar District was created as part of the Mountain (Gorskaya) People's Republic (also included present-day Chechnya, Ingushetiya, Karachayevo-Cherkessiya and North Osetiya), but was integrated into the Kabardino-Balkar Autonomous Province the following year. The Kabardino-Balkar ASSR was established on 5 December 1936. In 1943 the Balkars were deported to Kazakhstan and Central Asia and the Balkar administrative district within the Republic was disbanded. The Balkars were not recognized as a people until 1956, when they were allowed to return to the Caucasus region.

Thus, although greatly outnumbered by Kabardins and Russians, the Balkars had developed a strong sense of ethnic identity. In 1991 they joined the Assembly of Turkic Peoples and, on 18 November, the first congress of the National Council of the Balkar People declared the sovereignty of Balkariya and the formation of a 'Republic of Balkariya' within the Russian Federation. Kabardino-Balkariya declared its sovereignty on 31 December 1991, and signed a bilateral treaty with the federal authorities during 1995. The Republic also developed links with its neighbours: on 21 February 1996 its President, Valerii Kokov, declared that Kabardino-Balkariya would not abide by the Commonwealth of Independent States decision to impose sanctions on Abkhazia (Georgia), as that would run counter to a treaty between the two polities. In May 1998, at the second session of an interparliamentary council with the Republics of Adygeya and Karachayevo-Cherkessiya, a programme was adopted on the co-ordination of legislative, economic, environmental and legal activities.

Kabardino-Balkariya has an executive presidency and a bicameral Legislative Assembly or Parliament, consisting of an upper chamber known as the Soviet of the Republic and a lower chamber known as the Soviet of Representatives. The old nomenklatura class remained firmly in control, although their allegiance was divided between the federal Government and the Communist Party. The republican leadership took a pragmatic approach to reform and encouraged foreign investment. Kokov resigned from the centrist Our Home is Russia movement in May 1998.

Economy

Gross regional product in Kabardino-Balkariya amounted to 2,627,100m. roubles in 1995, equivalent to 3,325,800 roubles per head. The Republic's main industrial centres are at Nalchik, Tyrnyauz and Prokhladnyi. Prokhladnyi is an important junction on the North Caucasus Railway. There is an international airport at

Nalchik, from which there are regular flights to the Middle East, as well as to other cities within the Russian Federation. At the end of the 1990s foreign investment was being sought to finance the construction of a new international airport.

Karbardino-Balkariya's main agricultural products are maize and sunflowers. Animal husbandry, horticulture and viniculture are also important. In 1995 around 16.6% of the Republic's work-force was engaged in the agricultural sector, the output of which was worth a total of 1,240,500m. roubles. By 1997 there were over 600 private agricultural enterprises in the Republic, covering some 5,500 ha. Like the rest of the North Caucasus region, the Republic is rich in minerals, with reserves of petroleum, natural gas, gold, iron ore, garnet, talc and barytes. It is a net importer of electricity, producing less than one-10th of its requirement. The Republic's main industries, which employed some 21.9% of the work-force in 1995, are mechanical engineering, metal working, non-ferrous metallurgy, food processing and light industry, manufacture of building materials and the production and processing of tungsten-molybdenum ores. Total industrial output in 1995 was worth 1,396,000m. roubles. Most of the Republic's exports (of which raw materials comprise some 70%) are to Finland, Germany, the Netherlands, Turkey and the USA. Some four-fifths of its imports are from Europe.

The economically active population in Kabardino-Balkariya in 1995 totalled 258,000, of which 9,800 were registered unemployed. Those in employment were earning an average of 266,000 roubles per month. There was a budgetary deficit of 57,700m. roubles. Foreign investment in the Republic in that year amounted to US $2.45m. At 1 January 1996 there was a total of 4,100 small businesses in operation.

Directory

President: VALERII MUKHAMEDOVICH KOKOV; respublika Kabardino-Balkariya, Nalchik, Dom Pravitelstva; tel. (86622) 2-20-64.

Vice-President: GENNADII SERGEYEVICH GUBIN; respublika Kabardino-Balkariya, Nalchik, Dom Pravitelstva; tel. (86622) 2-21-62.

Prime Minister: KHUSEIN DZHABRAILOVICH CHECHENOV; respublika Kabardino-Balkariya, Nalchik, Dom Pravitelstva; tel. (86622) 2-21-26.

Legislative Assembly (Parliament): respublika Kabardino-Balkariya, Nalchik, ul. Lenina 55, Dom Sovetov.

    Chairman of the Soviet of the Republic: ZAURBI AKHMEDOVICH NAKHUSHEV; tel. (86622) 7-13-74.

    Chairman of the Soviet of Representatives: ILYAS BORISOVICH BECHELOV; tel. (86622) 7-33-04.

Permanent Representative of the President of the Russian Federation: PETR PETROVICH MARCHENKO (based in Stavropol Krai).

Permanent Representative in Moscow: ANATOLII GUZEROVICH EMUZOV; tel. (095) 271-18-52.

Head of Nalchik City Administration: MUKHAMED MAYEVICH SHOGENOV; respublika Kabardino-Balkariya, Nalchik, ul. Sovetskaya 70; tel. (86622) 2-20-04.

Kalmykiya

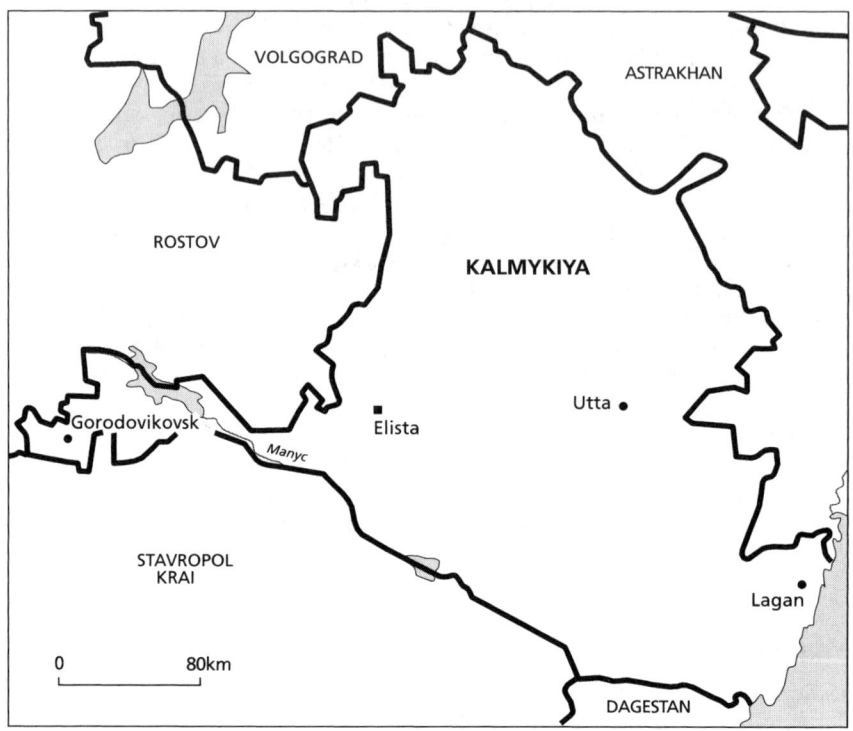

The Republic of Kalmykiya (known as the Republic of Kalmykiya-Khalmg Tangch from February 1992 until February 1996) is situated in the north-western part of the Caspian Sea lowlands. It forms part of the Volga Economic Area. The south-eastern part of the Republic lies on the Caspian Sea. It has a southern border with the Republic of Dagestan and a south-western border with Stavropol Krai, while Rostov, Volgograd and Astrakhan Oblasts lie to the west, north-west and north-east, respectively. The Republic occupies an area of 75,900 sq km (29,300 sq miles), one-half of which is desert, and comprises 13 administrative districts and three cities. At 1 January 1996 it had an estimated population of 319,000, of which 61.5% lived in urban areas, and a population density of 4.2 per sq km. One year later the total population was estimated at 320,000. In 1989, according to the census, some 45.4% of the total population were Kalmyks and 37.7% Russians. Unusually for Europe, the dominant religion among the Kalmyks is Lamaism (Tibetan Buddhism). Their native language is from the Mongol division of the Uralo-Altaic family and is spoken as a first language by some 90% of the indigenous population. The capital of Kalmykiya is at Elista, which had an estimated 96,200 inhabitants at 1 January 1996. The Republic's other cities are Lagan (15,600) and Gorodovikovsk (10,700).

History

The Kalmyks (also known as the Kalmuks, Kalmucks, Khalmgs and Oirots) originated in Eastern Turkestan (Central Asia—Dzungaria or Sungaria, mostly now part of the province of Xinjiang, People's Republic of China) and were a semi-nomadic Mongol-speaking people. Displaced by the Han Chinese, some 100,000 Kalmyks migrated westwards, in 1608 reaching the Volga basin, an area between the Don and Ural rivers which had been under Russian control since the subjugation of the Astrakhan khanate in 1556. The region, extending from Stavropol in the west to Astrakhan in the east, became the Kalmyk khanate (Kalmykiya), but was dissolved by Russia in 1771. By this time the Kalmyk community was severely depleted, the majority having been slaughtered during a mass migration eastwards to protect the Oirots from persecution by the Chinese. Those that remained were dispersed: some settled along the Ural, Terek and Kuma rivers, some were moved to Siberia, while others became Don Cossacks. Many ethnic Russians and Germans invited by Catherine II (the 'Great') settled in Kalmykiya during the 18th century. In 1806 the Kalmyks' pasture lands were greatly reduced by the tsarist government, forcing many to abandon their nomadic lifestyle and find work as fishermen and salt miners. A Kalmyk Autonomous Oblast was established by the Soviet Government on 4 November 1920 and the Kalmyks living in other regions of Russia were resettled there. Its status was upgraded to that of an ASSR in 1935. In 1943 the Republic was dissolved as retribution for the Kalmyks' alleged collaboration with German forces. The Kalmyks were deported to Central Asia, where they lived until their *de facto* rehabilitation in 1956. A Kalmyk Autonomous Oblast was reconstituted in 1957 and an ASSR in 1958.

During the late 1980s a growing Kalmyk nationalist movement began protesting against the treatment of the Kalmyks under Stalin (Iosif Dzhugashvili) and demanding local control of the region's mineral resources. A declaration of sovereignty by the Republic was adopted on 18 October 1990. On 28 December 1993 the Kalmyks were formally rehabilitated by the Russian President. On 11 March 1994 the President of Kalmykiya, Kirsan Ilyumzhinov, abrogated the republican Constitution and decreed that from 25 March only the Russian basic law would be valid in the Republic. However, a new republican constitution, known as the Steppe Legislation, was adopted on 5 April 1994. The loyalty of the republican political establishment, as far as the Federation was concerned, was demonstrated by the high level of support for Our Home is Russia (headed by Viktor Chernomyrdin, the federal premier) in the all-Russian general election of December 1995. This might also be interpreted as a result of political coercion, however: during the mid-1990s it became obvious that Ilyumzhinov, who suspended all local councils and suppressed political parties and publications critical of his regime, was adopting an increasingly autocratic style of government in Kalmykiya.

In 1995 Ilyumzhinov was the sole, unopposed candidate in the presidential election, in contravention of federal legislation. There was little serious challenge to his rule in the second half of the decade, although he attracted an increasing degree of controversy. (There were rumours that Ilyumzhinov was one of Russia's richest politicians, possessing US $1m. in income and assets which included six Rolls-Royce automobiles.) On 16 February 1998 he issued a decree abolishing the republican Government, in order to reduce public spending and bureaucracy. Of particular concern, however, was the arrest of one of the President's former aides in connection with the alleged murder, on 6 June, of Larisa Yudina, editor of an opposition newspaper. Local authorities subsequently banned a rally in the journalist's memory. The controversy surrounding Yudina's death added to outside interest in the 1998 Chess Olympiad, held in September in Elista. The event, promoted by Ilyumzhinov (head of the International Chess Federation—FIDE), was allegedly funded by government money intended for social security and investment in agriculture and industry. In June there had been other reports of financial irregularities on the part of the republican authorities—the federal legislature instructed the Audit Chamber to investigate the legitimacy of federal budget spending in 1996–98. Such investigations probably prompted Ilyumzhinov's controversial hint of secession in November 1998, although he denied such intentions following a strong federal reaction and, indeed, indicated his ambitions for the presidency of the Federation.

Legislative elections were held in Kalmykiya on 19 October 1998, to a 27-seat Parliament. Early in November a new premier, Viktor Baturin, was appointed. The architect of 'Chess City', built in Elista that year, he was also the brother-in-law of the Mayor of Moscow. Ilyumzhinov hoped to cement alliances elsewhere in Russia, but also expected economic assistance for the new government programme of social assistance (mainly housing) and economic expansion.

Economy

Kalmykiya is primarily an agricultural territory, with agricultural production comprising over one-half of its total output (gross regional product), which in 1995 amounted to 890,200m. roubles, or 2,789,900 roubles per head. In the mid-1990s, however, much of its agricultural land was in danger of desertification, owing to its irresponsible exploitation by the Soviet authorities during the 1950s, when the fragile black topsoil on the steppe was ploughed up or grazed all year round by sheep and cattle. (The sheep were even the wrong kind, they had sharp hooves which damaged the fragile grass.) With the collapse of the centralized economy, however, the number of sheep in the Republic fell by 80% and numbers of the indigenous saigak antelope began to increase. Kalmykiya's major industrial centres are at Elista and Kaspiisk. The Republic has an advanced road network and is intersected by the Astrakhan–Kizlyar railway line. Elista airport acquired international status in August 1996. The Republic has serious problems with its water supply, with a deficit of fresh water affecting almost all regions.

Kalmykiya's agriculture consists mainly of grain production and animal husbandry. The sector employed 33.9% of the Republic's work-force and generated 478,400m. roubles in 1995. Its industry, which engaged just 9.5% of the working population at that time, consists mainly of mechanical engineering, metal working, manufacture of building materials, food and timber processing and the production of petroleum and natural gas. In 1995 industrial output was equivalent to 337,000m. roubles. The Republic has major hydrocarbons reserves. In 1995 Kalmykiya extracted an estimated 500,000 metric tons of crude petroleum, which was exported to neighbouring regions in return for manufactured goods. In August 1995 Kalmykiya began negotiations with several foreign countries to build a petroleum refinery in Elista with an annual capacity of 500,000 metric tons of petroleum products. This US $22m. project was to be implemented by the new republican energy ministry, established in January 1996. The Oman Oil Company and LUKoil (a Russian company) showed interest in exploiting the Republic's petroleum and natural-gas deposits. It was estimated that Kalmykiya's hydrocarbons production could be increased by some 2m.–3m. tons per year. Despite its potential, Kalmykiya is currently a net importer of energy. The construction and services sectors benefited from preparations for and the hosting of the Chess Olympiad in Elista in September 1998.

The economically active population in the Republic amounted to 128,100 in 1995. Some 13,000 of these were registered unemployed. The average monthly wage at this time was 232,000 roubles and there was a budgetary surplus of 1,400m. roubles. Indeed, from 1996 Kalmykiya was declared a 'donor' region (one of only 13 such in the Federation during 1998), although at the beginning of 1999 the federal Government objected to the republican authorities' failure to hand over certain revenues in full. In 1995 there was some $1.64m.-worth of foreign investment in the Republic. By the beginning of 1997 the Republic had some 1,500 small businesses, almost one-half of which were involved in catering and trade.

Directory

President: KIRSAN NIKOLAYEVICH ILYUMZHINOV; respublika Kalmykiya, 358000 Elista, pl. Lenina, Dom Pravitelstva; tel. (84722) 5-06-55; fax (84722) 6-28-80.

Chairman of the Government: VIKTOR BATURIN; respublika Kalmykiya, 358000 Elista, pl. Lenina, Dom Sovetov; tel. (84722) 6-17-36.

Chairman of the Parliament: KONSTANTIN NIKOLAYEVICH MAKSIMOV; respublika Kalmykiya, 358000 Elista, pl. Lenina, Dom Sovetov; tel. (84722) 6-17-76.

Permanent Representative of the President of the Russian Federation: VYACHESLAV ANATOLIYEVICH BEMBETOV.

Permanent Representative in Moscow: ALEKSEI MARATOVICH ORLOV; tel. (095) 291-48-32.

Head of Elista City Administration: VYACHESLAV MIKHAILOVICH SHAMAYEV; respublika Kalmykiya, 358000 Elista, ul. Lenina 249; tel. (84722) 5-23-14; fax (84722) 5-42-56.

Karachayevo-Cherkessiya

The Republic of Karachayevo-Cherkessiya (formerly an Autonomous Oblast) is situated on the northern slopes of the Greater Caucasus. It forms part of Stavropol Krai and the North Caucasus Economic Area. Krasnodar Krai borders it to the north-west, Stavropol Krai proper to the north-east and the Republic of Kabardino-Balkariya to the east. There is an international boundary with Georgia (mainly with Abkhazia) to the south. Its major river is the Kuban. The total area of the Republic occupies some 14,100 sq km (5,440 sq miles). The territory measures 140 km (87 miles) from north to south and 160 km from west to east. Karachayevo-Cherkessiya consists of eight administrative districts and four cities. It had an estimated population of 436,000 at 1 January 1996 (of which some 46% inhabited urban areas) and a population density, therefore, of 30.9 per sq km. Of the Republic's inhabitants, some 119,900 were estimated to inhabit the capital, Cherkessk, at this time. Figures from the 1989 census showed that the Karachai accounted for 31.2% of the Republic's population, the Cherkess (Circassians) for 9.7% and ethnic Russians for 42.4%. Both the Karachai and the Cherkess are Sunni Muslims of the Hanafi school. The Cherkess speak a language close to Kabardin, from the Abkhazo-Adyge group of Caucasian languages, while the Karachais' native tongue, from the Kipchak group, is the same as that of the Balkars. The other cities in the Republic are Ust-Dzheguta (with an estimated 31,500 inhabitants at 1 January 1996) and Karachayevsk (20,900).

History

The Karachais, traditionally a transhumant group, descended from Kipchak tribes, were driven into the highlands of the North Caucasus by marauding Mongol tribes in the 13th century. Their territory was annexed by the Russian Empire in 1828, although, like their neighbouring North Caucasian peoples, they continued to resist Russian rule throughout the 19th century. In the 1860s and 1870s many Karachais migrated to the Ottoman Empire to escape oppression by the tsarist regime. Many of the Cherkess, a Circassian people descended from the Adyges who inhabited the region between the lower Don and Kuban rivers, also fled across the Russo-Turkish border at this time. They had come under Russian control in the 1550s, having sought protection from the Crimean Tatars and some Turkic tribes, including the Karachais. Relations between the Cherkess and Russia deteriorated as many Russians began to settle in Cherkess territory. Following the Treaty of Adrianople in 1829, by which the Ottomans abandoned their claim to the Caucasus region, a series of rebellions by the Circassians and reprisals by the Russian authorities occurred. In 1864 Russia completed its conquest of the region and many Cherkess fled.

The Cherkess Autonomous Oblast was established in 1928 and was subsequently merged with the Karachai Autonomous Oblast to form the Karachayevo-Cherkess Autonomous Oblast. This represented part of Stalin's (Iosif Dzhugashvili) policy of 'divide and conquer', by which administrative units were formed from ethnically unrelated groups (the same applied to the Kabardino-Balkar ASSR). The Karachai were among the peoples Stalin deported during the Second World War (they were moved to Central Asia in late 1943) but the Cherkess remained in the region, which was renamed the Cherkess Autonomous Oblast, until the Karachai were rehabilitated and permitted to return in 1957. Ethnic separatism in the territory, which was upgraded to republican status under the terms of the 1992 Federation Treaty, was minimal, compared to other Republics in the Caucasus region. There was, however, sympathy for the secessionist regime of the Abkhazians (another Circassian people) in Georgia. On 6 March 1996 a new constitutional system was adopted in the Republic, based on the results of a referendum on a republican presidency. The Republic had already, in the previous year, agreed on a division of responsibilities by treaty with the Russian Federation. A conservative territory, the Communists remained the predominant party (winning 40% of the republican vote in federal parliamentary elections at the end of 1995). In May 1998, at the second session of an interparliamentary council with the Republics of Adygeya and Kabardino-Balkariya, a programme was adopted on the co-ordination of the Republics' legislative, economic, environmental and legal activities. On 22 September enabling legislation providing for direct elections to the republican presidency was finally enacted. A poll was expected during 1999.

Economy

In 1995 gross regional product in Karachayevo-Cherkessiya totalled 1,701,700m. roubles, or 3,903,000 roubles per head. The predominant sector within the economy, in terms of volume of output and number of employees, is industry. The Republic's major industrial centres are at Cherkessk, Karachayevsk and Zelenchukskaya. It contains 52 km of railway track and 3,800 km of roads (of which 2,300 km are paved), including the Stavropol–Sukhumi (Georgia) highway.

Karachayevo-Cherkessiya's agriculture, which employed some 18.2% of the working population in 1995, consists mainly of animal husbandry. At 1 January 1995 there were some 182,100 cattle, 16,200 pigs, 555,400 sheep and goats and 16,900 horses in the Republic. The production of grain, sunflower seeds, sugar-beets and vegetables is also important. Owing to agricultural reforms in the region following the collapse of the centralized economy, by 1 January 1995 there were 835 private farms, occupying just under 2,000 ha. Total agricultural production in that year amounted to a value of 727,800m. roubles. The Republic's main industries are petrochemicals, chemicals, mechanical engineering and metal working. Light industry, the manufacture of building materials, timber processing and coal production are also important. In 1995 industry's total output was equivalent to 999,000m. roubles, while it employed around 24.3% of the work-force.

In 1995 the economically active population in the Republic amounted to 137,500 of its inhabitants, although 7,900 of these were registered unemployed. The average wage was 232,000 roubles per month. There was a large budgetary deficit in that year, amounting to 643,800m. roubles. At 1 January 1996 there were 2,100 small businesses registered in the Republic.

Directory

Head of the Republic: VLADIMIR ISLAMOVICH KHUBIYEV; respublika Karachayevo-Cherkessiya, 357100 Cherkessk, pr. Lenina, Dom Sovetov; tel. (87822) 2-40-40.

Chairman of the Government: ANATOLII GALIMZHANOVICH OZOV.

Chairman of the People's Assembly: IGOR VLADIMIROVICH IVANOV.

Permanent Representative of the President of the Russian Federation: PETR PETROVICH MARCHENKO (based in Stavropol Krai).

Permanent Representative in Moscow: MAGOMED KADEVICH KAITOV; tel. (095) 124-85-87.

Head of Cherkessk City Administration: STANISLAV EDUARDOVICH DEREV; respublika Karachayevo-Cherkessiya, 357100 Cherkessk, pr. Lenina 54A; tel. (87822) 5-42-24; fax (87822) 5-78-43.

Kareliya

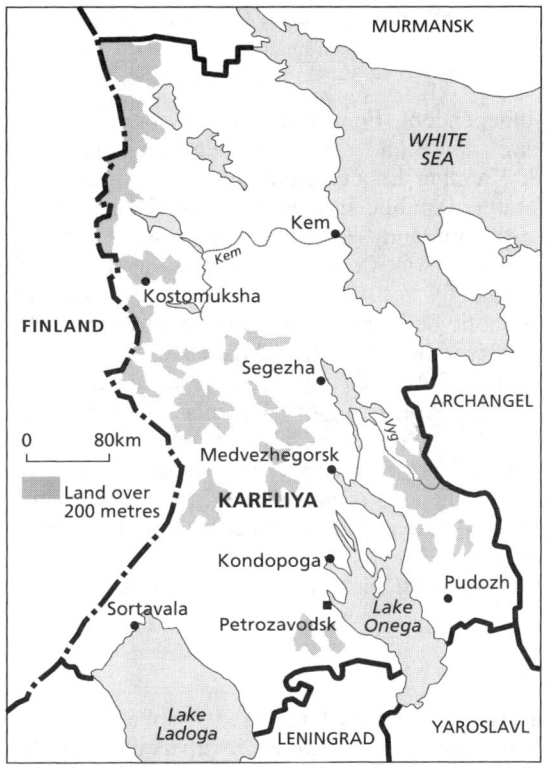

The Republic of Kareliya (Karelia) is situated in the north-west of the country, on the edge of the Eastern European Plain. The Republic forms part of the Northern Economic Area. It is bordered by Finland to the west. The White Sea lies to the north-east, Murmansk Oblast to the north and Vologda and Archangel Oblasts to the south. It contains some 83,000 km (51,540 miles) of waterways, including its major rivers, the Kem and the Vyg, and its numerous lakes (the Ladoga, Ladozhskoye, and the Onega, Onezhskoye, being the largest and second-largest lakes in Europe). A canal system 225 km long, the Belomorkanal, connects the Karelian port of Belomorsk to St Petersburg. One-half of its territory is forested and much of the area on the White Sea coast is marshland. It lies, on average, 300–400 m above sea level. Kareliya measures some 600 km south–north and 400 km west–east and occupies an area of 172,400 sq km (66,560 sq miles). It comprises 16 administrative districts and 13 cities. At 1 January 1996 it had an estimated population of 785,000, of whom some 74.0% inhabited urban areas, and a population density of some 4.6 per sq km. In 1989 some 10.0% of the population were Karelians (Finnish—also known as Karjala or Karyala, Korela and Karyalainen) and 73.6% Russians. The dominant religion among Karelians, and in the Republic as a whole, is Orthodox Christianity. The Karelian language consists of three dialects of Finnish

(Livvi, Karjala and Lyydiki), which are all strongly influenced by Russian. In 1989, however, more than one-half of the Karelian population spoke Russian as their first language. The capital of Kareliya is at Petrozavodsk, with an estimated population of 282,200 at 1 January 1996. Other major cities are Kondopoga (36,700), Segezha (36,300), Kostomuksha (31,600) and Sortavala (21,500).

History

Kareliya was an independent, Finnish-dominated state in medieval times. In the 16th century the area came under Swedish hegemony, before being annexed by Russia in 1721. A Karelian Labour Commune was formed on 8 June 1920 and became an autonomous republic in July 1923. A Karelo-Finnish SSR, including territory annexed from Finland, was created in 1940 as a Union Republic of the USSR. However, part of its territory was ceded to the Russian Federation in 1946 and Kareliya subsequently resumed its status of an ASSR within the Russian Federation. The Republic declared sovereignty on 9 August 1990. It was renamed on 13 November 1991 as the Republic of Kareliya. Its Constitution was adopted on 20 January 1994. On 17 April elections took place to a new bicameral legislature, the Legislative Assembly (consisting of a Chamber of the Republic and a Chamber of Representatives). The premier, who was vested with a quasi-presidential status as the republican head, Viktor Stepanov, was a critic of the federal Government and, in 1995, was prominent in urging greater decentralization. On 17 May 1998 Stepanov was narrowly defeated in the second round of direct elections to the premiership by the former Mayor of Petrozavodsk, Sergei Katanandov. A total of 49.5% of the votes were cast in favour of Katanandov, while Stepanov secured 43.4%.

Economy

The economy of Kareliya is largely based on its timber industry. In 1995 its gross regional product was 8,065,300m. roubles, equivalent to 10,245,500 roubles per head. Its major industrial centres are at Petrozavodsk, Sortavala, Kem, Kondopoga, Medvezhegorsk, Belomorsk and Segezha. In the mid-1990s Russia's first commercial railway was constructed on the territory of Kareliya. The Republic is at an important strategic point on Russia's roadways, linking the industrially developed regions of Russia with the major northern port of Murmansk. Its main port is at Petrozavodsk.

Kareliya's agriculture, which employed just 5.9% of the work-force in 1995, consists mainly of animal husbandry, fur farming and fishing. Total production within the sector was equivalent to 773,100m. roubles. The Republic has important mineral reserves, which attracted some 4,300m. roubles in investment during 1996, of which 44% was from foreign companies. An important agreement with the city of Moscow, which had need for construction materials, promised an increase in natural-stone procuction from some 3,000 cu m in 1998 to 20,000 cu m by 2002. Its main industries, apart from the processing of forestry products, are mechanical engineering, metallurgy and the extraction of iron ore and muscovite (mica). Industry engaged some 27.6% of the Republic's labour force in 1995, while total output within the sector was worth 6,163,000m. roubles. The Republic's major enterprise, Segezhabumprom, is one of the world's largest pulp and paper manufacturers. In July 1997 the Swedish group, AssiDomän, purchased a controlling stake

Autonomous Republics (Kareliya)

in the company. In 1995 the value of trade, which had increased by almost five times since 1992, was just under US $800m.

The economically active population in that year amounted to 370,600, of whom 21,900 were unemployed. The average monthly wage in the Republic was 232,000 roubles. The republican budget showed a surplus of 1,204,800m. roubles in 1995. Foreign investment in Kareliya at that time amounted to US $1.95m. There were some 400 foreign joint enterprises in Kareliya in 1997, of which more than one-half had Finnish partners. At 1 January 1996 there were some 4,700 small businesses operating in the Republic.

Directory

Chairman of the Government (Head of the Republic): SERGEI LEONIDOVICH KATANANDOV; respublika Kareliya, 185028 Petrozavodsk, pr. Lenina 19; tel. (8142) 76-41-41; fax (8142) 77-41-48.

Legislative Assembly: respublika Kareliya, 185610 Petrozavodsk, ul. Kuibysheva 5; tel. (8142) 7-27-44.

Chairman of the Chamber of the Republic: IVAN PETROVICH ALEKSANDROV.

Chairman of the Chamber of Representatives: VALENTINA NIKOLAYEVNA PIVMENKO.

Permanent Representative of the President of the Russian Federation: VYACHESLAV NIKOLAYEVICH USHAKOV.

Permanent Representative in Moscow: GEORGII ALEKSANDROVICH KUTS; tel. (095) 207-87-24.

Head of Petrozavodsk City Administration: (vacant); tel. (81400) 77-35-70; (81400) 77-49-47.

Khakasiya

The Republic of Khakasiya is situated in the western area of the Minusinsk hollow, on the left bank of the River Yenisei, which flows northwards towards, ultimately, the Arctic Ocean. In the heart of Eurasia, it lies on the eastern slopes of the Kuznetsk Alatau and the northern slopes of the Western Sayan Mountains. It lies within Krasnoyarsk Krai and is part of the Eastern Siberian Economic Area. The Republic of Tyva lies to the south-east and the Republic of Altai to the south-west. To the west is Kemerovo Oblast, while Krasnoyarsk Krai proper is beyond its northern and eastern frontiers. Its major rivers are the Yenisei and the Abakan. Khakasiya occupies 61,900 sq km (23,900 sq miles) and comprises eight administrative regions and five cities. At 1 January 1996 it had an estimated population of 586,000 and a population density, therefore, of 9.5 per sq km. In 1989 ethnic Khakassians were found to number 11.1% of the population, compared to 79.5% Russians. However, at this time over 76% of the Khakass spoke the national language, primarily derived from the Uigur group of Eastern Hunnic languages of the Turkic family, as their native tongue. Khakasiya's capital is at Abakan, with an estimated 163,100 inhabitants in 1996. Other major cities are Chernogorsk (79,600) and Sayanogorsk (56,000).

History

The Khakassians were traditionally known as the Minusinsk (Minusa), the Turki, the Yenisei Tatars or the Abakan Tatars. They were semi-nomadic hunters, fishermen and livestock-breeders. Khakasiya was a powerful state in Siberia, owing to its trading links with Central Asia and the Chinese Empire. Russian settlers began to arrive in the region in the 17th century and their presence was perceived as valuable protection against Mongol invasion. The annexation of Khakassian territory by the Russians was eventually completed during the reign of Peter I ('the Great') with the construction of a fort on the River Abakan. The Russians subsequently imposed heavy taxes, seized the best land and imposed Orthodox Christianity on the Khakassians. After the construction of the Trans-Siberian Railway in the 1890s the Khakassians were heavily outnumbered. Following the Revolution in Russia the Khakass National Okrug was established in 1923, which became the Khakass Autonomous Oblast on 20 October 1930, as part of Krasnoyarsk Krai. In 1992 it was upgraded to the status of an Autonomous Republic under the terms of the Federation Treaty, having declared its sovereignty on 3 July 1991.

Resentment at perceived neglect by the central authorities was encouraged by Communist propagandists, and that party remained the most popular in the Republic in the 1990s. The Russian nationalist ideas of Vladimir Zhirinovskii also enjoyed a significant degree of support. On 25 May 1995 the Republic adopted its Constitution. Elections for a head of government and a new legislature were held on 23 December 1996. Aleksei Lebed, an independent candidate and younger brother of the politician and former general, Aleksandr Lebed (Governor of Krasnoyarsk Krai from May 1998), was elected to the presidency. A former representative of the Republic in the State Duma, he had based his electoral campaign on the issues of administrative, budgetary, social and economic reform. His Government convinced the federal authorities to increase financial transfers to the Republic for 1999.

Economy

Khakasiya's gross regional product amounted to 5,094,000m. roubles in 1995, or 8,704,000 roubles per head. The Republic's industrial output is one of the highest in the Russian Federation. Khakasiya's major industrial centres are at Abakan, Sorsk, Sayanogorsk, Chernogorsk and Balyksa.

The Republic's agriculture, which employed around 13.4% of the working population in 1995, consists mainly of grain production and animal husbandry. Total agricultural production in 1995 was worth 928,400m. roubles. Industry was a far more important sector of the economy, although a major element of industrial activity was the processing of natural resources. In 1997 Khakasiya was estimated to have reserves of 36,000m. metric tons in coal and 1,500m. tons of iron ore. Other mineral reserves included those of molybdenum, lead, zinc, barytes, aluminium and clay. There was also the potential for extraction of petroleum and natural gas. The Republic's main industries are forestry (it contained some 2.8m. ha of forests and had an estimated 170m. cu m in reserves of timber in 1997), ore mining, light manufacturing, mechanical engineering, non-ferrous metallurgy and processing of agricultural products. The Republic's industrial output amounted to a value of 4,417,000m. roubles in 1995, one of the highest levels in Russia. The industrial sector employed 29.5% of the work-force in 1995.

The Republic's economically active population numbered 233,300 in that year, of whom 8,800 were registered unemployed. The average monthly wage stood at 465,000 roubles. The republican budget for 1995 showed a deficit of 12,000m. roubles. Foreign investment in Khakasiya at this time was worth US $1.3m. At 1 January 1996 there were 2,300 small businesses registered in the Republic.

Directory

Chairman of the Government: ALEKSEI IVANOVICH LEBED; respublika Khakasiya, 662600 Abakan, ul. Lenina 67; tel. (39022) 6-33-22; fax (39022) 6-50-96; e-mail mishakov@khakassia.ru.

Chairman of the Supreme Soviet: VLADIMIR NIKOLAYEVICH SHTYGASHEV.

Permanent Representative of the President of the Russian Federation: ALEKSANDR CHERNYAVSKII.

Permanent Representative in Moscow: VIKTOR ALEKSEYEVICH PETROV; tel. (095) 203-83-45.

Head of Abakan City Administration: NIKOLAI GENRICHOVICH BULAKIN; respublika Khakasiya, 662600 Abakan, ul. Shchetinkina 10; tel. (39022) 6-37-91.

Komi

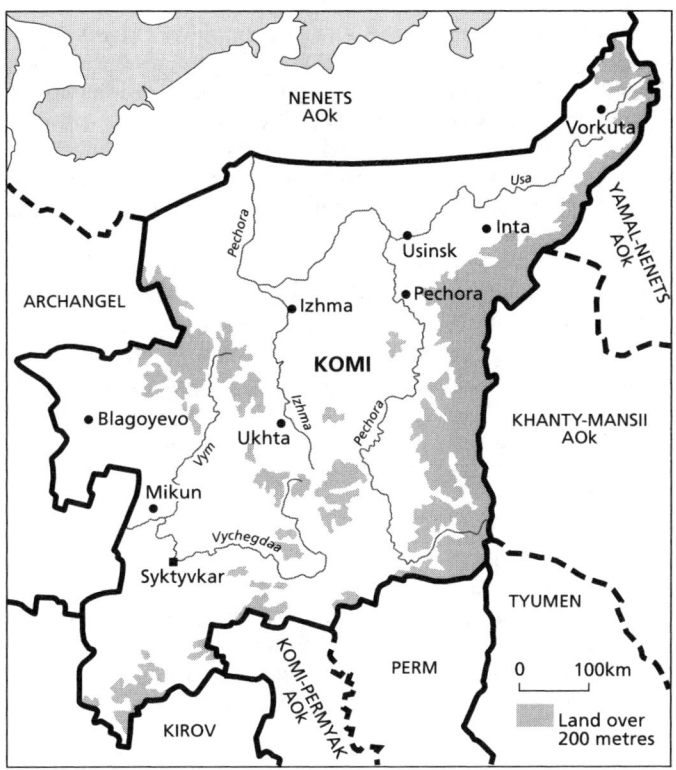

The Republic of Komi is situated in the north-east of European Russia. Its northern border lies some 50 km within the Arctic Circle. It forms part of the Northern Economic Area. Mountains of the Northern, Circumpolar and Polar Urals occupy the eastern part of the Republic. Its major rivers are the Pechora, the Vychegda and the Mezen. Komi is bordered to the north and west by Archangel Oblast, and to the east by the Yamal-Nenets AOk. To the south it has borders with Kirov Oblast, the Komi-Permyak AOk and Perm Oblast, Sverdlovsk Oblast and the Khanty-Mansii AOk (part of Tyumen Oblast). Some 90% of its territory is taiga (forested marshland), while the extreme north-east of the Republic lies within the Arctic tundra zone. The Republic occupies an area of 415,900 sq km (160,580 sq miles). It comprises 12 administrative districts and 10 cities and had an estimated population of 1,185,000 at 1 January 1996, and a population density, therefore, of 2.9 per sq km. Of these, some 23.3% of the Republic's inhabitants were Komis and 57.7% were ethnic Russians. The predominant religion in the region is Orthodox Christianity, although among the Komi this faith is combined with strong animist traditions. Their language, spoken as a native tongue by some 74% of the Komi population, belongs to the Finnic branch of the Uralo-Altaic family. Komi's capital is at Syktyvkar (known as Ust-Sysolsk before 1930), which had an estimated population of 230,400 in 1998. The Republic's other major cities are Ukhta (103,100), Vorkuta (99,000) and Pechora (61,300).

History

The Komi (known historically as the Zyryans or the Permyaks) are descended from inhabitants of the river basins of the Volga, the Kama, the Pechora and the Vychegda. From the 12th century Russian settlers began to inhabit territory along the Vychegda, and later the Vym, rivers. The Vym subsequently acquired a strategic significance as the main route along which Russian colonists advanced to Siberia and Ust-Sysolsk (now Syktyvar), the territory's oldest city, was founded in 1586. The number of Slavs increased after the territory was annexed by Russia in 1478. The region soon acquired importance as the centre of mining and metallurgy, following the discovery of copper and silver ores in 1491 by a search party sent by Ivan III. In 1697 petroleum was discovered in the territory; the first refinery was built by F. Pryadunov in 1745. The Komi were renowned as shrewd commercial traders and exploited important trade routes between Archangel and Siberia, via the Vyatka-Kama basin. Trade in fish, furs and game animals developed in the 17th century, while coal, timber, iron ore and paper became significant in the years prior to the Russian Revolution. The Komi Autonomous Oblast was established on 22 August 1921 and an ASSR in 1931.

The Komi Republic declared its sovereignty on 30 August 1990. A new republican Constitution was adopted on 17 February 1994, establishing a quasi-presidential premier at the head of government and a State Council as the legislature. The territory became known as the Republic of Komi. In March 1996 the republican and federal Governments signed a power-sharing treaty, which included agreements on foreign relations, energy, education, natural resources and employment. In mid-1998 the republican Government came under pressure from local miners, who were owed more than 400m. roubles in wage arrears. In November the Government retained federal revenues in order to pay pensioners.

Economy

The Republic of Komi is Russia's second-largest fuel and energy base. Apart from a wealth of natural resources, it is strategically placed close to many of Russia's major industrial centres and has a well-developed transport network. It also contains Europe's largest area of virgin forest—approximately one-third of its massive forest stock (amounting to 2,800m. cu m) has never been cut. In the 1990s Komi had a high ranking within the Federation in terms of gross domestic product (GDP) per head and it possessed a wealth of natural resources. However, in order to fulfil its economic potential the Republic needed to improve its export performance and diversify its economy into higher value-added activities. In 1995 gross regional product in the Republic amounted to 19,395,100m. roubles. This was equivalent to 162,507 roubles per head—one of the highest figures in Russia. Komi's major industrial centres are at Syktyvkar, Ukhta and Sosnogorsk.

Komi's agriculture, which employed 13.4% of the work-force, consists mainly of animal husbandry, especially reindeer-breeding. Total production within the sector amounted to a value of 1,011,400m. roubles in 1995. Ore-mining was developing in the mid-1990s: the Republic contained the country's largest reserves of bauxite, titanium, manganese and chromium ore. It also accounted for around one-half of northern Europe's petroleum stock and one-third of its natural-gas reserves. Total output from industry, which was based on the processing of forestry products, the production of coal and the production and processing of petroleum and natural gas, was worth 10,668,000m. roubles in 1995. Foreign trade was encouraged, with, for example, an agreement being reached with Iran in December 1998.

In 1995 the economically active population numbered 545,500, of whom 35,700 were unemployed. The average monthly wage in the Republic was relatively high, at 666,000 roubles. There was a budgetary deficit of 68,900m. roubles in 1995. Foreign investment in Komi in that year was considerable, amounting to US $33,812m. During the mid-1990s a number of joint ventures were established in Komi, with investment from France, the United Kingdom and the USA. These included Komi Arctic Oil, Sever TEK, and Northern Lights. At 1 January 1996 there were 5,400 small businesses in operation.

Directory

Chairman of the Government (Head of the Republic): YURII ALEKSEYEVICH SPIRIDONOV; respublika Komi, 167000 Syktyvkar, Kommunisticheskaya ul. 8; tel. (8212) 42-07-80; fax (8212) 42-37-70.

Chairman of the State Council: VLADIMIR ALEKSANDROVICH TORLOPOV; respublika Komi, 167000 Syktyvkar, Kommunisticheskaya ul. 8; tel. (8212) 42-07-76; fax (8212) 42-37-21.

Permanent Representative of the President of the Russian Federation: ALEKSANDR ALEKSANDROVICH POPOV.

Permanent Representative in Moscow: NIKOLAI NIKOLAYEVICH KOCHURIN; Moscow, Novyi Arbat 21; tel. (095) 291-47-03.

Head of Syktyvkar City Administration: YEVGENII NIKOLAYEVICH BORISOV; respublika Komi, 167000 Syktyvkar, ul. Babushkina 22; tel. (8212) 42-10-04.

Marii-El

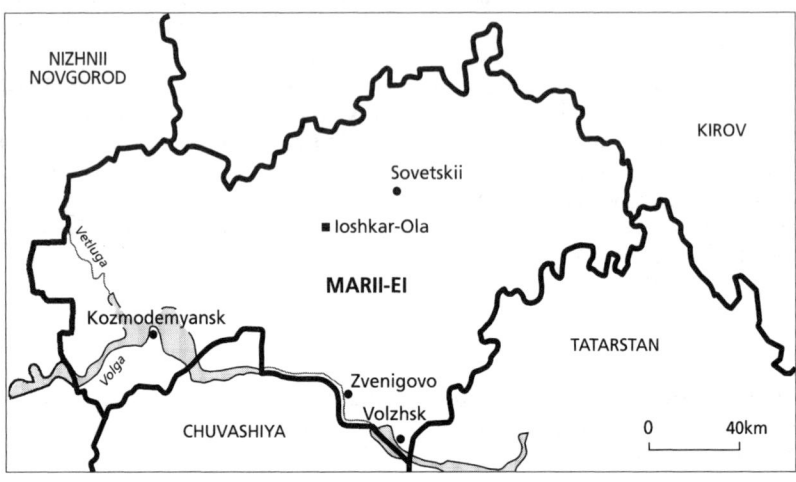

The Republic of Marii-El is situated in the east of the Eastern European Plain in the middle reaches of the River Volga. It forms part of the Volga-Vyatka Economic Area. Tatarstan and Chuvashiya neighbour it to the south-east and to the south, respectively. Nizhnii Novgorod Oblast lies to the west and Kirov Oblast to the north and north-east. Its major rivers are the Volga and the Vetluga and about one-half of its territory is forested. Marii-El measures 150 km (over 90 miles) from south to north and 275 km from west to east. It occupies an area of 23,200 sq km (9,000 sq miles) and consists of 14 administrative districts and four cities. At 1 January 1996 the estimated population was 766,000 and the population density approximately 33.0 per sq km. In 1989 some 43.3% of the Republic's inhabitants were Maris (also known as Cheremiss) and 47.5% ethnic Russians. Orthodox Christianity is the predominant religion in Marii-El, although many Maris have remained faithful to aspects of their traditional animistic religion. Their native language belongs to the Finnic branch of the Uralo-Altaic family. The capital of the Republic is at Ioshkar-Ola, with an estimated population of 250,900 at 1 January 1996. The Republic's other major cities are Volzhsk (62,100), Kozmodem-yansk (25,100) and Zvenigovo (14,600).

History

The Mari emerged as a distinct ethnic group in the sixth century. In the eighth century they came under the influence of the Khazar empire, but from the mid-ninth to the mid-12th century they were ruled by the Volga Bulgars. In the 1230s Mari territory was conquered by the Mongol Tatars and remained under the control of the Khanate of Kazan until its annexation by Russia in 1552. Nationalist feeling on the part of the Maris did not become evident until the 1870s, when a religious movement, the Kugu Sorta (Great Candle), attacked the authority of the Orthodox Church in the region. A Mari Autonomous Oblast was established in 1920. On 5 December 1936 the territory became the Mari ASSR.

The Republic declared its sovereignty on 22 October 1990. A presidential election was held on 14 December 1991. In December 1993 elections were held to a new 300-seat parliament, the State Assembly, which was dominated by the Communist Party and members of the old nomenklatura. The high proportion of ethnic Russians in the Republic also ensured support for Slav nationalists. The new legislature adopted the republican Constitution in June 1995, when the territory became known as the Republic of Marii-El. Continuing support for the opponents of the federal regime of Boris Yeltsin was demonstrated in the Russian parliamentary elections of 1995 and the federal presidential election of 1996.

Economy

In 1995 the Republic's gross regional product amounted to 3,927,200m. roubles, equivalent to 5,124,800 roubles per head. Its major industrial centres are at Ioshkar-Ola and Volzhsk.

Marii-El's agriculture, which in 1995 employed 20.5% of the work-force, consists mainly of animal husbandry and flax and grain production. Total agricultural output in 1995 was worth 1,676,400m. roubles. The Republic's main industries are mechanical engineering, metal working, light industry and the processing of forestry products. The total value of production within the industrial sector (which employed 27.5% of the work-force) was 2,581,000m. roubles in 1995. Marii-El is a net importer of energy: in July 1998 Yedinaya Electricheskaya Sistema, the state-owned power grid, imposed energy rationing on the Republic, owing to an accumulation of debts for electricity supplied. In 1995 the value of trade in the Republic amounted to US $70m. (of which exports were worth $46m. and imports $24m.). Exports primarily comprised raw materials, machine parts and medical supplies. Its major trading partners were Belarus, Finland, France, Germany, Ireland, Italy, Kazakhstan, the Netherlands, Ukraine, the United Kingdom and the USA.

In 1995 the economically active population in the Republic numbered 322,400. Some 17,000 of these were officially unemployed: those in employment earned an average of 259,000 roubles per month. There was a budgetary surplus in 1995, of 16,800m. roubles. Foreign investment in Marii-El is minimal, amounting to US $75,000 in 1995. The situation in the Republic prompted the federal Government to offer increased aid for 1999. At 1 January 1996 there was a total of 2,400 small businesses registered in the Republic.

Directory

President and Head of the Government: VYACHESLAV ALEKSANDROVICH KISLITSYN; respublika Marii-El, 424001 Ioshkar-Ola, Leninskii pr. 29; tel. (8362) 55-66-64; fax (8362) 55-69-64.

First Deputy Head of the Government: NIKOLAI NIKANDROVICH GAVRILOV; tel. (8362) 55-68-33.

Chairman of the State Assembly: MIKHAIL MIKHAILOVICH ZHUKOV; respublika Marii-El, 424001 Ioshkar-Ola, pr. Lenina 29; tel. (8362) 55-68-12.

Permanent Representative of the President of the Russian Federation: ANATOLII GENNADIYEVICH POPOV.

Permanent Representative in Moscow: YELENA ANATOLIYEVNA SKOROBOGA-TOVA; tel. (095) 291-48-38.

Head of Ioshkar-Ola City Administration: VENIAMIN VASILIYEVICH KOZLOV; respublika Marii-El, 424001 Ioshkar-Ola, Leninskii pr. 27; tel. (8362) 55-64-01; fax (8362) 55-64-22.

Mordoviya

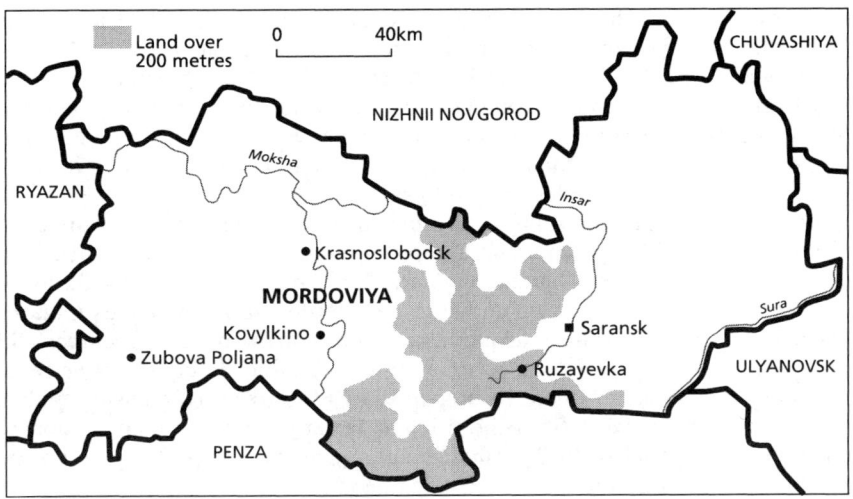

The Republic of Mordoviya is situated in the Eastern European Plain, in the Volga river basin. The north-west of the Republic occupies a section of the Oka-Don plain and and the south-east lies in the Volga Area Highlands (Privolzhskaya Vozvyshennost). The region forms part of the Volga-Vyatka Economic Area. The Republic of Chuvashiya lies to the north-east of Mordoviya. The neighbouring oblasts are Ulyanovsk to the east, Penza to the south, Ryazan to the west and Nizhnii Novgorod to the north. The major rivers in Mordoviya are the Moksha, the Sura and the Insar; one-quarter of its land area is forested. The territory of Mordoviya straddles the two major natural regions in Russia, forest and steppe, and occupies an area of 26,200 sq km (10,110 sq miles). The Republic consists of 22 administrative districts and seven cities. Its climate is continental, but with unpredictable levels of precipitation. At 1 January 1996 the Republic had a population of 955,800 (of whom 58.8% inhabited urban areas) and a population density, therefore, of approximately 36.5 per sq km. In 1990 some 32.6% of the total population were Mordovians and 60.8% Russians. The majority of Mordovians inhabited the agricultural regions of the west and north-east. The dominant religion amongst the Republic's inhabitants is Orthodox Christianity. The native tongue of the Mordovians belongs to the Finnic group of the Uralo-Altaic family, although this is spoken as a first language by less than two-thirds of the ethnic group. Mordoviya's capital is at Saransk, which lies on the River Insar and had an estimated population of 319,700 at 1 January 1996. The Republic's other major cities are Ruzayevka (52,800 inhabitants) and Kovylkino (23,100).

History

The Mordovians (Mordvinians) first appear in historical records of the sixth century, when they inhabited the area between the Oka and the middle Volga rivers. Their territory's capital was, possibly, on the site of Nizhnii Novgorod, before it was conquered by the Russians in 1172. In the late 12th and early 13th centuries a feudal society began to form in Mordoviya. One of its most famous fiefdoms was Purgasov Volost, headed by Prince Purgas, which was recorded in the Russian chronicles. The Mordovians came under the control of the Mongols and Tatars between the 13th and the 15th centuries and, at the fall of the Khanate of Kazan in 1552, they were voluntarily incorporated into the Russian state. Many thousands of Mordovians fled Russian rule in the late 16th and early 17th centuries to settle in the Ural Mountains and in southern Siberia, while those that remained were outnumbered by ethnic Russian settlers. The region was predominantly agricultural until the completion of the Moscow–Kazan railway in the 1890s, when it became more commercial and its industry developed.

Mordovians became increasingly assimilated into Russian life from the end of the 19th century, although in 1919 a Mordovian section was established in the People's Commissariat for Nationalities. The Mordovian Autonomous Okrug was created in 1928, and this was upgraded to the Mordovian Autonomous Oblast on 10 January 1930. The territory acquired republican status on 20 December 1934. It declared its sovereignty on 8 December 1990. A politically conservative region, the territory was only renamed the Republic of Mordoviya (dispensing with the words Soviet and Socialist from the title) in January 1994. Its Constitution was adopted on 21 September 1995, establishing an executive presidency and a State Assembly as the legislature.

Economy

In 1995 the gross regional product of Mordoviya was 5,012,000m. roubles, or 5,223,400 roubles per head. Industry is the dominant sector of the economy, with output amounting to a value of 3,537,000m. roubles in the same year. The territory's major industrial centres are at Saransk and Ruzayevka.

The principal crops in Mordoviya are grain, sugar-beets, potatoes and vegetables. Animal husbandry (especially cattle) and bee-keeping are also important. Agriculture employed 20.7% of the working population in 1995, while total agricultural production was worth 1,788,200m. roubles. Its main industries are mechanical engineering and metal working. There is also some light industry, production of chemicals and construction materials, and food processing. Total employment in industry was equal to 27.7% of the Republic's work-force. Mordoviya is the centre of the Russian lighting-equipment industry and contains the Rossiiskii Svet (Russian Light) association. In December 1995 the federal Government approved a programme for the economic and social development of Mordoviya, to be implemented in 1996–2000 at a cost of around 10,000m. roubles. The programme was to include 60 investment projects to assist the re-equipping and development of the high-technology sectors of Mordoviya's industry and to improve the efficiency of its agro-industrial complex.

In 1995 the economically active population was 400,700, although 29,300 of these were registered unemployed. The average monthly wage in the Republic was 284,000 roubles and there was a budgetary deficit of 86,200m. roubles. At 1 January 1996 there were some 2,100 small businesses in the Republic.

Directory

President: NIKOLAI IVANOVICH MERKUSHKIN; respublika Mordoviya, 430002 Saransk, ul. Sovetskaya 35; tel. and fax (8342) 17-45-26.

Chairman of the Government (Prime Minister): VLADIMIR DMITRIYEVICH VOLKOV; respublika Mordoviya, 430002 Saransk, ul. Sovetskaya 26; tel. (8342) 17-45-11.

Chairman of the State Assembly: VALERII ALEKSEYEVICH KECHKIN; respublika Mordoviya, 430002 Saransk, ul. Sovetskaya 20; tel. and fax (8342) 17-04-95.

Permanent Representative of the President of the Russian Federation: VALENTIN VASILIYEVICH KONAKOV; tel. (8342) 24-06-74.

Permanent Representative in Moscow: VIKTOR IVANOVICH CHINDYASKIN; tel. (095) 219-40-49.

Head of Saransk City Administration: IVAN YAKOVLEVICH NENYUKOV; respublika Mordoviya, 430002 Saransk, ul. Sovetskaya 34; tel. (8342) 17-64-16; fax (8342) 17-67-70.

North Osetiya
(ALANIYA)

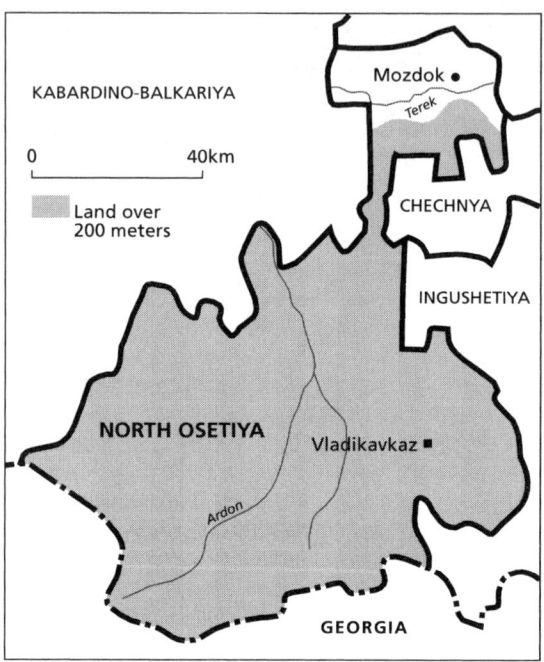

The Republic of North Osetiya (Severnaya Osetiya), Alaniya, is situated on the northern slopes of the Greater Caucasus and forms part of the North Caucasus Economic Area. Of other federal subjects, Kabardino-Balkariya lies to the west, Stavropol Krai to the north and Chechnya and Ingushetiya to the east. There is also an international boundary with Georgia (South Osetiya or Ossetia) in the south. Its major river is the Terek. In the north of the Republic are the steppelands of the Mozdok and Osetian Plains, while further south in the foothills are mixed pasture and beechwood forest (about one-fifth of the territory of the Republic is forested). Narrow river valleys lie in the southernmost, mountainous region. The territory of North Osetiya covers a total of 8,000 sq km (3,090 sq miles) and comprises eight administrative districts and six cities. It had an estimated population of 663,000 at 1 January 1996, some 69.3% of which inhabited urban areas. North Osetiya is extremely densely populated, with a rate of 82.8 per sq km in 1996. In 1989 some 53.0% of the population were Osetians and 29.9% ethnic Russians. The Osetians speak an Indo-European language of the Persian (Iranian) group. At the beginning of 1996 an estimated 313,300 of the region's inhabitants lived in the capital, Vladikavkaz (Ordzhonikidze 1932–90), situated in the east of the Republic. In 1997 there were 35,560 registered refugees from the conflict with Ingushetiya and from armed hostilities between South Osetian and Georgian government forces.

History

The Osetians (Ossetins, Oselty) are descended from the Alans, a tribe of the Samartian people. The Alans were driven into the foothills of the Caucasus by the Huns in the fourth century and their descendants (Ossetes) were forced further into the mountains by Tatar and Mongol invaders. Although the Osetians had been converted to Orthodox Christianity in the 12th and 13th centuries by the Georgians, a sub-group, the Digors, adopted Islam from the neighbouring Kabardins in the 17th and 18th centuries. Perpetual conflict with the Kabardins forced the Osetians to seek the protection of the Russian Empire, and their territory was eventually ceded to Russia by the Ottoman Turks at the Treaty of Kuçuk Kainavci in 1774 and confirmed by the Treaty of Iaşi (Jassy) in 1792. (Transcaucasian Osetiya, or South Osetiya, subsequently became part of Georgia.) The Russians fostered good relations with the Osetians, as they represented the only Christian group among the hostile Muslim peoples of the North Caucasus. Furthermore, both ends of the strategic Darial pass were situated in the region. The completion of the Georgian Military Road in 1799 facilitated the Russian conquest of Georgia (Kartli-Kakheti) in 1801.

After the Russian Revolution and having briefly been part of a Mountain (Gorskaya) People's Autonomous Republic, North Osetiya was established as an Autonomous Oblast on 7 July 1924. It became an ASSR on 5 December 1936. The Osetians were rewarded for their loyalty to the Soviet Government during the Second World War: in 1944 their territory was expanded by the inclusion of former Ingush territories to the east and of part of Stavropol Krai to the north. Furthermore, for 10 years the capital, renamed Ordzhonikidze in 1932, was known as Dzaudzikau, the Osetian pronunciation of Vladikavkaz. The Digors, however, were deported to Central Asia, along with other Muslim peoples, in 1944.

The Republic declared sovereignty in mid-1990. From 1991 there was considerable debate about some form of unification with South Osetiya. This resulted in armed hostilities between the South Osetians and Georgian troops, during which thousands of refugees fled to North Osetiya. Meanwhile, the Republic's administration refused to recognize claims by the Ingush to the territory they were deprived of in 1944 (the Prigorodnyi raion), which led to the onset of violence in October 1992 and the imposition of a state of emergency in the affected areas (see Ingushetiya, above). In spite of the cessation of armed hostilities in 1994 and a subsequent peace settlement, the region remained unstable. Under the terms of its Constitution, adopted on 7 December 1994, the Republic reverted to its old name of Alaniya. A power-sharing agreement was signed with the federal authorities the following year. The territory was a redoubt of the Communist Party, and was the only one of the 89 federal units in which any single party gained more than one-half of all votes cast at the December 1996 general election (52% for the Communist Party of the Russian Federation). Relations with Ingushetiya began to deteriorate again in 1996, particularly with attempts by Ingush refugees to return to the Prigorodnyi raion in mid-1997, prompting the intervention of the federal President, Boris Yeltsin, in August. The following month the republican President, Akhsarbek Galazov, signed an agreement with his Ingush counterpart, Ruslan Aushev, aimed at normalizing relations between the two territories. However, the Osetian authorities favoured a gradual return of refugees and continued to be accused of obstruction by the Ingush, as, for example, after a border incident at the end of December 1998. The territory also had a significant refugee population of its own (some 30,000 at this time), mainly from Chechnya, Ingushetiya, Georgia and Tajikistan. Relations with the federal President deteriorated in November of that year, following the introduction legislation providing for appointed, rather than elected, local government. It was also reported that the Russian Government, under Yevgenii Primakov, nevertheless continued to enjoy good relations with Aleksandr Dzassokhov (who had succeeded Galazov as the republican President in 1997).

Economy

In 1995 gross regional product in North Osetiya—Alaniya totalled 2,329,000m. roubles, equivalent to 3,526,600 roubles per head. Its major industrial centres are at Vladikavkaz, Mozdok and Beslan. It contains about 149 km of railway track, including a section of the North Caucasus Railway, and the only direct road route from Russia to the Transcaucasus. There is an international airport at Vladikavkaz.

Agriculture in North Osetiya, which employed some 11.5% of the labour force in 1995, consists mainly of vegetable and grain production, horticulture, viniculture and animal husbandry. The rate of reform in agriculture during the 1990s was slow. Agricultural production in 1995 amounted to a value of 666,300m. roubles. In the same year industrial output was worth 3,537,000m. roubles and the sector employed 27.7% of the working population. The Republic's main industries are radio electronics (until the 1990s largely used for defence purposes), non-ferrous metallurgy, mechanical engineering, wood-working, light industry, chemicals, glass-making and food processing. There are also five hydroelectric power-stations, with an average capacity of around 80 MWh. By the mid-1990s almost three-quarters of industrial production within the defence sector had been converted to civilian use.

The economically active population totalled 229,100 in 1995, of whom 26,000 were unemployed. Those in employment earned an average wage of 394,000 roubles per month. The republican budget in that year showed a deficit of 4,800m. roubles. Foreign investment remained deterred by the instability endemic to much of the North Caucasus region. At 1 January 1996 there was a total of 2,500 small businesses in operation on Osetian territory.

Directory

President of the Republic: ALEKSANDR SERGEYEVICH DZASSOKHOV; respublika Severnaya Osetiya, 362038 Vladikavkaz, pl. Svobody 1, Dom Sovetov; tel. (8672) 53-35-24.

Chairman of the Government: TAIMURAZ DZAMBEKOVICH MAMSUROV; respublika Severnaya Osetiya, 362038 Vladikavkaz, pl. Svobody 1, Dom Sovetov; tel. (8672) 53-35-56.

Chairman of the Parliament: VYACHESLAV SEMENOVICH PARINOV; respublika Severnaya Osetiya, 362038 Vladikavkaz, pl. Svobody, Dom Sovetov; tel. (8672) 53-35-53.

Permanent Representative of the President of the Russian Federation: VLADIMIR ADVASHEVICH KALAMANOV.

Permanent Representative in Moscow: KAZBEK MULDAROVICH DULAYEV; tel. (095) 239-38-57.

Head of Vladikavkaz City Administration (Mayor): MIKHAIL MIKHAILOVICH SHATALOV; respublika Severnaya Osetiya, 362040 Vladikavkaz, pl. Shtyba 1; fax (8672) 75-34-35.

Republic of Sakha
(YAKUTIYA)

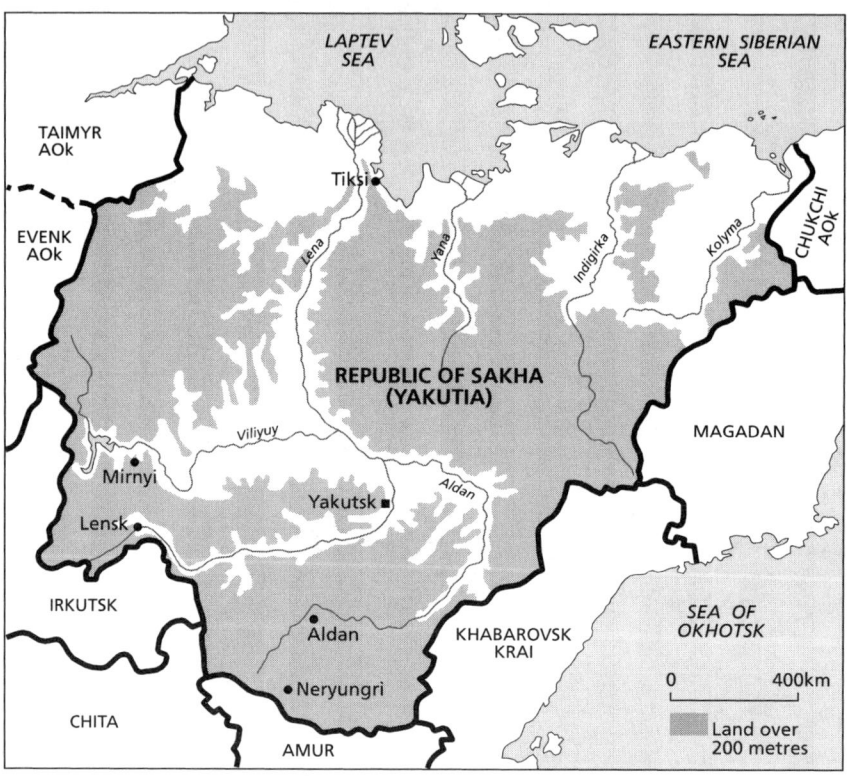

The Republic of Sakha (Yakutiya) is situated in eastern Siberia on the Laptev and Eastern Siberian Seas. Some two-fifths of the Republic's territory lies within the Arctic Circle. It forms part of the Far Eastern Economic Area. To the west it borders Krasnoyarsk Krai (the Taimyr and Evenk AOks), while Irkutsk and Chita Oblasts lie in the south-west, Amur Oblast to the south and Khabarovsk Krai and Magadan Oblast in the south-west. In the north-eastern corner of the territory there is a border with the Chukchi AOk, which lies to the east. Its main river is the Lena, which drains into the Laptev Sea via a large swampy delta; other important rivers are the Lena's tributaries, the Aldan and the Viliyuy, the Olenek, the Yana, the Indigirka and the Kolyma. Apart from the Central Yakut Plain, the region's territory is mountainous and four-fifths is taiga (forested marshland). Yakutiya is the largest federal unit in Russia, occupying an area of 3,103,200 sq km (1,198,150 sq miles), making it larger than Kazakhstan, itself the second-largest country in Eastern Europe and the former USSR (after Russia). It consists of 33 administrative districts and 11 cities. Its climate, owing to its size, is varied: temperatures in January can be as low as −48°C in some northern areas, while in more temperate regions in July they are around 18°C. At 1 January 1996 the Republic had an estimated population of just 1,023,000 and a population density, therefore, of 0.3 per sq km. Some 64.3% of the population inhabited urban areas at this time. In the mid-1990s there was a continuous outflow of population from the Republic. In 1989 some 33.4% of the total population were the indigenous Yakuts (who represent the largest ethnic group in Siberia, apart from Russians) and 50.3% Russians. Orthodox Christianity is the dominant religion in the region. The Yakuts' native tongue, spoken as a first language by over 93% of the indigenous population, is part of the North-Eastern branch of the Turkic family, although it is considerably influenced by Mongolian. The capital is at Yakutsk, which had an estimated population of 191,400 at 1 January 1996. The Republic's other major cities are Neryungri (76,700), Mirnyi (37,900), Lensk (29,300) and Aldan (24,000).

History

The Yakuts (Iakuts), also known as the Sakha (Saka), were historically known as the Tungus, Jekos and the Urangkhai Sakha. They are believed to be descended from various peoples from the Lake Baikal area, Turkish tribes from the steppe and the Altai Mountains, and indigenous Siberian peoples, including the Evenks. They were traditionally a semi-nomadic people, with those in the north of the region occupied with hunting, fishing and reindeer-breeding, while those in the south were pastoralists who bred horse and cattle and were also skilled blacksmiths. Their territory, briefly united by the toion (chief), Tygyn, came under Russian rule in the 1620s and a fur tax was introduced. This led to violent opposition from the Yakuts between 1634 and 1642, although all rebellions were crushed. Increasing numbers of Russians began to settle in the region as Yakutiya became a link between eastern and western Siberia. The completion of the mail route also increased the Russian population, as did the construction of camps for political opponents to the tsars and the discovery of gold in 1846. The territory became commercialized after the construction of the Trans-Siberian Railway in the 1880s and 1890s and the development of commercial shipping on the River Lena. The economic resources of the territory enabled the Yakut to secure a measure of autonomy as an ASSR in 1922 (its first leader was the Yakut poet, Platon Oyunskii). Collectivization and the purges of the 1930s greatly reduced the Yakut population during the Soviet era, and the region was rapidly industrialized, largely involving the extraction of gold, coal and timber.

Nationalist feeling, which first found voice in Yakutiya in 1906 with the founding of the Yakut Union, but was subsequently suppressed, re-emerged during the period of *glasnost* (openness) in the late 1980s. Cultural, ecological and economic concerns led to the proclamation of a Yakut-Sakha SSR on 27 April 1990. The Yakut Republic was officially declared by the Supreme Soviet on 15 August 1991, which demanded local control over the Republic's reserves of gold, diamonds, timber, coal, petroleum and tin. On 22 December 1991 elections for an executive presidency were held, and were won by the former Chairman of the Supreme Soviet, Mikhail Nikolayev. The Republic was renamed the Republic of Sakha in March 1992 and a new Constitution was promulgated on 27 April. On 12 October 1993 the Supreme Soviet dissolved itself and set elections to a 60-seat bicameral legislature for 12 December. On 26 January 1994 the new parliament (previously the Legislative State Assembly) named itself the State Assembly; it consisted of an upper Chamber of the Republic and a lower Chamber of Representatives. Although Communist support was relatively high in Yakutiya, the federal Government's willingness to concede a significant degree of local control over natural resources ensured that it too enjoyed some confidence. Local officials also proved concerned to address the problems of the minority indigenous peoples or 'small-numbered nations'. Native languages were designated official in certain areas and attempts to protect traditional lifestyles even involved the restoration of land. Thus, a Yeven-Bytantai Okrug was established on traditional Yeven territory in the mid-1990s. In June 1997 the Republic was honoured at a UN special session on the environment held in New York (USA) for its commitment to preserving its natural heritage (around one-quarter of its territory had been set aside as protected areas). Meanwhile, in December 1996 Nikolayev was re-elected President by an overwhelming majority and continued his efforts to win greater autonomy from the centre. In March 1998 a framework agreement on co-operation for five years was signed by the federal and republican Governments, which provided for collaboration on a series of mining and energy projects.

Economy

Owing to the Republic's wealth of mineral reserves, its gross regional product in 1995 was 20,334,800m. roubles, equivalent to 19,756,000 roubles per head, the highest figure in the Russian Federation. The Republic's major industrial centres are at Yakutsk, Mirnyi, Neryungra, Aldan and Lensk. Its main port is Tiksi.

Yakutiya's agriculture, in which 13.6% of the working population was engaged in 1995, consists mainly of animal husbandry (livestock- and reindeer-breeding), hunting and fishing. Grain and vegetable production tends to be on a small scale. Total agricultural output in 1995 was worth 1,612,000m. roubles (compared to a figure of 12,274,000m. roubles for the industrial sector). Yakutiya's industrial sector employed 15.5% of its working population in 1995: its main industries are ore mining (gold, diamonds, tin, muscovite—mica, antimony and coal), manufacture of building materials, processing of timber and agricultural products, and natural-gas production. Industrial output in Yakutiya increased in 1994 and 1995, with a rise in production of diamonds, natural gas, coal and building materials. In the same period, foreign trade increased by 50%. In September 1997 a local diamond producer, Almazy Rossii-Sakha—ARS, signed a preliminary one-year trade accord with the South African diamond producer, De Beers. The agreement had been delayed following allegations made by the federal Government against ARS (closely linked to the republican Government) of tax fraud. The accord was extended the following August, until 2001. In 1995 Yakutiya accounted for some 70% of Russia's total tin production and was the country's sole producer of antimony.

The social situation in Yakutiya in the mid-1990s was typical of the northern regions of the Russian Federation. Growth in the cost of goods and services (133% in December 1994–December 1995) was compounded by a weak economic structure, poorly developed social services and inappropriate conditions for people to grow their own food. In terms of a 'consumer basket' the Republic was one of the most expensive regions in the country, and Yakutiya the most expensive city. Unemployment, however, was relatively low: the official figure for 1995 was 4,800 out of an economically active population of 537,000. The average monthly wage in that year was 957,000 roubles (considerably higher than the national average, but obviously offset by the high cost of living). There was a large budgetary surplus of 4,270m. roubles. Foreign investment in Yakutiya in 1995 amounted to

US $5.23m. At 1 January 1996 there were 3,800 small businesses registered on its territory.

Directory

President: MIKHAIL YEFIMOVICH NIKOLAYEV; respublika Sakha, 677022 Yakutsk, ul. Kirova 11; tel. (4112) 43-50-50; fax (4112) 24-06-24.

Vice-President: SPARTAK STEPANOVICH BORISOV; respublika Sakha, 677022 Yakutsk, ul. Kirova 11.

Chairman of the Government: VASILII MIKHAILOVICH VLASOV; respublika Sakha, 677022 Yakutsk, ul. Kirova 11; tel. (4112) 43-55-55.

State Assembly: respublika Sakha, 677022 Yakutsk, ul. Kirova 11.

    Chairman of the Chamber of the Republic: VASILII VASILIYEVICH FILIPPOV; tel. (4112) 43-53-04.

    Chairman of the Chamber of Representatives: NIKOLAI IVANOVICH SOLOMOV; tel. (4112) 43-52-03.

Permanent Representative in Moscow: KLIMENT YE. IVANOV; tel. (095) 926-82-98.

Head of Yakutsk City Administration (Mayor): ILYA FILIPPOVICH MIKHALCHUK; respublika Sakha, 677022 Yakutsk, ul. Kirova 11; tel. (4112) 42-30-20; fax (4112) 43-52-03.

Tatarstan

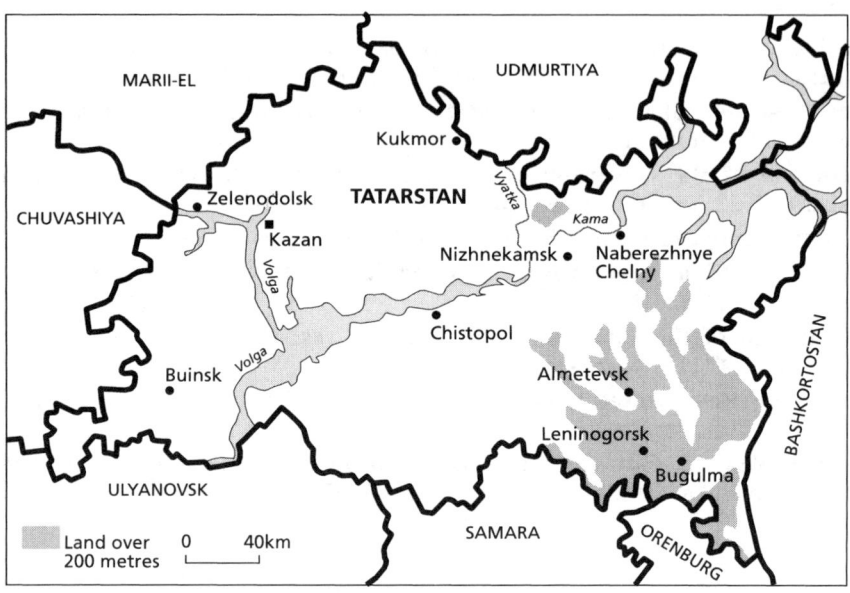

The Republic of Tatarstan is situated in the east of European Russia and forms part of the Volga Economic Area. It neighbours several other Republics: Bashkortostan to the east; Udmurtiya to the north; Marii-El to the north-west; and Chuvashiya to the west. The regions of Ulyanovsk, Samara and Orenburg lie to the south. Its major rivers are the Volga and the Kama and one-fifth of its total territory, of 67,836 sq km (26,260 sq miles), is forested. It measures 290 km (180 miles) from south to north and 460 km from west to east. The Republic is divided into 43 administrative districts and 19 cities. At 1 January 1996 it had an estimated population of 3,760,000 and, therefore, a population density of 55.4 per sq km. In 1989 some 48.5% of the total population were Tatars and 32.0% Russians. Tatarstan's capital is at Kazan, which lies on the River Volga and had an estimated population of 1,084,700 in 1996. Other major cities include Naberezhnye Chelny (formerly Brezhnev—525,500), Nizhnekamsk (212,700), Almetevsk (139,100) and Zelenodolsk (101,100).

History

After the dissolution of the Mongol Empire the region became the Khanate of Kazan, the territory of the Golden Horde. It was conquered by Russia in 1552. Some of the Muslim Tatars succumbed to Russian pressures to convert to Orthodox Christianity (the Staro-Kryashens still exist, using Tatar as their spoken and liturgical tongue), but most did not. A modernist school of thought in Islam, Jadidism, originated among the Volga Tatars, who attained an exceptionally high cultural level in the 19th-century Russian Empire, despite being a subject people. A Tatar ASSR was established on 27 May 1920.

Autonomous Republics (Tatarstan)

On 31 August 1990, the then Chairman of the Supreme Soviet of Tatarstan, Mintimer Shamiyev (elected President of the Republic in 1991), declared Tatarstan a sovereign republic. As President, Shamiyev continued to strive for the Republic's independence from the Federation Government. Apart from secessionist Chechnya, Tatarstan was the only republic to reject the Federation Treaty and adopted its own Constitution on 6 November 1992. The Constitution provided for a presidential republic with a legislative, bicameral State Council. On 15 February 1994 Shamiyev won important concessions from Russia's central Government by signing a treaty which ceded extensive powers to Tatarstan, including full ownership rights over its petroleum reserves and industrial companies, the right to retain most of its tax revenue (an arrangement considered likely to be continued when due for renewal in 1999) and the right to pursue its own foreign-trade policy. It was also allowed to retain its Constitution. The division of responsibilities was confirmed by treaty with the Federation in 1995.

In December 1995 the local success of the federal pro-government party, Our Home is Russia, in elections to the Federal Assembly, indicated the extent of co-operation between the national and republican ruling groups. In a presidential election, held on 24 March 1996, in which some 76% of the electorate participated, the incumbent President was re-elected, winning some 93% of the votes cast. Shamiyev's political victory was partly owing to the success of his economic policy: his Government adapted the reforms of *perestroika* (restructuring) to the conditions of the region, thereby averting excessive inflation and social upheaval. Tatarstan became a model for other territories seeking greater autonomy and economic security. On 28 August 1997 the Presidents of the Republics of Tatarstan and Bashkortostan signed a treaty on co-operation at the second World Congress of Tatars, held in Kazan. The Congress adopted a resolution praising the development of Tatarstan into a 'new kind of sovereign state'.

Economy

In 1995 the Republic's gross regional product stood at 37,829,500m. roubles, or 10,067,200 roubles per head. The territory is one of the most developed economic regions of the Russian Federation and has vast agricultural and industrial potential. Its main industrial centres are Kazan, Naberezhnye Chelny, Zelenodolsk, Nizhnekamsk, Almetyevsk, Chistopol and Bugulma. Kazan is the most important port on the Volga and a junction in national rail, road and air transport systems. Russia's second primary petroleum export pipeline to Europe starts in Almetyevsk.

Tatarstan's agriculture, in which some 14.7% of the work-force were engaged in 1995, consists mainly of grain production, animal husbandry, horticulture and bee-keeping. Total output in this sector amounted to a value of 404,400m. roubles in 1995. Mineral natural resources are more important—in early 1998 the Republic was ranked 18th in the world in terms of its hydrocarbons reserves. The region is an important industrial centre (industry accounts for 28.8% of its working population): its capital, Kazan, and the neighbouring towns of Zelendolsk and Vasilyevo are centres for light industry, the manufacture of petrochemicals and building materials, and mechanical engineering. The automobile and petroleum industries (in particular, the truck manufacturer KAMAZ, based at Naberezhnye Chelny, and Tatneft, the fourth-largest petroleum company in Russia), are major employers in the region. Kazanorgsintez, a petrochemicals giant, is one of the largest polyethylene producers in Europe. Industries connected with the extraction, processing and use of petroleum represent around one-half of the Republic's total industrial production, which was worth 31,761,000m. roubles in 1995 (in the same year a decline in petroleum production was halted for the first time in 20 years). In January 1996 the republican Government signed a co-operation agreement with the LUKoil petroleum company on extracting and refining petroleum and transporting petroleum and petroleum products. Under the terms of the agreement the LUKoil Tatarstan company was created, which was to use the Republic's industrial and labour resources to develop oilfields in western Siberia.

By the mid-1990s Tatarstan was also attracting foreign investors, owing to its reformist policies. For example, the US automobile company, General Motors, signed a contract to manufacture 50,000 automobiles per year at the Yelabuga plant. In April 1996 a programme on the Republic's social and economic development, drafted with French and US assistance, was adopted by the Council of Ministers. It envisaged the transformation of Tatarstan's economy from a military to a socially orientated system. A five-year credit agreement was signed with Germany in the same year to implement social programmes and the conversion of former military plants to civilian use. France also granted US $215m. credit for the reconstruction of Kazan's international airport and the development of the agricultural-tool industry. The 1994 Law on Foreign Investment in the Republic of Tatarstan, which conformed to international law, provided for specific advantages to investors, including a three-year tax exemption for major projects. In 1996 an International Centre for Investment Assistance was created, with offices in five countries. Foreign investment in the Republic during 1996 amounted to around $1,000m.: with over 230 companies attracting foreign capital from Finland, Germany, the Netherlands, Poland, Turkey, the United Kingdom and the USA. In November 1998 some anxiety was caused when Tatarstan defaulted on a debt to a Western bank, although the republican authorities blamed the general economic crisis in Russia.

The economically active population in the Republic amounted to 1,686,700 in 1995, of whom 26,000 were unemployed. The average wage at this time was 394,000 roubles per month. The 1995 budget saw a deficit of 247,000m. roubles. By the beginning of 1997 over 1,000 large and medium-sized enterprises in Tatarstan had been privatized, while some 190,000 people were employed in small businesses.

Directory

President: MINTIMER SHARIPOVICH SHAMIYEV; respublika Tatarstan, 420014 Kazan, Kreml; tel. (8432) 32-74-66; fax (8432) 36-70-88.

Prime Minister: FARID KHAIRULLOVICH MUKHAMETSHIN; respublika Tatarstan, 420060 Kazan, pl. Svobody 1; tel. (8432) 32-79-03; telex 224847; fax (8432) 36-28-24.

Chairman of the State Council: VASILII NIKOLAYEVICH LIKHACHEV; respublika Tatarstan, 420060 Kazan, pl. Svobody 1; tel. (8432) 32-14-02; fax (8432) 36-88-45.

Permanent Representative in Moscow: FARID MUBARAKSHEVICH MUKHAMETSHIN; tel. (095) 975-17-36.

Head of Kazan City Administration: KAMIL SHAMILYEVICH ISKHAKOV; tel. (8432) 35-56-94.

Tyva

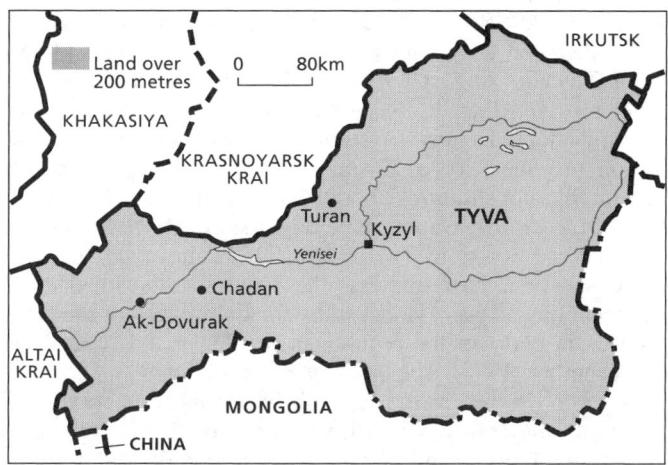

The Republic of Tyva (Tuva) is situated in the south of eastern Siberia in the Sayan Mountains. It forms part of the Eastern Siberian Economic Area. Tyva has an international border with Mongolia to the south. The Republic of Altai lies to the west, Khakasiya is in the north-west and the rest of Krasnoyarsk Krai in the north, Irkutsk Oblast lies to the north-east and Buryatiya forms part of the eastern border. Its major river is the Yenisei, which rises in the Eastern Sayan mountain range. The territory of the Republic consists of a series of high mountain valleys. One-half of its area is forested. The Republic has numerous waterways, including over 12,000 rivers and 8,400 freshwater lakes. Tyva occupies 170,500 sq km (65,830 sq miles) and consists of 16 administrative districts and five cities. At 1 January 1996 it had an estimated population of 309,000 and a population density of only 1.8 per sq km. Some 48.6% of the population lived in urban areas at this time. In 1989 some 64.3% of inhabitants were Tyvans (Tuvinians) and 32.0% Russians. Lamaism (Tibetan Buddhism) is the predominant religion in the Republic. The Tyvan language belongs to the Old Uigur group of the Turkic branch of the Uralo-Altaic linguistic family. The capital of Tyva is at Kyzyl, which had an estimated population of 95,400 at 1 January 1996.

History

The Tyvans (known at various times as Soyons, Soyots and Uriankhais, emerged as an identifiable ethnic group in the early 18th century. The territory of what is now Tyva was occupied in turn between the sixth and the ninth centuries by the Turkish khanate, the Chinese, the Uigurs and the Yenisei Kyrgyz. The Mongols controlled the region from 1207 to 1368. In the second half of the 17th century the Dzungarians (Sungarians) seized the area from the Altyn Khans. In 1758 the Manzhous (Manchus) annexed Dzungaria and the territory thus became part of the Chinese Empire. Russian influence dates from the Treaty of Peking (Beijing) of 1860, after which trade links were developed and a number of Russians settled there. One year after the Chinese Revolution of 1911 Tyva declared its independence. In 1914, however, Russia established a protectorate over the territory, which became the Tannu-Tuva People's Republic. This was a nominally independent state until October 1944, when it was incorporated into the USSR as the Tuvinian Autonomous Oblast. It became an ASSR on 10 October 1961, within the Russian Federation.

The Republic declared sovereignty on 11 December 1990 and renamed itself the Republic of Tuva in August 1991. On 21 October 1993 the Tyvan (Tuvin) Supreme Soviet resolved that the Republic's name was Tyva (as opposed to the russified Tuva) and adopted a new Constitution which came into effect immediately. The Constitution provided for a 32-member working legislature, the Supreme Hural, and a supreme constitutional body, the Grand Hural. The new parliament was elected on 12 December. On the same day, the new Constitution was approved by 62.2% of registered voters in Tyva. Only 32.7%, however, voted in favour of the Russian Constitution. Nevertheless, the federal authorities had secured the loyalty of the local élite, as was evidenced by the dominance of the pro-government Our Home is Russia party in the republican results of the federal parliamentary elections of December 1995. The victory of a nationalist Liberal Democratic candidate, Aleksandr Kashin, in the April 1998 mayoral elections in Kyzyl was, perhaps, a sign of intolerance with the reformism of the federal Government (certainly among the predominantly ethnic Russian population of the city). Apathy was also a likely cause, as a low turn-out in the general election of the same month meant that only 21 of the 38 seats in the enlarged Supreme Hural were filled. Further rounds later in the year failed to resolve the situation and, indeed, in December the parliament was rendered inquorate by the death of a deputy (a by-election was scheduled for February 1999).

Economy

Tyva's economy is largely agriculture-based. In 1995 its gross regional product stood at 1,087,900m. roubles, or 3,523,000 roubles per head. The Republic's main industrial centres are at Kyzyl and Ak-Dovurak. There are road and rail links with other regions, although the distance from Kyzyl to the nearest railway station is over 400 km (250 miles).

The Republic's agriculture, which employed 24.1% of the work-force in 1995, consists mainly of animal husbandry, although forestry and hunting are also important. Total agricultural production in 1995 was almost the highest of any federal unit, amounting to a value of 8,180,300m. roubles. At 1 January 1997 there were some 780,400 sheep and goats, 174,000 cattle, 45,600 pigs, 39,200 horses, 10,000 yaks, 3,000 deer and 2,000 camels in the Republic. Gold extraction was being developed in the mid-1990s: in 1996 it amounted to almost one metric ton. Its main industries were ore mining (asbestos, coal, cobalt and mercury), production of electricity, the processing of agricultural and forestry products, light manufacturing, manufacture of building materials and metal working. Industry in 1995 employed 10.6% of the working population and total production within the sector was worth just 259,000m. roubles.

The economically active population of Tyva in 1995 totalled 134,200, of whom 4,200 were unemployed. The average monthly wage in the Republic at this time was 314,000 roubles, while the 1995 budget showed a deficit of 29,200m. roubles. At 1 January 1996 there was a total of 2,000 small businesses registered in the Republic.

Directory

President: SHERIG-OOL DIZIZHIKOVICH OORZHAK; respublika Tyva, 667000 Kyzyl, ul. Chulduma 18; tel. (39422) 3-69-12; fax (39422) 3-74-59.

Vice-President: ALEKSEI ALEKSANDROVICH MELNIKOV; tel. (39422) 3-63-20.

Chairman of the Supreme Hural: KAADYR-OOL BICHELDEY; respublika Tyva, 667000 Kyzyl, ul. Lenina 32; tel. (39422) 3-75-03.

Permanent Representative of the President of the Russian Federation: KALINDUU CHADAMBAYEVICH MONGUSH.

Permanent Representative in Moscow: BORIS MIKHAILOVICH LAVROV; tel. (095) 291-45-25.

Head of Kyzyl City Administration (Mayor): ALEKSANDR KASHIN; respublika Tyva, 667000 Kyzyl, ul. Lenina 32; tel. (39422) 3-50-55.

Udmurtiya

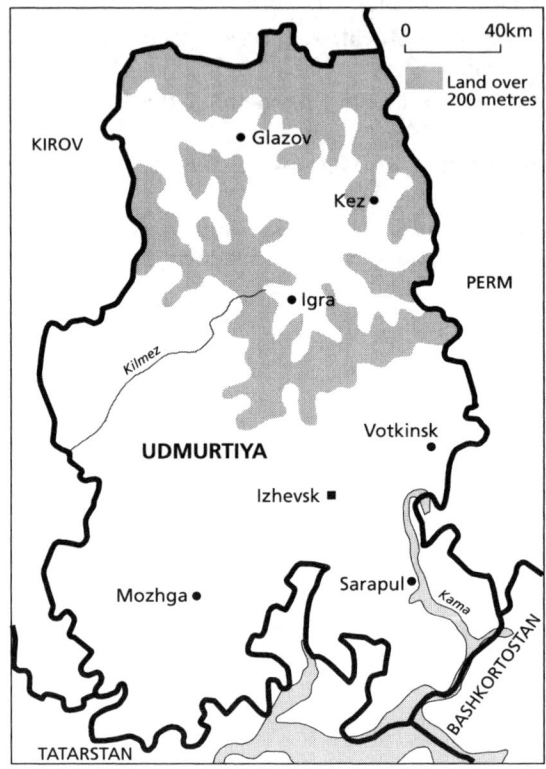

The Udmurt Republic occupies part of the Upper Kama Highlands. It forms part of the Urals Economic Area. Tatarstan lies to the south, Bashkortostan to the south-east, Perm to the east and Kirov to the north and west. Its major river is the Kama, dominating the southern and eastern borderlands, while the Vyatka skirts the territory in the west. About one-half of its territory is forested. Its total area covers some 42,100 sq km (16,250 sq miles). The Republic consists of 25 administrative districts and six cities. At 1 January 1996 Udmurtiya had an estimated population of 1,639,000, of which some 69.7% inhabited urban areas. The population density in the Republic at this time was 38.9 per sq km. In 1989 some 30.9% of the total population were Udmurts and 58.9% ethnic Russians. The dominant religion in the Republic is Orthodox Christianity. The 1989 census showed that some 70% of Udmurts spoke their native tongue, from the Permian group of the Finnic branch of the Uralo-Altaic family, as their first language. The capital of Udmurtiya is at Izhevsk (known as Ustinov for much of the Soviet period), which had an estimated population of 654,000 in 1997. Other major towns in the region are Sarapul (109,300), Glazov (106,200), Votkinsk (103,100) and Mozhga (48,400).

History

The first appearance of the Votyaks (the former name for Udmurts) as a distinct ethnic group occurred in the sixth century. The territories inhabited by Votyaks were conquered by the Khazars in the eighth century, although Khazar influence gave way to that of the Volga Bulgars in the mid-ninth century. In the 13th century the Mongol Tatars occupied the region, but were gradually displaced by the Russians from the mid-15th century. By 1558 all Votyaks were under Russian rule. A Votyak Autonomous Oblast was established on 4 November 1920. On 1 January 1932 it was renamed the Udmurt Autonomous Oblast, which became an ASSR on 28 December 1934.

The Republic declared sovereignty on 21 September 1990, although a new republican Constitution was not adopted until 7 December 1994. According to this basic law, the Chairman of the legislature, the State Council, remained head of the Republic, and a premier chaired the Government. In 1995 the Government of Udmurtiya agreed a power-sharing treaty with the Federation. It remained subject to the Constitution, however, although in 1996 the Udmurt parliament was accused of having virtually eliminated local government in the Republic, in contravention of federal law.

Economy

The Republic's gross regional product in 1995 amounted to 12,452,100m. roubles, equivalent to 7,593,200 roubles per head. Udmurtiya possesses significant hydrocarbons reserves and is an important arms-producing region. Its major industrial centres are at Izhevsk, Sarapul and Glazov. Its main river-ports are at Sarapul and Kambarka. In 1997 there were 878 km of railway track on its territory, of which 504 km were electrified. In the same year there were 4,469 km of paved roads and 178 km of navigable waterways. Twelve major gas pipelines and two petroleum pipelines pass through the Udmurt Republic.

Udmurtiya's agriculture employed 15.2% of the working population in 1995 and consists mainly of livestock breeding, grain production and flax growing. Total agricultural production in 1995 was worth 2,563,000m. roubles. There are substantial reserves of coal and of petroleum (prospected resources are estimated at 379,543m. metric tons), which in the late 1990s the Republic hoped to exploit with the aid of foreign investment. In 1995 some 34.0% of its working population was engaged in industry. The main industries in Udmurtiya, apart from the manufacture of weapons, are mechanical engineering (in 1996 the Republic produced some 65% of all the motor cycles manufactured in Russia), metal working, metallurgy, processing of forestry and agricultural products, petroleum production, glass-making, light manufacturing and the production of peat. Total industrial output in 1995 amounted to a value of 9,142,000m. roubles. External trade in Udmurtiya in 1995 amounted to US $566.5m., of which $449.7m. was with partners outside the CIS. Exports largely comprised metallurgical products, engines and machinery and rifles. In the mid-1990s the Republic had particularly active trade links with Syria.

In 1995 the economically active population amounted to 707,000. Some 69,900 of these were registered unemployed; those in employment earned an average of 319,000 roubles. The budget in 1995 showed a slight deficit, of 4,700m. roubles. There was $6.06m. of foreign investment in the Republic in that year. At 1 January

1996 there were approximately 7,000 small businesses registered in the Republic. In the mid-1990s the disposal of chemical weapons on the territory of Udmurtiya was proving to be a serious social and ecological problem—the Republic was thought to contain around one-quarter of Russia's entire arsenal of such weapons. It was hoped that an undertaking by the federal Government in July 1998 to repay its debts of over 560m. roubles to the military-industrial complex in the Republic would help alleviate the situation.

Directory

Chairman of the State Council: ALEKSANDR ALEKSANDROVICH VOLKOV; respublika Udmurtiya, 426007 Izhevsk, ul. 50 let Oktyabrya 15; tel. (3412) 75-39-80.

Chairman of the Government: PAVEL NIKOLAYEVICH VERSHININ; respublika Udmurtiya, 426007 Izhevsk, Pushkinskaya ul. 276; Dom Pravitelstva; tel. (3412) 25-45-67; fax (3412) 25-50-89.

Permanent Representative of the President of the Russian Federation: VIKTOR VASILIYEVICH BALAKIN.

Permanent Representative in Moscow: ANATOLII NIKOLAYEVICH KOVIN; tel. (095) 203-53-53.

Head of Izhevsk City Administration (Mayor): ANATOLII IVANOVICH SALTYKOV; respublika Udmurtiya, 426008 Izhevsk, ul. Pushkinskaya 276; tel. (3412) 22-45-90; fax (3412) 22-84-94.

Krais (Provinces)

Altai Krai

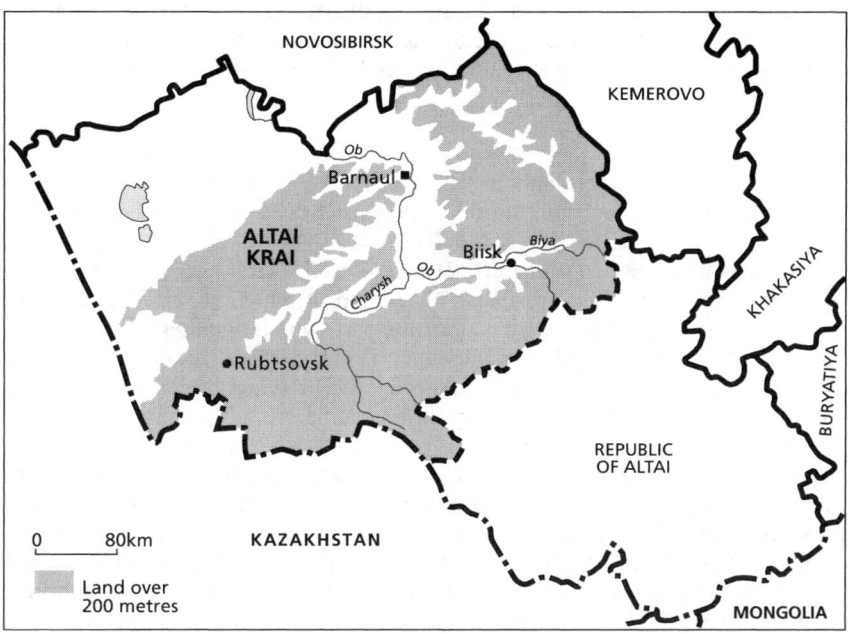

Most of Altai Krai lies within the Western Siberian Plain. Part of the Western Siberian Economic Area, it has international boundaries to the south with Kazakhstan, the People's Republic of China and Mongolia. To the north lie the federal subjects of Novosibirsk Oblast, Kemerovo Oblast and the Republic of Khakasiya (formally part of Krasnoyarsk Krai) and the Republic of Tyva lies beyond the eastern border. The eastern part of the Krai is constituted as the Republic of Altai (see above—formerly the Gorno-Altai Autonomous Oblast). Its major river is the Ob, which has numerous tributaries (there are altogether some 17,000 rivers within the territory). It has one main lake, the Teletskoye, although there are a total of 13,000 lakes, one-half of which are fresh water. About one-third of its total area is forested. In the east of the Krai are mountains, in the west steppe. The Krai (including the Altai Republic) occupies a total area of 261,700 sq km (101,040 sq miles). It is divided into 60 administrative districts and 12 cities, as well as the autonomous republic. It had an estimated population of 2,690,000 at 1 January 1996, of whom 52.5% lived in urban areas. Its population density at this time was 10.3 per sq km. In 1996 ethnic Russians comprised an estimated 90.3% of the population, Germans 4.8%, Ukrainians 2.4% and Altais just 0.1%. The Krai's administrative centre is at Barnaul, which had an estimated population of 593,000 at 1 January 1996. Other major cities are Biisk (227,400) and Rubtsovsk (168,400).

History

The territory of Altai Krai was annexed by Russia in 1738. The region was heavily industrialized during the Soviet period, particularly in the years 1926–40. Altai Krai was formed on 28 September 1937. On 13 March 1994, in accordance with a federal presidential decree of October 1993, a new provincial legislature, the Legislative Assembly, was elected, in place of the Provincial Soviet. The new legislature was bicameral, comprising a lower chamber of 25 deputies and an upper chamber of 73 deputies (one from each district in the Krai). The Legislative Assembly speaker, Aleksandr Surikov, a Communist, defeated the incumbent governor, Lev Korshunov, in the gubernatorial election of November 1996.

Economy

Altai Krai's gross regional product in 1995 totalled 14,887,600m. roubles, equivalent to 5,526,800 roubles per head. Its main industrial centres are at Barnaul, Biisk, Rubtsovsk, Novoaltaisk and Slavgorod. There are major river-ports at Barnaul and Biisk. It has well-developed transport networks—1,803 km (1,067 miles) of railway lines in 1997 and 15,673 km of roads, 13,860 km of which are paved. About one-quarter of its territory is served by water transport, which operates along a network of some 1,000 km of navigable waterways. There are five airports, including an international airport at Barnaul, with a service to Düsseldorf (Germany). The Krai is bisected by the main natural-gas pipeline running from Tyumen to Barnaul via Novosibirsk.

The Krai's principal crops are grain, flax, sunflowers and sugar-beets. Horticulture, animal husbandry and fur-animal breeding are also important. In 1995 some 23.2% of its work-force was engaged in agriculture, while total production in the sector amounted to 5,822,000m. roubles. The Krai contains substantial mineral resources, including salt, iron ore, soda and precious stones, most of which are not industrially exploited. Its main industries are mechanical engineering (including tractor manufacturing, primarily by the Rubtsovsk tractor plant), metallurgy, chemicals and petrochemicals, the manufacture of building materials, ore mining (complex ores, gold, mercury, salt), food processing (the Krai's agro-industrial complex is one of the largest in the country), textiles and light manufacturing. Barnaul contains one of the largest textile enterprises in Russia, producing cotton fibre and yarn for cloth. Industry employed 23.9% of the population in 1995 and total production in the sector amounted to a value of 9,976,000m. roubles.

In 1995 the economically active population in Altai Krai totalled 1,109,100, of whom 36,000 were unemployed. The average monthly wage at that time was 349,000 roubles, while the local budget showed a deficit of 88,900m. roubles in 1995. Continuing deficit problems contributed to the federal Government's decision of January 1999 to increase central subsidies to the province in that year. There was US $28.53m. of foreign investment in the territory in 1995. At 1 January 1996 there were 1,500 small businesses registered in the Krai.

Directory

Head of the Provincial Administration (Governor): ALEKSANDR ALEKSANDROVICH SURIKOV; Altaiskii krai, 656035 Barnaul, pr. Lenina 59; tel. (3852) 22-68-14.

Chairman of the Legislative Assembly: ALEKSANDR GRIGORIYEVICH NAZARCHUK; tel. (3852) 22-86-61; fax (3852) 22-85-42.

Permanent Representative of the President of the Russian Federation: VLADIMIR FEDROVICH RAIFIKESHT; tel. (3852) 22-28-36; fax (3852) 22-22-09.

Head of the Provincial Representation in Moscow: TAIMURAZ SURENOVICH BABLUMYAN; tel. (095) 202-44-43.

Head of Barnaul City Administration: VLADIMIR N. BAVARIN; Altaiskii krai, 656035 Barnaul, pr. Lenina 18; tel. (3852) 23-65-41.

Khabarovsk Krai

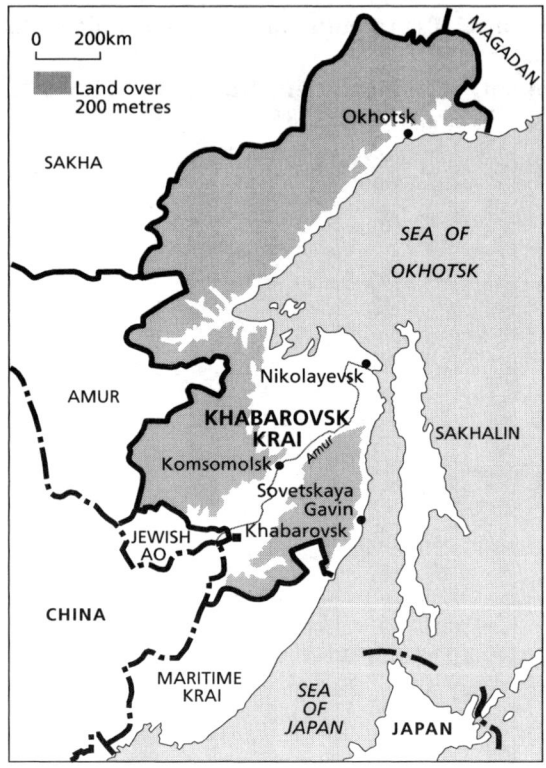

Khabarovsk Krai is situated in the Far East on the Sea of Okhotsk and the Tatar Strait. The region forms part of the Far Eastern Economic Area. Maritime Krai lies to the south, the Jewish Autonomous Oblast (Birobidzhan—part of the Krai until 1991) is to the south-west, Amur Oblast lies to the west, the Republic of Sakha (Yakutiya) to the north-west and, in the north of the province, Magadan Oblast lies to the east. The island of Sakhalin (part of Sakhalin Oblast) lies off shore to the east, across the Tatar Strait. There is a short international border with the People's Republic of China in the south-west. Its main river is the Amur, which rises near the Russo-Chinese border and flows into the Tatar Strait at the town of Nikolayevsk-on-Amur (Nikolayevsk-na-Amure). More than one-half of the Krai's total area of 788,600 sq km (304,400 sq miles) is forested and almost three-quarters comprises mountains or plateaux. The territory, one of the largest in the Federation, measures 1,780 km (1,105 miles) south to north and 7,000 km west to east. Its coastline is 2,500 km long. It is divided into 17 administrative districts and seven cities. The climate is monsoon-like in character, with hot, humid summers. Annual average precipitation in mountain areas can be as much as 1,000 mm (40 inches), while in the north it averages 500 mm. The total population in Khabarovsk Krai at 1 January 1996 was an estimated 1,571,200, of whom a large proportion (80.9%) lived in urban areas. The population density of the Krai was 1.9 per sq km. Khabarovsk Krai's administrative centre is at Khabarovsk, which had an estimated population of 616,300 in 1996. Other major cities are Komsomolsk-on-Amur (304,700), Amursk (56,700), Nikolayevsk-on-Amur (34,900) and Sovetskaya Gavan (33,500).

History

Khabarovsk city was established as a military outpost in 1858. It was named after Yerofei Khabarov, a Cossack who in 1650 led an expedition to the junction of the Amur and Ussuri rivers, the approximate location of Khabarovsk. The region prospered significantly with the construction of the Trans-Siberian Railway, which reached Khabarovsk in 1905. The Krai was formally created on 20 September 1938. The area was industrialized in 1946–80. Following the dissolution of the Provincial Soviet in late 1993, elections to a new legislative body, the Duma, were held in the Krai on 6 March 1994. A conservative territory, the greatest proportion of votes was won by the Communist Party, followed by the nationalist Liberal Democrats. This pattern was repeated in the federal general election of December 1995. In April 1996 the Russian President, Boris Yeltsin, and the head of the provincial administration, Viktor Ishayev, signed an agreement on the division of powers between the provincial and federal governments.

Economy

The Krai's principal land use is forestry. In 1995 its gross regional product totalled 15,074,100m. roubles, or 9,543,000 roubles per head. Its main industrial centres are at Khabarovsk, Komsomolsk-on-Amur, Sovetskaya Gavan, Nikolayevsk-on-Amur and Amursk. Its principal ports are Vanino (the port of Sovetskaya Gavan), Okhotsk and Nikolayevsk-on-Amur. It is traversed by two major railways, the Trans-Siberian and the Far Eastern (Baikal–Amur). A ferry service runs between the Krai and Sakhalin Oblast. The Krai is the most important Far Eastern territory in terms of its national and international air services, which connect Moscow and other European cities with Japan.

Agriculture, which employed just 4.6% of the working population in 1995 and generated 1,193,000m. roubles, consists mainly of grain production, animal husbandry, bee-keeping, fishing and hunting. Hunting is practised on about 97.5% of the Krai's territory. In August 1997 the federal Government approved a programme to rescue the Siberian tiger (435 of which inhabited the forests of Khabarovsk and Maritime Krais) from extinction at the hands of poachers.

Its main industries are mechanical engineering, metal working, ferrous metallurgy, the processing of forestry products, extraction of coal, ores and non-ferrous metals, shipbuilding (including oil rigs) and petroleum refining. Some 25.9% of the territory's work-force was engaged in industry in 1995. Total industrial output in that year amounted to a value of 9,180,000m. roubles. In the 1990s the territory began to develop its trade links with 'Pacific Rim' nations apart from Japan (with which it had a long trading history), such as Canada, the People's Republic of China, the Democratic People's Republic of Korea (North Korea) and the Republic of Korea (South Korea), Australia, New Zealand, Singapore and the USA. Its exports largely consisted of raw materials (timber, petroleum products, fish and metals).

Khabarovsk Krai's economically active population was 676,800 in 1995, of whom 40,500 were registered as unemployed. Its unemployment rate had reached almost 11% by the start of 1996. The figure for the town of Komsomolsk-on-Amur was as high as 52%, while in Amursk the number of people without work had increased 29-fold in two years, owing to the lack of funds to convert former military enterprises to civilian production. In 1995 the average monthly wage was 528,000 roubles. The provincial administration achieved a budgetary surplus in that year, of 7,600m. roubles. Total foreign investment amounted to US $28,529,000. At 1 January 1996 there were 7,600 small businesses in operation.

Directory

Head of the Provincial Administration (Governor): VIKTOR IVANOVICH ISHAYEV; Khabarovskii krai, 680000 Khabarovsk, ul. Karla Marksa 56; tel. (4212) 33-55-40; fax (4212) 33-87-56.

Chairman of the Provincial Duma: VIKTOR ALEKSEYEVICH OZEROV; Khabarovskii krai, 680000 Khabarovsk.

Permanent Representative of the President of the Russian Federation: KONDRAT MIKHAILOVICH YEVTUSHENKO; tel. (4212) 33-70-88.

Head of Khabarovsk City Administration (Mayor): PAVEL DMITRIYEVICH FILIPPOV; Khabarovskii krai, 680000 Khabarovsk, ul. Karla Marksa 66; tel. (4212) 22-58-67; fax (4212) 33-53-46.

Krasnodar Krai

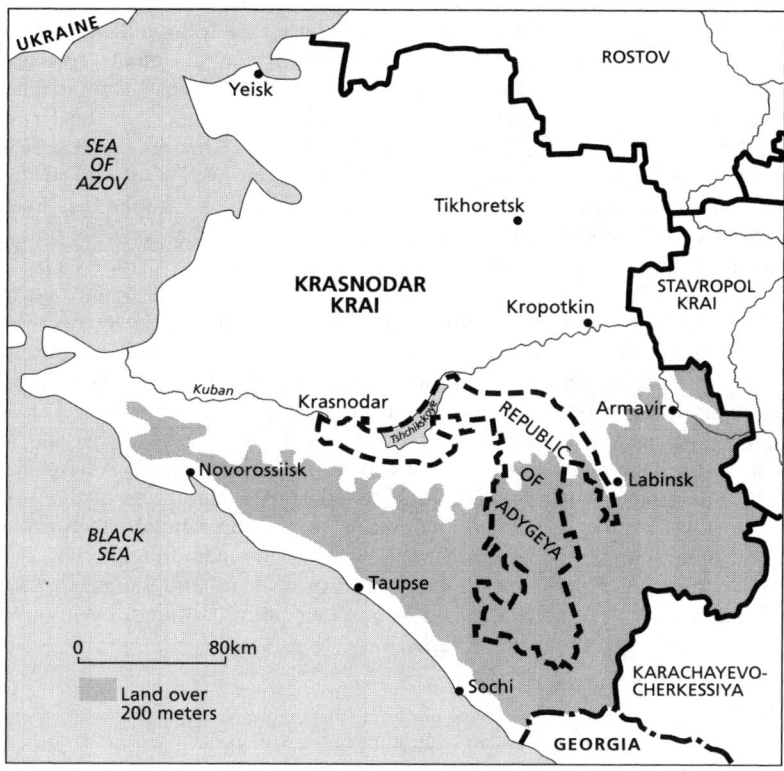

Krasnodar Krai, often known as the Kuban region, is situated in the south of European Russia, in the north-western region of the Greater Caucasus and Kuban-Azov lowlands. The Krai forms part of the North Caucasus Economic Area. It has a short international border with Georgia in the south, while Karachayevo-Cherkessiya and the rest of Stavropol Krai lie to the east and Rostov Oblast to the north-east. The Krai's territory includes and encloses the Republic of Adygeya. The Krai lies on the Black Sea (on the shores of which is sited the famous resort town of Sochi) in the south-west and on the Sea of Azov in the north-west. The narrow Kerch Gulf, in places only 10 km (six miles) wide, separates the western tip of the province from the Crimean Peninsula (Ukraine). Its major river is the Kuban. The territory of Krasnodar Krai, including Adygeya, covers some 83,600 sq km (32,280 sq miles) and measures 372 km south to north and 380 km west to east. The region is divided into 38 administrative districts and 26 cities. It had an estimated population of 5,044,000 at 1 January 1996. Its population density at this time was, therefore, 60.3 per sq km, a considerably higher figure than the national average. Krasnodar, the Krai's administrative centre, had an estimated population of 648,300.

History

Krasnodar city (known as Yekaterinodar until 1920) was founded as a military base in 1793, during the campaign of Catherine II ('the Great') to win control of the Black Sea region for the Russian Empire, which was eventually achieved in 1796. Dominated by the 'Whites' in the civil wars that followed the collapse of the tsarist regime, by the end of the Soviet period the area's innate conservatism was confirmed by its support for the Communists in independent Russia. The Krai had been formed on 13 September 1937. On 22 September 1993 the Krasnodar Provincial Soviet condemned President Boris Yeltsin's Decree 1,400 which dissolved the federal legislature. The following month the Soviet refused to dissolve itself but announced that elections would be held to a new 32-member provincial legislative assembly in March 1994, although this poll was subsequently postponed. Communist leadership of the new Provincial Soviet was not seriously challenged by other forces. The general tenor of popular sympathies was confirmed by the federal parliamentary and presidential elections of 1995 and 1996, respectively. In January 1996 the Krai signed a power-sharing treaty with the federal authorities.

During 1996 the incumbent governor, Nikolai Yegorov, attempted to use the regional courts to postpone the gubernatorial elections scheduled for December. He failed, however, and Nikolai Kondratenko, a member of the CPRF and former Chairman of the Provincial Soviet (later known as the Legislative Assembly), was elected by a large majority. The Communists and other supporters of the governor retained control of the legislative assembly in the provincial elections of 22 November 1998, winning 37 of the 50 seats. At this time Kondratenko was courting national notoriety by denouncing criminal control of Azov and the Black Sea ports and, in what was widely considered to be another populist move, by involvement in a scandal about anti-Semitic remarks.

Economy

In 1995 gross regional product in Krasnodar Krai amounted to 30,943,400m. roubles, or 6,159,000 roubles per head. Krasnodar is one of the Krai's main industrial centres, as are Armavir, Novorossiisk, Kropotkin, Tikhoretsk and Yeisk. Novorossiisk, Tuapse, Yeisk, Temryuk and Port Kavkaz are important sea-ports. The Krai has a road network, which was some 2,000 km (1,240 miles) in length in 1997. There were also 2,200 km of railway track at this time.

The Krai's principal crops are grain, sugar-beets, rice, tobacco, essential-oil plants, tea and hemp. Horticulture, viniculture and animal husbandry are also important. Agricultural output was worth 9,474,600m. roubles in 1995. Some 23.0% of the working population was engaged in agriculture at this time. There are important reserves of petroleum and natural gas in Krasnodar Krai: in 1996 around 1.7m. metric tons of petroleum were extracted, while 4.3m. tons were refined on the Krai's territory. Its main industries are food processing (which comprised around two-fifths of industry in the mid-1990s), electricity generation, chemical and light manufacturing, mechanical engineering, metal working and timber processing. Total production in the sector (which employed 18.2% of the territory's population in 1995) amounted to a value of 14,143,000m. roubles. The tourism sector is also important: the Kuban region's climate, scenery and mineral and mud springs attracted around 6m. visitors annually in the mid-1990s, when some 400,000 people were employed in tourism. The Krai contains the resort town of Sochi, as well as Anapa and Gelendbaz. In 1997 there were over 50 commercial banks operating in Krasnodar Krai. It was hoped that the transport and refinery of Caspian Sea hydrocarbons reserves would bring economic benefits by the end of the 1990s, particularly in Novorossiisk (the terminus of a major petroleum pipeline running from the Azerbaijani capital, Baku).

In 1995 the economically active population numbered 2,007,200, of whom 40,000 were registered unemployed, and the average monthly wage was 358,000 roubles. There was a small budgetary surplus in 1995, of 700m. roubles. Foreign investment in that year amounted to US $26.69m. At 1 January 1996 there were 31,800 small businesses in operation in the Krai.

Directory

Head of the Provincial Administration: NIKOLAI IGNATOVICH KONDRATENKO; Krasnodarskii krai, 350014 Krasnodar, ul. Krasnaya 35; tel. (8612) 68-57-16; fax (8612) 68-45-38.

Chairman of the Legislative Assembly: VLADIMIR ANDREYEVICH BEKETOV; tel. (8612) 52-50-07; fax (8612) 52-88-80.

Permanent Representative of the President of the Russian Federation: VITALII YEVGENIYEVICH SPIRIDONOV; tel. (8612) 52-45-63.

Head of Krasnodar City Administration (Mayor): VALERII ALEKSANDROVICH SAMOILENKO; Krasnodarskii krai, 350014 Krasnodar, ul. Krasnaya 122; tel. (8612) 55-43-48; fax (8612) 55-01-56.

Krasnoyarsk Krai

Krasnoyarsk Krai is the second-largest federal unit in Russia. It occupies the central part of Siberia and extends from the Arctic Ocean coast in the north to the western Sayan Mountains in the south. The Krai forms part of the Eastern Siberian Economic Area. It is bordered by the Republic of Sakha and Irkutsk to the east and Tyva to the south. Khakasiya, an autonomous republic which is, formally, part of the Krai, gives it a border with the Republic of Altai in the south-west. Otherwise, to the west lie the regions of Kemerovo and Tomsk, as well as Tyumen Oblast's Khanty-Mansii and Yamal-Nenets AOks. Its major river is the Yenisei, one of the longest in Russia, measuring 4,102 km (2,547 miles). Most of its area is covered by taiga (forested marshland). The Krai, including its two autonomous okrugs (Evenk and Taimyr or Dolgan-Nenets), covers a total area of 2,339,000 sq km (902,850 sq miles) and measures almost 3,000 km from south to north (a map of the entire territory can be found at the end of Part Two, on p. 279). It is divided into 48 administrative districts and 25 cities. The Krai lies within three climatic zones—arctic, sub-arctic and continental. It had an estimated total population of 3,106,000 at 1 January 1996 and a population density, therefore, of 1.3 per sq km. Some 73.9% of the population inhabited urban areas at this time. The Krai's administrative centre is at Krasnoyarsk, which had an estimated population of

871,100 at 1 January 1996. Other major cities include Norilsk (156,000), Achinsk (123,000), Kansk (108,500) and Zelenogorsk (93,500).

History

The city of Krasnoyarsk was founded in 1628 by Cossack forces as an ostrog (military transit camp) during the period of Russian expansion across Siberia (1582–1639). The region gained importance after the discovery of gold, and with the construction of the Trans-Siberian Railway. The Krai was formed on 7 December 1934. During the Soviet era the region was closed to foreigners, owing to its nuclear-reactor and defence establishments.

A gubernatorial election in December 1992 was won by Valerii Zubov (the incumbent, a supporter of President Boris Yeltsin), and elections to a new parliament, the Legislative Assembly, were held on 6 March 1994. The dominance of the old nomenklatura in the Krai was indicated by the high level of support for the Communists (mainly in the countryside), but also by the mainly urban support for pro-Yeltsin and reformist parties, which tended to be represented by respected members of the old establishment. During the mid-1990s, however, Zubov's regime, though enlightened, proved to be increasingly ineffectual—in 1997 the provincial administration collected less than one-half of the taxes it was owed and had one of the worst records on wage arrears in the country. This largely contributed to the victory in the 1998 gubernatorial elections of Aleksandr Lebed, who was perceived by many as a suitably strong leader capable of defending the interests of the territory against the federal Government. Lebed, who allegedly had strong support for his campaign from powerful industrial figures in the Krai, defeated Zubov in the second round of elections, held on 17 May, with 57.3% of the votes cast, compared to Zubov's 38.2%. He remained a controversial figure, mainly in national politics, but his popular rhetoric would be tested by provincial government. In January 1999 just over one-half of the deputies in the Legislative Assembly urged him to take a firm grip of policy and to appoint experienced administrators. At the same time they were engaged in a dispute over the establishment of a provincial government, with Lebed arguing that he would not have sufficient control of the executive and that his deputy should chair the cabinet.

Economy

Krasnoyarsk Krai is potentially one of Russia's richest regions, containing vast deposits of minerals, gold and petroleum. It also has serious economic problems, many of them typical of northern regions. In 1995 its gross regional product (including the autonomous okrugs) amounted to 44,098,900m. roubles, equivalent to 6,159,000 roubles per head. The Krai's major industrial centres are at Krasnoyarsk, Norilsk, Achinsk, Kansk and Minusinsk.

The principal crops are grain, flax, and hemp. Animal husbandry, fur farming and hunting are also important. The agricultural sector employed just 9.9% of the working population in 1995. Total output within the sector was worth 5,588,600m. roubles. At the beginning of 1999 the provincial assembly considered the state of farming to be critical, reported no sign of a revival of industry and expressed concern at the continued deterioration in living standards. Its main industries are non-ferrous metallurgy, mechanical engineering, metal working, ore mining (particularly bauxite, for aluminium), chemicals, forestry, light manufacturing and food processing. Industry employed 28.4% of the Krai's work-force in 1995. The combined industrial output of Krasnoyarsk Krai and its two autonomous okrugs amounted to a value of 33,664,000m. roubles. The Krai contains the world's second-largest aluminium smelter, Krasnoyarsk Aluminium, which in 1998 was 20%-owned by the British-based company, Trans-World.

In 1995 the territory's economically active population totalled 1,389,800. The number of registered unemployed for the entire province was 46,600 at this time. The average monthly wage in the Krai was 594,000 roubles, while the local budget, which included the two autonomous okrugs, showed a surplus of 46,900m. roubles. There was little foreign investment in the Krai at that time (US $363,000), but it increased in the second half of the 1990s. At the beginning of 1996 there were 18,154 small businesses in Krasnoyarsk Krai, of which 93.2% were privately owned.

Directory

Head of the Provincial Administration (Governor): ALEKSANDR IVANOVICH LEBED; Kranoyarskii krai, 660009 Krasnoyarsk, pr. Mira 110; tel. (3912) 22-22-63; fax (3912) 22-11-78.

Chairman of the Legislative Assembly: ALEKSANDR V. USS; Krasnoyarskii krai, 660009 Krasnoyarsk, pr. Mira 110; tel. (3912) 49-32-70; fax (3912) 22-27-37.

Permanent Representative of the President of the Russian Federation: VALERII KAZAKOV; tel. (3912) 49-36-12.

Head of the Provincial Representation in Moscow: (vacant); tel. (095) 299-45-83.

Head of Krasnoyarsk City Administration (Mayor): PETR IVANOVICH PIM-ASHKOV; Krasnoyarskii krai, 660049 Krasnoyarsk, ul. Karla Marksa 93; tel. (3912) 22-22-31; fax (3912) 22-25-12.

Maritime (Primorye) Krai

Maritime (Primorye) Krai is situated in the extreme south-east of the country on the Tatar Strait and the Sea of Japan. The province is part of the Far Eastern Economic Area. Its only border with another federal subject is with Khabarovsk Krai to the north. There are international borders with the People's Republic of China to the west and the People's Democratic Republic of Korea (North Korea) in the south-west. Its major river is the Ussuri. The territory occupies 165,900 sq km (64,060 sq miles), two-thirds of which is forested. It is divided into 25 administrative districts and 12 cities. At 1 January 1996 the total number of inhabitants in the territory was estimated at 2,255,500 and the population density was, therefore, 13.6 per sq km. Of this total, some 77.9% lived in urban areas. Maritime Krai's administrative centre is at Vladivostok, which had an estimated 626,500 inhabitants. Other major cities are Nakhodka (161,700), Ussuriisk (formerly Voroshilov—161,200), Arsenev (69,900) and Artem (69,000).

History

The territories of the Maritime Krai were recognized as Chinese possessions by Russia in the Treaty of Nerchinsk in 1687. They became part of the Russian Empire in 1860, however, being ceded by China under the terms of the Treaty of

Peking (Beijing), and the port of Vladivostok was founded. Along with other Transbaikal and Pacific regions of the former Russian Empire, the territory was part of the Far Eastern Republic until its 1922 reintegration into Russia under Soviet rule. Maritime Krai was created on 20 October 1938.

The territory declared itself a republic in mid-1993 but was not recognized as such by the federal authorities. On 28 October 1993 the head of the provincial administration, the Governor, disbanded the Provincial Soviet as it had failed to muster a quorum. Elections for a Governor of the territory were set for 7 October 1994, but were cancelled by presidential decree, after alleged improprieties by the incumbent, Yevgenii Nazdratenko, during his election campaign. Nazdratenko was elected, however, on 17 December 1995, having won some 76% of the votes cast. The intervention of the federal authorities against him only served to increase support for Nazdratenko in an area that strongly favoured the nationalist Liberal Democrats, as well as the Communists. His populist style of government and control of the local media reinforced his position, particularly outside the more pro-reform Vladivostok.

The Governor's disputes with the central Government, particularly with President Boris Yeltsin's reformist chief of staff, Anatolii Chubais, continued after his election—in October 1996 Chubais publicly blamed Nazdratenko for the serious energy crisis in the region, citing his failure to introduce market reforms, including liberalization of energy prices. In May 1997 the federal interior minister, Anatolii Kulikov, was forced to intervene in a prolonged strike by miners protesting at six-month wage arrears. Later that year a long-standing feud between Nazdratenko and the liberal Mayor of Vladivostok, Viktor Cherepkov, resulted in the latter's resignation in November (he eventually remained in office until August 1998). Throughout that year, the Governor's uncompromising demands for subsidies and his outspoken attacks over border issues against the Chinese Government had further alienated him from the federal Government. On 9 July 1998, following several months of industrial action by miners and defence and public-sector workers, an agreement 'on measures to improve finances' was signed. This rescheduled until 1999 the budget loan which the Krai received to repay its wage debt and envisaged the repayment of the federal debt of 2,000m. roubles to military and defence enterprises over the following 18 months. Controversy over the mayoral election in Vladivostok continued, with the poll of September 1998 being deemed invalid and a new contest scheduled for 17 January 1999. Meanwhile, Cherepov was ousted from office (although he resisted this move) and declared that he would stand for re-election. However, legal moves further delayed a mayoral contest until after a city duma had introduced a local charter—Vladivostok remained the only city in Russia not to have such a charter or a legislative assembly. On 17 January a duma was duly elected, although the provincial authorities challenged the results, which were overwhelmingly in favour of Cherepov and his supporters.

Economy

Maritime Krai's gross regional product totalled 19,290,200m. roubles in 1995, equivalent to 8,519,300 roubles per head. Its major industrial centres are at Vladivostok, the terminus of the Trans-Siberian Railway, Ussuriisk, Nakhodka, Dalnegorsk, Lesozavodsk, Dalnorechensk and Partizansk. The Krai's most important ports are at Vladivostok, Nakhodka and Vostochnyi (formerly Vrangel). Vessels based in these ports comprise around four-fifths of maritime transport services in the Far East. Maritime Krai has rail links with Khabarovsk Krai and, hence, other regions, as well as international transport links with North Korea and the Republic of Korea (South Korea).

Its agriculture, which employed just 9.4% of the labour force in 1995, consists mainly of grain and soya production, animal husbandry, fur farming, bee-keeping and fishing. Despite the Krai's serious economic problems the fishing industry thrived in the mid-1990s. Total agricultural output in 1995 amounted to a value of 1,972,700m. roubles. In August 1997 the federal Government approved a programme to rescue the Siberian tiger, 435 of which inhabited the forests of Khabarovsk and Maritime Krais, from extinction at the hands of poachers. Illicit agricultural activities were also thought to include the cultivation of marijuana, an illegal drug, particularly in the Khankai district. Serious pollution of the Krai's gulfs and bays (which some estimated to contain over 800,000 metric tons of metallic waste) resulted in September 1997 in the start of a cleaning operation assisted by US and Norwegian funds. The Krai contains some 1,200m. metric tons of coal reserves. The hydroelectric-energy potential of the region's rivers is estimated at 25,000m. kWh, while timber reserves are estimated at 1,500m.–1,800m. cu m. Its main industries are fuel and energy production, non-ferrous metallurgy, ore mining, the processing of fish and forestry products, mechanical engineering and ship repairs, metal working and chemicals. Total industrial production was worth 1,972,700m. roubles in 1995, while the sector employed 23.8% of the working population. Energy production in the Krai was hindered in the mid-1990s by political mismanagement. Dalenergo, its electricity-generation monopoly, was notorious as one of the worst-performing utilities in the country, unable to collect accounts, service debts or pay for fuel. The territory is ideally placed, in terms of its proximity to the Pacific nations, for international trade, although in the late 1990s the perception of widespread corruption restrained its development.

The economically active population in Maritime Krai was 970,600 in 1995, of whom 32,400 were unemployed. The average monthly wage at this time was 538,000 roubles. There was a budgetary deficit in 1995 of 295,700m. roubles. According to the European Bank for Reconstruction and Development, the Krai had huge investment potential: foreign investment in 1995 totalled US $18.3m. In late 1997 Hyundai (of South Korea), opened a $100m. hotel and business centre in Vladivostok. South Korea also planned to create an industrial park for high-technology industries in Nakhodka should the Russian Government create a free economic zone in the city. At 1 January 1996 there were 14,500 small businesses registered in the territory.

Directory

Head of the Provincial Administration (Governor): YEVGENII IVANOVICH NAZDRATENKO; Primorskii krai, Vladivostok, ul. Svetlanskaya 22; tel. (4232) 22-38-00; fax (4232) 22-50-10.

Chairman of the Provincial Duma: NIKOLAI ILIARIONOVICH LITVINOV; tel. (4232) 22-13-66; fax (4232) 22-52-77.

Permanent Representative of the President of the Russian Federation: VIKTOR YEVGENIYEVICH KONDRATOV; tel. (4232) 22-39-13.

Head of the Provincial Representation in Moscow: MIKHAIL NIKOLAYEVICH MALGINOV; tel. (095) 203-53-36.

Head of the Vladivostok City Administration (Mayor): YURII MIKHAILOVICH KOPYLOV (acting); Primorskii krai, Vladivostok, Okeanskii pr. 20; tel. (4232) 22-30-16; fax (4232) 22-68-40.

Stavropol Krai

Stavropol Krai is situated in the central Caucasus region and extends from the Caspian lowlands in the east to the foothills of the Greater Caucasus Mountains in the south-west. It is part of the North Caucasus Economic Area. Krasnodar Krai lies to the west, there is a short border with Rostov Oblast in the north-west of the Krai and it shares rather longer borders with Kalmykiya to the north-east and Dagestan to the east. Chechnya, North Osetiya (Ossetia) and Kabardino-Balkariya lie to the south. The autonomous republic of Karachayevo-Cherkessiya forms a south-western arm of the Krai, giving it an international border with Georgia further south still. The Krai's major rivers are the Kuban, the Kuma and the Yegorlyk. Much of its territory is steppe. Its total area, excluding that of Karachayevo-Cherkessiya, is 66,500 sq km (25,670 sq miles). It is divided into 26 administrative districts and 18 cities. The population of Stavropol Krai numbered 2,667,000 at 1 January 1996. The Krai's population density, therefore, was 40.1 per sq km. Its administrative centre is at Stavropol (known as Voroshilovsk 1935–43), which had an estimated population of 344,400. Other major cities are Pyatigorsk, Nevinnomyssk and Kislovodsk.

History

Stavropol city was founded in 1777 as part of the consolidation of Russian rule in the Caucasus. It was named Voroshilovsk in 1935–43. The territory was created on 13 February 1924, although it was originally known as South-Eastern Oblast and, subsequently, the North Caucasus Krai. It was named Ordzhonikidze Krai in 1937–43, before adopting its current title.

On 27 March 1994 elections were held to a new representative body, the State Duma. Further local elections took place on 29 February 1996, in which the

Communist Party won approximately one-third of the parliamentary seats. In June 1995 the town of Budennovsk, situated about 150 km north of the Chechen border, was the scene of a massive hostage-taking operation by rebel Chechen forces; over 1,000 civilians were seized, but were released after a few days. In the gubernatorial elections of November 1996 the Communist candidate, Aleksandr Chernogorov (a former State Duma deputy), defeated the government-backed incumbent, Petr Marchenko, winning 55% of the votes cast, as against Marchenko's 40%. Marchenko was subsequently appointed the Permanent Representative of the federal President in many of the territories of the North Caucasus. In March 1998 Chernogorov came under attack by the Russian Prosecutor-General over the establishment of his own administration, which violated a number of local laws on the status of government and territorial government. This move also brought him into conflict with the provincial Duma, which wished to approve all the ministry heads, not just the premier. In late 1998, however, the courts supported the Governor.

Economy

In 1995 Stavropol Krai's gross regional product was 18,171,700m. roubles, or 6,835,100 roubles per head. Its main industrial centres are at Stavropol, Nevinomyssk, Cherkessk (Kabardino-Cherkessiya), Georgiyevsk and Budennovsk. In September 1997 the federal Government announced that a new section of the petroleum pipeline from Baku (Azerbaijan) would cross Stavropol Krai, rather than run through Chechnya. The construction of the section was expected to take between 18 months and two years.

The Krai contains extremely fertile soil. Its agricultural production, which amounted to a value of 5,179,400m. roubles in 1995, consists mainly of grain, sunflower seeds, sugar-beets and vegetables. Horticulture, viniculture and animal husbandry are also important. The sector employed 24.1% of the working population in 1995. The Krai's main industries are food processing, light manufacturing, mechanical engineering, chemicals and the production of natural gas, petroleum, non-ferrous metal ores and coal. Around 16.3% of the labour force worked in industry in 1995; total industrial output for that year was worth 5,179,400m. roubles.

The economically active population in Stavropol Krai in 1995 was 1,012,700, of whom 20,500 were registered unemployed. The average wage at that time was 332,000 roubles per month and there was a budgetary surplus of 23,700m. roubles. Foreign investment in the territory in 1995 amounted to US $19.6m. At 1 January 1996 there were 8,000 small businesses in operation.

Directory

Head of the Provincial Administration (Governor): ALEKSANDR LEONIDOVICH CHERNOGOROV; Stavropolskii krai, 355025 Stavropol, pl. Lenina; tel. (8652) 35-22-52; fax (8652) 35-03-30.

Chairman of the Provincial Government: STANISLAV VALENTINOVICH ILYASOV; Stavropolskii krai, 355025 Stavropol.

Chairman of the Provincial Duma: ALEKSANDR AKIMOVICH SHIYANOV; tel. (8652) 34-82-55.

Permanent Representative of the President of the Russian Federation: PETR PETROVICH MARCHENKO; tel. (8652) 4-82-85.

Head of Stavropol City Administration (Mayor): MIKHAIL VLADIMIROVICH KUZMIN; Stavropolskii krai, 355000 Stavropol, pr. Karla Marksa 95; tel. (8652) 26-03-10; fax (8652) 26-28-23.

Oblasts (Regions)

Amur

Amur Oblast is situated in the south-east of the Russian Federation, to the west of Khabarovsk Krai. It forms part of the Far Eastern Economic Area. The Jewish Autonomous Oblast lies to the south-east, Chita Oblast to the west and the Republic of Sakha (Yakutiya) to the north. Southwards it has an international border with the People's Republic of China. The Oblast's main river is the Amur, which is 2,900 km (1,800 miles) long. A large reservoir, the Zeya, is situated in the north of the region. A little under three-quarters of the Oblast's territory is forested. Its total area occupies 361,900 sq km (139,690 sq miles) and measures 750 km south to north and 1,150 km south-east to north-west. It is divided into 20 administrative districts and nine cities. The territory's inhabitants numbered some 1,037,800 at 1 January 1996 and the population density was, therefore, 2.9 per sq km. Most people (65.3%) lived in urban areas. Amur Oblast's administrative centre is at Blagoveshchensk, near the Chinese border, and had an estimated population of 215,300 in 1996. Other major cities in the region are Belogorsk (75,300), Svobodnyi (73,400) and Tynda (53,000).

History

The Amur region was first discovered by European Russians in 1639 and came under Russian control in the late 1850s. Part of the pro-Bolshevik Far Eastern Republic (based in Chita) until its reintegration into Russia in 1922, an Amur Oblast was formed on 20 October 1932.

In the first year of post-Soviet Russian independence there was a struggle for power in the territory, which the federal President, Boris Yeltsin, decided should be resolved by a gubernatorial election in December 1992. However, his appointed head of the administration was defeated, leaving both executive and legislature in the region opposed to him. On 21 July 1993 Amur Oblast declared itself a republic, a move which was condemned by the federal authorities. During the constitutional crisis of September–October, President Yeltsin was denounced by all the regional authorities. The Governor was, therefore, later dismissed and the Regional Soviet dissolved. Contention between executive and legislative organs resumed following the election of a new Regional Assembly in 1994. In January 1996 the Regional Administration brought action against the Regional Assembly for adopting a Charter, a republican constitution, some of the clauses of which ran counter to federal laws and presidential decrees. In the same month, in accordance with the Charter, the Assembly changed its name to the Soviet of People's Deputies. In elections to the Soviet of People's Deputies, held in March 1996, Communist Party candidates won between 35% and 40% of the votes cast. In response to these developments President Yeltsin again dismissed the Governor in June, and appointed Yurii Lyashko, formerly the chief executive of Blagoveshchensk city, in his place. A further gubernatorial election was held on 22 September. It was won by the Communist-backed candidate by a narrow margin, but the results were subsequently annulled by a controversial court decision. An election in 1997 was won by Anatolii Belonogov, hitherto speaker of the regional legislature, a Communist.

Economy

Amur Oblast's gross regional product was 8,326,300m. roubles in 1995, equivalent to 8,011,400 roubles per head. Its main industrial centres are at Blagoveshchensk, Belogorsk, Raichikhinsk, Zeya, Shimanovsk, Svobodnyi and Tynda. In 1997 there were 15,999 km of roads in the Oblast. Construction of a major highway, running from Chita to Khabarovsk, was under way on its territory. There were 3,652 km of railway track, of which 1,110 km were electrified. Two major railways, the Trans-Siberian and the Far Eastern (Baikal–Amur), crossed the territory of the Oblast. There are five river-ports, at Blagoveshchensk, Svobodnensk, Poyarkovsk, Amursk (all of which transport cargo to and from the People's Republic of China) and Zeisk. There is an international airport at Blagoveshchensk which operates flights to Japan, the Democratic People's Republic of Korea (North Korea), the Republic of Korea (South Korea) and Turkey.

Agriculture in Amur Oblast, which employed 19.2% of its work-force in 1995, consists mainly of grain and vegetable production, animal husbandry and bee-keeping. The soil in the south of the region is particularly fertile—in 1998 Amur Oblast contained 57% of the arable land in the Russian Far East and produced 30% of its agricultural output. The value of output in this sector in 1995 was 1,512,300m. roubles. In 1998 timber reserves were estimated at 2,000m. cu m. Raw-material deposits in the Oblast include those of bituminous and brown coal and kaolin. There are also substantial reserves of iron, titanium, silver and gold ores. In the mid-1990s around 10–12 metric tons of gold were extracted annually. Coal-mining is also important, as are mechanical engineering, electricity generation, electro-technical industry and the processing of agricultural and forestry products. Some 16.5% of the Oblast's work-force were employed in industry in 1995, while total output in the sector amounted to a value of 3,847,000m. roubles. The region contains the Amur Shipbuilding Plant, which produced nuclear submarines until the early 1990s. In 1997, having hitherto failed to convert to civilian use, the plant was contracted to build a 111-sq-km steel platform for a foreign consortium, intended to exploit the petroleum and natural-gas fields of Sakhalin Oblast. There is a hydroelectric power plant at Zeya, with a reservoir of 2,400 sq km. Another power-station was under construction at Bureya in 1998. The Oblast's main trading partners were the People's Republic of China, Japan and North Korea.

The Oblast's economically active population numbered 475,300 in 1995, of whom 29,700 were officially registered as unemployed. Those in employment earned, on average, 489,000 roubles per month. There was a budgetary deficit in the region of 27,900m. roubles in that year, while foreign investment totalled US $883,000. At 1 January 1996 there was a total of 6,455 small businesses, with a combined work-force of 56,900 employees, registered in Amur.

Directory

Head of the Regional Administration: ANATOLII NIKOLAYEVICH BELONOGOV; Amurskaya obl., 675023 Blagoveshchensk, ul. Lenina 135; tel. (4162) 42-42-03; fax (4162) 44-62-01.

Chairman of the Soviet of People's Deputies (Regional Assembly): VIKTOR VASILIYEVICH MARTSENKO; tel. (4162) 42-46-75; fax (4162) 44-38-58.

Permanent Representative of the President of the Russian Federation: VALERII VASILIYEVICH VOSCHEVOZ; tel. (4162) 42-47-81; fax (4162) 44-17-54.

Head of Blagoveshchensk City Administration (Mayor): ALEKSANDR MIKHAILOVICH KOLYADIN; Amurskaya obl., 675000 Blagoveshchensk, ul. Lenina 133; tel. (4162) 42-49-85.

Archangel

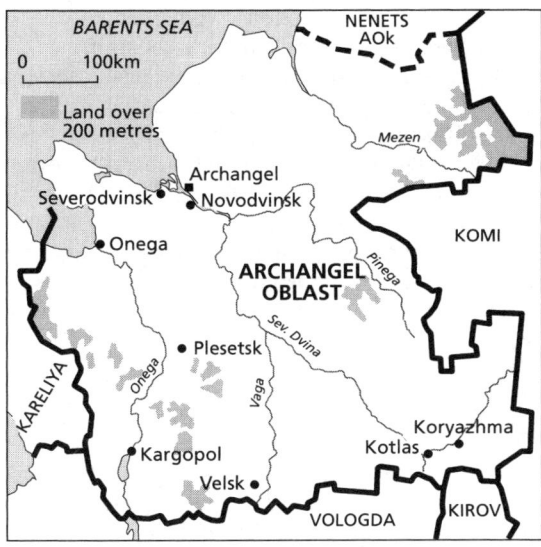

Archangel Oblast is situated in the north of the Eastern European Plain. It lies on the White, Barents and Kara Seas (parts of the Arctic Ocean) and includes the archipelago of Zemlya Frantsa-Iosifa and the Novaya Zemlya islands. The Oblast forms part of the Northern Economic Area. In the north-east the Nenets Autonomous Okrug, a constituent part of the Oblast (a complete map of which can be found at the end of Part Two, on p. 279), runs eastwards along the coast to end in a short border with the Yamal-Nenets AOk (part of Tyumen Oblast). The Republic of Komi lies to the south of the Nenets AOk and to the east of Archangel proper. Kirov and, mainly, Vologda Oblasts form the southern border and the Republic of Kareliya lies to the west. The Oblast contains several large rivers (the Severnaya Dvina, the Onega, the Mezen, the Pinega, the Vaga and the Pechora) and some 2,500 lakes. Some two-fifths of its entire area is forested—much of the north-west of the territory is taiga (forested marshland). The Oblast, including the autonomous okrug, occupies an area of 587,400 sq km (226,800 sq miles) and is divided into 20 administrative districts and 14 cities. It spans three climatic zones—arctic, sub-arctic and continental. The total population at 1 January 1996 was an estimated 1,521,000 and its population density, therefore, stood at 2.6 per sq km. Its administrative centre is at Archangel (Arkhangelsk), which had an estimated population of 372,100 at that time. Other major cities are Severodvinsk (238,700), Kotlas (67,600), Novodvinsk (49,400) and Koryazhma (44,300).

History

The city of Archangel (Arkhangelsk) was founded in the 16th century, to further Muscovite trade. It was the first Russian seaport and the country's main one until the building of St Petersburg in 1703. The port played a major role in the attack by the Entente fleet (British and French navies) against the Red Army in 1918.

It was an important route for supplies from the Allied Powers during the Second World War. Archangel Oblast was founded on 23 September 1937.

On 13 October 1993 the Archangel Regional Soviet transferred its responsibilities to the Regional Administration. On 12 December, simultaneously with the elections to the Russian Federal Assembly, elections were held to a new parliament, the Deputies' Assembly, which consisted of an upper chamber of 27 members and a lower chamber of 11 members. Communist candidates formed the largest single group elected to the legislature, and the predominance of the party was confirmed by the results of the Russian general election of December 1995. However, supporters of the federal Government and the liberal reformists also enjoyed respectable levels of support in the cities. In March 1996 the unpopular head of the regional administration was replaced and subsequently investigated on charges of corruption. A gubernatorial election took place in December, when Pavel Pozdeyev, the central government appointment, was displaced by Anatolii Yefremov. Local elections, held in March 1998, were declared invalid, owing to a turn-out of less than 25%.

Economy

Including the Nenets district, Archangel Oblast's gross regional product totalled 14,263,000m. roubles in 1995, equivalent to 9,336,300 roubles per head. The Oblast's main industrial centres are at Archangel, Kotlas, Severodvinsk and Novodvinsk. Its main ports are Archangel, Onega, Mezen and Naryan Mar (sea- and river-ports).

The Oblast's agriculture, which employed just 7.4% of the labour force in 1995, consists mainly of grain and vegetable production, animal husbandry (livestock and reindeer) and hunting. Agricultural output in the Oblast, still including the autonomous okrug, amounted to a value of 1,692,800m. roubles in 1995. Its industry, which employed 29.1% of the working population in 1995, is based on the extraction of minerals (the Oblast's reserve of bauxite is the third largest in the world), petroleum and natural gas, processing of agricultural and forestry products and mechanical engineering. Industrial output across the entire Oblast was worth 11,102,000m. roubles in 1995. In July 1998 it was announced that the federal finance ministry was to allocate credit worth US $30m. for development of a diamond field in the Oblast, one of Russia's largest, run by Severoalmaz.

From 1992 the economic situation in the region rapidly deteriorated, causing widespread shortages in food and power, and resulting in the migration from the region of hundreds of thousands of the Oblast's inhabitants. However, at the beginning of 1997 the Oblast's economically active population amounted to some 703,000, or 48% of its total inhabitants. At the end of 1996 some 55,900 people, or 8.0% of the economically active population, were registered unemployed. These figures seemed to indicate that the level of emigration had declined, as had unemployment. The average wage in 1995 was 505,000 roubles per month. There was a budgetary deficit in the Oblast in that year, amounting to 103,400m. roubles. At the end of 1998 Archangel was cited as the sixth-worst region in the Federation for wage-payment arrears (on average, almost six months behind). Total foreign investment in the Oblast in 1995 was US $2.72m. At 1 January 1996 there were 5,200 small businesses registered on its territory.

Oblasts (Archangel)

Directory

Head of the Regional Administration (Governor): ANATOLII ANTONOVICH YEFREMOV; Arkhangelskaya obl., 163400 Archangelsk, pr. Troitskii 49; tel. (8182) 43-79-12; fax (8182) 43-21-12.

Chairman of the Regional Deputies' Assembly: VYACHESLAV IVANOVICH KALYAMIN; tel. (8182) 43-66-81; fax (8182) 43-73-03.

Permanent Representative of the President of the Russian Federation: MARINA NIKOLAYEVNA BELUGUBOVA; tel. (8182) 43-74-82; fax (818) 3-77-51.

Head of Archangel City Administration: PAVEL NIKOLAYEVICH BALAKSHIN; Arkhangelskaya obl., 163061 Arkhangelsk, pl. Lenina 5; tel. (8182) 43-86-84; fax (8182) 43-20-71.

Astrakhan

Astrakhan Oblast is situated in the Caspian lowlands and forms part of the Volga Economic Area. Lying between the Russian federal subject of Kalmykiya southwards and the former Soviet state of Kazakhstan eastwards, Astrakhan is a long, relatively thin territory which flanks the course of the River Volga as it flows out of Volgograd Oblast in the north-west and into the Caspian Sea in the south-east. The Volga drains into the Caspian via a large delta at Astrakhan. The delta is one of the largest in the world and occupies more than 24,000 sq km (9,260 sq miles) of the Caspian lowlands. It gives the Oblast some 200 km (over 120 miles) of coastline. It has one lake, the Baskunchak, measuring 115 sq km. Astrakhan occupies some 44,100 sq km (17,000 sq miles) and is divided into 11 administrative districts and six cities. At 1 January 1996 its total population was an estimated 1,029,000 and its population density, therefore, was 23.3 per sq km. The Oblast's administrative centre is at Astrakhan (formerly Khadzhi-Tarkhan), which had an estimated population of 488,300 at this time. The city lies at 22 m (72 feet) below sea level and is protected from the waters of the Volga delta by 75 km of dykes. It is the most important river- and seaport in the Volga-Caspian basin. Other major cities are Akhtyubinsk (50,400) and Znamensk (34,700).

History

The Khanate of Astrakhan, which was formed in 1446 following the dissolution of the Golden Horde, was conquered by the Russians in 1556. The region subsequently became an important centre for trading in timber, grain, fish and petroleum. It was occupied by Bolshevik forces in 1917. Astrakhan Oblast was founded on 27 December 1943.

There was considerable hardship in the region with the dissolution of the USSR and the economic reforms of the early 1990s. Dissatisfaction was indicated by the relatively high level of support for the nationalist Liberal Democrats in the 1995 early federal parliamentary elections, although the Communists remained the leading party. The Governor, Anatolii Guzhvin, originally a federal appointment, retained his post in local elections in 1997.

Economy

Astrakhan Oblast's gross regional product was 5,746,600m. roubles in 1995, equivalent to 5,597,700 roubles per head. The Oblast's main industrial centres are at Astrakhan and Akhtyubinsk. The rise in the level of the Caspian Sea (by some 2.6 m between the late 1970s and the late 1990s) and the resulting erosion of the Volga delta caused serious environmental problems in the region. These were exacerbated by the pollution of the water by petroleum products, copper, nitrates and other substances, which frequently contributed to the death of a significant proportion of fish reserves.

The Oblast remains a major producer of vegetables and cucurbits (gourds and melons). Grain production and animal husbandry are also important. Total agricultural production in 1995 amounted to a value of 1,231,700m. roubles. The sector employed 13.5% of the working population in that year. The Oblast is rich in natural resources, including gas and gas condensate, sulphur, petroleum and salt. Its main industries are light manufacturing, food processing, mechanical engineering, metal working, wood-working, pulp and paper manufacturing, chemicals and the production of petroleum and natural gas. It was hoped that this last activity would improve the economic fortunes in the region by the end of the 1990s, as the exploitation of Caspian hydrocarbons reserves increased. Industrial output in 1995 was worth 3,066,000m. roubles, while the sector employed 21.0% of the Oblast's labour force. Regional trade was also important to the economy of Astrakhan. In the mid-1990s the Lakor freight company established important shipping links with Iran, and in 1996 handled around 940,000 metric tons of cargo. In September 1997 the company, with an Iranian group, Khazar Shipping, registered the Astrakhan–Nowshahr joint shipping line. Astrakhan's exports to Iran mainly comprised paper, metals, timber, mechanical equipment, fertilizers and chemical products.

Astrakhan Oblast's economically active population numbered 437,200 in 1995, of whom 22,600 were registered unemployed. The average monthly wage at that time was 321,000 roubles and there was a budgetary deficit of 39,300m. roubles. Foreign investment in the territory amounted to only US $92,000. At 1 January 1995 there were 5,100 small businesses in operation.

Directory

Head of the Regional Administration (Governor): ANATOLII PETROVICH GUZHVIN; Astrakhanskaya obl., 414008 Astrakhan, ul. Sovetskaya 15; tel. (8512) 22-17-67; fax (8512) 22-95-14.

Chairman of the Representative Assembly: VALERII VASILIYEVICH BORODAYEV; tel. (8512) 22-13-09; fax (8512) 22-22-48.

Permanent Representative of the President of the Russian Federation: VALERII MIKHAILOVICH ADROV; tel. (8512) 22-56-44.

Head of Astrakhan City Administration (Mayor): IGOR ALEKSANDROVICH BEZRUKAVNIKOV; Astrakhanskaya obl., 414000 Astrakhan, ul. Chernyshevskogo 6; tel. (8512) 22-55-88; fax (8512) 22-24-47.

Belgorod

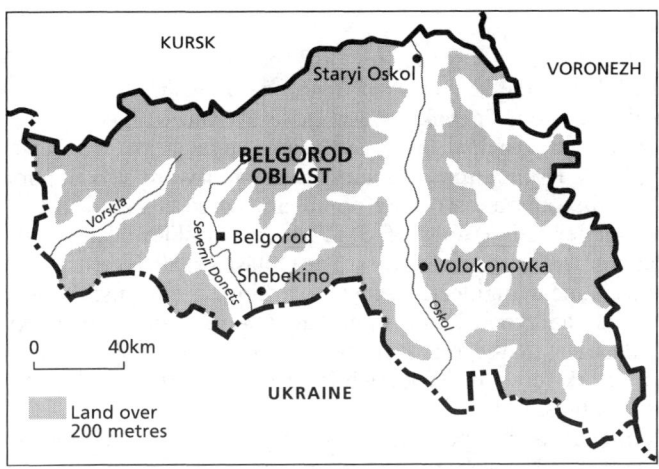

Belgorod Oblast is situated in the south-west of the Central Russian Highlands. It forms part of the Central Chernozem Economic Area. The Oblast lies on the international border with Ukraine, with Kursk to the north and Voronezh to the east. Its main rivers are the Severnii Donets, the Vorskla and the Oskol. The territory occupies 27,100 sq km (10,460 sq miles) and measures around 260 km (160 miles) from west to east. It is divided into 21 administrative districts and nine cities. It had an estimated population of 1,469,000 at 1 January 1996, of whom some 64.8% inhabited urban areas, and a population density of 54.2 per sq km. According to the 1989 census, 92.9% of the Oblast's inhabitants were ethnic Russians. The Oblast's administrative centre is at Belgorod, which had an estimated 326,400 inhabitants in 1996. Other major cities include Staryi Oskol (201,800), Gubkin (85,300) and Shebekino (46,000).

History

Belgorod was established as a bishopric during the early days of Orthodox Christianity. The region was part of Lithuania until 1503, when it was annexed by the Muscovite state. The new city of Belgorod was founded in 1593. Belgorod Oblast was formally established on 6 January 1954. Briefly a 'White' stronghold in the civil wars following the 1917 Russian Revolution, in the 1990s the region was still considered conservative. However, it was now as part of the so-called 'red belt' of loyal Communist support.

During the 1993 confrontation of the federal presidency and parliament, both the regional executive and soviet were critical of President Boris Yeltsin. He, therefore, dismissed the governor and arranged for elections to a new Regional Duma in 1994. The Communists enjoyed a majority in this body too, and there was constant conflict with the administration, the head of which, however, also enjoyed popular support. For this reason, the Oblast was one of only 12 areas in the Federation to be permitted gubernatorial elections in December 1995. The incumbent, Yevgenii Savchenko, a supporter of the federal Government, was duly elected, despite the continued strength of the Communists. Local elections were held in the Oblast on 17 March 1996.

Economy

In 1995 Belgorod Oblast's gross regional product amounted to 12,585,900m. roubles, or 8,598,700 roubles per head. The main industrial centres in the territory are situated at Belgorod, Shebekino, Alekseyevka and Valuiki.

Belgorod Oblast's principal crops are grain, sugar-beets, sunflower seeds and essential-oil plants. Horticulture and animal husbandry are also important. In 1995 some 21.6% of the region's working population were engaged in the agricultural sector, which generated a total of 3,327,600m. roubles. There are substantial reserves of bauxite, iron ore and apatites. The Oblast's main industries are ore mining (iron ores), mechanical engineering, metal working, chemicals, the manufacture of building materials and food processing. There were plans to develop the mining and metal industries in the region between 1996 and 2000. Industry employed 24.4% of the work-force in 1995, while total industrial production was worth 11,228,000m. roubles.

The economically active population in Belgorod Oblast numbered 648,500 in that year, of whom 7,000 were registered unemployed. The average monthly salary was 340,000 roubles and there was a budgetary deficit of 3,700m. Foreign investment in the Oblast in 1995 totalled just US $53,000. In 1997 there were 3,600 small businesses (double the figure for 1995), which employed 40,000 people.

Directory

Head of the Regional Administration (Governor): YEVGENII STEPANOVICH SAVCHENKO; Belgorodskaya obl., 308005 Belgorod, pl. Revolyutsii 4; tel. (072) 22-42-47; fax (072) 22-33-43.

Chairman of the Regional Duma: ANATOLII ZELIKOV; tel. (072) 22-36-76; fax (072) 22-33-43.

Permanent Representative of the President of the Russian Federation: SERGEI N. KISIN; tel. (072) 22-33-02.

Head of Belgorod City Administration: GEORGII GEORGIYEVICH GOLIKOV; Belgorodskaya obl., 308800 Belgorod, ul. Lenina 38; tel. (072) 27-72-06.

Bryansk

Bryansk Oblast is situated in the central part of the Central Russian Highlands and is in the Central Economic Area. It has international borders on its west (Belarus) and south (Ukraine), with Kursk and Orel Oblasts lying to the east, Kaluga to the north-east and Smolensk to the north-west. Bryansk's main river is the Desna, a tributary of the Dnepr (Dnieper), and just under one-third of its area is forested. The Oblast occupies 34,900 sq km (13,480 sq miles) of territory and measures 245 km (152 miles) from south to north and 270 km from west to east. It is divided into 27 administrative districts and 16 cities. At 1 January 1996 the total number of inhabitants in the region was estimated at 1,480,000 (of whom some 68.4% inhabited urban areas) and the population density was, therefore, 42.4 per sq km. Bryansk, with an estimated population of 463,000 at 1 January 1996, is the Oblast's administrative centre. Other major cities are Klintsy (70,100), Novozybkov (43,300) and Dyatkovo (34,800).

History

The ancient Russian city of Bryansk was part of the independent principality of Novgorod-Serversk until 1356. It was an early Orthodox Christian bishopric. The Muscovite state acquired the city from Lithuania in the 16th century. After the German invasion during the Second World War had been repelled, Bryansk Oblast was founded on 5 July 1944.

In the 1990s the region was considered part of the Communist-dominated 'red belt'. Bryansk was one of eight federal territories permitted gubernatorial elections in December 1992. The incumbent, a supporter of the federal President, Boris Yeltsin, was defeated by the Communist-backed candidate, Yurii Lodkin. During the constitutional crisis of 1993 the regional authorities were thus united in condemning President Yeltsin's Decree 1,400, which dissolved the all-Russian parliament. Lodkin was then dismissed and the soviet disbanded, being replaced by a Regional Duma. The Communists secured about 35% of the votes cast in the region for the Federation Assembly in December 1995, indicating their continued popular support, and their candidate in the gubernatorial election of December 1996, Lodkin, was returned to office. In the local elections held in June 1997 Communist candidates were dominant, including Nikolai Sarviro, who was elected Mayor of Bryansk.

Economy

Bryansk Oblast is one of the Russian Federation's major industrial regions. The territory's gross regional product was 7,801,500m. roubles in 1995, equivalent to 5,272,300 roubles per head. Its main industrial centres are at Bryansk and Klintsy. There are 1,055 km (656 miles) of railway track on its territory, and 11,265 km of roads, of which 9,431 km are paved.

The Oblast's agriculture, which employed 21.6% of its work-force in 1995, consists mainly of grain and vegetable production and animal husbandry. Around one-half of its area is used for agricultural purposes. Total production in the sector in 1995 was worth 3,327,600m. roubles. The Oblast's main industries are mechanical engineering, metal working, the manufacture of building materials, light manufacturing, food processing and timber working. Industry employed 28.3% of the workforce in 1995 and generated 4,056,000m. roubles.

At 1 January 1997 a total of 37,900, or 5.9% of the Oblast's work-force, were registered unemployed. In 1995 the average monthly wage was 340,000 roubles. There was a regional government budgetary deficit of 50,300m. roubles. Although in the late 1990s the economy of the Oblast was suffering severe difficulties, initially with a crisis in wage arrears, foreign investment remained relatively high (in 1995 it had amounted to US $3.09m.). At 1 January 1996 there were 5,100 small businesses operating in the territory.

Directory

Head of the Regional Administration (Governor): YURII YEVGENIYEVICH LODKIN; Bryanskaya obl., 241002 Bryansk, pr. Lenina 33; tel. (0832) 46-26-11; fax (0832) 41-31-10; e-mail gwo@admin.bryansk.ru; internet http://www.admin.bryansk.ru.

Chairman of the Regional Duma: STEPAN NIKOLAYEVICH PONASOV; tel. (0832) 46-36-91.

Permanent Representative of the President of the Russian Federation: VLADIMIR ILYCH GAIDUKOV; tel. (0832) 74-38-60.

Head of Bryansk City Administration: NIKOLAI KONSTANTINOVICH SARVIRO; Bryanskaya obl., 241002 Bryansk, pr. Lenina 35; tel. (0832) 74-30-13; fax (0832) 74-47-30.

Chelyabinsk

Chelyabinsk Oblast is situated in the Southern Urals, in the Transural (Asian Russia). It forms part of the Urals Economic Area. Orenburg Oblast lies to the south, the Republic of Bashkortostan to the west, Sverdlovsk Oblast to the north and Kurgan Oblast to the east. There is an international border with Kazakhstan in the south-west. Much of the region lies on the eastern slopes of the southern Ural Mountains. The major rivers in the Oblast are the Ural and the Miass. It has over 1,000 lakes, the largest of which are the Uvildy and the Turgoyak. The Oblast covers an area of 87,900 sq km (34,940 sq miles) and is divided into 24 administrative districts and 30 cities. With an estimated population of 3,689,000 at 1 January 1996 (of whom 81.3% inhabited urban areas), the population density in the region was 42.0 per sq km. The Oblast's administrative centre is at Chelyabinsk, which had an estimated population of 1,083,400 at that time. Other major cities are Magnitogorsk (425,300), Zlatoust (201,300), Miass (167,200), Troitsk (85,600) and Kopeisk (73,300).

History

Chelyabinsk city was established as a Russian frontier post in 1736, but was deep within Russian territory by the 19th century. The Oblast was created on 17 January 1934. The region was heavily industrialized during the Soviet period and was dominated by Communist cadres well into the 1990s. In December 1992, at elections for the head of the regional administration, the incumbent governor, a supporter of Boris Yeltsin, the Russian President, was defeated. President Yeltsin re-established his authority in late 1993 and required the election of a Duma during 1994. Both in this body and in the local results of the general election of 1995 pro-Yeltsin and reformist forces also gained significant levels of support. In the gubernatorial election of late 1996, however, Petr Sumin was returned to power. Sumin, a Communist, had been removed as head of the regional administration following the attempted Soviet coup of 1991. Even a Communist administration (albeit one that was pragmatic in its acceptance of some economic reform) could not prevent an accumulation in wage arrears, however, and there were strikes by coal-miners in mid-1998. The federal authorities nevertheless considered the region able to sustain a lower central subsidy for 1999.

Economy

Chelyabinsk Oblast is one of the most industrialized territories of the Russian Federation, with around two-fifths of its economically active population working in industry in 1997. A major cost, however, is that the Oblast is one of the most polluted in the Federation, with high levels of radioactivity in many areas. In 1995 its gross regional product amounted to 33,126,800m. roubles, equivalent to 8,967,300 roubles per head. The region's major industrial centres are at Chelyabinsk, Magnitogorsk, Miass, Zlatoust, Kopeisk, Korkino and Troitsk. The Oblast is a major junction of the Trans-Siberian Railway. There are 2,200 km (1,370 miles) of railway track in the Oblast and 20,000 km of paved roads.

The Oblast's agriculture, which employed 9.9% of the working population in 1995, consists mainly of animal husbandry, horticulture and the production of grain and vegetables. Total agricultural output in 1995 was worth 3,377,200m. roubles. Its main industries are ferrous and non-ferrous metallurgy, ore mining, mechanical engineering, metal working, fuel and energy production and the manufacture of building materials. In the north-west, at Snezhinsk and Ozersk, there is a major centre for the nuclear industry, while in the west are centres for weapons manufacturing and space technology. In 1995 the industrial sector generated 37,384,000m. roubles.

The economically active population numbered 1,546,200 in 1995; some 32,300 of these were registered unemployed. Those in employment earned an average wage of 415,000 roubles per month. The 1995 budget showed a deficit of 28,900m. roubles. In order to create favourable conditions for economic growth in the region, the administration created two funds: one for the support of strategic sectors of the economy; the other concerned with development. Attempts to attract foreign investment in the Oblast in the mid-1990s were largely successful: foreign capital amounted to US $17.22m. in 1995 and increased thereafter. The Oblast contained the highest number of joint enterprises in the Urals Economic Area. At 1 January 1996 there were 13,900 small businesses registered on its territory.

Directory

Governor: PETR IVANOVICH SUMIN; Chelyabinskaya obl., 454089 Chelyabinsk, ul. Tsvillinga 28; tel. (3512) 33-92-41; fax (3512) 33-12-83.
Chairman of the Regional Government: VLADIMIR PETROVICH UTKIN.
Chairman of the Regional Duma: VIKTOR FEDROVICH DAVIDOV.

Permanent Representative of the President of the Russian Federation: NIKOLAI RODIONOVICH SUDENKOV; Chelyabinskaya obl., 454113 Chelyabinsk, pl. Revolyutsii 2; tel. (3512) 33-38-05; fax (3512) 33-38-55.

Head of the Regional Representation in Moscow: YEVGENII ANATOLIYEVICH MELCHAKOV; tel. (095) 203-62-47.

Head of Chelyabinsk City Administration (Mayor): VYACHESLAV MIKHAILOVICH TARASOV; Chelyabinskaya obl., 454113 Chelyabinsk, pl. Revolyutsii 2; tel. (3512) 33-38-05; fax (3512) 33-38-55.

Chita

Chita Oblast is situated in Transbaikal. It forms part of the Eastern Siberian Economic Area. The Transbaikal region of Buryatiya lies to the west, Irkutsk Oblast in the north, Sakha and Amur to the east. To the south Chita has international borders with the People's Republic of China and Mongolia. The Aga-Buryat Autonomous Okrug lies within the Oblast, in the south. The western part of the region is situated in the Yablonovii Khrebet mountain range. Chita Oblast's major rivers are those in the Selenga, the Lena and the Amur basins. More than one-half of the Oblast's territory is forested. Its entire territory covers an area of 431,500 sq km (166,600 sq miles) and is divided into 31 districts and 10 cities. The total population of the Oblast, including that of the autonomous okrug, was estimated at 1,295,000 at 1 January 1996 and its population density was, therefore, 3.0 per sq km (almost three times lower than the national average). In the same year, some 62.9% of the region's inhabitants were found to live in urban areas. The Oblast's administrative centre is at Chita, which had an estimated population of 321,300 at that time. The region's other major cities are Krasnokamensk (57,000), Borzya (32,200), Petrovsk-Zabaikalskii (24,000) and Balei (renowned as the birthplace of Temujin—Chinghiz or Genghis Khan—20,100).

History

The city of Chita was established by the Cossacks in 1653, at the confluence of the Chita and Ingoda rivers. It was named Ingodinskoye Zirnove for a time. Chita was pronounced the capital of the independent, pro-Bolshevik Far Eastern Republic upon its establishment in April 1920. It united the regions of Irkutsk, Transbaikal, Amur and the Pacific coast (Maritime Krai, Khabarovsk Krai, Magadan and

Kamchatka), but merged with Soviet Russia in November 1922. Chita Oblast was founded on 26 September 1937.

Along with the other oblasts, Chita was acknowledged as a Russian federal unit by participation in the Federation Treaty of March 1992. A new Regional Duma was elected in 1994. The Communists and the nationalist Liberal Democrats were the most popular parties in the mid- and late 1990s. The region experienced problems with wage arrears, which provoked strikes by coal-miners in December 1998.

Economy

Chita Oblast's gross regional product amounted to 10,0371,100m. roubles in 1995, equivalent to 7,738,700 roubles per head. The region's main industrial centres are at Chita, Nerchinsk, Darasun, Olovyannaya and Tarbagatai. There are some 2,900 km (1,800 miles) of railway track in the territory, including sections of the Trans-Siberian and the Far Eastern (Baikal–Amur) Railways. There are also 15,300 km of roads, of which 11,400 km are paved, and 1,000 km of navigable waterways. The Chita–Khabarovsk highway was under construction in the late 1990s. There is an international airport at Chita.

Chita Oblast's agriculture, which employed some 16.7% of its working population in 1995, consists mainly of animal husbandry (livestock- and reindeer-breeding) and fur-animal hunting. In 1995 total agricultural output amounted to a value of 1,964,600m. roubles. The region's major industries are ferrous metallurgy, mechanical engineering, fuel extraction, processing of forestry and agricultural products and ore mining. Industry employed some 19.5% of the work-force in 1995; total industrial production in that year was worth 3,259,000m. roubles. Coal mining in the Oblast was centred around the Vostochnaya mine; gold and tin mining were based at Sherlovaya Govra; and lead- and zinc-ore mines are situated at Hapcheranga, 200 km south-east of Yakutsk. In 1992 it was revealed that thorium and uranium had been mined until the mid-1970s at locations just outside Balei. The resulting high levels of radiation had serious consequences among the town's population, with abnormally high incidences of miscarriages and congenital defects in children. The regional Government lacked sufficient funds to relocate Balei's inhabitants and reduce radiation in the area. In 1997, however, the Australian mining company, Balgold, announced that it planned to seal the abandoned mines and exploit the nearby gold deposits. In 1996 the Oblast's exports, largely comprising ferrous metals and fertilizers, amounted to US $104.3m.

The territory had an economically active population in 1995 of 483,300, including those in the autonomous okrug. Some 16,900 were registered unemployed at that time; the average monthly wage was 421,000 roubles (although, in the first quarter of 1997, it was reported that some 74% of the Oblast's economically active population earned less than the subsistence level, compared to 21% in Russia as a whole). In 1995 the budget (including for the autonomous okrug) showed a surplus of 6,500m. roubles. There was US $124,000-worth of foreign investment in the Oblast in that year, but levels increased later in the decade. At 1 January 1996 a total of 3,800 small businesses were in operation in Chita.

Directory

Head of the Regional Administration (Governor): RAVIL FARITOVICH GENIATULIN; Chitinskaya obl., 672021 Chita, ul. Chaikovskogo 8; tel. (30222) 3-34-93; fax (30222) 6-33-19.

Chairman of the Regional Duma: VITALII YEVGENIYEVICH VISHNYAKOV.
Permanent Representative of the President of the Russian Federation: VLADIMIR ILYCH MELNIKOV; tel. (30222) 3-34-92.
Head of Chita City Administration (Mayor): ALEKSANDR FEDOROVICH SEDIN; Chitinskaya obl., 672000 Chita, ul. Butina 39; tel. (30222) 3-21-01.

Irkutsk

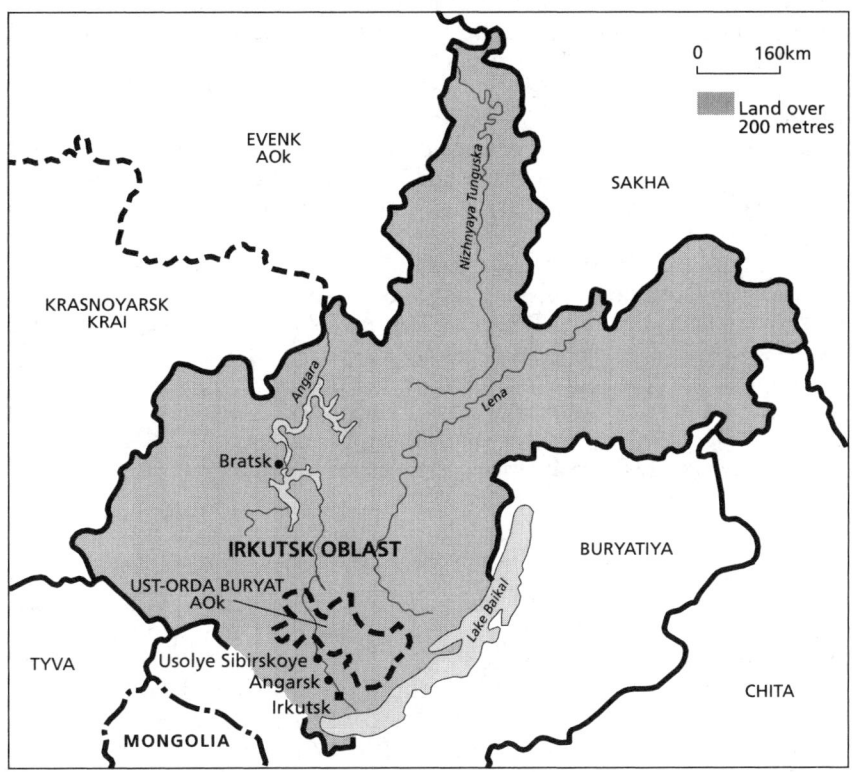

Irkutsk Oblast is situated in eastern Siberia in the south-east of the Central Siberian Plateau. Irkutsk Oblast forms part of the Eastern Siberian Economic Area. The Republic of Sakha lies to the north-east, Krasnoyarsk Krai (including the Evenk AOk) to the north-west and Tyva to the south-west. Most of the long south-eastern borders are with the Transbaikal territories of Buryatiya and, in the east, Chita. Irkutsk Oblast includes the Autonomous Okrug of the Ust-Orda Buryats. The one lake, Baikal, is the deepest in the world, possessing over 80% of Russia's, and 20% of the world's, freshwater resources. The Oblast's main rivers are the Angara (the only river to drain Lake Baikal), the Nizhnyaya Tunguska, the Lena, the Vitim and the Kirenga. More than four-fifths of the region's territory is covered with forest (mainly coniferous). The total area of the Oblast, including that of the autonomous okrug, is 767,900 sq km (296,490 sq miles) and stretches 1,400 km (850 miles) from south to north and 1,200 km west to east. It is divided into 33 administrative districts and 22 cities. The Oblast's estimated population was 2,790,000 in January 1997. The overall population density in the region was 3.6 per sq km. Its administrative centre is at Irkutsk, which had an estimated population of 591,000 in 1998. Other major cities in the region include Bratsk (281,000), Angarsk (272,000) and Usolye-Sibirskoye (105,000).

TERRITORIAL SURVEYS

History

The city of Irkutsk was founded as an ostrog (military transit camp) in 1661, at the confluence of the Irkut and Angara rivers 66 km to the west of Baikal. Irkutsk became one of the largest economic centres of eastern Siberia. After the collapse of the Russian Empire, the region was part of the independent, pro-Bolshevik Far Eastern Republic (based in Chita), which was established in April 1920 and merged with Soviet Russia in November 1922. On 26 September 1937 an Irkutsk Oblast was formed.

In late 1993, following the federal presidency's forcible dissolution of parliament, the executive branch of government secured the dissolution of the Regional Soviet, and in 1994 a Legislative Assembly was elected in its place. In January 1996 Yurii Nozhikov, the Governor of the region, signed a law extending the term of the Assembly for an additional two years. According to the law, all branches of power were to be elected simultaneously no later than 27 March 1998. In April 1996 it was announced that a Polish consulate was to open in the region (owing to the presence of a community of ethnic Poles, descendants of Second World War deportees) and the following month a power-sharing agreement was signed by the regional and federal authorities. On 27 July 1997 the government-nominated candidate, Boris Govorin, was elected Governor, receiving 50.3% of the votes cast, in an election result that was interpreted as an endorsement of the federal Government's reform programmes.

Economy

Irkutsk Oblast is one of the most economically developed regions in Russia, largely owing to its significant fuel, energy and water resources, minerals and timber. In 1995 its gross regional product totalled 34,301,200m. roubles, or 12,251,300 roubles per head. The region's main industrial centres are at Irkutsk, Bratsk, Ust-Ilimsk, Angarsk and Usoliye Sibirskoye. The Oblast, which is traversed by the Trans-Siberian and the Far Eastern (Baikal–Amur) Railways, contains 2,700 km of railway track. There are more than 10,000 km of roads in the region, which carry some 30m. metric tons of freight and 350m. passengers annually. It has two international airports, at Irkutsk and Bratsk, from which there are direct and connecting flights to Japan, the People's Republic of China, the Republic of Korea (South Korea), Mongolia and some western European destinations. In the late 1990s approximately one-10th of the region's freight was transported by river—there are two major river-ports on the Lena river at Kirensk and Osetrovo (Ust-Kut). These are used to transport freight to the Republic of Sakha and the northern seaport of Tiksi.

The Oblast's agriculture, which employed just 9.1% of its work-force in 1995, consists mainly of grain production, animal husbandry (fur-animal, reindeer- and livestock-breeding), hunting and fishing. Total agricultural production in the territory generated 4,149,800m. roubles in 1995. The region contains the huge Kovyikinskoye oilfield, which in the late 1990s was awaiting an international consortium with the resources to construct an export pipeline across the People's Republic of China. The Oblast's development as a centre for heavy industry originated in the city of Irkutsk's position as a major junction on the Trans-Siberian Railway. In the late 1990s more than 45% of its fixed assets were concentrated in its industrial sector and more than one-third of its economically active population were engaged in industrial production. Its main industries were mining (coal, iron ore, gold, muscovite or mica, gypsum, talc and salt), mechanical engineering, metal working, chemicals and petrochemicals, petroleum refining, non-ferrous metallurgy, fuel extraction, electricity generation, the manufacture of building materials and the processing of forestry products. The total value of manufactured goods in the Oblast in 1996 was 33,667,000m. roubles, of which extraction contributed 12% and processing 88% (including 31% by the fuel industry, 15% by electricity generation and the non-ferrous metallurgy industry and 13% by the timber and timber-processing industries).

The economically active population in Irkutsk Oblast totalled 1,160,000 in 1995. Some 40,800 in the entire territory were unemployed at this time. For those in employment, the average wage amounted to 580,000 roubles per month. In 1995 there was a budgetary deficit of 29,000m. roubles. Foreign investment in the territory was worth US $19.79m. At 1 January 1996 there was a total of 13,700 small businesses in operation.

Directory

Governor: BORIS ALEKSANDROVICH GOVORIN; Irkutskaya obl., 664027 Irkutsk, ul. Lenina 1A; tel. (3952) 27-67-60; fax (3952) 24-13-79.

Chairman of the Legislative Assembly: IVAN ZIGMUNDOVICH ZELENT; tel. (3952) 24-15-83; fax (3952) 27-44-27.

Permanent Representative of the President of the Russian Federation: ALEKSANDR ADAMOVICH SUVOROV; tel. (3952) 34-24-19.

Head of the Regional Representation in Moscow: NIKOLAI V. EROSHCHENKO; tel. (095) 203-60-41.

Head of Irkutsk City Administration: VLADIMIR VIKTOROVICH YAKUBOVSKII; tel. (3952) 27-56-90; fax (3952) 33-65-22.

Ivanovo

Ivanovo Oblast is situated in the central part of the Eastern European Plain. It forms part of the Central Economic Area. It is surrounded by the Oblasts of Kostroma (to the north), Nizhnii Novgorod (east), Vladimir (south) and Yaroslavl (north-west). Its main river is the Volga and one-half of its territory is forested. The Oblast covers a total area of 21,500 sq km (9,230 sq miles), which includes 21 administrative districts and 17 cities. Its estimated population at 1 January 1996 was 1,266,000, of whom as many as 82.3% inhabited urban areas; its population density was 57.9 per sq km. Its administrative centre, Ivanovo, had an estimated population of 485,000 in 1996.

History

The city of Ivanovo was founded in 1871 and was known as Ivanovo-Voznesensk until 1932. It was an important centre of anti-government activity during the strikes of 1883 and 1885 and in the 1905 Revolution. Ivanovo Oblast was founded on 20 July 1918.

At the end of the 20th century the region was more conservative than at the beginning, although there was a great deal of unease at federal economic policy. Thus, in the general election of 1995, both the Communists and the supporters of Vladimir Zhirinovskii, a maverick nationalist, received the same level of support. This was also evidenced in the region's Legislative Assembly (elected in 1994). The stabilization of Russia's political and economic situation was reflected, however, in the results of the gubernatorial and legislative elections, held in the Oblast on 1 December 1996, in which moderates won a majority.

Economy

In 1995 Ivanovo Oblast's gross regional product totalled 6,442,700m. roubles, equivalent to 5,070,600 roubles per head. The region's main industrial centres are at Ivanovo (a major producer of textiles), Kineshma, Shuya, Vichuga, Furmanov,

Teikovo and Rodniki. There are well-developed rail, road and river transport networks in the region and the largest international airport in central Russia.

Ivanovo Oblast was the historic centre of Russia's cotton-milling industry and was known as the 'Russian Manchester' at the beginning of the 20th century. Flax production was still an important agricultural activity in the region in the 1990s, as were grain and vegetable production and animal husbandry. Owing to the Oblast's high degree of urbanization, agriculture employed just 9.9% of its workforce in 1995, while total agricultural production in that year amounted to a value of 1,463,800m. roubles. The region's main industries were light manufacturing (especially textiles), mechanical engineering, chemicals, food processing, woodworking and handicrafts (especially lacquerware). Some 37.0% of its working population were engaged in the sector, which generated 5,333,000m. roubles in 1995.

The economically active population in that year amounted to 517,400, of whom 76,000 were registered unemployed. The average wage was 306,000 roubles per month. The 1995 budget showed a deficit of 24,700m. roubles. Although foreign investment totalled only US $761,000 in 1995, in 1997 Alfabank and the federal Chamber of Commerce and Industry initiated a campaign to attract foreign capital to the Oblast, in conjunction with the adoption of federal and regional laws to protect the interests of overseas investors. By 1998 joint ventures had already been established with companies from Germany, Japan, the Republic of Korea (South Korea) and the United Kingdom, while businesses within the region had trading relations with more than 60 countries. At 1 January 1996 there was a total of 5,900 small businesses registered in the region.

Directory

Head of the Regional Administration (Governor): VLADISLAV NIKOLAYEVICH TIKHOMIROV; Ivanovskaya obl., 153002 Ivanovo, ul. Baturina 5; tel. (0932) 41-77-05; fax (0932) 37-24-85.

Chairman of the Legislative Assembly: VALERII GRIGORIYEVICH NIKOLOGORSKII; Ivanovskaya obl., Ivanovo, ul. Pushkina 9; tel. (0932) 32-82-80.

Permanent Representative of the President of the Russian Federation: VLADIMIR ILYCH TOLMACHEV; Ivanovskaya obl., Ivanovo, ul. Pushkina 9; tel. (0932) 32-70-05; fax (0932) 32-92-25.

Head of Ivanovo City Administration: VALERII VASILIYEVICH TROYEGLAZOV; Ivanovskaya obl., 153000 Ivanovo, pl. Revolyutsii 6; tel. (0932) 32-70-20; fax (0932) 41-25-12.

Kaliningrad

Kaliningrad Oblast is the westernmost part of the Russian Federation, being an enclave separated from the rest of the country by Lithuania (which borders it to the north and east) and Belarus. Poland lies to the south. It is sometimes included in the North-Western Economic Area. The city of Kaliningrad (formerly Königsberg) is sited at the mouth of the River Pregolya (Pregel), where it flows into the Vistula Lagoon, an inlet of the Baltic Sea. The other main river is the Neman (Memel). The Oblast occupies 15,100 sq km (5,830 sq miles), of which only 13,300 sq km are dry land, the rest of its territory comprising the freshwater Kurshskaya Lagoon, in the north-west, and the Vistula Lagoon. The coastline is 140 km (87 miles) long. The Oblast is divided into 13 administrative districts and 22 cities. It had an estimated population of 936,000 at 1 January 1997 (of whom some 78.0% inhabited urban areas) and its population density was, therefore, 62.0 per sq km. Its administrative centre is at Kaliningrad, which had an estimated population of 422,100 at 1 January 1996. Other major cities in the Oblast are Sovetsk (formerly Tilsit—43,100), Chernyakhovsk (formerly Insterburg—42,500), Baltiisk (formerly Pillau—30,500) and Gusev (28,200).

History

The city of Kaliningrad was founded in 1255, as Königsberg, during German expansion eastwards. The chief city of East Prussia, it was the original royal capital of the Hohenzollerns (from 1871 the German Emperors). After the Second World War it was annexed by the USSR and received its current name (1945). Most of the German population was deported. On 7 April 1946 the region became an administrative-political entity within the Russian Federation.

In mid-1993 Kaliningrad Oblast requested the status of a republic, a petition refused by the federal authorities. On 15 October the Regional Soviet was disbanded by the head of the regional administration for failing to support the state presidency's struggle against the federal parliament. A new regional legislature, the Duma, was later formed. On 12 January 1996 Yurii Matochkin was one of the very first oblast governors to sign a power-sharing agreement with the federal Government. Elections to the governorship were held in October, and were won by Leonid Gorbenko, an independent candidate.

Despite ambitions to transform the enclave into a progressive special economic zone, Kaliningrad was bedevilled by corruption and excessive and arbitrary taxation. In March 1998 there were reports of a power struggle in the main city, in the course of which all powers were transferred from the mayor to the head of the city council. The acting mayor, Yurii Savenko, won the mayoral election of October in the second round of voting, with 60% of the votes cast. Another power struggle, this one between the regional executive and legislature, was declared settled in November, after almost one year, although there was scepticism as to whether this would be the case. Meanwhile, in July, as the Russian Government planned to curtail the Oblast's special economic benefits, a proposal that the region be awarded the status of autonomous Russian Baltic republic was submitted to the Federation Council. On 8 September it was reported that the regional authorities had declared a state of emergency, owing to the deterioration in the Oblast's social and economic conditions (that winter, of 1998/99, the population was reliant on food aid from their Baltic neighbours).

Economy

Kaliningrad Oblast is noted for containing more than 90% of the world's reserves of amber. Within Russia it is also noted for its reputedly flourishing parallel ('black') market, with federal officials suggesting in January 1999 that the region had become a major transhipment point for illegal drugs. In 1995 its gross regional product totalled 5,258,200m. roubles, or 5,658,200 roubles per head. Its main industrial centres are at Kaliningrad, Gusev, Sovetsk and Chernyakhovsk. There are rail services to Lithuania and Poland and the Oblast's road network is one of the most highly developed in the Federation, consisting of 4,581 km of paved roads. Its main ports are at Kaliningrad and Baltiisk.

Kaliningrad Oblast's agricultural sector, which employed some 11.6% of its work-force in 1995, consists mainly of animal husbandry, vegetable growing and fishing. Total agricultural output in 1995 was worth 1,463,800m. roubles. The Oblast has substantial reserves of petroleum (around 275m. metric tons), more than 2,500m. cu m in peat deposits and 50m. metric tons of coal. The industrial sector employed 21.1% of its working population and generated 3,278,000m. roubles in 1995. The region's main industries are mechanical engineering, electro-technical industry, the processing of agricultural and forestry products, natural-gas production, light manufacturing and the production and processing of amber. In 1996 some 757,000 tons of petroleum were extracted, but were refined outside the Oblast.

The economically active population, of whom 25,000 were registered unemployed, numbered 392,000 in 1995. The average monthly wage at this time was 379,000 roubles. In the mid-1990s there was some foreign investment (US $8.33m. in 1995) and hopes continued that the region would be favoured as a legitimate entry point to the Russian market proper. Much of the foreign investment was from Germany, which alarmed nationalist Russians that the ethnic Germans expelled 50 years previously might wish to return. At 1 January 1996 there was a total of 4,700 small businesses registered in the region.

Directory

Head of the Regional Administration (Governor): LEONID PETROVICH GORBENKO; Kaliningradskaya obl., 236007 Kaliningrad, ul. Dmitriya Donskogo 1; tel. (0112) 46-46-43; fax (0112) 46-38-62.

Chairman of the Regional Duma: VALERII NIKOLAYEVICH USTYUGOV; tel. (0112) 46-46-32; fax (0112) 46-35-54.

Permanent Representative of the President of the Russian Federation: ALEKSANDR VLADIMIROVICH ORLOV; tel. (0112) 46-46-32.

Head of Kaliningrad City Administration (Mayor): YURII SAVENKO; Kaliningradskaya obl., 236040 Kaliningrad, ul. Pobedy 1; tel. (0112) 21-48-98; fax (0112) 21-16-77.

Kaluga

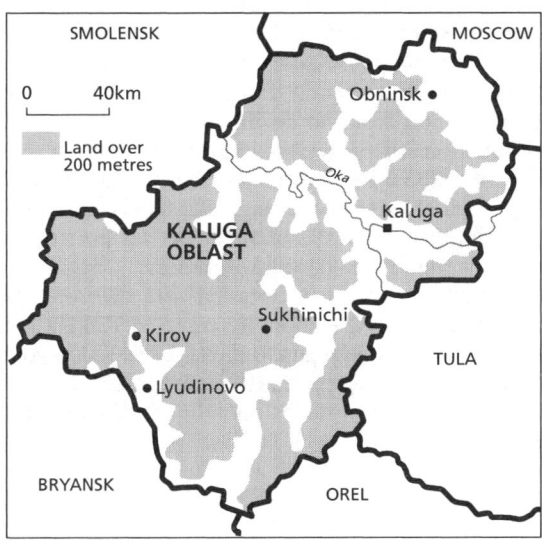

Kaluga Oblast is situated in the central part of the Eastern European Plain, its administrative centre, Kaluga, being 188 km (177 miles) south-west of Moscow. It forms part of the Central Economic Area. Tula and Orel Oblasts lie to the south-east, Bryansk Oblast to the south-west and Smolensk Oblast to the north-west. Kaluga's main river is the Oka and some two-fifths of its territory is forested. It occupies 29,900 sq km (11,540 sq miles) and is divided into 23 administrative districts and 17 cities. The Oblast had a population of 1,093,200 in 1997 (74% of whom inhabited urban areas) and a population density, therefore, of 36.6 per sq km. Its administrative centre is at Kaluga, a river-port on the Oka river, which had an estimated population of 367,000 in 1997. Other major cities in the Oblast include Obninsk (110,000), Lyudinovo (45,000) and Kirov (41,000).

History

The city of Kaluga, first mentioned in the letters of a Lithuanian prince, Olgerd, in 1371, was founded as a Muscovite outpost. The region was the scene of an army mutiny in 1905 and was seized by Bolshevik troops at the end of 1917. Kaluga Oblast was founded on 5 July 1944.

Kaluga remained a loyally Communist region into the 1990s, with managers of industrial and agricultural bodies dominating the new representative body, the Legislative Assembly, which was elected in March 1994. The Communist Party won over one-quarter of the region's votes in the 1995 elections to the State Duma of the Federation. Viktor Sudarenkov was elected Governor in 1996 with twice as many votes as his nearest rival. Further elections to the Legislative Assembly took place in 1996.

Economy

In 1995 gross regional product in Kaluga Oblast totalled 8,124,400m. roubles, equivalent to 7,413,400 roubles per head. Apart from Kaluga, the region's main industrial centres are at Lyudinovo, Kirov, Maloyaroslavets, Sukhinichi and Borovsk. There are 1,237 km (769 miles) of railway track in the Oblast and 6,177 km of roads.

Only some areas of the Oblast contain fertile black earth (*chernozem*). Agriculture employed just 11.6% of the work-force in 1995 and consists mainly of animal husbandry and production of vegetables, grain and flax. Agricultural output amounted to a value of 2,206,100m. roubles in 1995. The Oblast's main industries are mechanical engineering, wood-working, chemicals and light manufacturing. Industry as a whole employed 29.4% of the working population in 1995, while the industrial sector generated 4,360,000m. roubles.

The economically active population totalled 497,100, of whom 14,000 were registered unemployed. The average monthly wage in Kaluga Oblast in 1995 was 435,000 roubles. There was a budgetary deficit of 10,000m. roubles in that year. Total foreign investment in the region in 1995 amounted to US $666,000. In 1997 there were around 7,000 small businesses operating in the region, with a combined work-force of 70,000.

Directory

Head of the Regional Administration (Governor): VALERII VASILIYEVICH SUDARENKOV; Kaluzhskaya obl., 248661 Kaluga, pl. Staryi torg 2; tel. (0842) 56-23-57; fax (0842) 53-13-09; e-mail postmaster@admobl.kaluga.su.

Chairman of the Legislative Assembly: VIKTOR MIKHAILOVICH KOSLESNIKOV; tel. (0842) 56-21-89; fax (08422) 4-63-81.

Permanent Representative of the President of the Russian Federation: ANATOLII IVANOVICH MINAKOV; tel. (0842) 57-46-37; fax (08422) 4-63-88.

Head of Kaluga City Administration: VALERII GRIGORIYEVICH BELOBROVSKII; Kaluzhskaya obl., 248630 Kaluga, ul. Lenina 93; tel. (0842) 56-26-46; fax (08422) 4-41-78.

Kamchatka

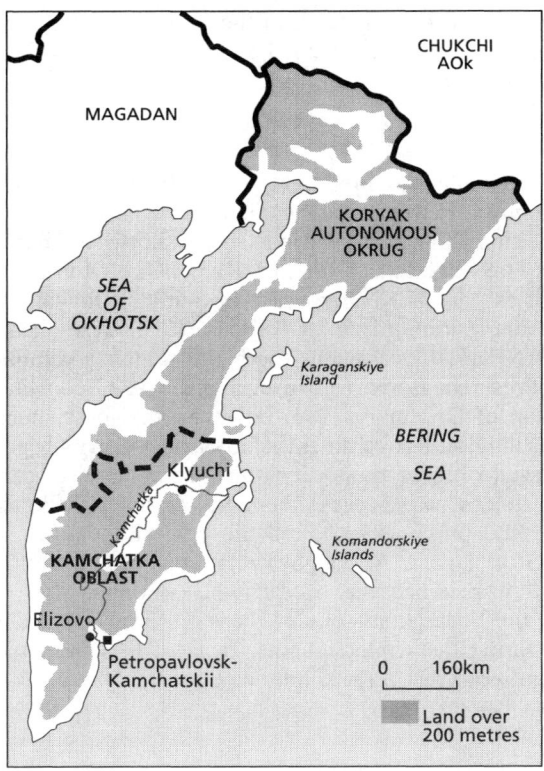

Kamchatka Oblast occupies the Kamchatka Peninsula in the easternmost part of Russia and is, therefore, part of the Far Eastern Economic Area. The Peninsula, some 1,600 km (1,000 miles) in length and 130 km (80 miles) in width, separates the Sea of Okhotsk, in the west, from the Bering Sea, in the east. The Oblast also includes the Karaginskiye and Komandorskiye Islands and the southernmost part of the Chukhotka Peninsula. In the latter area there there are land borders with other Russian federal territories, the Chukchi AOk to the north and Magadan Oblast to the west. This part of the Oblast, together with the northern section of the Kamchatka Peninsula, comprises the Koryak Autonomous Okrug. The region is dominated by the Sredinnii Khrebet mountain range, which is bounded to the west by a broad, poorly drained coastal plain, and to the east by the Kamchatka river valley. The territory's other main river is the Avacha. Two-thirds of its area is mountainous (including the highest point in the Russian Far East, Mt Klyuchevskaya, at 4,685 m—15,961 feet) and it contains many hot springs. Kamchatka Oblast covers an area of 472,300 sq km (182,350 sq miles), including the autonomous okrug, and is divided into 11 administrative districts and four cities. There is a high annual rate of precipitation in the region, sometimes as much as 2,000 mm, and temperatures vary considerably according to region. January temperatures are between –9°C and –22°C, while those for July are between 11°C and 34°C. At 1 January 1996 the estimated total population in the region was 411,000 and the population density, therefore, was just 0.9 per sq km. An estimated 80.8% of the region's population inhabited urban areas. The Oblast's administrative centre is at Petropavlovsk-Kamchatskii, in the south-east, which was inhabited by around 204,800 people. The Oblast's other cities are Elizovo (40,600), Vilyuchinsk (35,800) and Klyuchi (10,700).

History

The Kamchatka Peninsula was first sighted in 1697 and was annexed by Russia during the 18th century. Petropavlovsk came under Russian control in 1743. After the Russian Revolution Kamchatka was part of the short-lived Far Eastern Republic (which had its capital at Chita). A distinct Kamchatka Oblast was formed on 20 October 1923, but as part of Khabarovsk Krai until 23 January 1956.

Following the dissolution of the USSR in 1991, Kamchatka tended to be supportive of the federal Government (both the regional administration and the soviet supported President Boris Yeltsin during the 1993 constitutional crisis). In the general election of December 1995, however, the most successful party was the liberal, and usually anti-government, Yabloko bloc, which gained 20% of the votes in the Oblast (a higher proportion than the reformists gained even in the great cities). This success was because the local candidate, Mikhail Zadornov, was a popular figure, who previously chaired the powerful budget committee in the previous federal State Duma. Although a relatively wealthy region, however, by the late 1990s public patience was tried by the continued lack of economic and social stability in the Federation—one of the main issues for Kamchatka was the shortage of fuel during the winter months. In late 1998 the situation became so serious that it required direct federal intervention.

Economy

The waters around Kamchatka Oblast (the Sea of Okhotsk, the Bering Sea and the Pacific Ocean) being extremely rich in marine life, fishing, especially of crabs, is the dominant sector of Kamchatka Oblast's economy, accounting for over 90% of its trade in the mid-1990s. The region's fish stocks comprise around one-half of Russia's total. In 1995 the Oblast's gross regional product (GRP) amounted to 5,415,200m. roubles, or 12,973,700 roubles per head (one of the highest per-head GRPs in the Russian Federation). These figures all include the Koryak AOk. Petropavlovsk is one of two main industrial centres and ports in the territory, the other being Ust-Kamchatka. There is an international airport, Yelizovo, situated 30 km from Petropavlovsk-Kamchatskii.

Apart from fishing, agriculture in Kamchatka Oblast consists of animal husbandry (livestock, reindeer, mostly in the Koryak AOk, and fur animals), poultry farming and hunting. Just 6.9% of the working population were employed in agriculture in 1995. Agricultural output for the entire territory amounted to a value of 676,200m. roubles in that year. There are deposits of gold, silver, natural gas, sulphur and other minerals in Kamchatka Oblast, which by the late 1990s had been explored and were in the process of development. Industry had been developed in the Soviet period, but only to a limited extent. The sector, which employed 26.8% of the work-force in 1995, is based on the processing of agricultural and forestry products and coal production. Total industrial output was worth 4,076,000m. roubles in 1995. With trade dominated by the fishing industry, one of the Oblast's main foreign markets was Japan.

In 1995 the economically active population of Kamchatka region numbered 194,900; some 9,800 inhabitants of the entire territory were registered unemployed. Those in employment in Kamchatka Oblast earned an average of 949,000 roubles per month, a relatively high wage compared to the rest of the Russian Federation. There was a budgetary deficit of 9,100m. roubles in 1995. In May 1998 10-hour reductions in power and heating supplies to homes were introduced, owing to debts owed by the region's energy supplier, Kamchatenergo. Shortages of fuel then reached critical levels by the end of the year. Foreign investment in the Oblast amounted to US $794,000 in 1995. At 1 January 1995 there were some 3,500 small businesses registered in the region.

Directory

Governor: VLADIMIR AFANASIYEVICH BIRYUKOV; Kamchatskaya obl., 683040 Petropavlovsk-Kamchatskii, pl. Lenina 1; tel. (41522) 11-20-96; fax (41522) 7-38-43.

Chairman of the Legislative Assembly: LEV N. BOITSOV; Kamchatskaya obl., 683040 Petropavlovsk-Kamchatskii; tel. (41522) 2-56-06; fax (41522) 2-47-12.

Permanent Representative of the President of the Russian Federation: (vacant); tel. (41522) 2-29-88.

Head of the Regional Representation in Moscow: MIKHAIL M. SITNIKOV; tel. (095) 241-39-29.

Head of Petropavlovsk-Kamchatskii City Administration: ALEKSANDR KUZMICH DUDNIKOV; Kamchatskaya obl., 683040 Petropavlovsk-Kamchatskii, ul. Leninskaya 14; tel. (4152) 11-21-00; fax (4152) 11-26-70.

Kemerovo

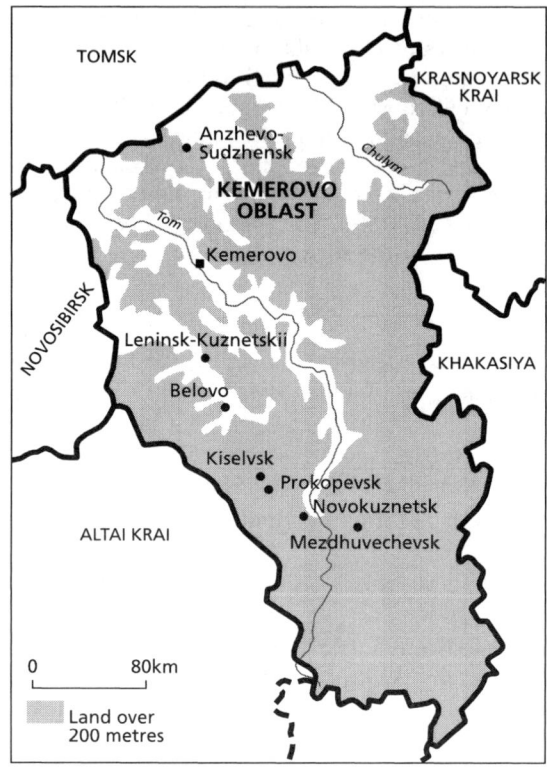

Kemerovo Oblast, also known as the Kuzbass (a Russian acronym for the Kuznetsk coalfields) region, is situated in southern central Russia and forms part of the Western Siberian Economic Area. It lies to the west of Krasnoyarsk Krai and Khakasiya (an autonomous republic, nominally part of that province). Tomsk lies to the north, Novosibirsk to the west and Altai (including the Republic of Altai) to the south-west. The region lies in the Kuznetsk basin, the area surrounding its main river, the Tom. The territory of the Oblast occupies 95,500 sq km (36,870 sq miles) and is divided into 19 administrative districts and 20 cities. At 1 January 1996 the total population was 3,063,000 and the population density in the region was 32.1 per sq km. Some 86.8% of the population inhabited urban areas. The region's administrative centre is at Kemerovo, which had an estimated population of 501,400 at this time. Other major cities are Novokuznetsk (568,600), Prokopevsk (250,000), Leninsk-Kuznetskii (119,400), Kiselevsk (114,700), Mezhdurechevsk (104,100) and Anzhero-Sudzhensk (100,200).

History

Kemerovo (formerly Shcheglovsk) was founded in 1918 and became the administrative centre of the Oblast at its formation on 26 January 1943. The city was at the centre of Russia's principal coal-mining area, the Kuzbass. Although disaffection in the region was instrumental in the disintegration of the USSR, it maintained its strong Communist tradition throughout the 1990s. In the first part of the decade a former head of the Kuzbass workers, Mikhail Kislyuk, was governor of the region and widely respected. He was a supporter of President Boris Yeltsin, but could not distract the population from their support of the Communist Party. Moreover, he earned criticism, as did the federal authorities, for refusing to schedule elections to a new duma (to replace the bicameral Regional Assembly—elected in March 1994, its activities suspended in 1995).

In the December 1995 federal general election, the Communists won 48% of the regional vote, their highest proportion (and the highest of any party) in the Federation outside the ethnic republic of North Osetiya. Much of this support was secured because of the leadership of Aman Tuleyev, speaker of the suspended local assembly (and a candidate in the federal presidential election of mid-1996). Tuleyev, who at one time served in President Yeltsin's cabinet, was overwhelmingly elected Governor in October 1997, winning almost 95% of the votes cast. This result was perceived by many as a dramatic rejection of the federal Government's reformist policies and as a protest against declining social conditions in the region. Tuleyev, however, assumed a pragmatic style of government, preferring to co-operate rather than confront President Yeltsin's regime. In May 1998, however, widespread industrial action by coal-miners in Anzhero-Sudzhensk and Prokopevsk over wage arrears threatened to bring the regional administration into direct confrontation with the federal Government. The workers blockaded a section of the Trans-Siberian Railway, which seriously affected rail transportation throughout the country. Failure by the federal Ministry of Fuel and Energy to comply with a schedule of payment resulted in Tuleyev threatening legal action and the continuation of the strike until the end of July. At this time Tuleyev's administration signed a framework agreement (negotiated by a commission headed by the energy ministry) with the federal Government on the delimitation of powers, and accompanied by 10 accords aimed at strengthening the economy of the Kuzbass region. However, at the end of 1998 Kemerovo Oblast was considered to be the federal region with the fourth-worst record on wage arrears (six months behind, on average); civil servants were to be on leave in January 1999, in order to save money. An indication that many of Russia's endemic economic problems were blamed on the federal authorities is that, at this time, Tuleyev was widely considered to be the country's most popular regional leader.

Economy

The economy of Kemerovo Oblast is based on industry. The region ranks seventh among the federal units in Russia in terms of industrial production. It is rich in mineral resources, particularly coal, containing the Kuzbass basin, one of the major coal reserves of the world. The region produced 38% of Russia's coal in 1997, but intensive mining in the Soviet period had resulted in severe environmental degradation. In 1995 Kemerovo's gross regional product amounted to 36,371,100m. roubles, equivalent to 11,844,800 roubles per head. The Oblast's main industrial centres are at Kemerovo, Novokuznetsk, Prokopevsk, Kiselevsk, Leninsk-Kuznetskii, Anzhero-Sudzhensk and Belovo. The region has 38.3 km (24 miles) of railway track and 91.2 km of roads per 1,000 km of its territory.

Kemerovo Oblast's agriculture, which employed just 6.5% of the work-force in 1995, consists mainly of vegetable production, animal husbandry, bee-keeping and fur-animal hunting. The value of agricultural output for 1995 stood at 3,421,000m. roubles. In the mid-1990s reserves of coal to a depth of 1,800 m (5,900 feet) were estimated at 733,400m. metric tons. In the same period deposits of iron ore were considered to amount to some 5,250m. metric tons. Production of complex ores, ferrous and non-ferrous metallurgy, chemicals, mechanical engineering, metal working, food processing, light manufacturing and wood-working are also important industries in the region. The industrial sector as a whole employed 37.4% of the working population in 1995 and generated 35,559,000m. roubles.

The economically active population in 1995 numbered 1,349,900, of whom 25,300 were registered unemployed. The average monthly wage was 701,000 roubles. The 1995 budget showed a relatively large deficit compared to other federal subjects, of 79,400m. roubles. During the mid-1990s foreign investors were showing some interest in exploiting the region's coal reserves. Total foreign investment in the Oblast in 1995 only amounted to US $1.36m. Economic reforms introduced after 1992 were fairly effective; by 1995 some 61% of employees were working in the private sector. The regional government elected in October 1997 aimed to promote small businesses, of which there were 14,500 in operation at 1 January 1996.

Directory

Head of the Regional Administration (Governor): AMAN GUMIROVICH TULEYEV; Kemerovskaya obl., 650099 Kemerovo, pr. Sovetskii 62; tel. (3842) 36-43-33; fax (3842) 36-34-09.

Chairman of the Council of People's Deputies: ALEKSANDR ALEKSEYEVICH FILATOV; tel. (3842) 23-41-42; fax (3842) 23-57-32.

Permanent Representative of the President of the Russian Federation: VALERII GRIGORIYEVICH BELORUS; tel. (3842) 26-41-54; fax (3842) 23-57-32.

Head of the Regional Representation in Moscow: IGOR S. KOZHUKHOVSKII; tel. (095) 202-00-63.

Head of Kemerovo City Administration: VLADIMIR VASILIYEVICH MIKHAILOV; Kemerovskaya obl., 650099 Kemerovo, pr. Sovetskii 54; tel. (3842) 36-18-41; fax (3842) 23-18-91.

Kirov

(VYATKA)

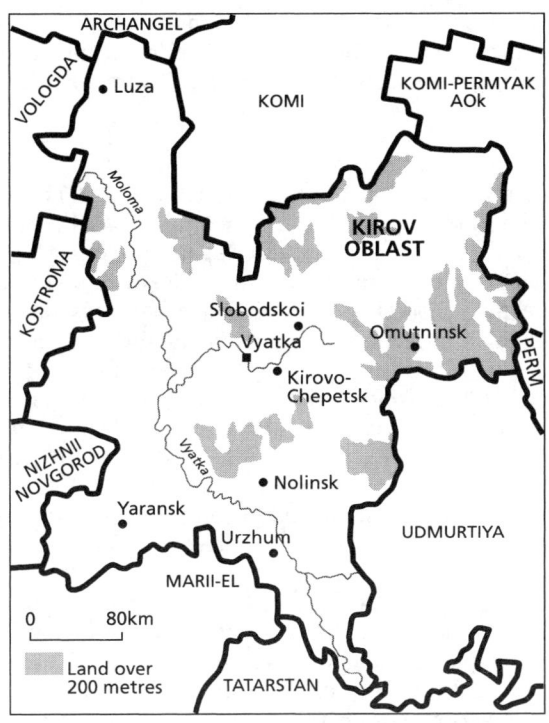

Kirov Oblast is situated in the east of the Eastern European Plain. It forms part of the Volga-Vyatka Economic Area. It is bordered by Archangel and Komi to the north, the Komi-Permyak AOk (part of Perm Oblast) and Udmurtiya to the east, Tatarstan and Marii-El to the south, and Nizhnii Novgorod, Kostroma and Vologda to the west. Its main rivers are the Kama and the Vyatka; in addition there are almost 20,000 rivers and more than 1,000 lakes on its territory. Kirov occupies a total area of 120,800 sq km (46,640 sq miles) and measures 570 km (354 miles) from south to north and 440 km from west to east. It is divided into 39 administrative districts and 18 cities. The total population at 1 January 1996 was 1,635,400 and the population density was, therefore, 13.5 per sq km. Around 70.4% of the population inhabited urban areas at this time. At the census of 1989 ethnic Russians comprised 90.4% of the population. The Oblast's administrative centre is at Vyatka (formerly Kirov), a river-port, which had an estimated 464,800 inhabitants in 1996. Other major cities are Kirovo-Chepetsk (93,600), Vyatskiye Polyany (42,600), Slobodskoi (35,700), Kotelnich (33,300) and Omutninsk (29,200).

History

The city and its region were known as Kirov from the formation of the latter on 7 December 1934, but the city was renamed Vyatka in the early 1990s. In September

1993 a draft constitution for Kirov Oblast was prepared; this referred to the Oblast as Vyatka Krai and provided for a universally elected governor and a new legislature, a provincial duma. On 18 October the Kirov Regional Soviet voted to disband itself. The federal authorities refused to acknowledge the area's redesignation as a krai and, during 1994, a Regional Duma was elected. The most popular party throughout the mid-1990s consisted of the nationalist supporters of Vladimir Zhirinovskii, although members of the old Communist establishment were well represented in its ranks. Election to the headship of the administration in the Oblast was held in October 1996 and was won by the Communist candidate, Vladimir Sergeyenkov.

Economy

In 1995 the Oblast's gross regional product (GRP) stood at 11,753,600m. roubles, equivalent to 7,168,100 roubles per head. Its main industrial centres are at Vyatka, Slobodskoi, Kotelnich, Omutninsk, Kirovo-Chepetsk and Vyatskiye Polyany. There are 1,600 km of railway track in the region, 155 km of roads per 1,000 km of territory and more than 2,000 km of navigable waterways on the Vyatka river. Owing to the density of rivers in the region its soil is high in mineral salts, reducing its fertility.

The Oblast's agriculture, which employed 16.2% of the working population in 1995, consists mainly of animal husbandry and production of grain, flax and vegetables. Total output within the sector in 1995 amounted to 3,755,300m. roubles. Kirov Oblast has significant deposits of peat, estimated at 435m. metric tons, and phosphorites, reserves of which amounted to some 2,000m. metric tons in the mid-1990s. Its main industries are mechanical engineering, metal working, ferrous and non-ferrous metallurgy, chemicals, the processing of agricultural products and light manufacturing. In March 1998 the regional administration signed a protocol with the federal ministries of defence and economy on the restructuring of the Oblast's military-industrial complex, which was significantly underachieving (in 1997 the sector accounted for just one-10th of the Oblast's GRP, despite owning 58% of its main assets). The region was also renowned for the manufacturing of toys and wood products (especially skis). Industry employed 31.1% of the work-force in 1995 and generated 8,405,000m. roubles. In 1997 exports largely comprised chemical and petrochemical goods, while imports were dominated by automobiles and equipment and food products.

In 1995 the economically active population numbered 698,800, with 57,000 registered as unemployed. This latter figure barely deteriorated in the next few years (at 1 January 1997 there were 57,300 registered unemployed), but average earnings and government finances also remained weak into the late 1990s. In 1995 the average monthly wage was 381,000 roubles, while the budget deficit was 31,400m. roubles. Economic reform in the region was, nevertheless, well advanced by the mid-1990s: in 1996 the private sector accounted for some 90% of total industrial output, while in 1997 there were some 3,400 small businesses operating in Kirov Oblast, employing around 50,000 people.

Directory

Head of the Regional Administration (Governor): VLADIMIR NILOVICH SERGEYENKOV; Kirovskaya obl., 610019 Vyatka, ul. K. Libknekhta 69; tel. (8332) 62-95-64; fax (8332) 62-89-58.

Chairman of the Regional Duma: MIKHAIL ALEKSANDROVICH MIKHEYEV.

Permanent Representative of the President of the Russian Federation: NIKOLAI ALEKSEYEVICH MARTYANOV; tel. (8332) 62-24-94.

Head of Kirov City Administration: VASILII ALEKSEYEVICH KISELEV; Kirovskaya obl., 610000 Vyatka, ul. Vorovskogo 39; tel. (8332) 62-89-40; fax (8332) 67-69-91.

Kostroma

Kostroma Oblast is situated in the central part of the Eastern European Plain. It forms part of the Central Economic Area. It borders Vologda Oblast to the north, Kirov Oblast to the east, Nizhnii Novgorod and Ivanovo Oblasts to the south and Yaroslavl Oblast to the west. Its main rivers are the Volga, the Kostroma, the Unzha, the Vokhma and the Vetluga. It has two major lakes—the Galichskoye and the Chukhlomskoye. The total area of Kostroma Oblast is 60,100 sq km (23,200 sq miles), almost three-quarters of which is forested. It is divided into 24 administrative districts and 12 cities. The region had an estimated population of 806,000 at 1 January 1996, some 66.3% of whom inhabited urban areas. Its population density at this time was 13.4 per sq km. The Oblast's administrative centre is at Kostroma, a river-port situated on both banks of the Volga, which had an estimated 285,900 inhabitants. Other major cities include Bui (29,300), Nerekhta (29,200), Sharya (26,700), Manturovo (21,900) and Galich (21,200).

History

The city of Kostroma was founded in the 12th century. In the Russian heartland, Kostroma Oblast was formed on 13 August 1944. The region remained loyal to the Communist nomenklatura in the 1990s—its local council supported the federal parliament in its 1993 defiance of the Russian President, Boris Yeltsin, and was replaced by a new representative body in 1994. The main party was the Communists; its domination of the region was secured in the gubernatorial election that took place in December 1996.

Economy

In 1995 gross regional product in Kostroma Oblast amounted to 5,918,200m. roubles, or 7,330,800 roubles per head. The Oblast's main industrial centres are at Kostroma, Sharya, Nerekhta, Galich, Bui, Manturovo and Krasnoye-on-Volga (Krasnoye-na-Volge). The region has major road and rail networks—there are 646 km (401 miles) of railways in use on its territory and 9,843 km of roads. There are also 985 km of navigable waterways.

Agriculture in Kostroma Oblast, which employed 12.9% of the work-force in 1995, consists mainly of production of grain, flax (the region is one of Russia's major producers of linen) and vegetables and animal husbandry. Total agricultural output in 1995 was worth 1,655,800m. roubles, while industrial production amounted to a value of 3,533,000m. roubles. The region has an energy surplus, exporting some four-fifths of electrical energy produced. Electricity generation comprises 41.8% of total industrial production in Kostroma Oblast. The other main industries in the region are light manufacturing, wood-working, mechanical engineering, food and timber processing and handicrafts (especially jewellery). The territory is also an important military centre, with numerous rocket silos, of which 23 had already been converted to agricultural use by early 1996, with plans to recultivate a further 20. Some 25.9% of the Oblast's working population was engaged in industry in 1995. In 1996 imports into the region amounted to US $25.1m., of which $14.3m. were from countries outside the former USSR. Exports amounted to $63.8m.

The economically active population numbered 351,800 in 1995, of whom 30,300 were registered unemployed. The average wage in the Oblast was 391,000 roubles per month. There was a budgetary deficit of 10,200m. roubles in that year. Although the amount of foreign trade was significant, foreign investment was equivalent to only US $21,000m. in 1995. At 1 January 1996 there were 3,200 small businesses in operation.

Directory

Head of the Regional Administration (Governor): VIKTOR ANDREYEVICH SHERSHUNOV; Kostromskaya obl., 156006 Kostroma, ul. Dzerzhinskogo 15; tel. (0942) 31-34-72; fax (0942) 31-33-95.

Chairman of the Regional Duma: ANDREI IVANOVICH BYCHKOV; Kostromskaya obl., 156000 Kostroma, Sovetskaya pl. 2; tel. (0942) 57-62-52.

Permanent Representative of the President of the Russian Federation: LEONORII NIKITICH BABENKOV; tel. (0942) 7-24-82.

Head of the Regional Representation in Moscow: GALINA MIKHAILOVNA PSHENITSYNA; tel. (095) 203-41-56.

Head of Kostroma City Administration: BORIS KONSTANTINOVICH KOROBOV; Kostromskaya obl., 156000 Kostroma, pl. Sovetskaya 1; tel. (0942) 31-44-40; fax (0942) 31-23-04.

Kurgan

Kurgan Oblast is situated in the south of the Western Siberian Plain. It forms part of the Urals Economic Area. Chelyabinsk Oblast lies to the west, Sverdlovsk Oblast to the north and Tyumen Oblast to the north-east. There is an international border with Kazakhstan in the south-east. The main rivers flowing through Kurgan Oblast are the Tobol and the Iset and there are numerous lakes (more than 2,500) in the south-east of the region. The Oblast occupies 71,000 sq km (27,400 sq miles) and measures 290 km (180 miles) from south to north and 430 km from east to west. It is divided into 24 administrative districts and nine cities. It had an estimated population of 1,112,000 at 1 January 1996 (of whom some 54.9% inhabited urban areas, the lowest urban population of the Urals Economic Area) and a population density, therefore, of 15.7 per sq km. Its administrative centre is at Kurgan, which had an estimated population of 362,700. Other major cities are Shadrinsk (88,100), Shumikha (21,600), Kurtamysh (18,900), Dalmatovo (16,900), Kataisk (16,700) and Petukhovo (15,100).

History

The city of Kurgan was founded as a tax-exempt settlement in 1553, on the edge of Russian territory. By the Soviet period, when there was some industrialization, it was a firmly Russian area. Kurgan Oblast was formed on 6 February 1943. In the 1990s it was still dominated by the Communists, who led the Regional Duma elected on 12 December 1993. Two years later, as indicated by the regional results of the all-Russian parliamentary election, the Communists remained the most popular party, but were closely followed by the Liberal Democrats, an immoderate nationalist grouping. In the gubernatorial election of late 1996 the Communist candidate, Oleg Bogomolov, hitherto speaker of the Regional Duma, was voted into office.

Economy

Kurgan Oblast, with its fertile soil and warm, moist climate, is the agricultural base of the Urals area, producing around one-10th of the region's grain, meat and milk. In 1995 its gross regional product amounted to 6,342,500m. roubles, equivalent to 5,690,900 roubles per head. Its main industrial centres are at Kurgan, a river-port in the south-east of the region, and Shadrinsk. The Trans-Siberian Railway passes through the Oblast's territory, as do several major petroleum and natural-gas pipelines.

The Oblast's important agricultural sector employed 24.1% of the work-force in 1995 and consists mainly of grain production and animal husbandry. Total agricultural production in the region was worth 2,625,000m. roubles in 1995. Its main industries are mechanical engineering, metal working, manufacturing of building materials, light manufacturing and food and timber processing. The industrial sector employed 23.7% of the working population and generated 4,250m. roubles in 1995.

The economically active population in 1995 numbered 441,000; around 31,400 of these were registered unemployed. Those in employment earned, on average, 275,000 roubles per month. There was a budgetary deficit of 33,300m. roubles in 1995, while foreign investment totalled a mere US $24,000. Government deficit problems continued into the late 1990s and, in January 1999, with wage arrears having provoked teachers' strikes, central government announced that federal transfers to the region would be increased in that year. In 1997 there were around 3,000 small businesses operating in the Oblast, employing some 28,000 people.

Directory

Head of the Regional Administration (Governor): OLEG ALEKSEYEVICH BOGOMOLOV; Kurganskaya obl., 640024 Kurgan, ul. Gogolya 56; tel. (35222) 2-25-34; fax (35222) 2-74-64.

Chairman of the Regional Duma: LEV GRIGORIYEVICH YEFREMOV; tel. (35222) 2-41-29.

Head of the Regional Representation in Moscow: OLEG YEVGENIYEVICH PANTELEYEV; tel. (35222) 2-22-33.

Head of Kurgan City Administration (Mayor): ANATOLII FEDOROVICH YELCHANINOV; Kurganskaya obl., 640000 Kurgan, pl. Lenina; tel. (35222) 2-24-52; fax (35222) 2-42-88.

Kursk

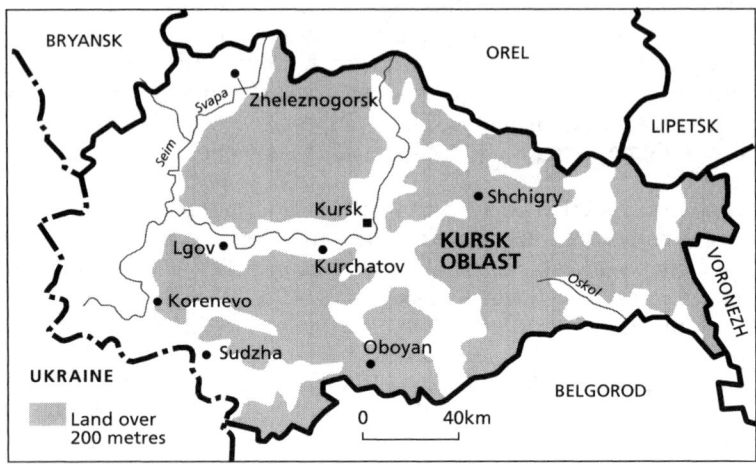

Kursk Oblast is situated within the Central Russian Highlands. It forms part of the Central Chernozem Economic Area. The former Soviet state of Ukraine lies to the south-west, with neighbouring Russian federal territories consisting of Bryansk in the north-west, Orel and Lipetsk in the north, Voronezh in the east and Belgorod in the south. Its main river is the Seim. The Oblast measures 171 km (106 miles) from south to north and 305 km from west to east. It occupies 29,800 sq km (11,500 sq miles) and is divided into 28 administrative districts and 10 cities. It had a population of 1,342,900 in 1996, of whom some 803,000 (59.9%) inhabited urban areas. Its population density was, therefore, 45.1 per sq km—over five times the national average. The Oblast's administrative centre is at Kursk, which had an estimated 442,300 inhabitants at 1 January 1996. Other major cities in the region are Zheleznogorsk (94,900), Kurchatov (48,200), Lgov (25,100) and Shchigry (21,200).

History

The city of Kursk, one of the most ancient in Russia, was founded in 1032 and became famous for its nightingales and Antonovka apples. The region was the scene of an army mutiny in 1905 and, in 1943, of a decisive battle against German forces during the Second World War. Kursk Oblast was formed on 13 July 1934. The Communists dominated the regional assembly, a Duma, elected in 1994. In December 1995 the party's candidates to the federal State Duma secured 28% of the regional vote. It was, therefore, unsurprising when the Communist candidate, the former Russian Vice-President, Aleksandr Rutskoi, defeated the incumbent regional chief executive in the gubernatorial election of 20 October 1996. In December 1998 the Governor forced the legislature to approve the establishment of a regional government.

Economy

Kursk Oblast's gross regional product in 1995 stood at 9,621,000m. roubles, equivalent to 7,137,800 roubles per head. Its main industrial centres are at Kursk and Zheleznogorsk.

The region's agriculture, which employed 23.0% of the working population in 1995, consists mainly of sugar-beets and grain production, horticulture and animal husbandry. Total agricultural production in 1995 amounted to a value of 2,993,200m. roubles. The territory contains a major iron-ore basin, with significant deposits of Kursk magnetic anomaly. Kursk Oblast's main industries were production and enrichment of iron ores, mechanical engineering, electro-technical products and chemicals, food processing, light manufacturing and production of building materials. Some 26.7% of the work-force was engaged in industry, while output within the sector was worth 7,449,000m. roubles in 1995. In the mid-1990s the Oblast's main foreign trading partners were Poland and the Czech Republic, although it also had economic links with other European countries, North America, India and Turkey. It exports largely comprised iron ore and concentrate, automobiles and machinery.

The economically active population in Kursk Oblast was 557,900 strong in 1995. Just 9,000 of these were registered unemployed at that time. The average monthly wage in the region was 309,000 roubles and there was a budgetary deficit, of 24,700m. roubles. Foreign investment in that year amounted to US $901,000. At 1 January 1996 around 3,200 small businesses were operating in the Oblast.

Directory

Head of the Regional Administration (Governor): ALEKSANDR VLADIMIROVICH RUTSKOI; Kurskaya obl., 305002 Kursk, Krasnaya pl., Dom Sovetov; tel. (07122) 2-62-62; fax (07122) 56-58-89.

Chairman of the Regional Duma: VIKTOR DMITRIYEVICH CHERNYKH; tel. (07122) 56-09-91; fax (07122) 56-20-06.

Permanent Representative of the President of the Russian Federation: (vacant); tel. (07122) 2-30-02.

Head of Kursk City Administration: SERGEI IVANOVICH MALTSEV; Kurskaya obl., 305000 Kursk, ul. Lenina 1; tel. (07122) 2-63-63; fax (07122) 2-43-16.

Leningrad

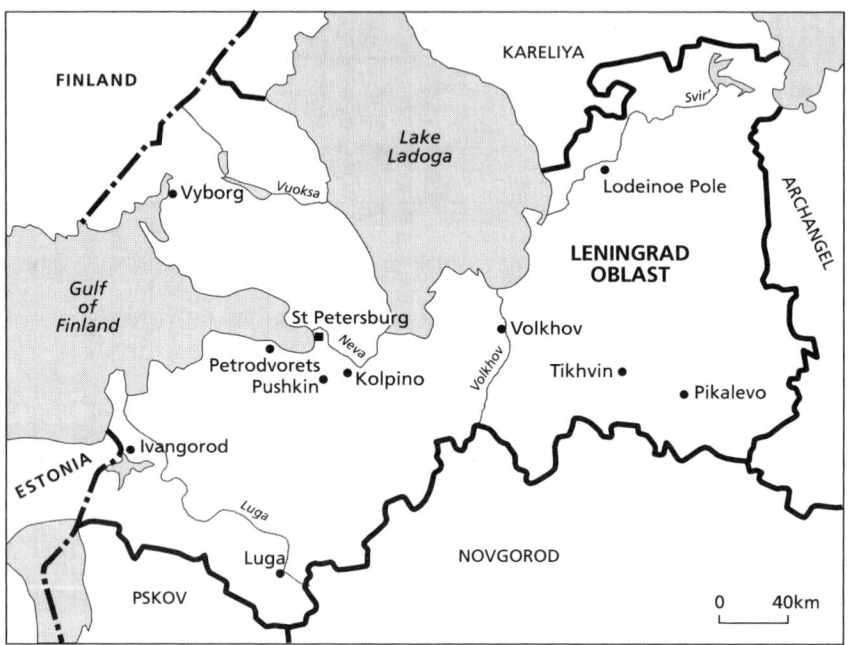

Leningrad Oblast is situated in the north-west of the Eastern European Plain. It lies on the Gulf of Finland, an inlet of the Baltic Sea, and forms part of the North-Western Economic Area. The Republic of Kareliya (Karelia) lies to the north and the oblasts of Archangel to the east and Novgorod and Pskov to the south. There is an international border with Estonia to the west and with Finland to the north-west. Two-thirds of the Oblast is forested and over one-10th is swampland. Its main rivers are the Neva, the Sayas, the Luga and the Vuoksa. Lake Ladoga (Ladozhskoye), the largest lake in Europe, with a surface area of 17,800 sq km, forms a partial border with Kareliya, and the southern tip of Lake Onega (Onezhskoye—9,700 sq km) also lies within Leningrad. The Oblast occupies 84,500 sq km (32,620 sq miles) and is divided into 17 administrative districts and 29 cities. Its total population at 1 January 1996, excluding the St Petersburg city region, was 1,676,000, of whom 66.1% inhabited urban areas. Its administrative centre is at St Petersburg.

History

The city of St Petersburg (known as Petrograd 1914–24 and Leningrad until 1991) was built in 1703. Leningrad Oblast, which was formed on 1 August 1927 out of territories of five regions (Cherepovetskoi, Leningrad, Murmansk, Novgorod and Pskov), was heavily industrialized during the Soviet period, particularly during 1926–1940. The region did not change its name when the city reverted to the name of St Petersburg in October 1991.

Although the city was a strong base for reformists and supporters of the federal Government in the early and mid-1990s, and the Oblast evinced a greater degree of approval for the Communists, the region generally produced a significant number of votes for Our Home is Russia and Yabloko. The former, led by the federal premier, won 11% of the poll in December 1995, while the reformists gained 8%. The Oblast administration and the Regional Legislative Assembly (elected on 20 March 1994) were criticized in mid-1996 for restrictions on the responsibilities of the lower tiers of local government, despite federal constitutional stipulations. At around the same time an agreement delimiting the division of powers between the federal and regional governments was signed. Later that year gubernatorial elections were held, which were won by an independent candidate, Vadim Gustov. On 24 September 1998 the federal President, Boris Yeltsin, approved a proposal to merge the Oblast with the federal city of St Petersburg, although any immediate implementation seemed unlikely.

Economy

Leningrad Oblast's gross regional product amounted to 12,507,100m. roubles in 1995, equivalent to 7,466,000 roubles per head. Its main industrial centres are at St Petersburg, Vyborg (both major seaports), Sestroretsk and Kingisepp. At the beginning of 1995 the region contained 2,229 km (1,384 miles) of railway track, of which 1,352 km were electrified, and 9,669 km of roads, of which all but 53 km were paved.

The Oblast's agriculture, which employed 14.0% of the working population in 1995, consists mainly of animal husbandry and vegetable production. Total agricultural output was worth 3,769,600m. roubles in 1995. The region's timber reserves are estimated to be covering 6.1m. ha (15m. acres). Its major industries are mechanical engineering, ferrous and non-ferrous metallurgy, chemicals and petrochemicals, petroleum refining, the processing of forestry and agricultural products, production of electrical energy, light manufacturing and the production of building materials, bauxites, slate and peat. Some 28.1% of the Oblast's work-force was engaged in industry in 1995. Industrial output in that year amounted to a value of 10,701,000m. roubles.

The economically active population numbered 677,700, of whom 40,800 were registered unemployed. The average monthly wage in 1995 was 371,000 roubles. The budget for 1995 showed a surplus of 47,100m. roubles. At the beginning of 1996 there were 171 joint enterprises, which were mainly in the Vyborg raion, bordering Finland, and established with investment by Finnish companies. In 1995 there had been more than US $20m.-worth of foreign investment in the region, primarily in the timber, chemical and petrochemicals industries.

Directory

Head of the Regional Administration (Governor): VADIM ANATOLIYEVICH GUSTOV; Leningradskaya obl., 193311 St Petersburg, Suvorovskii 67; tel. (812) 274-35-63; fax (812) 271-56-27.

Chairman of the Regional Legislative Assembly: Vasiliyevich Ivanov; tel. (812) 274-65-31.

Permanent Representative of the President of the Russian Federation: FEDR DMITRIYEVICH SHKRUDNEV; tel. (812) 274-13-08; fax (812) 310-43-54.

Lipetsk

Lipetsk Oblast is situated within the Central Russian Highlands, some 508 km (315 m) south-east of Moscow. It forms part of the Central Chernozem Economic Area. It is bordered by Voronezh and Kursk Oblasts to the south, Orel Oblast to the west, Tula Oblast to the north-west, Ryazan Oblast to the north and Tambov Oblast to the east. Its main rivers are the Don and the Voronezh. The Oblast occupies 24,100 sq km (9,300 sq miles) and is divided into 18 administrative districts and eight cities. It had an estimated population of 1,250,000 at 1 January 1996, of whom some 63.5% inhabited urban areas. Its population density at this time was 51.9 per sq km. Its administrative centre is at Lipetsk, which had an estimated population of 475,600 in 1996. Other major cities are Yeletsk (118,300), Gryazi (48,300), Dankov (24,800) and Lebedyan (22,600).

History

Lipetsk was founded in the 13th century and was later famed for containing one of Russia's oldest mud-bath resorts and spas. In the late tsarist and Soviet period the region became increasingly industrialized. Lipetsk Oblast was formed on 6 January 1954. By the 1990s it was considered part of the 'red belt' of Communist support across central Russia. Thus, in December 1992, when Lipetsk was one of eight territorial units permitted to hold gubernatorial elections (in an attempt to resolve the dispute between the head of the administration and the regional assembly), the incumbent, a supporter of the federal Government, was defeated by the Communist candidate. In September 1993 both the Regional Soviet and the governor, therefore, denounced the Russian President's dissolution of the federal parliament. Subsequently, the territory was obliged to comply with the directives of the federal Government. Legislative elections were held in the region on 6 March 1994, but were invalidated, owing to a low level of attendance. Further elections were held later that year. Political apathy also contributed to a low level of support, compared to other regions on the 'red belt', for the Communists in the federal general election of December 1995—a still high 29%. On 12 April 1998 the Chairman of the Regional Assembly, Oleg Korolev, won an overwhelming victory (some 79% of the votes cast) in the gubernatorial election.

Economy

In 1995 Lipetsk Oblast's gross regional product totalled 13,794,700m. roubles, or 11,034,900 roubles per head. Its main industrial centres are at Lipetsk, Yeletsk, Dankov and Gryazi. Yeletsk and Gryazi contain the region's major railway junctions.

The region's agriculture consists mainly of animal husbandry, horticulture and the production of grain, sugar-beets, makhorka tobacco and vegetables. Some 18.0% of the work-force was engaged in agriculture in 1995. Agricultural output in that year amounted to a value of 2,672,300m. roubles. The Oblast's main industries are ferrous metallurgy (ferrous metallurgy comprised two-thirds of the region's total industrial output in the mid-1990s), mechanical engineering, metal working, electro-technical industry, food processing and the production of building materials. Novolipetsk Metallurgical Group, based in the region, is one of the country's major industrial companies. The industrial sector employed 28.4% of the region's working population and generated 16,055,000m. roubles.

The economically active population in 1995 totalled 546,400; 6,900 of these were registered unemployed. Those in employment earned, on average, 376,000 roubles per month. Foreign investment in Lipetsk Oblast in 1995 amounted to US $3.65m. At 1 January 1996 there were around 3,700 small businesses registered in the territory.

Directory

Head of the Regional Administration (Governor): OLEG PETROVICH KOROLEV; Lipetskaya obl., 398014 Lipetsk, pl. Sobornaya 1; tel. (0742) 24-25-65; fax (0742) 72-24-26.

Chairman of the Regional Assembly: ANATOLII IVANOVICH SAVENKOV.

Permanent Representative of the President of the Russian Federation: ANATOLII NIKOLAYEVICH LARIN; tel. (0742) 24-03-65.

Head of Lipetsk City Administration: ALEKSANDR KOROBEINIKOV; Lipetskaya obl., 398600 Lipetsk, ul. Sovetskaya 22; tel. (0742) 77-66-17; fax (0742) 77-44-30.

Magadan

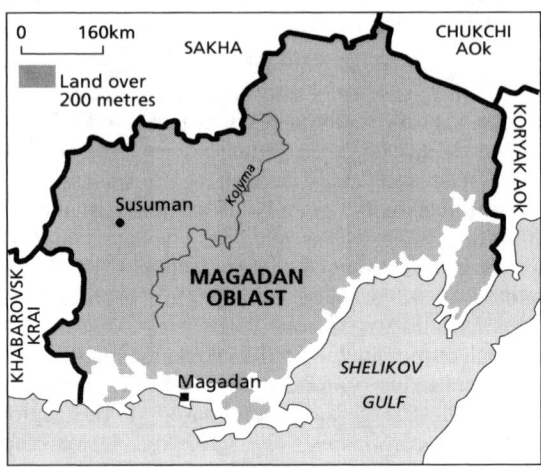

Magadan Oblast is situated in the north-east of Russia and forms part of the Far Eastern Economic Area. To the north-east, on the Chukotka Peninsula, lies the Chukchi AOk, which, until 1992, formed part of Magadan Oblast. The rest of its border with territory on Chukotka is with the Koryak AOk (Kamchatka Oblast), which lies to the east. Magadan has a coastline on the Sea of Okhotsk in the south-east. Khabarovsk Krai lies to the south-west of the region and the Republic of Sakha (Yakutiya) to the north-west. Its main river is the Kolyma, which flows north, through Yakutiya, and drains into the Arctic Ocean. Much of the territory of the region is mountainous, while the area around the Anadyr estuary is low marshland. Much of the Oblast is tundra or forest-tundra. The Oblast occupies a total area of 461,400 sq km (178,150 sq miles—much reduced from when it included the Chukchi, or Chukot, AOk). It is divided into eight administrative districts and two cities. The climate in the region is severe, with winters lasting between six and over seven months. The average annual temperature in all areas of the region is below nought (Celsius). The Oblast had an estimated population of 258,000 at 1 January 1996. It is one of the most sparsely populated regions, with a population density of just 0.6 per sq km. The majority of the population (89.7%) inhabited urban areas. Its administrative centre is at Magadan, which had an estimated population of 124,200 in 1996. The second city of the territory is Susuman (10,400).

History

Russians first reached the Magadan region in the mid-17th century. At the start of the Soviet period it was in the Far Eastern Republic, which in 1922 was reintegrated into Russia. A distinct Magadan Oblast was formed on 3 December 1953, although it then included the Chukot (now Chukchi) AOk. The successful rejection of Magadan's jurisdiction on the Chukotka Peninsula (acknowledged by the federal authorities in 1992) massively reduced Magadan's territory and contributed to local feeling of remoteness and of neglect by the centre. Thus, in the elections to the State Duma of the Federation Assembly of December 1995, candidates of the Liberal Democrats secured 22% of the votes cast in the region. Both the Communists and the existing federal authorities were too identified with the political establishments, to the benefit of the nationalists. However, the Regional Duma (elected in 1994) was still dominated by the old nomenklatura class. The outcome, therefore, of the gubernatorial election, held on 3 November 1996, was far from certain, but was won by an independent candidate, Valentin Tsvetkov.

Economy

Magadan Oblast is Russia's principal gold-producing region. Its gross regional product in 1995 amounted to 3,373,700m. roubles, equivalent to 7,466,900 roubles per head. The Oblast's main industrial centres are at Magadan and Susuman. Magadan and Nagayevo are its most important ports. There are no railways in the territory, but there are 2,645 km (1,643 miles) of paved roads. There is an international airport at Magadan.

The region's primary economic activities are fishing, animal husbandry and hunting. These and other agricultural activities, which employed just 5.8% of the region's work-force, generated 219,400m. roubles in 1995. Ore mining is also important: apart from gold, the region contains considerable reserves of silver, tin and wolfram (tungsten). It is also rich in peat and timber. In early 1998 the regional Government hired a prospecting company to explore offshore petroleum deposits in the Sea of Okhotsk, in a zone thought to hold around 5,000m. metric tons of petroleum and natural gas. The Kolyma river is an important source of hydroelectric energy. Other industry includes food processing, mechanical engineering and metal working. Some 24.1% of the working population was engaged in industry in 1995. Total industrial output in that year was worth 2,796,000m. roubles.

In 1996 a total of 134,000 of the Oblast's inhabitants were economically active, of whom 118,000 were in employment. The average monthly wage in 1995 was 961,000 roubles, while the budget showed a large deficit, of 139,500m. roubles. Persistent deficit problems, not helped by high wages, meant continuing problems with payment arrears and, in December 1998, Magadan was cited as the fifth-worst territory in the Federation for wage arrears. Foreign investment in the Oblast amounted to US $13.78m. in 1995. At 1 January 1996 there were an estimated 2,400 small businesses in operation.

Directory

Governor: VALENTIN IVANOVICH TSVETKOV; Magadanskaya obl., 685000 Magadan, ul. Gorkogo 6; tel. (41322) 2-31-34; fax (41322) 2-04-25.

Chairman of the Regional Duma: VLADIMIR ALEKSEYEVICH PEKHTIN.

Permanent Representative of the President of the Russian Federation: SERGEI SERGEYEVICH PETRISHCHEV; tel. (41322) 2-55-32.

Head of Magadan City Administration (Mayor): NIKOLAI BORISOVICH KARPENKO; Magadanskaya obl., 685000 Magadan, pl. Gorkogo 1; tel. (41322) 2-50-47; fax (41322) 2-49-00.

Moscow

(MOSCOW OBLAST)

Moscow Oblast is situated in the central part of the Eastern European Plain, at the Volga-Oka confluence. It forms part of the Central Economic Area. Moscow is surrounded by seven other oblasts: Tver and Yaroslavl to the north, Vladimir and Ryazan to the east, Tula and Kaluga to the south-west and Smolensk to the west. Most of the region is forested and its main rivers are the Moskva and the Oka. The territory of the Oblast covers an area of 46,000 sq km (17,760 sq miles) and has 39 administrative districts and 74 cities. Its total population at 1 January 1996 was estimated at 6,597,000 (excluding Moscow City region). It is the most densely populated region in Russia, having a total of 143.4 inhabitants per sq km. Inhabitants of urban areas comprise around 79.7% of the region's total population. The Oblast's administrative centre is in Moscow city.

History

The city of Moscow was established in the mid-12th century and became the centre of a burgeoning Muscovite state. The region soon became an important trade route between the Baltic Sea in the north and the Black and Caspian Seas in the south. It first became industrialized in the early 18th century, with the development of the textile industry, in particular the production of wool and cotton. The region and the city of Moscow were captured by the troops of Emperor Napoleon I of France in 1812, but the invaders were forced to retreat later that year. German invaders reached the Moscow region (which had been formed as Moscow Oblast on 14 January 1929) in 1941, and the Soviet Government removed from the city until 1943. In the winter of 1941/42 the German forces were driven from the Oblast's territory. Otherwise, the region and the city have benefited from Moscow being the Soviet, and the Russian, capital.

As the seat of government, in the 1990s the federal executive could rely on a reasonable level of support in the Moscow region. Our Home is Russia, the party of Viktor Chernomyrdin, the federal Prime Minister, achieved 14% of the votes in the general election (not as high as in the city itself, and not as high as the Communists, on 22%) in 1995. In simultaneous local elections for a governor, the pro-government incumbent won, but only after a second round of voting. Anti-government forces were also well represented in the 50-member Regional Duma (elected in December 1993). Relative prosperity kept discontent minimal, however, with the region not experiencing the problems of wage arrears to the same extent as elsewhere in the Federation—it was among the three regions with the best record for timely payment during 1998.

Economy

Moscow Oblast's gross regional product (GRP) amounted to 47,607,700m. roubles, or 7,201,200 roubles per head in 1995. The main industrial centres are at Podolsk, Lyubertsy, Kolomna, Mytishchi, Odintsovo, Noginsk, Serpukhov, Orekhovo-Zuyevo, Shchelkovo and Sergiyev-Posad (formerly Zagorsk).

The Oblast's agriculture, which employed just 7.2% of the region's work-force in 1995, consists mainly of animal husbandry and the production of vegetables and grain. Total agricultural production generated 6,613,900m. roubles in 1995. Moscow Oblast's industry, in which some 30.8% of the working population were engaged in 1995, mainly comprised heavy industry (which accounted for approximately one-third of GRP during the mid-1990s). The region's major industries are mechanical engineering, radio electronics, chemicals, light manufacturing, textiles, ferrous metallurgy, metal working, the manufacture of building materials, wood-working and handicrafts (ceramics, painted and lacquered wooden ornaments). The region's military-industrial complex is also important. Industrial output in 1995 was worth 29,896m. roubles.

The economically active population in the Oblast in 1995 was 2,429,200, of whom 71,000 were registered unemployed. The average monthly wage at that time was 395,000 roubles. There was a regional budgetary surplus of 29,200m. roubles. Total foreign investment in Moscow Oblast amounted to US $29.90m. in 1995. In 1997 there was a total of 110 joint enterprises operating in the Oblast, of which 78 had foreign partners, particularly from Germany, Italy and the USA.

Directory

Governor: ANATOLII STEPANOVICH TYAZHLOV; Moskovskaya obl., 103070 Moscow, Staraya pl. 6; tel. (095) 206-60-93; fax (095) 975-26-42.

First Deputy Governors: VLADIMIR VASILIYEVICH SEMAYEV; VIKTOR OLEGOVICH VLASOV; tel. (095) 206-65-49.

Chairman of the Regional Duma: ALEKSANDR YEVGENIYEVICH ZHAROV.

Permanent Representative of the President of the Russian Federation: GENNADII VLADIMIROVICH VERETENNIKOV; tel. (095) 206-03-56.

Murmansk

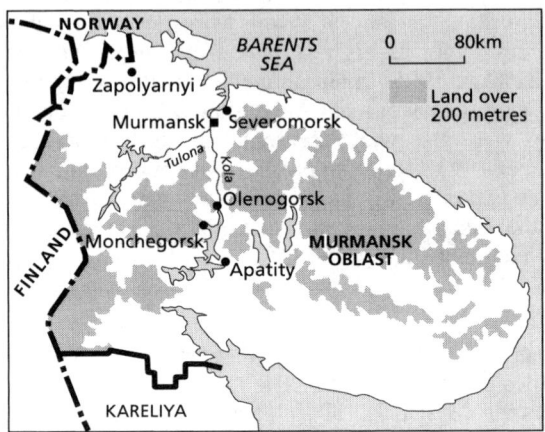

Murmansk Oblast occupies the Kola Peninsula, which is washed by the Barents Sea to the north and the White Sea to the east. It forms part of the Northern Economic Area. It has international borders with Norway and Finland to the west and the Russian federal subject of Kareliya (Karelia) lies to the south. Much of its territory lies within the Arctic Circle. The major rivers in the Oblast are the Ponoi, the Varguza, the Umba, the Kola, the Niva and the Tulona. It has several major lakes, including the Imandra, Umbozero and Lovozero. The territory of the Oblast covers an area of 144,900 sq km (55,930 sq miles), extending some 400 km (250 miles) from south to north and 500 km from west to east. The climate in the Oblast is severe and changeable, influenced by cold fronts from the Arctic and warm, moist weather from the Atlantic. Its total population was estimated at 1,048,000 at 1 January 1996 (of whom 92.0% inhabited urban areas) and it had a population density, therefore, of 7.2 per sq km. It is divided into five districts and 16 cities. Its administrative centre is at Murmansk, a major seaport and tourist centre, with an estimated population of 399,000 in 1996. Other major cities in the region are Apatity (73,000), Monchegorsk (61,100), Severomorsk (58,700) and Kandalaksha (48,500).

History

Murmansk city was founded in 1916, as a fishing port on the Barents Sea and was known as Romanov-on-Murman (Romanov-na-Murmane) until the following year. After the Bolshevik Revolution of 1917 Murmansk region was a centre of anti-Communist resistance until a peace treaty was signed with the Soviet Government on 13 March 1920. Murmansk Oblast was formed on 28 May 1938.

The development of industry in the region, particularly after the Second World War, resulted in a steady increase in population until the late 1950s. However, heavy industry, particularly the sulphurous emissions from the vast nickel-smelting works on the Kola Peninsula, were accused of causing major environmental damage by the neighbouring Nordic nations (agreement on the monitoring and limiting of this was achieved, to an extent, in mid-1996). The concentration of nuclear reactors on the Kola Peninsula, considered to be the world's most hazardous, is also a major source of concern—in 1993–97 Norway, Finland and the European Bank for Reconstruction and Development committed considerable funds to improving atomic safety in the region.

In the 1990s political allegiances in the Oblast as a whole were fairly evenly balanced, although disparity by area was immense. As measured by the regional results of the 1995 all-Russian general election, the reformist Yabloko movement achieved a relatively high 11% of the votes cast (about the same proportion as for the Communists and the government party). Most of the liberal votes, however, were concentrated in Murmansk city while the countryside gave Vladimir Zhirinovskii's Liberal Democrats over 12%. In fact it was a candidate favoured by Aleksandr Lebed, Yurii Yevdokimov, who was elected in the Oblast's first ever direct poll to the governorship, held in November 1996.

Economy

Murmansk Oblast's gross regional product in 1995 stood at 14,357,700m. roubles, or 13,577,000 roubles per head. The Oblast's principal industrial centres are at Murmansk, Monchegorsk, Kirovsk, Zapolyarnyi, Apatity and Kandalaksha. There are 1,013 km of railway track in the region, with Murmansk, Apatity, Olenegorsk and Kandalaksha the main railway junctions, and 4,159 km of roads. The port at Murmansk is Russia's principal unfrozen port in the Arctic Circle, through which some 12m. metric tons of cargo pass every year. This is also the base for the world's only nuclear ice-breaker fleet, the Northern Fleet. There is an international airport at Murmansk, which operates flights to destinations in Finland, Norway and Sweden.

The Oblast's agriculture sector, which owing to its extreme climate employed just 2.1% of the work-force in 1995, consists mainly of fishing (the region produces 45% of the country's fish supplies) and animal husbandry. The territory is rich in natural resources, including phosphates, iron ore and rare and non-ferrous metals. In 1985 the Shtokmanov gas-condensate deposit, thought to contain reserves exceeding 3,000,000m. cu m of gas, was opened on the continental shelf of the Barents Sea. It was hoped that after 2000 the deposit would supply most of the north and north-west of the country. The region produces almost all of Russia's apatites, 43.4% of its nickel, 14.4% of its refined copper and 11.7% of its concentrates of iron. Some 30.1% of the Oblast's working population was engaged in industry in 1995, while the industrial sector generated 12,276,000m. roubles. Its major industries are the production and enrichment of ores and ferrous metals, ore mining, ferrous metallurgy, the manufacture of building materials and food processing. The Oblast's major exports are non-ferrous metals, fish products and apatite concentrate.

In 1995 the region's economically active population numbered 471,700, of whom some 32,700 were registered unemployed. The average monthly wage in the Oblast was 740,000 roubles. The 1995 budget showed a surplus of 19,200m. roubles. Foreign investment in that year amounted to US $3.03m. The Kola Centre for Business Development, employing Russian and US specialists, opened in Murmansk in the mid-1990s and there was a regional fund for the development of small businesses. At 1 January 1996 there were some 6,100 small businesses operating in the Oblast.

Directory

Head of the Regional Administration (Governor): YURII ALEKSEYEVICH YEVDOKIMOV; Murmanskaya obl., 183006 Murmansk, pr. Lenina 75; tel. (8152) 55-65-40; fax (8152) 55-55-03.

Chairman of the Regional Soviet: PAVEL ALEKSANDROVICH SAZHINOV.

Permanent Representative of the President of the Russian Federation: IVAN IVANOVICH MENSHIKOV; tel. (8152) 5-51-31.

Head of the Regional Representation in Moscow: PETR IVANOVICH ZELENOV; tel. (095) 299-37-59.

Head of Murmansk City Administration: OLEG PETROVICH NAIDENOV; Murmanskaya obl., 183006 Murmansk, pr. Lenina 75; tel. (8152) 55-51-60; fax (8152) 55-43-66.

Nizhnii Novgorod

Nizhnii Novgorod (Nizhegorod) Oblast is situated on the middle reaches of the Volga river. It forms part of the Volga-Vyatka Economic Area. Mordoviya and Ryazan lie to the south, Vladimir and Ivanovo to the west, Kostroma to the north-west, Kirov to the north-east and Marii-El and Chuvashiya to the east. Its major rivers are the Volga, the Oka, the Sura and the Vetluga. The terrain in the north of the Oblast is mainly low lying, with numerous forests and extensive swampland. The southern part is characterized by fertile black soil (*chernozem*). The Oblast occupies a total area of 74,800 sq km (28,870 sq miles) and measures some 400 km (250 miles) from south to north and 300 km from east to west. It is divided into 48 administrative districts and 26 cities. At 1 January 1996 it had an estimated total population of 3,727,000 and a population density, therefore, of 49.8 per sq km, making it one of Russia's most densely populated regions. Some 77.9% of the Oblast's inhabitants resided in urban areas. Its administrative centre is at Nizhnii Novgorod (formerly Gorkii), which lies at the confluence of the Volga and Oka rivers. The city is Russia's third largest, with an estimated population of 1,375,500 in 1996. Other major cities include Dzerzhinsk (283,600), Arzamas (112,100), Sarov (82,300) and Pavlovo (71,700).

History

Nizhnii Novgorod city was founded in 1221 on the borders of the Russian principalities. With the decline of Tatar power the city was absorbed by the Muscovite state. The Sarov Monastery, one of Russian Orthodoxy's most sacred sites, was founded in the region. Industrialization took place in the late tsarist period. In 1905 mass unrest occurred among peasants and workers in the region, which was one of the first areas of Russia to be seized by the Bolsheviks in late 1917. Nizhnii Novgorod Oblast was formed on 14 January 1929. From 1932 until 1990 the city and region were known as Gorkii, and for much of the time the city was 'closed', owing to the importance of the defence industry.

In 1991 the Russian President, Boris Yeltsin, appointed a leading local reformer, Boris Nemtsov, head of the regional administration (governor). Nemtsov instituted a wide-ranging programme of economic reform which was widely praised by liberals and by the federal Government. Nemtsov, however, was careful not to be identified with any one party, but secured popular election in December 1995 with 60% of the votes cast (although the Communists and Liberal Democrats did rather better in simultaneous federal elections). Although occasionally accused of authoritarian tendencies, he was a prominent advocate of democratization and decentralization in the Federation. On 8 June 1996 Nemtsov signed a treaty on the delimitation of powers with the federal Government. This gave the Oblast greater budgetary independence and more control over its public property. In April 1997 Nemtsov was appointed to the federal Government; gubernatorial elections were subsequently held in which the pro-government candidate, Ivan Sklyarov (former Mayor of Nizhnii Novgorod), defeated Gennadii Khodyrev (who was backed both by the Communists and the Liberal Democrats) after a 'run-off' vote in mid-July. His victory was claimed by the federal Government as an endorsement of President Yeltsin's reform programme and a rejection of political extremism. On 1 April 1998 the mayoral elections in Nizhnii Novgorod were annulled, following the revelation that the winning candidate, Andrei Klimintyev (a former ally of Nemtsov) had been imprisoned in 1994. Klimentyev was subsequently sentenced for a further six years on charges of forgery, embezzlement and corruption. In October the former presidential representative in the region, Yurii Lebedev, was elected mayor. The election of a pro-government candidate was achieved in spite of the national financial crisis in August or the earlier industrial action by defence-sector workers over wage arrears and the withholding of funds by the federal Government for the conversion of the Oblast's defence industry.

Economy

The Oblast's gross regional product amounted to 35,172,300m. roubles, or 9,420,200 roubles per head. Its principal industrial centres are at Nizhnii Novgorod, Dzerzhinsk and Arzamas. Nizhnii Novgorod contains a major river-port, from which it is possible to reach the Baltic, Black, White and Caspian Seas and the Sea of Azov. There are over 14,000 km of roads and 1,200 km of railway track in the region. In 1985 an underground railway system opened in Nizhnii Novgorod and in 1994 an international airport, from which Lufthansa (of Germany) operated flights to the German city of Frankfurt. In late 1996 plans to extend the Second Trans-European Corridor to Nizhnii Novgorod were initiated by the Russian Government and the European Union.

Reform of the farming sector in the 1990s involved extensive privatization and investment in rural infrastructure. Agriculture in the region, which employed 10.0% of the working population in 1995, consists mainly of the production of grain, sugar-beets, flax and onions and other vegetables, although the Oblast lacks many areas with the fertile black topsoil typical of the European Plain. Animal husbandry and poultry farming are also important. Total agricultural output in 1995 was worth 4,004,500m. roubles. As one of the three most industrially developed regions in Russia, however, it was the Oblast's industry that provided some 80% of total production (industrial output generated as much as 29,631,000m. roubles in 1995). One of the principal industries in the Oblast is the manufacture of automobiles (especially at the Gorkii automobile plant—GAZ), mechanical engineering, metal working, ferrous metallurgy, chemicals, petrochemicals, the processing of agricultural and forestry products, the production of building materials and light manufacturing. In 1995 some 35.8% of the working population was engaged in industry. During the Soviet period the region was developed as a major military-industrial centre, with the defence sector accounting for around three-quarters of the regional economy, and Gorkii became a 'closed' city. The Oblast also contained the secret city of Arzamas-16, a centre of nuclear research. In the early 1990s much of Governor Nemtsov's reform programme was aimed at the conversion of as much of the industrial base to civilian use as possible, but this process was made increasingly difficult as federal funds became less readily available (they were withheld in 1998). Privatization and commercialization was not only confined to industry and agriculture; indeed, it started with transport services and the retail sector. The Oblast exports principally to Belarus, Belgium, France, Kazakhstan, Switzerland and the United Kingdom and imports goods from Austria, Belarus, the People's Republic of China, Germany, Kazakhstan, the Netherlands, Ukraine and the USA. In 1997 there were 1,153 joint-stock companies in the region, as well as 34 commercial banks and 35 insurance companies.

In 1995 the economically active population numbered 1,768,400, of whom 54,200 (3.1%) were registered unemployed. The average monthly wage in the Oblast was 382,000 roubles. The 1995 budget showed a deficit of 60,900m. roubles. Foreign investment in the region in that year totalled US $59.84m. Infrastructure for small-business development had resulted in the emergence of 99,000 small businesses, employing 254,000 people, by 1997.

Directory

Head of the Regional Administration (Governor): IVAN PETROVICH SKLYAROV; Nizhegorodskaya obl., 603082 Nizhnii Novgorod, Kreml, korp. 1; tel. (8312) 39-67-00; fax (8312) 39-06-29.

Chairman of the Legislative Assembly: ANATOLII ALEKSANDROVICH KOZERADSKII.

Permanent Representative of the President of the Russian Federation: (vacant); tel. (8312) 39-15-06.

Head of the Regional Representation in Moscow: (vacant); tel. (095) 203-77-41.

Head of Nizhnii Novgorod City Administration (Mayor): YURII ISAKOVICH LEBEDEV; Nizhegorodskaya obl., 603082 Nizhnii Novgorod, Kreml, korp. 5; tel. (8312) 39-15-06; fax (8312) 39-13-02.

Novgorod

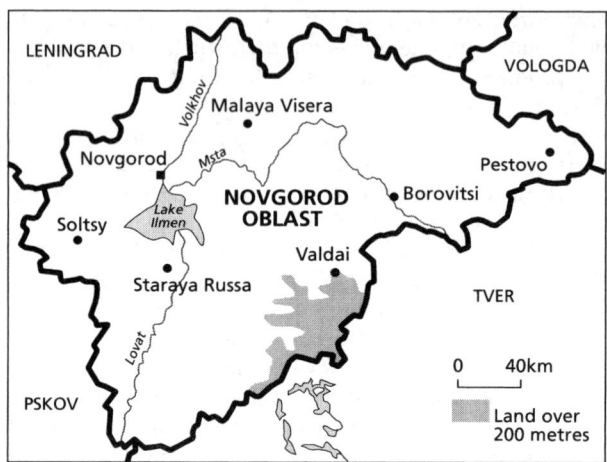

Novgorod Oblast is situated in the north-west of the Eastern European Plain, some 500 km (just over 300 miles) north-west of Moscow and 180 km south of St Petersburg. It forms part of the North-Western Economic Area. Tver Oblast lies to the south-east, Pskov Oblast to the south-west and Leningrad and Vologda Oblasts to the north. The territory's major rivers are the Msta, the Lovat and the outlet of Lake Ilmen, the Volkhov. Just over two-fifths of its territory is forested (either taiga—forested marshland—or mixed forest). The region contains the Valdai state national park. Its territory covers an area of 55,300 sq km (21,350 sq miles) and extends 250 km from south to north and 385 km from west to east. It is divided into 21 administrative districts and 10 cities. At 1 January 1996 the population of the Oblast was estimated at 743,000 and its population density, therefore, was 13.4 per sq km. The urban population was reckoned at 70.9% of the total. The region's administrative centre is at Novgorod, which lies on the River Volkhov, some 6 km from Lake Ilmen (it had an estimated population of some 31,100 in 1997).

History

One of the oldest Russian cities, Novgorod (or 'Great Novgorod') remained a powerful principality after the dissolution of Kievan Rus and even after the Mongol incursions. In 1478 Ivan III ('the Great'), prince of Muscovy and the first Tsar of All Russia, destroyed the Republic of Novgorod, a polity sometimes used as evidence for the rather spurious claim of a democratic tradition in Russia. Its wealth and importance, based on trade, declined after the foundation of St Petersburg. Novgorod Oblast was formed on 5 July 1944.

In the mid-1990s the region displayed a relatively high level of support for reformists and the centrist supporters of the federal Government of President Boris Yeltsin. The Oblast was permitted gubernatorial elections in December 1995, which were won by the pro-Yeltsin incumbent, Mikhail Prusak. Prusak's regime was characterized by his policy of pragmatic compromise with regard to the economy, spreading the region's economic benefits as widely as possible. Similar policies prevailed in the Duma, the members of which did not bear allegiance to any national political party.

Economy

In 1995 Novgorod Oblast's gross regional product amounted to 4,407,900m. roubles, equivalent to 5,923,800 roubles per head. The Oblast's major industrial centres are at Novgorod and Staraya Russa (a 19th century resort town famous for its mineral and radon springs and therapeutic mud). The major Moscow–St Petersburg road and rail routes pass through the region. The road system, comprising 10,200 km of roads, is the Oblast's major transport network.

The region's agriculture, which employed 13.9% of the work-force in 1995, consists mainly of flax production and animal husbandry. Its major natural resource is timber: in the mid-1990s some 2.5m. cu m were produced annually, but it was thought that there was potential for this amount to be expanded by four or five times. In 1995 total agricultural production amounted to a value of 1,296,200m. roubles. The region's major industries include mechanical engineering, chemicals, wood-working, light manufacturing and the processing of forestry and agricultural products. The industrial sector employed 29.2% of the working population in 1995 and generated 3,991,000m. roubles. Novgorod city is an important tourist destination, attracting around 1m. visitors annually.

The economically active population in 1995 totalled 333,300. Some 14,400 of these were registered unemployed. Those in employment earned an average wage of 434,000 roubles per month. Legislative conditions for foreign investors in Novgorod Oblast were considered to be favourable in the 1990s, owing to a foreign company's exemption from all local taxes until its project returned a profit. In 1995 total foreign investment in the region amounted to US $10.33m. By the end of 1997 a total of 197 foreign companies were established in the region, accounting for around 40% of Novgorod's output and more than 83% of exports (compared to figures of 3% and 9%, respectively, for Russia as a whole). None the less, in early 1998 the region's budgetary strength was slightly below average, with fiscal indicators, including revenues per head, federal taxes paid per head and the proportion of expenditure covered by its own revenue, appearing weak. At 1 January 1996 there were an estimated 3,800 small businesses registered in the region.

Directory

Head of the Regional Administration (Governor): MIKHAIL MIKHAILOVICH PRUSAK; Novgorodskaya obl., 173005 Novgorod, Sofiiskaya pl. 1; tel. (816) 7-47-79; fax (816) 7-70-88.

Chairman of the Regional Duma: ANATOLII ALEKSANDROVICH BOITSEV; tel. (816) 7-54-60; fax (816) 13-13-30.

Permanent Representative of the President of the Russian Federation: MIKHAIL SEMENOVICH DYAGILEV; tel. (816) 7-40-46; fax (816) 13-13-30.

Head of the Regional Representation in Moscow: VLADIMIR NIKOLAYEVICH PODOPRIGORA; tel. (095) 200-45-38.

TERRITORIAL SURVEYS

Head of Novgorod City Administration (Mayor): ALEKSANDR VLADIMIROVICH KORSUNOV; Novgorodskaya obl., 173007 Novgorod, ul. Bolshaya Vlasevskaya 4; tel. (816) 7-25-40; fax (816) 7-83-42.

Novosibirsk

Novosibirsk Oblast is situated in the south-east of the Western Siberian Plain, at the Ob-Irtysh confluence. The Oblast forms part of the Western Siberian Economic Area. Its south-western districts lie on the international border with Kazakhstan. The neighbouring federal territories are Omsk Oblast to the west, Tomsk Oblast to the north, Kemerovo Oblast to the east and Altai Krai to the south. The region's major rivers are the Ob and the Om. The Oblast has around 3,000 lakes, the four largest being Chany, Sartlan, Ubinskoye and Uryum. About one-third of its territory is swampland. It occupies a total area of 178,000 sq km (68,710 sq miles) and measures over 400 km (250 miles) from south to north and over 600 km from west to east. It is divided into 30 administrative districts and 14 cities. At 1 January 1996 the Oblast had an estimated population of 2,749,000 (of whom some 73.9% inhabited urban areas) and a population density of 15.4 per sq km. Around 92% of the Oblast's population is ethnic Russian. Just under one-half of the region's inhabitants live in its administrative centre, Novosibirsk, which had an estimated population of 1,367,700 in 1996. Other major cities are Bertsk (85,000), Iskitim (69,000), Kuibyshev (51,800) and Barabinsk (36,600).

History

The city of Novosibirsk (known as Novonikolayevsk until 1925) was founded in 1893, during the construction of the Trans-Siberian Railway. It became prosperous through its proximity to the Kuznetsk coal basin (Kuzbass). The Oblast, which was officially formed on 28 September 1937, increased in population throughout the Soviet period as it became heavily industrialized, and was a major centre of industrial production during the Second World War.

In October 1993 the Russian President, Boris Yeltsin, dismissed the head of the regional administration, Vitalii Mukha, because of the latter's outspoken criticism of the President. In the same month the Regional Soviet refused to disband itself until new elections were held. In 1994 elections were held to a new representative body, consisting of 48 members. However, the region is considered part of the 'red belt' of Communist support, and that party dominated the new Regional Soviet. It maintained an anti-Yeltsin stance and was constantly in dispute with the regional administration, the head of which was a presidential appointment. In an effort to resolve this power struggle, and in the hope that the incumbent would win, the President permitted the Oblast a gubernatorial election in December 1995. It was the Communist candidate, Mukha, who was returned to his former post by the electorate. Despite his support for the Communists, Mukha failed publicly to endorse any federal presidential candidates prior to the June 1996 elections. He was involved in further disagreements with the federal authorities during the late 1990s.

Economy

In 1995 Novosibirsk Oblast's gross regional product stood at 23,025,200m. roubles, or 8,377,400 roubles per head. Novosibirsk city is a port on the Ob river, and is also the region's principal industrial centre. There are four airports in the region, including Tomalchevo, an international airport.

The Oblast's agriculture employed 13.4% of its working population in 1995 and consists mainly of animal husbandry, fur-animal breeding and the production of grain, vegetables, potatoes and flax. Agriculture generated 11,287,000m. roubles in 1995, compared to a total of 58,445,000m. roubles contributed by the industrial sector. Extraction industries involved the production of coal, petroleum, natural gas, peat, marble, limestone and clay. Manufacturing industry includes ferrous and non-ferrous metallurgy, mechanical engineering, metal working, chemicals, electricity generation, food processing, light manufacturing, timber production and the manufacture of building materials. Industry employed some 24.4% of the region's work-force in 1995. Mechanical engineering and metallurgy accounted for some 80% of the city of Novosibirsk's total industrial output in the early 1990s. In the mid-1990s the region's defence industry was largely converted to civilian use—by 1995 only one-quarter of the output from the industrial sector was for military purposes.

The Oblast's economically active population totalled 1,197,900 in 1995, of whom 26,600 (2.2%) were registered unemployed. The average monthly wage in the region was 340,000 roubles. The 1995 budget showed a deficit of 163,300m. roubles. In February 1996 a 'social contract' was agreed between the region's trade unions, administration and employers' union, according to which average civil-service pay was to be maintained at no less than 85% of the average wage in industry and unemployment was to be kept below 6% of the able-bodied population. Some commentators claimed that this arrangement contributed to the problem of the late payment of wages, with arrears provoking teachers into withdrawing their labour in January 1999, for instance. The regional and federal governments each blamed the other, but one pertinent statistic was that 56% of the regional budget was expended on servicing the state debt and only 23% on wages. Foreign investment in Novosibirsk Oblast totalled US $58.45m. roubles in 1995. At 1 January 1996 there were some 16,900 small businesses registered in the region.

Directory

Head of the Regional Administration (Governor): VITALII PETROVICH MUKHA; Novosibirskaya obl., 630011 Novosibirsk 11, Krasnyi pr. 18; tel. (3832) 23-08-62; fax (3832) 23-57-00.

Chairman of the Regional Soviet: VIKTOR VASILIYEVICH LEONOV.

Permanent Representative of the President of the Russian Federation: IGOR VIKTOROVICH SCHMIDT; tel. (3832) 23-08-13.

Head of the Regional Representation in Moscow: NINA MIKHAILOVNA PIRYAZEVA; tel. (095) 203-27-20.

Head of Novosibirsk City Administration (Mayor): VIKTOR ALEKSANDROVICH TOKOLONSKII; Novosibirskaya obl., 630099 Novosibirsk 99, Krasnyi pr. 34; tel. (3832) 22-49-32; fax (3832) 22-08-58.

Omsk

Omsk Oblast is situated in the south of the Western Siberian Plain on the middle reaches of the Irtysh river. Kazakhstan lies to the south. Other federal subjects which neighbour the Oblast are Tyumen to the north-west and Tomsk and Novosibirsk to the east. Omsk forms part of the Western Siberian Economic Area. Its major rivers are the Irtysh, the Ishim, the Om and the Tara. Much of its territory is marshland and about one-quarter is forested. The total area of Omsk Oblast covers some 139,700 sq km (53,920 sq miles). It measures some 600 km (370 miles) from south to north and 500 km from west to east and is divided into 30 administrative districts and 14 cities. At 1 January 1996 the region had a total population of 2,176,000 and a population density, therefore, of 15.6 per sq km. Of the Oblast's inhabitants, some 1,448,600 (67.4%) lived in urban areas. Its administrative centre is at Omsk, which lies at the confluence of the Ob and Irtysh rivers and had an estimated population of 1,160,200 in 1996. Other major cities are Isilkul (26,800) and Kalachinsk (25,900).

History

The city of Omsk was founded as a fortress in 1716. In 1918 it became the seat of Admiral Aleksandr Kolchak's 'all-Russian Government' (in which he was

'Supreme Ruler'). However, Omsk fell to the Bolsheviks in 1919 and Kolchak 'abdicated' in January 1920. Omsk Oblast was formed on 7 December 1934.

In the 1990s the region was generally supportive of the Communists, although the nationalist, anti-government Liberal Democrats also enjoyed a significant level of popularity. The regional Governor, although a supporter of the federal state President, Boris Yeltsin, was well respected locally and, in December 1995, the federal authorities permitted an election to his post (one year in advance of the gubernatorial elections scheduled for most territories). The incumbent, Leonid Polezhayev, was duly elected. In May 1996 the regional and federal administrations signed a treaty on the delimitation of powers. Legislative elections were held in the Oblast on 22 March 1998, in which left-wing candidates won 30 assembly seats and 14 seats on Omsk city council.

Economy

Omsk Oblast's gross regional product in 1995 amounted to 20,762,400m. roubles, equivalent to 9,352,800 roubles per head. Omsk is one of the highest-ranking cities in Russia in terms of industrial output. The region lies on the Trans-Siberian Railway and is a major transport junction, containing 1,495 km of railway track, 11,418 km of paved roads and 1,252 km of navigable waterways. There are also 580 km of pipeline on its territory, carrying petroleum and petroleum products. There are two airports—a third, international one was under construction in the late 1990s.

The Oblast's soil is the fertile black earth (*chernozem*) characteristic of the region. Its agriculture, which generated a total of 5,307,000m. roubles in 1995 and employed some 20.4% of the work-force, consists mainly of the production of grain, flax, sunflower seeds and vegetables, and animal husbandry and hunting. The region's mineral reserves include clay, peat and lime. There are also deposits of petroleum and natural gas. Industry employed 20.7% of the work-force in 1995. The Oblast's main industries are electricity generation, fuel, chemical and petrochemical production, processing of forestry products, mechanical engineering, petroleum refining, light manufacturing, the manufacture of building materials and food processing. Total industrial production amounted to a value of 15,510,000m. roubles in 1995. The Omsk petroleum refinery is one of Russia's largest and most modern and is part of Sibneft, one of the country's newer vertically integrated petroleum companies. The region's exports primarily comprise chemical, petrochemical and petroleum products. External trade in 1995 amounted to US $1,000m., compared to $355m. in 1981. The Oblast's main trading partners are the People's Republic of China, Cyprus, Germany, Kazakhstan, Spain, Switzerland and the United Kingdom.

The economically active population in 1995 numbered 928,900, of whom 24,100 (2.6%) were registered unemployed. The 1995 budget showed a deficit of 27,600m. roubles. Foreign investment in the region in 1995 totalled US $1.53m. and was growing; by 1997 some 500 companies had been established with foreign participation. At 1 January 1996 there was a total of 9,500 small businesses registered in the region.

Directory

Head of the Regional Administration (Governor): LEONID KONSTANTINOVICH POLEZHAYEV; Omskaya obl., 644002 Omsk, ul. Krasnyi put 1; tel. (3812) 24-14-15; fax (3812) 24-23-72.

Chairman of the Legislative Assembly: VLADIMIR A. VARNAVSKII.

Permanent Representative of the President of the Russian Federation: ALEKSANDR VASILIYEVICH MINZHURENKO; tel. (3812) 23-18-20.

Head of Omsk City Administration (Mayor): VALERII PAVLOVICH ROSHCHUPKIN; Omskaya obl., 644099 Omsk, ul. Gagarina 34; tel. (3812) 24-30-33; fax (3812) 24-49-34.

Orel

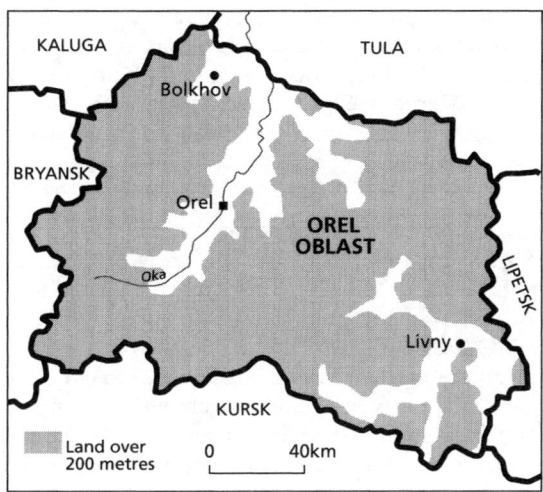

Orel Oblast is situated in the central part of the Eastern European Plain within the Central Russian Highlands. The Oblast forms part of the Central Economic Area. It is surrounded by five other oblasts: Kursk (to the south), Bryansk (west), Kaluga (north-west), Tula (north-east) and Lipetsk (east). The Ukrainian border lies some 180 km (just over 100 miles) to the south-west. The Oblast's major river is the Oka, the source of which is found in the south-west. There are a total of around 2,000 rivers, with a combined length of 9,100 km, although none are navigable. Just over 7% of the Oblast's area is forested. The territory of Orel Oblast covers an area of 24,700 sq km (9,530 sq miles) and is divided, for administrative purposes, into 24 districts and seven cities. At 1 January 1996 the estimated population of the Oblast was 914,000 (the smallest of any oblast in Russia) and the population density was 36.9 per sq km. Some 62.9% of the inhabitants of the region lived in urban areas at this time, while around 96.9% were ethnic Russians. The Oblast's administrative centre is at Orel, which had an estimated 347,600 inhabitants in 1996. Other major cities are Livny (53,400) and Mtsensk (50,900).

History

Orel was founded as a fortress in 1566. In the 1860s it served as a place of exile for Polish insurgents and was later a detention centre for prisoners on their way to exile in Siberia. Orel Oblast was formed on 27 September 1937. In the newly independent, post-Soviet Russia it remained very much part of the political 'red belt'. The Communist candidate defeated the pro-government incumbent in elections for a head of the regional administration in December 1992. The victor was eventually dismissed and the regional legislature dissolved by presidential decree, following their criticism of the federal government during the constitutional crisis of 1993. A 50-seat Regional Duma was elected in March 1994, but remained dominated by the Communists. That party received 45% of the votes cast in the Oblast during the 1995 elections to the State Duma of the Federal Assembly. Despite the loyalty to President Yeltsin shown by the head of the regional administration, Yegor Stroyev (a former cabinet member and the speaker of the upper house of the Russian parliament, the Federation Council), the greatest show of support in the presidential election of 1996 was for Gennadii Zyuganov, the Communist candidate. Orel Oblast was Zyuganov's home region. In the regional legislative elections of March 1998, however, just 11 Communist deputies were elected, compared to the 37 seats won by candidates nominated by initiative groups.

Economy

Orel Oblast's gross regional product amounted to 6,021,200m. roubles in 1995, equivalent to 6,580,500 roubles per head. The principal industrial centres in the region are at Orel, Livny and Mtsensk. Orel city lies on the Moscow–Simferopol (Ukraine) highway and is an important railway junction. There are 593 km of railway track in the Oblast and 3,800 km of paved roads.

Orel Oblast is an important agricultural trade centre. At 1 January 1996 around 21.6% of the economically active population were engaged in agriculture. Agricultural production consists mainly of grain, sugar-beets, sunflower seeds, potatoes, vegetables, hemp and animal husbandry and amounted to a value of 2,113,700m. roubles in 1995. There are some 17.5m. cu m of timber reserves in the Oblast and a major source of iron ore, at Novoyaltinskoye. However, this and reserves of other minerals in the region have generally not been exploited to their full potential. The industrial sector employed around 26.1% of the economically active population in 1996 and generated some 3,559,000m. roubles the previous year. The Oblast's main industries are mechanical engineering, metallurgy, chemicals, light manufacturing and food processing. It produces around one-third of its electrical-energy requirements, the remainder being supplied by neighbouring Oblasts (Tula, Kursk and Lipetsk).

The region's economically active population numbered 403,800 in 1995; some 9,700 of these were registered unemployed, while those in employment earned an average of 380,000 roubles per month. There was a budgetary surplus of 3,600m. roubles in that year, while total foreign investment in Orel Oblast was US $18.28m. At 1 January 1996 there were some 2,800 small businesses in operation.

Directory

Head of the Regional Administration (Governor): YEGOR SEMENOVICH STROYEV; Orlovskaya obl., 302000 Orel, pl. Lenina 1; tel. (08622) 41-63-13; (08622) 41-25-30.

Chairman of the Regional Duma: NIKOLAI ANDREYEVICH VOLODIN.

Permanent Representative of the President of the Russian Federation: ANATOLII ALEKSANDROVICH MERTSALOV; tel. (08622) 4-26-24.

Head of Orel City Administration (Mayor): ALEKSANDR GRIGORIYEVICH KISLYAKOV; Orlovskaya obl., 302000 Orel, Proletarskaya gora 1; tel. (08622) 6-33-12.

Orenburg

Orenburg Oblast is situated in the foothills of the Southern Urals. It forms part of the Urals Economic Area. Orenburg sprawls along the international border with Kazakhstan, which lies to the south and east. Samara Oblast lies to the west, and in the north-west of the territory there is a short border with the Republic of Tatarstan. The Republic of Bashkortostan and Chelyabinsk Oblast encroach on it from the north. Orenburg's major river is the Ural. The region occupies a total area of 124,000 sq km (47,860 sq miles) and is divided into 35 districts and 12 cities. At 1 January 1996 the total population of the Oblast was 2,229,600 and the population density was, therefore, 18.0 per sq km. Its administrative centre is at Orenburg, which had an estimated population of 532,100 in 1996. Other major cities are Orsk (274,600), Novotroitsk (110,500), Buzuluk (87,000) and Buguruslan (54,500).

History

The city of Orenburg originated, as a fortress, in 1743. During the revolutionary period Orenburg was a headquarters of 'White' forces and possession of it was fiercely contested with the Bolsheviks. The city was also a centre of Kazakh (then erroneously known as Kyrgyz) nationalists and was the capital of the Kyrgyz ASSR in 1920–25. The region was then separated from the renamed Kazakh ASSR. Orenburg Oblast was formed on 7 December 1934. Orenburg city was known as Chkalov between 1938 and 1957.

The Communists remained the most popular party into the 1990s, winning 24% of the votes cast in the region at the general election of December 1995. Simultaneous elections to the post of governor, however, were won by the incumbent, Vladimir Yelagin, who was popular in spite of expressing support for the Russian President, Boris Yeltsin. The region was considered strategically important, owing to its proximity to Kazakhstan, a fact which led to the signing, on 30 January 1996, of an agreement between the regional administration and President Yeltsin. The accord defined the powers and areas of remit of the federal and local authorities. In regional legislative elections held at the end of March 1998 the Communists maintained their high level of support, winning 16 out of 47 seats.

Economy

The Oblast's gross regional product was 18,136,100m. roubles in 1995, or 8,147,400 roubles per head. Its principal industrial centres are at Orenburg, Orsk, Novotroisk, Mednogorsk, Buzuluk, Buguruslan and Gai. Owing to the region's high degree of industrialization, and that of its neighbours, Chelyabinsk and Bashkortostan, there is a high level of pollution in the atmosphere. Around 1m. metric tons of harmful substances are emitted annually, including almost 700 tons of nickel and one ton of lead. In addition, the intensive exploitation of petroleum and gas deposits have caused serious damage to the land—around 60% of arable land is eroded or in danger of suffering erosion.

Agriculture in Orenburg Oblast, which employed some 19.7% of the work-force in 1995, consisted mainly of grain, vegetable and sunflower production and animal husbandry. In the mid-1990s the sector contributed an average of about one-sixth of the total agricultural output in the Urals Economic Area. This amounted to a value of 2,921,500 roubles in 1995. The Oblast's major industries are ferrous and non-ferrous metallurgy, mechanical engineering, metal working, natural-gas production, chemicals, light manufacturing, food processing and the production of petroleum, ores, asbestos (the region produces around two-fifths of asbestos produced in Russia) and salt. In 1995 some 21.2% of the working population was engaged in industry, which generated a total of 15,946,000m. roubles.

The economically active population at this time stood at 985,500, some 9,200 (0.9%) of whom (a relatively low proportion) were registered unemployed. The regional average monthly wage was 331,000 roubles. The Oblast's budget for 1995 showed a surplus of 12,900m. roubles. Total foreign investment in the region in 1995 amounted to US $720,000. At 1 January 1996 there were some 14,300 small businesses in operation.

Directory

Head of the Regional Administration (Governor): VLADIMIR VASILIYEVICH YELAGIN; Orenburgskaya obl., 460015 Orenburg, Dom Sovetov; tel. (3532) 77-69-31; fax (3532) 77-38-02.

Chairman of the Legislative Assembly: VALERII NIKOLAYEVICH GRIGOREV.

Permanent Representative of the President of the Russian Federation: VLADISLAV ALEKSANDROVICH SHAPOVALENKO; tel. (3532) 47-34-46.

Head of the Regional Representation in Moscow: ALEKSANDR IVANOVICH GRECHUSHKIN; tel. (095) 203-85-32.

Head of Orenburg City Administration (Mayor): GENNADII PAVLOVICH DONKOVTSEV; Orenburgskaya obl., 460000 Orenburg, ul. Sovetskaya 60; tel. (3532) 77-50-55; fax (3532) 72-11-53.

Penza

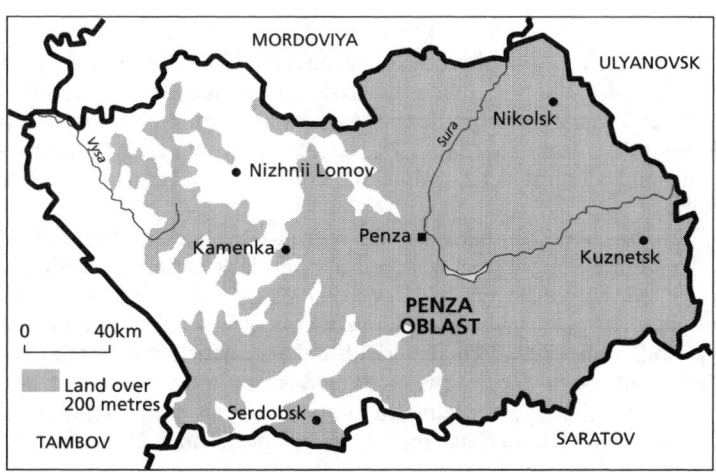

Penza Oblast is situated in the Volga Area Highlands (Privolzhskaya Vozvyshennost), to the south of the Republic of Mordoviya. It forms part of the Volga Economic Area and shares borders with Ulyanovsk Oblast to the east, Saratov Oblast to the south, Tambov Oblast to the south-west and touches Ryazan Oblast in the north-west. Penza's major river is the Sura, a tributary of the River Volga. Its territory covers an area of 43,200 sq km (16,750 sq miles) and is divided into 28 districts and 11 cities. At 1 January 1996 the population of the Oblast was estimated to be 1,562,000 (of whom some 64.2% inhabited urban areas) and its population density, therefore, stood at 36.1 per sq km. Its administrative centre, Penza, had an estimated population of 534,200 in 1996. The region's other major cities are Kuznetsk (99,500), Zarechnyi (63,400), Kamenka (45,900) and Serdobsk (45,500).

History

The city of Penza was founded in 1663 as an outpost on the south-eastern border of the Russian Empire. The region was annexed by Bolshevik forces in late 1917 and remained under the control of the Red Army throughout the period of civil war. Penza Oblast was formed on 4 February 1939. Described as part of the 'red belt' of Communist support in the 1990s, in 1992 the Communist candidate defeated the pro-Yeltsin governor in elections to head the regional administration. The Communists controlled the Legislative Assembly, elected in 1994 (although the federal presidency replaced the governor), and, almost exactly three years after the gubernatorial elections, still gained some 37% of the local vote in the federal general elections of December 1995. Although the presidentially appointed governor, Anatolii Kovlyagin, was a member of the pro-government movement, Our Home is Russia, he failed to give public support to the federal Government's reforms during the mid-1990s, apparently striving for a degree of popularity within the Oblast. Nevertheless, on 12 April 1998 a new governor, Vasilii Bochkarev, was elected. Later in the year, in November, there were public protests at plans to bury chemical weapons in the region (a munitions storage facility near Penza city contained 17% of Russia's chemical-weapons reserves).

Economy

In 1995 Penza's gross regional product was put at 7,475,300m. roubles or 4,779,300 per head. The Oblast's principal industrial centres are at Penza and Kuznetsk. There are around 890 km (550 miles) of railway track in the region, which include lines linking the territory to central and southern Russia as well as the Far East and Ukraine and Central Asia. Some 9,057 km of roads include several major highways.

Around 3m. ha (over 7m. acres) of the region's territory is used for agricultural purposes, some three-quarters of which is fertile black earth (*chernozem*). Agricultural activity, which employed 20.1% of the work-force in 1995, consists mainly of the production of grain, sugar-beets, potatoes, sunflower seeds and hemp. Animal husbandry is also important. Total agricultural production amounted to a value of 2,632,300m. roubles in 1995. The main industries are mechanical engineering, light manufacturing, the processing of timber and agricultural products and the production of building materials. Industry employed some 27.8% of the working population in 1995 and generated 5,086,000m. roubles.

In 1995 the economically active population in Penza Oblast numbered 676,300, of whom around 44,000 were registered unemployed. Those in employment earned an average of 301,000 roubles per month. The 1995 local budget showed a deficit of 81,300m. roubles. Foreign investment in the Oblast in that year amounted to US $1.16m. In 1996 there was a total of 7,100 small businesses in operation.

Directory

Head of the Regional Administration (Governor): VASILII BOCHKAREV; Penzenskaya obl., 440025 Penza, pl. Lenina; tel. (8412) 66-11-94; fax (8412) 55-04-11.

Chairman of the Legislative Assembly: YURII IVANOVICH VECHKASOV.

Permanent Representative of the President of the Russian Federation: IGOR ALEKSANDROVICH KUDINOV; tel. (841) 263-47-35.

Head of the Regional Representation in Moscow: LEV BORISOVICH YERMIN; tel. (095) 202-82-89.

Head of Penza City Administration: ALEKSANDR SERAFIMOVICH KALASHNIKOV; Penzenskaya obl., 440064 Penza, pl. Zhukova 4; tel. (8412) 63-14-63; fax (8412) 6-65-88.

Perm

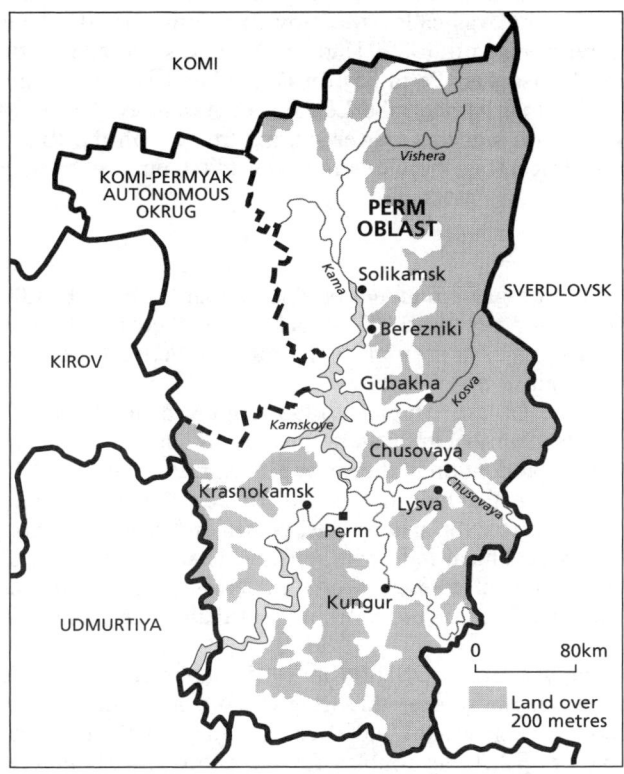

Perm Oblast is situated on the western slopes of the Central and Northern Urals and the eastern edge of the Eastern European Plain. It forms part of the Urals Economic Area. The Komi-Permyak Autonomous Okrug forms the north-western part of the Oblast, providing part of the northern border with the Republic of Komi and most of the western border with Kirov Oblast. The Republic of Udmurtiya also lies to the west, the Republic of Bashkortostan to the south and Sverdlovsk Oblast to the east. Apart from the Kama, its major rivers are the Chusovaya, the Kosva and the Vishera. The Kamsk reservoir lies in the centre of the region. Its territory, including that of the autonomous okrug, occupies an area of 160,600 sq km (61,990 sq miles) and extends some 600 km (370 miles) from south to north and 400 km from west to east. It is divided into 36 districts and 25 cities. Its total population at 1 January 1996 was estimated at 3,009,000, some 76.5% of whom inhabited urban areas, and its population density at that time was 18.7 per sq km. The Oblast's administrative centre is at Perm, which had an estimated population of 1,027,800. Other major cities include Berezniki (182,900), Solikamsk (107,300), Chaikovskii (89,700), Kungur (76,600) and Lysva (76,500).

History

Perm city was founded in 1723, with the construction of a copper foundry. Industrial development was such that by the latter part of the 20th century the city extended for some 80 km along the banks of the Kama. Perm Oblast was formed on 3 October 1938. The city was called Molotov for a time (1940–57) and entry was forbidden to foreigners until 1989. Until 1991 it was the site of the last Soviet camp for political prisoners (Perm-35). In December 1993 there were elections in the region for a new parliament, the Legislative Assembly. On 31 May 1996 the regional administration signed a power-sharing treaty with the Russian President, Boris Yeltsin. In December the Governor, Genadii Igumnov, retained his post in direct elections.

Economy

In 1995 Perm Oblast's gross regional product amounted to 37,081,000m. roubles, or 12,291,500 roubles per head. This included the contribution of the Komi-Permyak AOk. Its major industrial centres are at Perm, Berezniki, Solikamsk, Chusovoi, Krasnokamsk and Chaikovskii.

Agriculture in the Oblast, which in 1995 employed just 9.4% of the working population, consists mainly of grain and vegetable production and animal husbandry. In 1995 agricultural production in the entire Oblast was worth 4,102,100m. roubles, compared to a total in the industrial sector of 26,246,000m. roubles. The main industries are coal, petroleum, natural-gas, potash and salt production, mechanical engineering, electro-technical industries, chemicals and petrochemicals, petroleum refining, the processing of forestry products, ferrous and non-ferrous metallurgy and printing. Some 29.9% of the working population were engaged in industry in 1995.

The economically active population in 1995 numbered 1,363,100. There were 69,800 registered unemployed at this time (5.1%), including in the autonomous okrug. The average wage was 479,000 roubles per month. In 1995 there was a budgetary surplus of 72,200m. roubles for the entire Oblast. Foreign investment in 1995 amounted to US $15.75m. At 1 January 1996 there were some 12,200 small businesses registered in the region.

Directory

Governor: GENNADII VYACHESLAVOVICH IGUMNOV; Permskaya obl., 614006 Perm, ul. Kuibysheva 14; tel. (3422) 34-07-90; fax (3422) 34-89-52.

Chairman of the Legislative Assembly: YURII G. MEDVEDEV; tel. (3422) 30-60-81.

Permanent Representative of the President of the Russian Federation: GENNADII ALEKSANDROVICH ZAITSEV; tel. (3422) 34-33-44.

Head of Perm City Administration: YURII PETROVICH TRUTNEV; Permskaya obl., 614000 Perm, ul. Lenina 23; tel. (3422) 92-40-84; fax (3422) 34-94-91.

Pskov

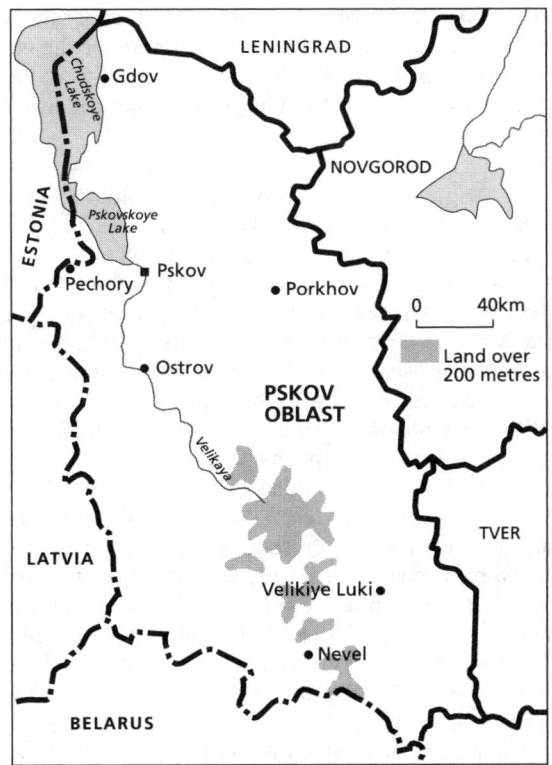

Pskov Oblast is situated on the Eastern European Plain. The Oblast forms part of the North-Western Economic Area. It has international borders with Belarus to the south and Latvia and Estonia to the west. During the first half of the 1990s Estonia questioned Russia's sovereignty of parts of Pskov Oblast. Smolensk Oblast lies to the south-east, Tver and Novgorod Oblasts to the east and Leningrad Oblast to the north-east. Pskov's major river is the Velikaya and around two-fifths of its territory is forested. On its border with Estonia lie the Pskovskoye (Pihkva) and Chudskoye (Peipsi) lakes. Pskov Oblast covers an area of 55,300 sq km (21,350 sq miles) and measures 380 km (236 miles) from south to north and 260 km from west to east. It is divided into 24 districts and 14 cities. The population at 1 January 1997 was estimated at 827,100 and the population density was, therefore, 15.0 per sq km. Around 94.0% of the territory's inhabitants were ethnic Russian and 65.7% inhabited urban areas in 1996. The Oblast's administrative centre is at Pskov, which had an estimated population of 206,200 in 1997. Other major towns are Velikiye Luki (117,200) and Ostrov (29,900).

History

Pskov region was acquired by the Muscovite state in 1510. The Oblast was formally created on 23 August 1944. Some territory to the south of Lake Pskov was transferred from Estonia to Pskov Oblast in 1945, remaining a cause for dispute between the newly independent Estonia and the Russian Federation in the 1990s. In 1995 Estonia formally renounced any territorial claim, but it remained eager to secure Russian acknowledgement of the 1920 Treaty of Tartu (by which Estonia had been awarded the disputed territory), which would render the Soviet occupation illegal. The Oblast was a traditional bastion of support for the extreme nationalist policies of Vladimir Zhirinovskii; gubernatorial elections were held on 21 October 1996, which were won by Yevgenii Mikhailov, a former Liberal Democrat deputy.

Economy

In 1995 Pskov Oblast's gross regional product amounted to 4,618,300m. roubles, equivalent to 5,538,900 roubles per head. The Oblast's principal industrial centres are at Pskov and Velikiye Luki. There are 1,100 km of railway track in the region and 9,900 km of paved roads. There is an international airport at Pskov.

Just over 1m. ha (2.5m. acres) of its territory was used for agriculture, of which about two thirds was arable land. Agricultural activity, which employed 16.6% of the work-force in 1995, consists mainly of animal husbandry and the production of grain, potatoes, vegetables and flax. Total output in the sector amounted to a value of 1,831,500m. roubles in 1995. The region's major industries are the manufacture of building materials, mechanical engineering, light manufacturing, food processing and wood-working. Industry employed some 25.4% of the working population in 1995 and generated 2,329,000m. roubles. By the mid-1990s the branches of industry concerned with food processing and the manufacture of building materials were almost entirely privatized. Foreign involvement was not uncommon. Owing to its three international borders, there are two representatives of foreign consulates, Latvian and Estonian, operating in the region. Its geopolitical situation is also conducive to foreign trade—in the mid-1990s turnover averaged US $180m.–$200m. Its main trading partners are Estonia, Finland and Germany.

At 1 January 1997 there were 23,700 registered unemployed in the Oblast, amounting to 7.2% of the economically active population. In 1995 those in employment earned, on average, 340,000 roubles per month. There was a budgetary deficit of 6,900m. roubles. A 1996–98 federal programme for the socio-economic development of Pskov Oblast invested some 1,500,000m. roubles in the improvement of agriculture in the region. A significant amount was also allocated to new housing projects, as over 51,000 families were homeless at the beginning of 1996. In 1995 foreign investment in the region totalled $792,000. At 1 January 1996 there were some 2,400 small businesses in operation.

Directory

Head of the Regional Administration (Governor): YEVGENII EDUARDOVICH MIKHAILOV; 180001 Pskovskaya obl., Pskov, ul. Nekrasova 23; tel. (81112) 16-22-03; fax (81112) 16-03-90.
Chairman of the Regional Assembly: YURII ANISIMOVICH SHCHMATOV; tel. (81112) 16-24-44.
Permanent Representative of the President of the Russian Federation: DMITRII KONSTANTINOVICH KHRITONENKOV; tel. (81112) 16-26-46.
Head of Pskov City Administration (Mayor): ALEKSANDR VASILIYEVICH PROKOFEV; Pskovskaya obl., 180000 Pskov, ul. Nekrasova 22; tel. (81112) 16-26-67.

Rostov

Rostov Oblast is situated in the south of the Eastern European Plain, in the North Caucasus Economic Area. It lies on the Taganrog Gulf of the Sea of Azov. Krasnodar and Stavropol Krais lie to the south and the Republic of Kalmykiya largely to the east. Volgograd Oblast lies to the north-east and Voronezh Oblast to the north-west. The region has an international border with Ukraine to the west. Its major rivers are the Don and the Severnii Donets. The Volga–Don Canal runs through its territory. Rostov Oblast covers an area of 100,800 sq km (38,910 sq miles) and consists of 43 districts and 23 cities. The region is densely populated, having an estimated 4,425,000 inhabitants at 1 January 1996, giving it a population density of 43.9 per sq km. Some 67.9% of the region's inhabitants resided in urban areas. Its administrative centre is at Rostov-on-Don (Rostov-na-Donu), which had an estimated population of 1,024,500. Other major cities are Taganrog (291,600), Shakhty (229,200), Novocherkassk (189,000), Volgo-Donsk (182,100) and Novoshakhtinsk (105,700).

History

Rostov-on-Don was established as a city in 1796. It became an important grain-exporting centre in the 19th century, and increased in economic importance after the completion of the Volga–Don Canal. Rostov Oblast was formed on 13 September 1937. The region became heavily industrialized after 1946 and, therefore, considerably increased in population.

Although a traditionally Communist region, with that party predominantly represented in the Legislative Assembly, the liberal Yabloko bloc here enjoyed its highest level of support outside the federal cities and Kamchatka. Just as in this last region, the local Yabloko candidates in the federal elections of December 1995 were widely respected and secured 14% of the votes cast in the Oblast (second only to the Communists with 27%), which increasingly gained a reputation as 'an island in the red zone'. The regional Government signed a power-sharing treaty with the federal authorities in June 1996. The Oblast directly elected the incumbent as Governor on 29 September. In regional legislative elections held on 29 March 1998 the Communists gained just nine out of 45 seats to the Legislative Assembly, the majority being won by local business leaders.

Economy

In 1995 Rostov Oblast's gross regional product stood at 26,338,600m. roubles, or 5,949,100 roubles per head. The Oblast's main industrial centres are at Rostov-on-Don, Taganrog, Novocherkassk, Shakhty, Kamensk-Shakhtinskii, Novoshakhtinsk and Volgo-Donsk. Its ports are Rostov-on-Don (connected by shipping routes to 16 countries) and Ust-Donetskii, both of which are river-ports.

The Oblast is one of the major grain-producing regions in Russia, with agricultural land comprising some 85% of its territory. The production of sunflower seeds, coriander, mustard, vegetables and cucurbits (gourds and melons) is also important, as are viniculture and horticulture. The sector employed some 16.5% of the working population in 1995. Total agricultural output amounted to a value of 6,877,900m. roubles in that year. The Oblast is situated in the eastern Donbass coal-mining region and contains some 6,500m. metric tons of coal, as well as significant deposits of anthracite. It is also rich in natural gas, reserves of which are estimated at 54,000m. cu m. Its other principal industry is mechanical engineering: Rostov-on-Don contained some 50 machine-building plants; in the early 1990s the industrial association, Rostselmash, produced 70% of all grain combines in Russia and Krasnyi Aksai manufactured 50% of all tractor-mounted cultivators; in Novocherkassk, Krasnyi Kotelshchii produced 70% of Russia's electric locomotives; and 60% of the country's steam boilers were made in Taganrog. Food processing, light manufacturing, chemicals and ferrous and non-ferrous metallurgy are also major economic activities. In 1995 some 27.8% of the Oblast's working population were employed in industry, while industrial production was worth 17,264,000m. roubles.

In 1995 the economically active population numbered 1,904,100, of whom some 25,900 (1.4%) were unemployed. Those in employment earned an average monthly wage of 333,000 roubles per month. The 1995 budget showed a surplus of 13,700m. roubles. Total foreign investment in the region amounted to US $99,000 in that year. At 1 January 1996 there were some 21,400 small businesses operating in the Oblast.

Directory

Head of the Regional Administration (Governor): VLADIMIR FEDOROVICH CHUB; Rostovskaya obl., 344050 Rostov-on-Don, ul. Sotsialisticheskaya 112; tel. (8632) 66-78-10; fax (8632) 65-67-73.

Chairman of the Regional Government: VIKTOR NIKOLAYEVICH ANPILOGOV; tel. (8632) 66-61-44.

Chairman of the Legislative Assembly: ALEKSANDR VASILIYEVICH POPOV; tel. (8632) 65-04-26.

Permanent Representative of the President of the Russian Federation: VIKTOR VASILIYEVICH USACHEV; tel. (8632) 66-37-59.

Head of Rostov-on-Don City Administration (Mayor): MIKHAIL ANATOLIYEVICH CHERNYSHEV; Rostovskaya obl., 344007 Rostov-on-Don, ul. Bolshaya Sadovaya 47; tel. (8632) 66-62-75; fax (8632) 66-62-62.

Ryazan

Ryazan Oblast is situated in the central part of the Eastern European Plain and forms part of the Central Economic Area. It lies some 192 km (just under 120 miles) south-east of Moscow. The other neighbouring regions are Vladimir (to the north), Nizhnii Novgorod (north-east), the Republic of Mordoviya (east), Penza (south-east), Tambov and Lipetsk (south), and Tula (west). There are some 2,800 lakes in the region (the largest being the Velikoye and the Dubovoye) and its major rivers are the Oka and its tributaries. The Oka extends 489 km (304 miles) between the borders with Moscow and Vladimir Oblasts. Its catchment area amounts to over 95% of the region's territory, which occupies an area of 39,600 sq km (15,290 sq miles) and is divided into 25 administrative districts and 12 cities. At 1 January 1996 its population was estimated at 1,325,000 (of whom some 68.0% inhabited urban areas) and its population density, therefore, was 33.5 per sq km. About 40% of the region's population inhabited its administrative centre, Ryazan, which had an estimated population of 535,600 in 1996. Other major cities are Kasimov (37,900), Sasovo (34,600), Skopin (28,700) and Ryazhsk (27,000).

History

Ryazan city was an early Orthodox Christian bishopric. The Oblast was formed on 26 September 1937. In the 1990s it was described as part of the 'red belt' of Communist support across the Russian heartland. With 31% of the Oblast's participating electorate voting Communist in the general election of December 1995, this party was also able to dominate the Regional Duma. There were elections to this at the end of 1993 and in April 1996. The region co-operated in a federal experiment with jury trials (introduced in 1993), although the Governor petitioned the central authorities in November 1998 to end the system.

Economy

In 1995 Ryazan Oblast's gross regional product amounted to 10,428,200m. roubles, or 7,847,300 roubles per head. The Oblast's industrial centres are at Ryazan, Skopin, Kasimov and Sasovo.

Its warm, moist climate is conducive to agriculture, which consists mainly of grain and vegetable production, horticulture and animal husbandry, and employed some 17.0% of the work-force in 1995. Total agricultural production amounted to a value of 2,827,800m. roubles in that year. There are 162.8m. cu m of timber reserves in the region and substantial reserves of brown coal and peat, estimated at around 302m. metric tons and 222m. metric tons, respectively. Deposits of peat are concentrated in the north, the east and the south-west of the region. The Oblast's main industries are mechanical engineering, petroleum processing, chemicals, the production of building materials, light manufacturing and food processing. In 1995 some 29.5% of the working population was engaged in industry, which generated a total of 9,699,000m. roubles.

The economically active population numbered 578,000 at this time. Some 11,500 of these (2.0%) were registered unemployed, while those in employment earned, on average, 335,000 roubles per month. The 1995 budget showed a deficit of 59,700m. roubles. Foreign investment in the region totalled US $1.36m. roubles in 1995, while at 1 January 1996 there were some 5,800 small businesses registered on its territory.

Directory

Head of the Regional Administration (Governor): VYACHESLAV NIKOLAYEVICH LYUBIMOV; Ryazanskaya obl., 390000 Ryazan, ul. Astrakhanskaya 30; tel. (0912) 77-40-32; fax (0912) 44-25-68.

Chairman of the Regional Duma: VLADIMIR NIKOLAYEVICH FEDOTKIN.

Permanent Representative of the President of the Russian Federation: GENNADI KONSTANTINOVICH MERKULOV; tel. (0912) 77-21-47.

Head of Ryazan City Administration (Mayor): PAVEL DMITRIYEVICH MAMARTOV; Ryazanskaya obl., ul. Radishcheva 28; tel. (0912) 77-34-85; fax (0912) 93-05-70.

Sakhalin

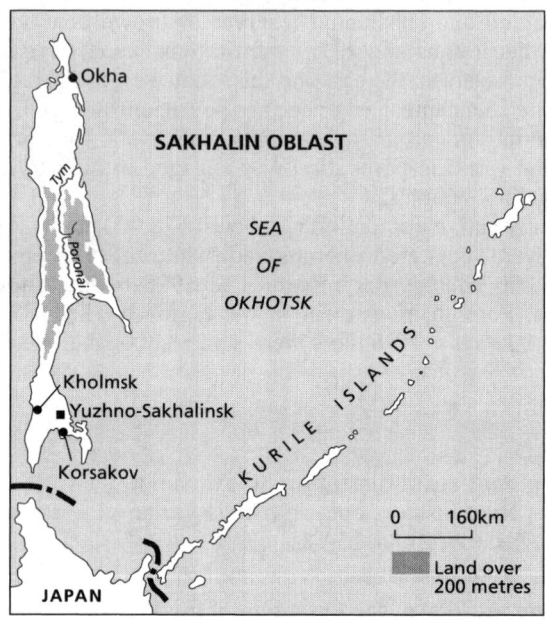

Sakhalin Oblast comprises the island of Sakhalin and the Kurile Islands in the Pacific Ocean. It forms part of the Far Eastern Economic Area. The island of Sakhalin lies off the coast of Khabarovsk Krai, separated from the mainland by the Tatar Strait. Eastward lie the Kurile (Kuril) Islands (annexed by the USSR in 1945, but claimed by Japan), which are an archipelago of some 56 islands extending from the Kamchatka Peninsula in the north-east, to Hokkaido Island (Japan) in the south-west. Sakhalin Island is 942 km (just over 580 miles) in length and contains two parallel mountain ranges running north to south and separated by a central valley. The highest peaks on the island, both belonging to the eastern range of mountains, are Lopatin (1,609 m or 5,281 feet) and Nevelskogo (1,397 m). The north-west coast of the island is marshland, and much of its area is forested. The Kurile Islands are actively volcanic and contain many hot springs. There are some 60,000 rivers on Sakhalin Island, the major ones being the Poronai (350 km in length), the Tym (330 km), the Viakhtu (131 km) and the Lyutoga (130 km), all of which are frozen during the winter months, December–April/May. The Kurile Islands contain around 4,000 rivers and streams and the largest waterfall in the Russian Federation, Ilya Muromets. Sakhalin Oblast covers a total area of 87,100 sq km (33,620 sq miles) and is divided into 17 districts and 18 cities. The estimated total population at 1 January 1996 was 648,000, the region's population density being 7.4 per sq km. Some 85.8% of the region's total population at that time was found to reside in urban areas. The Oblast's administrative centre is at Yuzhno-Sakhalinsk, which had an estimated population of 181,000. Other major cities are Kholmsk (144,900), Korsakov (42,300) and Okha (31,700). All these settlements are on Sakhalin Island.

History

Sakhalin Island was traditionally known as a place of exile for political opponents to the tsars. It was originally inhabited by the indigenous Gilyak people; Russians first reached the island in 1644, although the region was assumed to be a peninsula until the early 19th century. The island was conquered by the Japanese at the end of the 18th century, but Russia established a military base at Korsakov in 1853. Joint control of the island followed until 1875, when it was granted to Russia in exchange for the Kurile Islands. Karafuto, the southern part of the island, was won by Japan during the Russo-Japanese War (1904–05), but the entire island was ceded to the USSR in 1945. The Kurile Islands, which were discovered for Europeans by the Dutch navigator, Martin de Vries, in 1634, were divided between Japan and Russia in the 18th century and ruled jointly until 1875. Russia occupied the islands in 1945 and assumed full control in 1947. The southern Kuriles remained disputed between Japan and the newly independent Russia. Sakhalin Oblast had been formed on 20 October 1932 as part of Khabarovsk Krai. It became a separate administrative unit in 1947, when the island was united with the Kuriles.

On 16 October 1993 the Regional Soviet in Sakhalin Oblast was disbanded by the head of the regional administration. A Regional Duma was elected in its place. In May 1995 a major earthquake, one of the largest ever to occur in Russia, destroyed the town of Neftegorsk in the north of the region, and claimed an estimated 2,000 lives. In May 1996 the Russian President, Boris Yeltsin, signed a treaty with the regional Government on the delimitation of powers between the Federation and the federal territory. A gubernatorial election was held in the Oblast on 21 October 1996. In 1998 Russia and Japan agreed to attempt to settle their territorial dispute by 2000, although the regional administration objected to suggestions that the southern Kuriles might become a separate unit under federal jurisdiction. In December the Oblast authorities agreed to establish a commission to co-ordinate friendly and economic relations with the Japanese province of Hokkaido. In January 1999 President Yeltsin urged the rapid adoption of legislation establishing a special economic zone in the southern Kuriles.

Economy

In 1995 Sakhalin Oblast's gross regional product amounted to 6,929,000m. roubles, or 10,490,500 roubles per head. The Oblast's principal industrial centres are at Yuzhno-Sakhalinsk, Kholmsk, Okha (the administrative centre of the petroleum-producing region), Nevelsk, Dolinsk, Korsakov, Uglegorsk and Poronaisk. Its ports are Kholmsk (from where the Kholmsk-Vanino ferry connects Sakhalin Island with the mainland), Korsakov and Aleksandrov-Sakhalinskii. All these settlements are on the island of Sakhalin. There are flights to Moscow, Khabarovsk, Vladivostok, Petropavlovsk-Kamchatskii and Novosibirsk and international services to the Republic of Korea (South Korea) and Japan.

Agriculture in the region is minimal, owing to its unfavourable climatic conditions—agricultural land occupies only 130,000 ha (321,000 acres), or 1% of its territory. It employed just 5.6% of its working population. Agricultural activity consists mainly of potato and vegetable production, animal husbandry and fur farming. Total agricultural production amounted to a value of 923,300m. roubles in 1995. Annual catches of fish and other marine life amount to around 350,000 metric tons. Fishing and fish processing is the major traditional industry, accounting for just under one-third of industrial production, while timber and the processing of forestry products is likewise important. Manufacturing industry is minimal. The entire industrial sector employed some 28.6% of the region's work-force and generated 4,748,000m. roubles in 1995. There is some extraction of coal and, increasingly, petroleum and natural gas in the north of Sakhalin Island. Some petroleum is piped for refining to a plant in Komsomolsk-on-Amur (Komsomolsk-na-Amure), although from 1994 the territory had its own refinery, with a capacity of some 200,000 metric tons per year. Coal is the territory's primary source of energy. At 1 January 1997 there were nine shaft mines and four open-cast mines in operation, although in the mid-1990s coal production was falling annually. The further development of Sakhalin's rich hydrocarbons reserves, which, it was thought, could supply a large part of Asia's fuel needs, was the subject of negotiations between a number of Russian and foreign companies in the mid-1990s. By 1998 three major consortia had been formed. Sakhalin-1, a project to produce petroleum on the continental shelf of Sakhalin Island, comprised Rosneft (of which Sakhalin-morneftegas is a local subsidiary and which had a 40% stake), Exxon (of the USA) and Sodeco (of Japan), both of which had a 30% stake. Sakhalin-2, two fields containing an estimated 1,000m. barrels of petroleum and 408,000m. cu m of natural gas, was run by Sakhalin Energy Investment, comprising Mitsui and Mitsubishi (of Japan), Marathon (of the USA) and the Anglo-Dutch company, Shell. Sakhalin-3, backed by Mobil and Texaco (of the USA), was seeking to develop what was potentially the largest field on the Sakhalin shelf, containing an estimated 320m. metric tons of recoverable reserves. It was hoped that the proceeds from these projects would help to alleviate the high level of poverty in the region. Indeed, in July 1998 the then federal premier, Sergei Kiriyenko, signed a resolution extending a federal programme on social and economic development of the Oblast, to be financed by federal proceeds from Sakhalin-1 and Sakhalin-2, until 2005.

In 1995 the Oblast's economically active population totalled 290,100, of whom 18,000 (6.2%) were unemployed. The average monthly wage in the region amounted to 672,000 roubles. The 1995 budget showed a surplus of 6,700m. roubles. Total foreign investment in the region was equivalent to US $48.17m. in 1995 and increased thereafter. At 1 January 1996 there was a total of 4,100 small businesses.

Directory

Governor: IGOR PAVLOVICH FARKHUTDINOV; Sakhalinskaya obl., 693011 Yuzhno-Sakhalinsk, Kommunisticheskii pr. 39; tel. (42422) 3-14-02; fax (42422) 3-60-81.

Chairman of the Regional Duma: BORIS NIKITOVICH TRETYAK.

Permanent Representative of the President of the Russian Federation: VIKTOR NIKOLAYEVICH KAMORNIK; tel. (42422) 3-50-70.

Head of Yuzhno-Sakhalinsk City Administration (Mayor): FEDOR ILYCH SIDORENKO; Sakhalinskaya obl., Yuzhno-Sakhalinsk, ul. Lenina 173; tel. (42422) 2-25-11; fax (42422) 3-00-06.

Samara

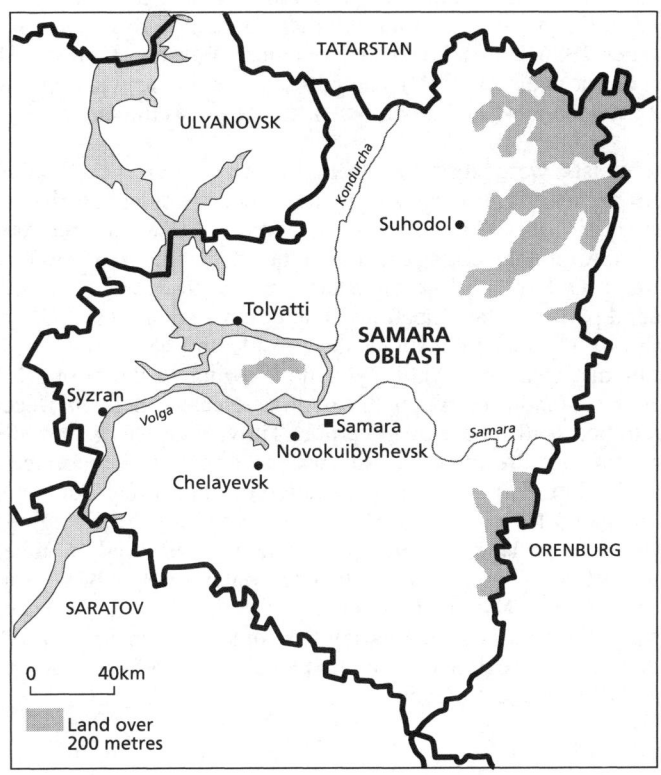

Samara Oblast (known as Kuibyshev between 1935 and 1991) is situated in the south-east of the Eastern European Plain on the middle reaches of the Volga river. It forms part of the Volga Economic Area. Its southernmost tip lies on the border with Kazakhstan. Saratov lies to the south-west, Ulyanovsk to the west, Tatarstan to the north and Orenburg to the east. The Volga snakes through the west of the territory. The Oblast's other major rivers are the Samara, the Sok, the Kunel, the Bolshoi Igruz and the Kondurcha. The region occupies an area of 53,600 sq km (20,690 sq miles). It is divided into 27 districts and 10 cities. Owing to its proximity to the Kazakh desert, the southernmost part of the Oblast is prone to drought. The region is densely populated, with an estimated population of 3,312,000 at 1 January 1996 (of whom 80.6% inhabited urban areas) and a population density, therefore, of 61.8 per sq km. The majority of the population, 83.4%, was ethnic Russian. Mordovians comprised 3.6%, as did both Tatars and Chuvashs, and 2.5% were Ukrainians. The administrative centre is at Samara (formerly Kuibyshev), which had an estimated 1,174,700 inhabitants in 1996. The region's other major towns are Tolyatti (709,500), Syzran (178,400), Novokuibyshevsk (115,900) and Chelayevsk.

TERRITORIAL SURVEYS

History

Samara city was founded in 1586 as a fortress. It increased in prosperity after the construction of the railways in the late 19th century. Samara Oblast was founded on 14 May 1928, as the Middle Volga (Sredne-Volzhskaya) Oblast. In 1929 it was upgraded to the status of a krai, which was renamed Kuibyshev Krai in 1935. On 5 December 1936 Kuibyshev Krai became Kuibyshev Oblast. (The territory assumed its current name in 1991.) The city became the headquarters of the Soviet Government between 1941 and 1943, when Moscow was threatened by the German invasion.

The Communists were still the strongest party after the dissolution of the Soviet system in 1991. The local legislature defied President Boris Yeltsin in the constitutional crisis of 1993 and was dissolved in October and replaced by a Regional Duma. Although geographically on the edge of the 'red belt' of Communist strength, Samara Oblast only provided the party with 22% of the local votes in the 1995 federal parliamentary elections. There was also more support in the region for the candidacy of Boris Yeltsin in the presidential election of mid-1996 than for his Communist rival, Gennadii Zyuganov, owing to the strong leadership of the governor, Konstantin Titov. In the popular election held in December 1996 Titov was returned to the post of governor. Titov, who was reportedly offered a senior cabinet post by President Yeltsin, was an ambitious economic reformer. In January 1998 he introduced a policy to defer the tax arrears of companies that managed to maintain tax payments. He also strongly urged the Regional Duma to approve legislation on land ownership, which was achieved in June. Although personally respected in Samara, Titov had to contend not only with a suspicious regional assembly, but also with a mayor of Samara from Aleksandr Lebed's nationalist party, the Congress of Russian Communities. On 13 July 1997, Georgii Limanskii, the party's regional head, had decisively defeated the government-approved candidate in local elections.

Economy

Economic growth in Samara Oblast during 1997 was 6%, in real terms, compared to around 1% in Russia as a whole. In 1995 its gross regional product amounted to 45,031,600m. roubles, or 13,611,700 roubles per head. The Oblast's major industrial centres are at Samara, Tolyatti, Syzran and Novokuibyshevsk.

Agriculture in the Oblast, which employed just 9.0% of the working population in 1995, consists mainly of animal husbandry and the production of grain, sugar-beets and sunflower seeds. Total agricultural production in 1995 was worth 4,221,900m. roubles. There are some reserves of petroleum and natural gas in the region. Its main industries are petroleum production and refining, food processing, mechanical engineering, metal working, petrochemicals and the manufacture of building materials. The Oblast's principal company is AvtoVAZ, manufacturer of the Lada automobile, which accounts for around 43% of industrial output in the region. In 1995 some 32.5% of the region's work-force was engaged in industry, which generated 40,653,000m. roubles.

In 1995 the economically active population numbered 1,555,400, of whom some 33,200 (2.1%) were unemployed. Those in employment earned an average wage of 476,000 roubles per month. This continued to rise above the national average into the late 1990s. In 1998 the rate of spending per head in the Oblast was one of the highest in the Federation. The 1995 budget showed a deficit of 22,000m. roubles, but regional government finances improved later in the decade—in December 1998 Samara was one of the three regions with the best record on the timely payment of wages (most Russian regions owed significant arrears). In 1995 total foreign investment in the region amounted to US $69.69m. By August 1998 some 300 foreign companies, including some of the world's largest, such as Coca-Cola and General Motors of the USA and Nestlé of Switzerland, had invested in the region, attracted by its technologically advanced industrial base and well-educated, urbanized labour force. At 1 January 1996 there were some 17,400 small businesses in operation.

Directory

Governor: KONSTANTIN A. TITOV; Samarskaya obl., 443006 Samara, ul. Molodogvardeiskaya 210; tel. (8462) 32-22-68; fax (8462) 32-13-40.

Chairman of the Regional Duma: LEON IOSIFOVICH KOVALSKII; tel. (8462) 32-19-44.

Permanent Representative of the President of the Russian Federation: YURII MIKHAILOVICH BORODULIN; tel. (8462) 32-22-06.

Head of Samara City Administration (Mayor): GEORGII SERGEYEVICH LIMANSKII; Samarskaya obl., 443010 Samara, ul. Kuibysheva 135; tel. (8462) 32-20-68; fax (8462) 33-67-41.

Saratov

Saratov Oblast is situated in the south-east of the Eastern European Plain. It forms part of the Volga Economic Area. On the border with Kazakhstan (to the south-east), the federal territories adjacent to Saratov are Volgograd (south), Voronezh and Tambov (west), and Penza, Ulyanovsk and Samara (north). Its main river is the Volga. The west of the Oblast (beyond the left bank of the Volga) is mountainous, the east low lying. The region's territory occupies an area of 100,200 sq km (38,680 sq miles). It comprises 38 districts and 17 cities. At 1 January 1996 it had a total of 2,739,000 inhabitants (of whom some 73.6% inhabited urban areas) and a population density of 27.3 per sq km. Its administrative centre is at Saratov, a major river-port on the Volga, with an estimated population of 891,500 in 1996. Other major cities were Balakovo (206,300), Engels (187,400), Balashov (98,400), Volsk (64,600) and Rtishchevo (45,100).

History

Saratov city was founded in 1590 as a fortress city, to protect against nomad raids on the Volga trade route. Strategically placed on the Trans-Siberian Railway, it was seized by Bolshevik forces in late 1917 and remained under Communist control, despite attacks by the 'White' forces under Admiral Aleksandr Kolchak during 1918 and 1919. The Oblast was formed on 10 January 1934, but on 5 December 1936 was upgraded to the status of a krai for a time. The region became heavily industrialized in the Soviet period, before the Second World War.

Saratov remained an important centre for the military and, indeed, of Communist support, into the 1990s. However, in September Dmitrii Ayatskov, a presidential appointment, retained his post heading the regional administration, having secured 81.35% of the popular vote. As Governor, Ayatskov carried out extensive reform to the region's agro-industrial sector, which culminated, in November 1997, in the passing in the Oblast of the first law in Russia to provide for the purchase and sale of agricultural land. The law greatly diminished the power base of Communists and nationalists in the region and by April 1998 land sales had already generated 3m. new roubles (i.e. 3,000m. pre-January 1998 roubles) for the regional economy. In that month Ayatskov announced his intention of creating a new party with a genuine power base at the regional level, following a deterioration in relations with Our Home is Russia. Later in the year he urged the replacement of Viktor Chernomyrdin, a former federal premier, as leader of Our Home is Russia.

Economy

Saratov Oblast's gross regional product in 1995 totalled 20,425,600m. roubles, equivalent to 7,456,200 roubles per head. The region's major industrial centres are at Saratov, Engels and Balakovo. The Oblast was the major Soviet/Russian arsenal for chemical weapons, provoking some local concern. In January 1996 it was announced that chemical weapons stored near the village of Gornyi would be destroyed, in accordance with international agreements.

Its agriculture, which employed some 20.7% of the working population in 1995, consists primarily of animal husbandry and the production of grain (the Oblast is one of Russia's major producers of wheat), sunflower seeds and sugar-beets. Total agricultural production in 1995 amounted to a value of 4,622,600m. roubles. Its main industries are mechanical engineering, petroleum refining, chemicals, the manufacture of building materials, wood-working, light manufacturing, food processing and the production of petroleum and natural gas. The region produces more than 30% of the cement and 20% of the mineral fertilizer produced in the Volga Economic Area. Total industrial production was worth 11,124,000m. roubles in 1995, while some 23.7% of the work-force was engaged in industry at that time. Foreign-trade turnover in 1996 amounted to around US $525m. Petroleum and chemical products accounted for two-thirds of exports in that year.

In 1995 the region's economically active population numbered 1,209,900; some 45,700 (3.8%) of these were registered unemployed, while those in employment earned an average wage of 326,000 roubles per month. Foreign investment in the Oblast amounted to US $18.04. In 1997 there were around 100 joint enterprises registered in the region, participated in by eight different countries. At 1 January 1996 there were some 12,300 small businesses in operation in the region.

Directory

Head of the Regional Administration (Governor): DMITRII FEDOROVICH AYATSKOV; Saratovskaya obl., 410600 Saratov, ul. Moskovskaya 72; tel. (8452) 24-50-86; fax (8452) 24-20-89.

Chairman of the Regional Duma: ALEKSANDR PETROVICH KHARITONOV.

Permanent Representative of the President of the Russian Federation: PETR PETROVICH KAMSHILOV; tel. (8452) 24-10-25; fax (8452) 24-49-91.

Head of Saratov City Administration (Mayor): YURII NIKOLAYEVICH ARSENENKO; Saratovskaya obl., 410600 Saratov, ul. Pervomaiskaya 78; tel. (8452) 24-04-77; fax (8452) 24-84-44.

Smolensk

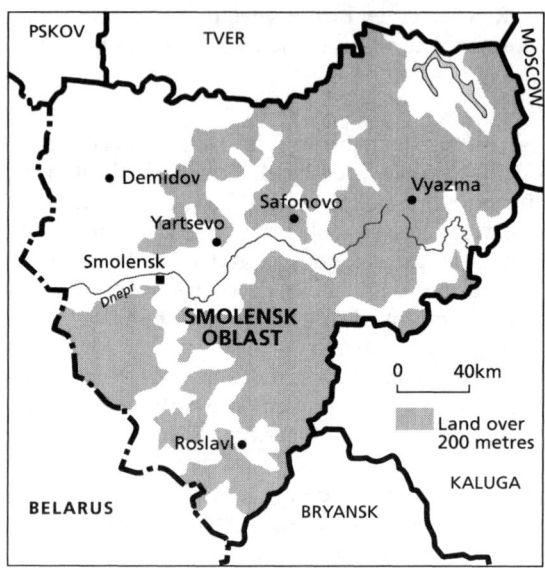

Smolensk Oblast is situated in the central part of the Eastern European Plain on the upper reaches of the Dnepr (Dnieper). It forms part of the Central Economic Area. The former Soviet state of Belarus lies to the south-west, while neighbouring Russian territories are Pskov and Tver Oblasts to the north, Moscow in the north-east and Kaluga and Bryansk to the south-east. The Oblast covers an area of 49,800 sq km (19,220 sq miles) and extends for some 280 km (175 miles) from south to north and 250 km from west to east. It is divided into 25 districts and 15 cities. The estimated population was 1,172,000 at 1 January 1996 and the population density 23.5 per sq km. Some 69.7% of the region's inhabitants lived in urban areas at this time. Its administrative centre is at Smolensk, a river-port on the Dnepr with an estimated 355,700 inhabitants in 1996. The Oblast's other major cities are Roslavl (61,100), Vyazma (60,500), Yartsevo (57,900) and Safonovo (55,700).

History

Smolensk city was first documented in 863, as the chief settlement of the Krivichi, a Slavic tribe. It became an Orthodox Christian bishopric in 1128. It achieved prosperity during the 14th and 15th centuries as it was situated on one of the Hanseatic trade routes. Smolensk was the site of a major battle in 1812, between the Russian imperial army and the forces of Emperor Napoleon I of France, who subsequently went on to occupy the city of Moscow for a time. It was seized by the Bolsheviks in late 1917 and remained under their control for the duration of the civil war. Smolensk Oblast was formed on 27 September 1937.

The Communist establishment remained in control of the region in the early years of Russia's restored independence. The party won the most seats in the Regional Duma elected in 1994 and, in December 1995, secured 32% of the regional poll in the elections to the Russian State Duma. Likewise, in a simultaneous gubernatorial election, the Communist candidate won, although the federal Government had only sanctioned this contest because its appointed chief executive was respected locally. In the gubernatorial election of April–May 1998, after a second round of voting, the Communist candidate and Mayor of Smolensk, Aleksandr Prokhorov, defeated the incumbent.

Economy

Smolensk Oblast's gross regional product amounted to 7,848,200m. roubles in 1995, or 6,692,400 roubles per head. Its major industrial centres are at Smolensk, Roslavl, Safonovo, Vyazma, Yartsevo, Gagarin and Verkhnedneprovskii. At 1 January 1997 there were 8,900 km of roads in the Oblast, of which all but 100 km were paved.

Agriculture in Smolensk Oblast, which employed some 17.0% of the work-force in 1995, mainly consists of animal husbandry and the production of grain, sugar-beets and sunflower seeds. Total agricultural output in 1995 was worth 2,420,300m. roubles. Its main industries are textiles, mechanical engineering, chemicals, light manufacturing, food processing, electrical-energy production and the production of coal and peat. In 1995 some 28.2% of the work-force was engaged in industry. Total industrial production in that year amounted to a value of 6,288,000m. roubles.

The region's economically active population numbered 474,500, of whom some 4,700 were registered unemployed. The average wage in the Oblast at that time stood at 366,000 roubles per month. The 1995 budget showed a deficit of 2,300m. roubles. Total foreign investment in the region in 1995 amounted to US $5.73m. At 1 January 1996 there were some 3,400 small businesses in operation.

Directory

Head of the Regional Administration (Governor): ALEKSANDR DMITRIYEVICH PROKHOROV (elected May 1998); Smolenskaya obl., 214008 Smolensk, ul. Lenina 1; tel. (08100) 3-66-11; fax (08100) 3-68-51.

Chairman of the Regional Duma: VLADIMIR IVANOVICH ANISIMOV.

Permanent Representative of the President of the Russian Federation: VIKTOR NIKOLAYEVICH TIMOSHENKOV; tel. (08100) 3-65-23.

Head of Smolensk City Administration: (vacant); Smolenskaya obl., 214000 Smolensk, ul. Oktyabrskaya revolyutsii 1–2; tel. and fax (08100) 3-11-81.

Sverdlovsk

Sverdlovsk Oblast is situated on the eastern, and partly on the western, slopes of the Central and Northern Urals and in the Western Siberian Plain. It forms part of the Urals Economic Area. Tyumen Oblast lies to the east (with its constituent district of the Khanty-Mansii AOk to the north-west), there is a short border with the Republic of Komi in the north-west and Perm Oblast lies to the west. To the south are Bashkortostan, Chelyabinsk and Kurgan. The region's major rivers are those of the Ob and Kama basins. The west of the region is mountainous, while much of the eastern part is taiga (forested marshland). The territory of the Oblast covers an area of 194,800 sq km (75,190 sq miles) and is divided into 30 districts and 47 cities. At 1 January 1996 the estimated population totalled 4,686,000 and the population density was 24.1 per sq km. As many as 87.6% of the region's inhabitants lived in urban areas. The Oblast's administrative centre is at Yekaterinburg (formerly Sverdlovsk), which had an estimated population of 1,277,800 in 1996. Other major cities are Nizhnii Tagil (407,300), Kamensk-Uralskii (195,000), Pervouralsk (137,100), Serov (100,400) and Asbest (83,200).

History

Yekaterinburg city was founded in 1821 as a military stronghold and trading centre. Like the Oblast (formed on 17 January 1934) it was renamed Sverdlovsk during the Soviet period but, unlike the Oblast, reverted to the name of Yekaterinburg in 1990. The city was famed as being where the last Tsar, Nicholas II, and his family were killed in 1918. The region became a major industrial centre after the Second World War.

Following the disintegration of the USSR, Sverdlovsk Oblast was the most forthright in demanding regional rights from the centre. On 29 September 1993 the Sverdlovsk Regional Soviet adopted a draft constitution for a 'Ural Republic'. The 'Republic' was officially proclaimed on 27 October by the Regional Soviet and the head of the regional administration. The Ural Republic was dissolved by presidential decree, however, and Eduard Rossel, the head of the regional administration, was dismissed on 9 November. In 1994 elections were held to a Regional Duma. In August 1995 Rossel was reinstated as Governor, having won the direct election to head the regional administration. His popularity enabled him to establish an independent Transformation of the Urals Movement that completely eclipsed support for the national parties in the region, a fact demonstrated in the federal elections of December 1995.

As Governor, Rossel continued to strive for more autonomy for the Oblast, one of the most powerful and potentially most prosperous regions in the Federation. On 12 January 1996 Rossel signed an agreement on the division of powers and spheres of competence between federal and regional institutions. This accord was the first of its kind to be signed with a federal territory that did not have republican status. On 7 April elections were held to the Regional Duma. Less than one-third of the electorate participated, but some 35% voted for Rossel's non-party Transformation bloc. Subsequently, however, the Governor's popularity began to decline: in April 1998 there were student protests in Yekaterinburg against delayed payment of grants and government plans to introduce tuition fees for higher education in the region. In the same month the Transformation bloc won just 9.3% of the votes to the regional legislature and claimed just two seats in the lower house, in which they had previously held a majority.

Economy

Sverdlovsk Oblast is a leading territory of the Russian Federation in terms of industry, producing around 5% of the country's total industrial output during the mid-1990s. The concentration of industry in the Oblast is around four times the average for a federal unit. In 1995 the territory's gross regional product amounted to 58,097,900m. roubles, equivalent to 12,376,000 roubles per head. Its most important industrial centres are at Yekaterinburg, Nizhnii Tagil, Pervouralsk, Krasnouralsk, Serov, Alapayevsk and Kamensk-Uralskii. There is an international airport, Koltsovo.

The Oblast's agriculture, which employed just 6.1% of its work-force in 1995, consists of grain production and animal husbandry. Total agricultural output in 1995 was worth 5,571,800m. roubles. There is some extraction of gold and platinum in the Oblast. Its main industries are ferrous and non-ferrous metallurgy, mechanical engineering (the most important plant being the Yekaterinburg-based Uralmash), chemicals, the processing of forestry and agricultural products, light manufacturing and the production of copper and other ores, bauxite, asbestos, petroleum, peat and coal. Industry employed some 36.0% of the working population in 1995 and generated as much as 48,265,000m. roubles. The service sector is also of increasing significance in the territorial economy: in 1996 there were 98 insurance companies, three stock exchanges and 42 commercial banks in the Oblast.

TERRITORIAL SURVEYS

Sverdlovsk's economically active population numbered 2,034,400 in 1995, of whom some 77,300 were registered unemployed. The average monthly wage in the region at that time was 503,000 roubles. The 1995 budget showed a deficit of 130,100m. roubles. Total foreign investment in that year was US $8.39m. At 1 January 1996 there were 26,900 small businesses registered in the region.

Directory

Governor: EDUARD ERGARTOVICH ROSSEL; Sverdlovskaya obl., 620031 Yekaterinburg, pl. Oktyabrskaya 1; tel. (3432) 51-13-65; fax (3432) 51-36-42.

Chairman of the Government: ALEKSEI PETROVICH VOROBEV; Sverdlovskaya obl., 620031 Yekaterinburg, pl. Oktyabrskaya 1; tel. (3432) 51-29-20.

Legislative Assembly: Sverdlovskaya obl., Yekaterinburg.

Chairman of the House of Representatives: ALEKSANDR YURIYEVICH SHASPOSHNIKOV.

Chairman of the Regional Duma: VYACHESLAV SERGEYEVICH SURGANOV.

Permanent Representative of the President of the Russian Federation: YURII ALEKSANDROVICH BRUSNITSYN; tel. (3432) 51-21-61.

Head of the Regional Representation in Moscow: ARTURO PAVLOVICH VEYER; tel. (095) 291-90-72.

Head of Yekaterinburg City Administration (Mayor): ARKADII MIKHAILOVICH CHERNETSKII; Sverdlovskaya obl., 620038 Yekaterinburg, pr. Lenina 24; tel. (3432) 58-92-18; fax (3432) 56-29-92.

Tambov

Tambov Oblast is situated in the central part of the Oka-Don plain. It forms part of the Central Chernozem Economic Area. Penza and Saratov Oblasts lie to the east, Voronezh Oblast to the south, Lipetsk Oblast to the west and Ryazan Oblast to the north. Tambov city lies about 300 km (just under 200 miles) south-east of Moscow. Its major rivers are the Tsna and the Vorona. Its territory occupies 34,300 sq km (13,240 sq miles) and measures around 250 km from south to north and 200 km from west to east. The Oblast is divided into 23 districts and eight cities. At 1 January 1996 its population was estimated at 1,310,000, of whom some 57.8% inhabited urban areas, and it had a population density of 38.2 per sq km. The administrative centre is at Tambov, which had an estimated population of 318,100 in 1996. Other major cities are Michurinsk (123,500), Morshansk (50,500) and Rasskazovo (50,400).

History

Tambov city was founded in 1636 as a fort to defend Moscow. The region was the scene of an army mutiny during the anti-tsarist uprising of 1905, and came under Bolshevik control immediately following the October Revolution in 1917. The Oblast was formed on 27 September 1937. It was still considered part of the 'red belt' of committed Communist adherence in the 1990s. The dissolution of the local council in October 1993, and its replacement by a Regional Duma, did not ease the tension between the still Communist-led assembly with the regional administration. In an attempt to resolve this conflict, and having appointed a locally respected governor, President Boris Yeltsin permitted a gubernatorial election in

Tambov in December 1995. With the Communist Party winning 40% of the regional votes in the simultaneous elections to the federal parliament, it was, perhaps, not unexpected that the incumbent was defeated by the Communist candidate, Aleksandr Ryabov, who became head of the regional administration. None the less, in elections held to the Regional Duma in March 1998 (at which the turn-out was just over 25%) the greatest number of seats was won by the Common Sense Party, comprised largely of young directors of firms and enterprises.

Economy

In 1995 Tambov Oblast's gross regional product amounted to 6,547,800m. roubles, equivalent to 4,987,300 roubles per head. The region's industrial centres are at Tambov, Michurinsk, Morshansk, Kotovsk and Rasskazovo. It is situated on the ancient trading routes from the centre of Russia to the lower Volga and Central Asia and contains several major road and rail routes.

The Oblast's agriculture, which employed a relatively high proportion of the work-force (some 23.3% in 1995) consists mainly of the production of grain, sugar-beets, sunflower seeds and vegetables. Animal husbandry and horticulture are also important. Total agricultural output in 1995 was worth 3,030,200m. roubles. The principal industries in the Oblast are mechanical engineering, metal working, chemicals and petrochemicals, the production of electrical energy, light manufacturing and food processing. In 1995 some 23.1% of the working population was engaged in industry. Total industrial production in that year amounted to a value of 3,793,000m. roubles.

In 1996 around 5.6% of the economically active population of some 572,000 was unemployed. In 1995 the average monthly wage in the Oblast was 307,000 roubles and there was a budgetary deficit of 13,700m. roubles. At 1 January 1996 there were some 2,900 small businesses operating in the region.

Directory

Head of the Regional Administration (Governor): ALEKSANDR IVANOVICH RYABOV; Tambovskaya obl., 392017 Tambov, ul. Internatsionalnaya 14; tel. (0752) 22-10-61; fax (0752) 22-10-43.

Chairman of the Regional Duma: VLADIMIR NIKOLAYEVICH KAREV.

Permanent Representative of the President of the Russian Federation: (vacant); tel. (0752) 22-12-25.

Head of Tambov City Administration (Mayor): ALEKSEI YURIYEVICH ILYIN (acting); tel. (0752) 22-20-30; fax (0752) 22-71-47.

Tomsk

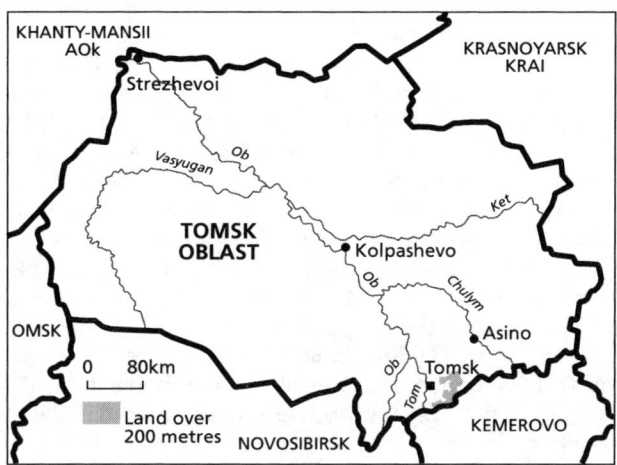

Tomsk Oblast is situated in the south-east of the Western Siberian Plain. It forms part of the Western Siberian Economic Area. The regions of Kemerovo and Novosibirsk lie to the south, Omsk Oblast to the south-west, the Khanty-Mansii AOk (part of Tyumen Oblast) to the north-west and Krasnoyarsk Krai to the east. Its major rivers are the Ob, the Tom, the Chulym, the Ket, the Tym and the Vasyugan. The Ob flows for about 1,000 km (almost 400 miles) from the south-east to the north-west of the territory. Its largest lake is the Mirnoye. Almost all the Oblast's territory taiga (forested marshland), and over one-half of its total area is forested. It occupies 316,900 sq km (122,320 sq miles) and is divided into 16 districts and six cities. At 1 January 1996 its total population was 1,078,000, of whom 65.7% inhabited urban areas. The region's population density was, therefore, 3.4 per sq km. Around 88.2% of the population were ethnic Russian at this time, 2.6% were Ukrainian and 2.1% Tatar. The administrative centre of the Oblast is at Tomsk, which had an estimated population of 473,000 in 1996. Other major cities are Seversk (110,900) and Strezhevoi (44,100).

History

Tomsk city was founded as a fortress in 1604. It was a major trading centre until the 1890s, when the construction of the Trans-Siberian Railway promoted other centres. Tomsk Oblast was formed on 13 August 1944. In 1993 the Regional Soviet was initially critical of President Boris Yeltsin's forcible dissolution of the federal parliament. It too, therefore, was disbanded and replaced (elections on 12 December) by a Regional Duma. The Communists remained the most popular party in the region, securing 19% of the vote in federal elections two years later. However, in a simultaneous gubernatorial election for the Oblast, the pro-Yeltsin incumbent, Viktor Kress, won the popular mandate to head the regional administration.

Economy

In 1995 the gross regional product of Tomsk Oblast amounted to 12,828,600m. roubles, equivalent to 11,896,000 roubles per head. The industrial sector plays a dominant role in the economy of Tomsk Oblast. Its major industrial centres are at Tomsk, Kopashevo, Asino and Strezhevoi.

The Oblast's agricultural sector, which generated 1,751,400m. roubles in 1995, consists mainly of animal husbandry, the production of grain, vegetables and flax, fishing, hunting and fur farming. Some 10.4% of the Oblast's working population was engaged in agriculture in 1995. Around 1.4m. ha (3.4m. acres) of the Oblast's territory was used for agricultural purposes, of which one-half was arable land. The Oblast has substantial reserves of coal as well as of petroleum and natural gas (estimated at 333.7m. metric tons and 300,000m. cu m, respectively). Its other main industries are mechanical engineering, metal working, the electro-technical industry, the processing of forestry and agricultural products and chemicals. Industry employed 26.3% of the working population in 1995, while industrial output amounted to a value of 7,798,000m. roubles in that year.

In 1996 around 4.5% of the economically active population of 441,900 were registered unemployed; this was four to five times higher than the average among Russia's oblasts. In 1995 the average monthly wage was 493,000 roubles. There was a budgetary deficit of 58,800m. roubles. Total foreign investment in that year amounted to US $44.34m. At 1 January 1996 there were some 5,200 small businesses in operation in the region.

Directory

Head of the Regional Administration (Governor): VIKTOR MELKHIOROVICH KRESS; Tomskaya obl., 63450 Tomsk, pl. Lenina 6; tel. (3822) 22-25-05; fax (3822) 22-47-30.

Chairman of the Legislative Assembly (Regional Duma): BORIS ALEKSEYEVICH MALTSEV; tel. (3822) 22-21-47.

Permanent Representative of the President of the Russian Federation: VLADIMIR ALEKSANDROVICH ZHIDKIKH; tel. (3822) 22-59-30.

Head of Tomsk City Administration (Mayor): ALEKSANDR SERGEYEVICH MAKAROV; Tomskaya obl., 634050 Tomsk, pr. Lenina 73; tel. (3822) 23-32-32.

Tula

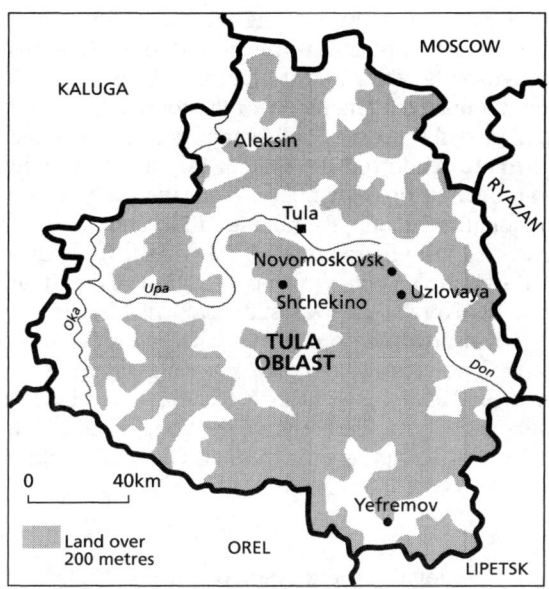

Tula Oblast is situated in the central part of the Eastern European Plain in the northern section of the Central Russian Highlands. It forms part of the Central Economic Area. Ryazan Oblast borders Tula to the east, Lipetsk Oblast to the south-east, Orel Oblast to the south-west, Kaluga Oblast to the north-west and Moscow Oblast to the north. Tula city is approximately 193 km (about 120 miles) south of Moscow. The region's major rivers are the Oka, the Upa, the Don and the Osetr. The territory of the Oblast covers an area of 25,700 sq km (9,920 sq miles) and extends for 230 km from south to north and 200 km from west to east. It is divided into 23 administrative districts and 21 cities. It is a highly populated area, with a total population of 1,785,600 at the beginning of 1998 and a population density of 70.0 per sq km. At 1 January 1996 some 81.3% of the Oblast's population inhabited urban areas. The Oblast's administrative centre is at Tula, a military town, which had an estimated population of 567,600 in 1998. Other major cities are Novomoskovsk (with an estimated 142,900 inhabitants in 1996), Aleksin (71,800), Shchekino (66,700), Uzlovaya (62,200) and Yefremov (55,800).

History

Tula, the city of armourers, was founded in the 12th century. It became an important economic centre in 1712, with the construction of the Imperial Small Arms Factory. In 1812 it successfully resisted the French invasion under Napoleon I and in 1941 it repeated its performance against the Germans. Tula Oblast was founded on 26 September 1937. Tula's armaments industry (the Kalashnikov AK-47 automatic rifle was invented here) meant that it was closed to foreigners for most of the Soviet period.

On 7 October 1993 the Tula Regional Soviet refused to disband itself, having opposed the federal President, Boris Yeltsin, in the recent constitutional crisis, but over 100 deputies resigned, thereby making the Soviet inquorate. The Soviet was subsequently dissolved and its functions transferred to the Regional Administration. A new representative body, the 48-seat Regional Duma, was later elected. The assembly remained dominated by members of the former Communist nomenklatura, and that party remained the most widely supported in the Oblast, but a number of respected local figures endorsed the federal regime. The regional results of the all-Russian general election of December 1995 gave the Communists 22% of the votes cast, the nationalist Liberal Democrats 13% and the pro-government Our Home is Russia party 10%. In February 1997 Aleksandr Korzhakov, former general and bodyguard to President Yeltsin, won a by-election to the State Duma, obtaining 26% of the votes cast. Korzhakov was supported in his campaign by Aleksandr Lebed (Governor of Krasnoyarsk from 1998), who had previously represented Tula in the federal parliament. Korzhakov had campaigned as a *gosudarstvennik*, a believer in a strong and nationally assertive state. Later in 1997 the successful Communist candidate in the gubernatorial election, Vasilii Starodubtsev, was a veteran of the 1991 coup attempt against Mikhail Gorbachev, the last Soviet leader.

Economy

Tula Oblast's gross regional product amounted to 12,436,900m. roubles, or 6,833,100 roubles per head. Its important industrial centres are at Tula, Novomoskovsk, Shchekino, Aleksin, Uzlovaya and Yefremov. The region's long history of industry is attested by its weapons manufacturing and its claim to have invented the samovar (the city possesses the world's only samovar museum).

Around 73.7% of the Oblast's territory is used for agricultural purposes. Agricultural activity, in which some 11.3% of the working population were engaged in 1995, consists primarily of animal husbandry and production of grain, potatoes and sugar-beets. Agricultural production was worth 3,462,400m. roubles in 1995. The Oblast's main industries are mechanical engineering, metal working, chemicals, ferrous metallurgy, manufacture of building materials, light manufacturing, food processing and the production of brown coal (lignite). Industry employed approximately 34.3% of the working population in 1995, while total industrial production amounted to a value of 12,149,000m. roubles. Ferrous metallurgy, mechanical engineering and metal working dominated exports in the region. A tourism sector is encouraged by the city's history and its location near to the Yasnaya Polyana country estate of Count Leo Tolstoy (1828–1910), the writer. Its main foreign trading partners are Germany, Italy, the Republic of Korea (South Korea), Switzerland and the USA.

In 1995 the economically active population in the Oblast numbered 814,900, of whom around 15,200 (1.9%) were registered unemployed. Those in employment at that time earned an average monthly wage of 398,000 roubles. The 1995 budget showed a deficit of 10,400m. roubles. Total foreign investment in Tula Oblast in 1995 amounted to US $12.93m. By 1997 around 350 companies in the Oblast had economic links with 75 foreign countries. At 1 January 1996 there were some 7,900 small businesses in operation on its territory.

Directory

Head of the Regional Administration (Governor): VASILII ALEKSANDROVICH STARODUBTSEV; tel. (0872) 27-84-36.

Chairman of the Regional Duma: IGOR VIKTOROVICH IVANOV; tel. (0872) 20-52-24.

Permanent Representative of the President of the Russian Federation: VIKTOR GEORGIYEVICH KUZNETSOV; tel. (0872) 20-57-51.

Head of the Regional Representation in Moscow: ANDREI FEDOROVICH FEDOTOV; tel. (095) 978-14-56.

Head of Tula City Administration (Mayor): SERGEI IVANOVICH KAZAKOV; tel. (0872) 27-80-85.

Tver

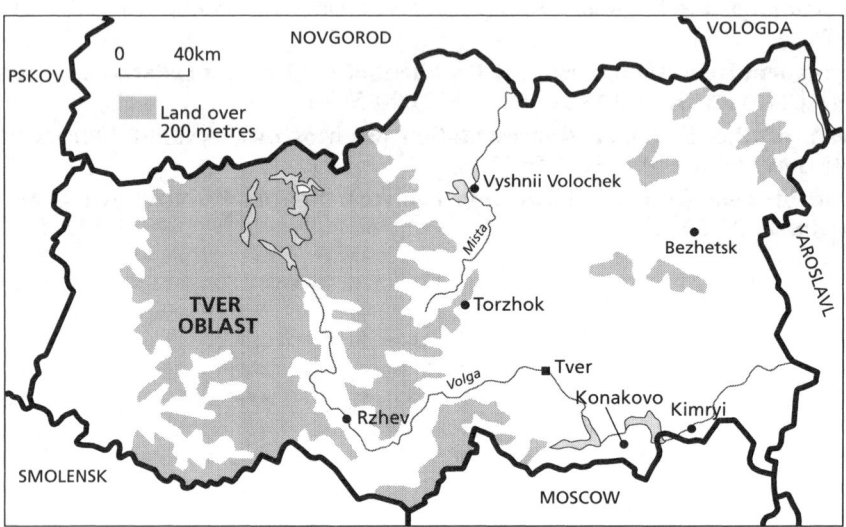

Tver Oblast (known as Kalinin from 1931 to 1990) is situated in the central part of the Eastern European Plain. It forms part of the Central Economic Area. Moscow and Smolensk Oblasts lie to the south, Pskov Oblast to the west, Novgorod and Vologda Oblasts to the north and Yaroslavl Oblast to the east. Its westernmost point lies some 50 km (just over 30 miles) from the border with Belarus. The major rivers in the region are the Volga, which rises within its territory, the Mologa and the Tvertsa. The Zapadnaya Dvina and the Msta rivers also have their sources in the Oblast. It has more than 500 lakes, the largest of which is the Seliger, and contains nine reservoirs. The western part of the territory is mountainous, containing the Valdai Highlands (Valdaiskaya Vozvyshennost). About one-third of the territory of the Oblast is forested. It occupies 84,100 sq km (32,460 sq miles). It is divided into 36 districts and 23 cities. The region had an estimated 1,649,600 inhabitants in 1997, of whom 75% inhabited urban areas, and its population density was 19.6 per sq km. Some 94% of its inhabitants are ethnic Russian. The administrative centre is at Tver (formerly Kalinin), a river-port, which at the beginning of January 1996 had an estimated population of 457,500. Other major cities are Vyshnii Volochek (62,700), Kimryi (60,700) and Torzhok (50,200).

History

The city of Tver was founded as a fort in the 12th century. The Oblast was officially formed on 29 January 1935. Although long in the heart of the Russian state, in the 1990s the region's relations with the central Government, led by President Boris Yeltsin, were not always cordial. Having criticized Yeltsin for his policy towards the federal parliament, in October 1993 the Tver Regional Soviet refused to disband itself. It was subsequently obliged to comply with the directives of the federal authorities and a new body, the Legislative Assembly, was elected the following year. This, too, was dominated by the Communists and was obstructive of executive action. President Yeltsin appointed a respected local figure to head the regional administration and decided to permit a gubernatorial election in December 1995. The incumbent was defeated by the Communist candidate, Vladimir Platov, and, in the simultaneous election to the Russian State Duma, the Communist Party secured 27% of the regional vote, compared to only 8% for the pro-Yeltsin bloc. The federal Government attempted to placate local opinion, therefore, and in June 1996 the regional authorities were granted greater autonomy with the signing of a power-sharing treaty.

Economy

In 1995 Tver Oblast's gross regional product amounted to 11,618,300m. roubles, equivalent to 7,033,700 roubles per head. Industry is the dominant branch of the Oblast's economy. The principal industrial centres are Tver, Vyshnii Volochek, Rzhev, Torzhok and Kimryi. The region is crossed by road and rail routes between Moscow and Rīga (Latvia) and a highway between Moscow and St Petersburg. The total length of railway track in the Oblast is 2,713 km, while the road network is 10,244 km long. There are 924 km of navigable waterways in the region, mainly on the Volga. There is an international airport at Tver.

Around 2.4m. ha (5.9m. acres) of the Oblast's territory is used for agricultural purposes, of which two-thirds is arable land. Agriculture in Tver Oblast, which employed around 15.3% of the work-force in 1995, consists mainly of animal husbandry and the production of vegetables, potatoes and flax (the region is traditionally a flax-growing area and grows around one-quarter of flax produced in Russia). Total agricultural output in 1995 amounted to a value of 2,793,300m. roubles. The region contains deposits of peat, lime and coal and is famous for its mineral-water reserves. Its major industries are mechanical engineering, metal working, light manufacturing, chemicals, wood-working, the processing of forestry and agricultural products, printing and glass-, china- and faience-making. In 1995 some 29.0% of the Oblast's working population was engaged in industry, while total industrial production was worth 7,606,000m. roubles. Its main trading partners in the mid-1990s were the People's Republic of China, Germany, Switzerland, Turkey and the USA. In 1998 there were 20 commercial banks and 100 insurance companies and branches in operation on its territory.

In 1995 the region's economically active population numbered 697,200, of whom some 14,100 (2.0%) were registered unemployed. The average wage at this time amounted to 344,000 roubles per month. The 1995 regional government budget showed a deficit of 18,700m. roubles. In 1998 a social and cultural development programme for Tver Oblast (for 1998–2005) was adopted by the federal Government. Total foreign investment in the Oblast in 1995 amounted to US $67.21m. In 1997 more than 4,000 small businesses were operating in the region, employing 60,000 people.

Directory

Head of the Regional Administration (Governor): VLADIMIR IGNATEVICH PLATOV; Tverskaya obl., 170000 Tver, ul. Sovetskaya 44; tel. (0822) 33-10-51; fax (0822) 42-55-08; e-mail tradm@tversu.ru.

Chairman of the Legislative Assembly: VYACHESLAV A. MIRONOV; tel. (0822) 33-10-11.

Permanent Representative of the President of the Russian Federation: TAMARA TERENTIYEVNA KARYAKINA; tel. (0822) 33-50-25.

Head of Tver City Administration (Mayor): ALEKSANDR PETROVICH BELUSOV; Tverskaya obl., 170640 Tver, ul. Sovetskaya 11; tel. (0822) 33-01-31; fax (0822) 42-59-39.

Tyumen

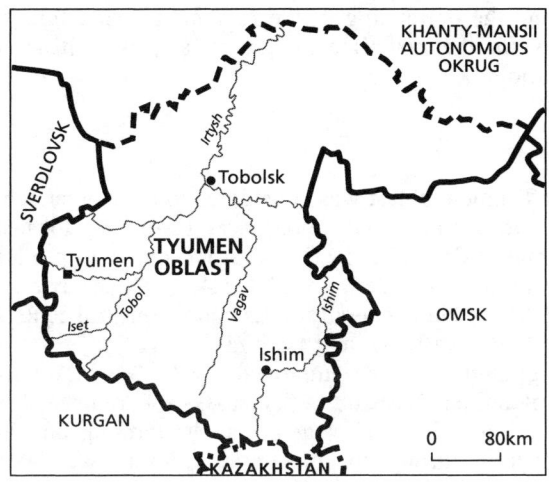

Tyumen Oblast is situated in the Western Siberian Plain, extending from the Kara Sea in the north to the border with Kazakhstan in the south. It forms part of the Western Siberian Economic Area. Much of its territory comprises the Khanty-Mansii and Yamal-Nenets Autonomous Okrugs (a map of the whole of Tyumen Oblast can be found at the end of Part Two, on p. 280). To the west (going south to north) lie Kurgan, Sverdlovsk, Komi and the Nenets AOk (part of Archangel Oblast); to the east lie Omsk, Tomsk and Krasnoyarsk (in the far north the border is with Krasnoyarsk's Taimyr AOk). The region has numerous rivers, its major ones being the Ob, the Taz, the Pur and the Nadym. Much of its territory is taiga (forested marshland). The territory of the Oblast, including that of the autonomous okrugs, occupies an area of 1,435,200 sq km (554,130 sq miles) and is divided into 38 districts and 26 cities. It is a sparsely populated region: the estimated total population at 1 January 1996 was 3,170,000 and the population density was 2.2 per sq km. Some 76.2% of the Oblast's inhabitants lived in urban areas. The Oblast's administrative centre is at Tyumen, which then had an estimated population of 496,500. Other major cities are Surgut (266,300), Nizhnevartovsk (236,100), Tobolsk (98,000), Nefteyugansk (96,800), Noyabrsk (95,500) and Urengoi (90,000).

History

Tyumen city was founded in 1585 on the site of a Tatar settlement. It subsequently became an important centre for trade with the Chinese Empire. Tyumen Oblast was formed on 14 August 1944. The region became industrialized after the Second World War. On 21 October 1993 the Regional Soviet in Tyumen Oblast repealed its earlier condemnation of government action against the federal parliament but refused to disband itself. Legislative elections were held in the Oblast on 6 March 1994, but the results in several constituencies were declared invalid, owing to a low level of participation. Eventually a new assembly, the Regional Duma, was elected. It remained led by the Communists, but the pro-government faction was well represented. This position was confirmed by regional results in the general election of 1995. During the mid-1990s the two Autonomous Okrugs, which wished to retain a greater share of the income from their wealth of natural resources, made an attempt to challenge the jurisdiction of the regional authorities. In 1998 a scandal involving the defrauding of the regional pension fund caused delays in pension payments for the first time in three years, as well as embarrassing the Oblast administration.

Economy

In the mid-1990s Tyumen Oblast was considered to have great economic potential, owing to its vast hydrocarbons and timber reserves (mainly located in the Khanty-Mansii and Taimyr AOks). In 1995 its gross regional product amounted to 108,885,100m. roubles, equivalent to 34,421,400 roubles per head (one of the highest figures in the Russian Federation). Its main industrial centres are at Tyumen, Tobolsk, Surgut, Nizhnevartovsk and Nadym.

The Oblast's agriculture, which employed just 8.1% of its work-force in 1995, consists mainly of animal husbandry (livestock- and reindeer-breeding), fishing, the production of grain, flax and vegetables, fur farming and hunting. In 1995 agricultural production throughout the entire territory was worth 3,805,200m. roubles. In the mid-1990s the Oblast's reserves of petroleum, natural gas and peat were estimated at 60%, 80% and 36%, respectively, of Russia's total supply. Tyumeneftegaz is the fourth-largest petroleum company in the country and produced 156m. barrels of crude petroleum in 1996. Its subsidiary, Nizhnevartovskneftegaz, in which it has a 38% stake, is its main production unit. In 1997 there were plans to privatize Tyumeneftegaz. Overall petroleum output in the region for 1997 was forecast at 191.6m. metric tons. The Oblast's other major industries are mechanical engineering, metal-working, chemicals and the processing of agricultural and forestry products. Industry employed some 15.9% of the Oblast's working population in 1995 and generated a total of 71,594,00m. roubles.

The economically active population in 1995 totalled 1,700,700. There was a total of 45,000 (2.6%) registered unemployed in the region at the time. The average monthly wage in 1995 was 312,000 roubles. The budget for that year, including for the two autonomous okrugs, showed a deficit of 417,000m. roubles. Total foreign investment in the Oblast amounted to US $102.58m. in 1995, while by the beginning of the next year there were some 33,600 small businesses in operation on its territory.

Directory

Governor: LEONID YULIANOVICH ROKETSKII; Tyumenskaya obl., 625004 Tyumen, ul. Vodoprovodnaya 45; tel. (3452) 36-77-20; fax (3452) 29-32-05.

Chairman of the Regional Duma: SERGEI YEVGENIYEVICH KOREPANOV.

Permanent Representative of the President of the Russian Federation: GENNADII ALEKSANDROVICH SHCHERBAKOV; tel. (3452) 26-29-84.

Head of the Regional Representation in Moscow: GEORGII VASILIYEVICH GLYBIN; tel. (095) 921-29-94.

Head of Tyumen City Administration: IVAN GRIGORIYEVICH KIRICHUK; Tyumenskaya obl., 625036 Tyumen, ul. Pervomaiskaya 20; tel. (3452) 23-67-43; fax (3452) 24-65-26.

Ulyanovsk

Ulyanovsk Oblast is situated in the Volga Area Highlands (Privolzhskaya Vozvyshennost). It forms part of the Volga Economic Area. The Republics of Mordoviya and of Chuvashiya and Tatarstan lie to the north-west and to the north, respectively. There are also borders with Samara Oblast in the south-east, Saratov Oblast in the south and Penza Oblast in the south-west. The region's major river is the Volga. It occupies an area of 37,300 sq km (14,400 sq miles) and is divided into 21 districts and six cities. The estimated total population of the Oblast was 1,495,000 in January 1996, of whom some 72.7% inhabited urban areas. It therefore had a population density of 40.1 per sq km. The administrative centre is at Ulyanovsk (formerly Simbirsk), which had an estimated population of 680,200 at this time. Other major cities include Dimitrovgrad (136,200), Inza (25,200) and Barysh (21,900).

History

Simbirsk city was founded in 1648. Lenin (Vladimir Ulyanov) was born there in 1870, and it was his home until 1887. The city and region assumed his family name following his death in 1924. Ulyanovsk Oblast, which was formed on 19 January 1943, remained very much part of the 'red belt' of Communist support in post-Soviet Russia. Thus, it refused to revert to its old name (as was common in the 1990s), but, more tangibly, it gave the party 37% of the regional vote in the 1995 elections to the federal State Duma. In December 1996, as predicted, the Communist-backed candidate, Yurii Goryachev, won the election to the governorship of the Oblast. Goryachev, whose support came largely from the Oblast's rural community, banned local privatization and collective-farm reforms, imposed restrictions on imports and exports, and subsidized bread prices until early 1997. As was common in post-Soviet politics, the region's administrative centre was run by a liberal, Vitalii Marusin. Consequently, the city which provided the Oblast's tax base was in open conflict with the regional government which spent the revenue.

Economy

In 1995 Ulyanovsk Oblast's gross regional product amounted to 10,695,800m. roubles, or 7,160,600 roubles per head. The Oblast's major industrial centres are at Ulyanovsk and Melekess.

Around 1.5m. ha of its territory is used for agricultural purposes, of which over four-fifths is arable land. Agriculture in the region, which employed some 16.0% of the working population in 1995, consists primarily of animal husbandry and the production of grain, sunflower seeds and sugar-beets. Total agricultural production amounted to a value of 2,829,400m. roubles in 1995. The Oblast's main industries are mechanical engineering and metal working, food processing, light manufacturing, the manufacture of building materials and wood-working. The region's major companies included the UAZ automobile plant and the Aviastar aeroplane manufacturer (both of which were working at 50% capacity in the mid-1990s). Industry employed approximately 32.2% of the working population in 1995 and generated some 9,586,000m. roubles.

The economically active population in Ulyanovsk Oblast in that year numbered 646,700, of whom some 23,000 were registered unemployed. Those in employment at this time earned an average of 312,000 roubles per month. There was a large budgetary deficit in 1995, of 225,300m. roubles. Total foreign investment in the Oblast in that year amounted to only US $260,000. At 1 January 1996 there were some 4,600 small businesses in operation.

Directory

Head of the Regional Administration (Governor): YURII FROLOVICH GORYACHEV; Ulyanovskaya obl., 423700 Ulyanovsk, pl. Lenina 1; tel. (8422) 41-20-78; fax (8422) 31-27-65.

Chairman of the Legislative Assembly: SERGEI NIKOLAYEVICH RYABUKHIN.

Permanent Representative of the President of the Russian Federation: VALERII ALEKSANDROVICH SYCHEV; tel. (8422) 31-91-30.

Head of the Regional Representation in Moscow: GENNADII VASILIYEVICH SAVINOV.

Head of Ulyanovsk City Administration (Mayor): VITALII VLADIMIROVICH MARUSIN; Ulyanovskaya obl., 432700 Ulyanovsk, ul. Kuznetsova 7; tel. (8422) 31-30-80; fax (8422) 31-90-64.

Vladimir

Vladimir Oblast is situated in the central part of the Eastern European Plain. It forms part of the Central Economic Area. It shares borders with Ryazan and Moscow to the south-west, Yaroslavl and Ivanovo to the north and Nizhnii Novgorod to the east. The Oblast's main rivers are the Oka and its tributary, the Klyazma. Over one-half of its territory is forested. It occupies a total of 29,000 sq km (11,200 sq miles) and measures around 170 km (over 100 miles) from south to north and 280 km from west to east. The Oblast is divided into 19 administrative districts and 22 cities. It had an estimated population of 1,645,000 at 1 January 1996, of whom 80.1% inhabited urban areas. Its population density in 1996 was 56.7 per sq km. Its administrative centre is at Vladimir, which had an estimated population of 339,700. Other major cities are Kovrov (162,500), Murom (126,000), Gus-Khrustalnyi (75,900) and Aleksandrov (68,600).

History

Founded in 1108 as a frontier fortress, after the disintegration of Kievan Rus, by Prince Vladimir Monomakh, Vladimir city is one of the oldest in Russia. It was the seat of the principality of Vladimir-Suzdal and an early Orthodox Christian bishopric. Vladimir fell under the rule of Moscow during the 14th century and was supplanted by that city as the seat of the Russian Orthodox patriarch, although Vladimir was chosen for the coronations of several Muscovite princes. It declined in importance from the 15th century. Vladimir Oblast was formed on 14 August 1944.

In a Russia restored to independence, in the 1990s Vladimir Oblast awarded a respectable level of support to all the main national parties. Thus, according to the regional results of the December 1995 general election, the Communists gained 21% of the votes cast, the nationalist Liberal Democrats 15%, the pro-government Our Home is Russia 12% and even the reformist Yabloko bloc 7%. The Communists, however, secured the election of Nikolai Vinogradov, former Chairman of the Legislative Assembly, to the post of Governor in late 1996.

Economy

Vladimir Oblast's gross regional product in 1995 totalled 10,679,300m. roubles, or 6,487,600 roubles per head. The Oblast's main industrial centres are at Vladimir, Kovrov, Murom, Aleksandrov, Kolchugino, Vyazniki and Gus-Khrustalnyi. There are 923 km of railway track and 8,600 km of roads on its territory.

Agriculture in the region, which employed just 8.5% of its work-force in 1995, consists mainly of animal husbandry, vegetable production and horticulture. Total agricultural output in 1995 stood at a value of 2,357,400m. roubles. Vladimir is rich in peat deposits and timber reserves but relies on imports for around 70% of its energy supplies. The Oblast's main industries are mechanical engineering, manufacture of building materials, metal working, light manufacturing, chemicals, glass-making and handicrafts. Industrial output in 1995 was worth 8,845,000m. roubles. In that year a total of 39.9% of the working population was engaged in industry. Vladimir city's largest employer is the Vladimirskii Traktornyi Zavod (Vladimir Tractor Factory), which struggled to survive in the 1990s, as interest rates increased and demand fell.

At 1 January 1997 approximately 5.7% of the economically active population were registered as unemployed. The average monthly wage in the Oblast in 1995 was 314,000 roubles. Total foreign investment in Vladimir Oblast in 1995 amounted to US $5.30m. In 1997 organizations with private or mixed forms of ownership, which employed 400,000 people, contributed around 90% of the Oblast's economic output. At 1 January 1996 there was a total of 8,000 small businesses registered on its territory.

Directory

Head of the Regional Administration (Governor): NIKOLAI VLADIMIROVICH VINOGRADOV; Vladimirskaya obl., 600000 Vladimir, Oktyabrskaya pr. 21; tel. (0922) 22-52-52; fax (0922) 22-60-13.

Chairman of the Legislative Assembly: VITALII YAKOVLEVICH KOTOV; Vladimirskaya obl., 600000 Vladimir, Oktyabrskaya pr. 21; tel. (0922) 22-64-42; fax (0922) 22-60-13.

Permanent Representative of the President of the Russian Federation: SERGEI NIKOLAYEVICH SOKOLOV; tel. (0922) 22-53-62.

Head of Vladimir City Administration: IGOR VASILIYEVICH SHAMOV; Vladimirskaya obl., 600000 Vladimir, ul. Gorkogo 36; tel. (0922) 23-28-17; fax (0922) 23-85-54.

Volgograd

Volgograd Oblast is situated in the south-east of the Eastern European Plain. It forms part of the Volga Economic Area and spreads westwards from an international border with Kazakhstan. The federal subjects of Astrakhan and Kalmykiya lie to the south-east, Rostov to the south-west, Voronezh to the north-west and Saratov to the north. The Oblast's main rivers are the Volga and the Don. Its terrain varies from fertile black earth (*chernozem*) to semi-desert. Volgograd city is the eastern terminus of the Volga–Don Canal. The region occupies an area of 113,900 sq km (43,980 sq miles) and is divided into 33 administrative districts and 19 cities. At 1 January 1996 it had an estimated total of 2,704,000 inhabitants, of whom some 74.3% lived in urban areas, and a population density of 23.7 per sq km. In 1997 around 89% of the population were ethnic Russians, while 3% were Ukrainians, 2% were Kazakhs and 1% were Tatars. Its administrative centre is at Volgograd (formerly Stalingrad), which had an estimated population of 1,003,300 in 1996. Other major cities are Volzhskii (289,900) and Kamyshin (128,200).

History

The city of Volgograd (known as Tsaritsyn until 1925 and Stalingrad from 1925 until 1961) was founded in the 16th century, to protect the Volga trade route. It was built on the River Volga, at the point where it flows nearest to the Don (the two river systems were later connected by a canal). The Oblast was formed on 10 January 1934. In 1942–43 the city was the scene of a decisive battle between the forces of the USSR and Nazi Germany.

In October 1993 the Regional Soviet in Volgograd Oblast eventually agreed to a reform of the system of government in the Oblast. It decided to hold elections to a new 30-seat Regional Duma, which took place the following year. The Communist Party was the largest single party. The continued pre-eminence of the old ruling élite was confirmed by the 27% share of the regional poll secured by the Communist list in the 1995 federal parliamentary election. Furthermore, the December 1996 elections to the post of Governor were won by Nikolai Maksyuta, a Communist and former speaker of the regional assembly. In December 1998 Communist candidates won a convincing 23 of the 32 seats in the regional legislative elections. On 24 September the Duma had voted for the principle of restoring the Oblast's previous name.

Economy

In 1995 Volgograd Oblast's gross regional product amounted to 19,629,800m. roubles, or 7,272,700 roubles per head. Its main industrial centres are at Volgograd, Bolzhskii and Kamyshyn. In 1997 there were more than 16,000 km of roads, of which 53% were paved. In 1996 construction began of a road bridge across the Volga river into Volgograd. The region's principal agricultural products are grain, sunflower seeds, fruit, vegetables, mustard and cucurbits (gourds and melons). Horticulture and animal husbandry are also important. In 1995 some 18.4% of the Oblast's work-force were engaged in agriculture. Total agricultural production amounted to a value of 4,371,800m. roubles in that year. The agricultural sector suffered a major reverse in mid-1998, however, when drought destroyed more than 1m. ha of grain, 200,000 ha of fodder crops and 80,000 ha of mustard. The Oblast's mineral reserves include petroleum, natural gas and phosphorites. The main industries in the Oblast are petroleum refining, chemicals and petrochemicals, mechanical engineering, metal working, ferrous and non-ferrous metallurgy, the manufacture of building materials, wood-working, light manufacturing, food processing and the production of petroleum and natural gas. Industry employed approximately 26.1% of the working population in 1995, while total industrial production was worth 15,277,000m. roubles. In 1995 the economically active population in the Oblast numbered 1,224,100, of whom around 18,300 (1.5%) were unemployed. The local average monthly wage was 331,000 roubles. There was a budgetary deficit of 76,600m. roubles in that year. Total foreign investment in 1995 amounted to US $17.34m. In 1997 there were more than 250 joint and foreign enterprises in the region. The joint enterprises had largely been established with investment from Bulgaria, Germany, Greece, Italy and the USA. At the beginning of the previous year there were some 18,600 small businesses in the region.

Directory

Head of the Regional Administration (Governor): NIKOLAI KIRILLOVICH MAKSYUTA; Volgogradskaya obl., 400098 Volgograd, pr. umeni V. I. Lenina 9; tel. (8442) 33-66-88; fax (8442) 93-62-12.

Chairman of the Regional Duma: LEONID VASILIYEVICH SEMERGEI; tel. and fax (8442) 36-52-79.

Permanent Representative of the President of the Russian Federation: (vacant); tel. (8442) 33-58-20.

Head of Volgograd City Administration (Mayor): YURII VIKTOROVICH CHEKHOV; Volgogradskaya obl., 400066 Volgograd, ul. Sovetskaya 11; tel. (8442) 33-50-10.

Vologda

Vologda Oblast is situated in the north-west of the Eastern European Plain. It forms part of the Northern Economic Area. It has a short border, in the north-west, with the Republic of Kareliya, which includes the southern tip of Lake Onega (Onezhskoye). Onega also forms the northern end of a border with Leningrad Oblast, which lies to the west of the Vologda region. Novgorod Oblast lies to the south-west and Tver, Yaroslavl and Kostroma Oblasts to the south. Kirov Oblast forms an eastern border and Archangel Oblast lies to the north. The region's main rivers are the Sukhona, the Yug, the Sheksna and the Mologa. There are three major lakes, in addition to Lake Onega—Beloye, Bozhe and Kubenskoye. Vologda Oblast occupies 145,700 sq km (56,250 sq miles) and extends for 385 km (240 miles) from south to north and 650 km from west to east. It is divided into 26 administrative districts and 15 cities. The Oblast's population at the beginning of 1996 was estimated at 1,350,000 and the population density was, therefore, 9.3 per sq km. Some 67.6% of the total population inhabited urban areas. The Oblast's administrative centre is at Vologda, which had an estimated population of 300,400 in 1996. Its other major city is Cherepovets (320,900).

History

Vologda province was annexed by the state of Muscovy in the 14th century. The city was, for a time, the intended capital of Tsar Ivan IV ('the Terrible', 1533–84). Until the Bolshevik Revolution of 1917 the province was administered by governors appointed by the Tsar. Vologda Oblast was formed on 23 September 1937.

In 1991 the newly elected Russian President, Boris Yeltsin, appointed a new head of administration of Vologda Oblast. In mid-1993 the Vologda Oblast declared itself a republic but failed to be acknowledged as such by the federal authorities. On 13 October the Regional Soviet transferred its responsibilities to the Regional Administration and elections were later held to a Legislative Assembly. In 1995 ballots implemented the Statutes of Vologda Oblast, according to which the region's

Governor would lead the executive. In the Russia of the 1990s many in the region considered Vologda neglected by the federal centre. There was, therefore, a high level of support for the nationalist Liberal Democrats, particularly in the countryside. In June 1996 it was reported that the exigencies of his campaign to be re-elected as President prompted Boris Yeltsin to dismiss the local governor, who was subsequently arrested and imprisoned on charges of corruption. The present Governor, Vyacheslav Pozgalev, won 80% of votes cast in a direct election in late 1996. On 22 March 1998 legislative elections were held in the region.

Economy

In 1995 Vologda Oblast's gross regional product amounted to 19,326,800m. roubles, equivalent to 14,292,900 roubles per head. Its main industrial centres are at Vologda, Cherepovets, Velikii Ustyug and Sokol. There are 771 km of railway track in general use on its territory, as well as 13,200 km of roads and 1,800 km of navigable waterways, including part of the Volga–Baltic route network.

Agriculture in Vologda Oblast, which employed some 13.1% of the work-force in 1995, consists mainly of animal husbandry and production of flax and vegetables. The region is famous for its butter. In 1995 total agricultural output was worth 2,553,800m. roubles. The territory imports around one-half of its electrical energy from other Oblasts (Kostroma, Kirov, Leningrad, Tver and Yaroslavl). Its main industries are ferrous metallurgy (the region produces 20% of Russia's iron, 19% of its rolled stock and 18% of its steel), chemicals (11% of the country's mineral fertilizers are manufactured in Vologda Oblast), the processing of forestry products, mechanical engineering, pharmaceuticals, glass-making, light manufacturing, food processing and handicrafts, such as lace-making. In 1995 approximately 31.6% of the region's working population were engaged in industry. The industrial sector generated a total of 18,603,000m. roubles.

The Oblast's economically active population numbered 600,800 in 1995, of whom 18,900 were registered unemployed. Those in employment earned, on average, 499,000 roubles per month. The 1995 budget showed a deficit of 37,300m. roubles. Total foreign investment in the Oblast in that year amounted to US $20.00m. In January 1996 there were some 4,400 small businesses in operation.

Directory

Governor: VYACHESLAV YEVGENIYEVICH POZGALEV; Vologodskaya obl., 160035 Vologda, ul. Gertsena 2; tel. (8172) 72-07-64; fax (8172) 25-15-54.

Chairman of the Legislative Assembly: GENNADII TIMOFEYEVICH KHRIPEL; tel. (8172) 25-11-33.

Permanent Representative of the President of the Russian Federation: ALEKSEI ALEKSEYEVICH TITOV; tel. (81722) 72-93-95.

Head of the Regional Representation in Moscow: VLADIMIR SERGEYEVICH SMIRNOV; tel. (095) 905-77-96.

Head of Vologda City Administration: ALEKSEI SERGEYEVICH YAKUNICHEV; Vologodskaya obl., 160035 Vologda, ul. Kamennyi most 4; tel. (81722) 72-00-42; fax (81722) 72-25-59.

Voronezh

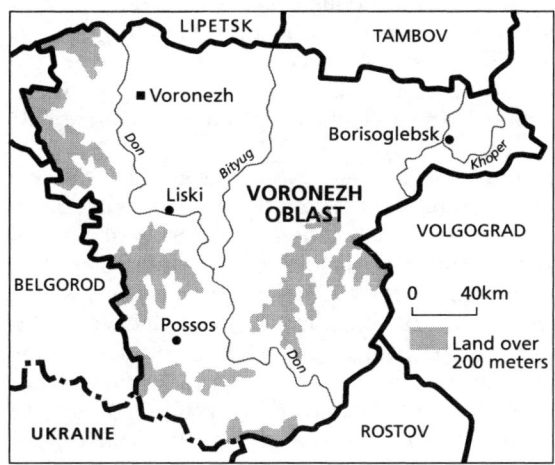

Voronezh Oblast is situated in the centre of the Eastern European Plain on the middle reaches of the Volga. It forms part of the Central Chernozem Economic Area. There is a short border with Ukraine in the south. Of the neighbouring Russian federal territories, Belgorod and Kursk lie to the west, Lipetsk and Tambov to the north, a short border with Saratov in the north-east, Volgograd to the east and Rostov to the south-east. The west of the territory is situated within the Central Russian Highlands and the east in the Oka-Don Lowlands. Its main rivers are the Don, the Khoper and the Bityug. The Voronezh region occupies an area of 52,400 sq km (20,230 sq miles) and is divided into 32 administrative districts and 15 cities. The Oblast's estimated population at 1 January 1996 was 2,504,000, of whom 61.6% lived in urban areas; its population density was 47.8 per sq km. The region's administrative centre is at Voronezh, which had an estimated population of 909,000 at this time. Other major cities are Borisoglebsk (69,500) and Liski (56,300).

History

Voronezh city was founded in 1586 as a fortress. The centre of a fertile region, the city began to industrialize in the tsarist period. Voronezh Oblast was formed on 13 June 1934. In the immediate post-Soviet years the region remained committed to the Communist Party, which controlled the Regional Duma and in the federal general election of 1995 secured 27% of the regional vote. It was also largely in support of the Communist candidate, Gennadii Zyuganov, in the presidential election of June 1996. Aleksandr Kovalev, the regional governor at the time, although a supporter of Viktor Chernomyrdin's centrist Our Home is Russia movement, did not publicly endorse the unpopular federal Government reforms or speak out in favour of President Boris Yeltsin during his 1996 election campaign. Nevertheless, a Communist and former speaker of the oblast assembly replaced him as Governor following an election held in late 1996.

Economy

In 1995 Voronezh Oblast's gross regional product amounted to 16,535,000m. roubles, equivalent to 6,600,000 roubles per head. The important industrial centres in the Oblast are at Voronezh, Borisoglebsk, Georgii u-Dezh, Rossosh and Kalach. The territory contains some 1,200 km (750 miles) of railway track (of which 60.2% are electrified) and 8,300 km of roads, all but 200 km being paved. The road network includes sections of major routes, such as the Moscow–Rostov, Moscow–Astrakhan and Kursk–Saratov highways. There are 640 km of navigable waterways.

Around 4.7m. ha (11.6m. acres—90% of the total) of Voronezh's territory is used for agricultural purposes, of which 3.1m. ha is arable land. In 1995 around 19.3% of the Oblast's working population were employed in the agricultural sector. The Oblast's agriculture consists mainly of the production of grain, sugar-beets, sunflower seeds, fruit and vegetables. Animal husbandry was also important. Total agricultural production in 1995 amounted to a value of 4,264,000m. roubles. Its main industries are mechanical engineering, metal working, chemicals and petrochemicals, the manufacture of building materials and food processing. In 1995 some 25.3% of the work-force were engaged in industry, the output of which was valued at a total of 9,598,000m. roubles. In 1997 there were five commercial banks, 18 insurance companies and six investment funds in operation on the Oblast's territory. Turnover from foreign trade in 1996 amounted to around US $500m.

The Oblast's economically active population numbered 1,048,000 in 1995, of whom around 23,200 were registered unemployed. The Oblast's average wage in that year was 343,000 roubles per month. There was a budgetary deficit of 20,700m. roubles in 1995. By 1997 some sectors of the economy, such as light industry, food processing and construction materials, were almost entirely privatized. Foreign investment in the region increased dramatically during the mid-1990s: while total foreign capital in 1995 amounted to just US $23,000, by 1997 there were 200 joint or foreign enterprises, established primarily with funds from Belarus, Bulgaria, the Czech Republic, Germany, Liechtenstein, Ukraine, the USA and Uzbekistan. At 1 January 1996 there were around 8,800 small businesses operating in the region.

Directory

Head of the Regional Administration: IVAN MIKHAILOVICH SHABANOV; Voronezhskaya obl., 394015 Voronezh, pl. Lenina 1; tel. (0732) 55-27-37; fax (0732) 55-38-78.

Chairman of the Regional Duma: ANATOLII SERGEYEVICH GOLINSOV; tel. (0732) 55-06-88; fax (0732) 55-38-78.

Permanent Representative of the President of the Russian Federation: BORIS SERGEYEVICH KUZNETSOV; tel. (0732) 55-34-24.

Head of the Regional Representation in Moscow: VLADIMIR PETROVICH ANISH-CHEV; tel. (095) 299-67-35.

Head of Voronezh City Administration (Mayor): ALEKSANDR NIKOLAYEVICH TSAPIN; Voronezhskaya obl., 394067 Voronezh, ul. Plekhanovskaya 10; tel. (0732) 55-34-20; fax (0732) 55-47-16.

Yaroslavl

Yaroslavl Oblast is situated in the central part of the Eastern European Plain. It forms part of the Central Economic Area. Ivanovo Oblast lies to the south-east, Vladimir and Moscow Oblasts to the south, Tver Oblast to the west, Vologda Oblast to the north and Kostroma Oblast to the east. Yaroslavl city, which lies on the Volga, is some 250 km (just over 150 miles) north-east of Moscow. The region has 2,500 rivers and lakes, its major two lakes being Nero and Pleshcheyevo, and there is a large reservoir at Rybinsk. The Volga river flows for 340 km through the region. Its territory, just over two-fifths of which is forested, covers a total area of 36,400 sq km (14,050 sq miles) and is divided into 17 administrative districts and 11 cities. The estimated total population in the Oblast at the outset of 1996 was 1,451,000, of whom 80.6% inhabited urban areas. The population density in the region was 39.9 per sq km. The Oblast's administrative centre is at Yaroslavl, which had an estimated population of 627,500 in 1996. Other major cities are Rybinsk (246,600), Tutayev (45,700), Pereslavl-Zalesskii (44,800), Uglich (38,900) and Rostov (36,600).

History

Yaroslavl city is reputed to be the oldest town on the River Volga, having been founded *circa* 1024. The region was acquired by the Muscovite state during the reign of Ivan III (1462–1505). Yaroslavl Oblast was formed on 11 March 1936. In the 1990s the region developed a liberal and diverse political climate. A range of interests was represented in the new, 23-seat Regional Duma elected on 27

February 1994. Thus, in December 1995 the federal President, Boris Yeltsin, permitted his appointed Governor to contest a direct election for the post, which he won. At the same time, in the regional results of the elections to the new federal parliament, the reformist Yabloko bloc gained a relatively high 12% of the votes cast (second only to the Communists on 15%). However, in July 1998 the Regional Duma passed a vote of 'no confidence' in President Yeltsin, in support of its federal counterpart.

Economy

In 1995 Yaroslavl Oblast's gross regional product amounted to 14,763,100m. roubles, equivalent to 10,155,500 roubles per head. The major industrial centres in the region are at Yaroslavl itself, Rybinsk, Tutayev, Uglich, Pereslavl-Zalesskii, Rostov and Gavrilov-Yam. There are river-ports at Yaroslavl, Rybinsk and Uglich. Its total length of railway track amounts to 697 km. The Oblast lies on the main Moscow–Yaroslavl–Archangel and Yaroslavl–Kostroma highways. The total length of roads in the territory is 6,689 km, of which 5,926 km were paved. There are also 789 km of navigable waterways.

The climate and soil quality in the region is not favourable to agriculture. Agricultural activity, which employed just 9.5% of the working population in 1995, consists primarily of animal husbandry and the production of vegetables, flax and grain. Total agricultural output in 1995 was worth 2,116,600m. roubles. The main industries are mechanical engineering (Rybinsk Motors is Russia's largest manufacturer of aircraft engines), chemicals and petrochemicals, petroleum refining, light manufacturing, peat production and the processing of agricultural and forestry products. In 1995 industrial output in the region amounted to a value of 12,961,000m. roubles and accounted for an estimated 2% of total production in the Russian Federation (while its inhabitants numbered about 1% of the total population). Industry employed some 35.8% of the work-force in that year.

The economically active population, of whom around 61,100 (9.4%) were registered unemployed, numbered 651,800 in 1995. The average wage was 472,000 roubles per month. There was a regional budgetary deficit in 1995 of 47,500m. roubles. However, Yaroslavl was considered sufficiently viable to have its federal transfers reduced in amount for 1999. Total foreign investment in the region amounted to US $395,000, while at 1 January 1996 there were some 8,300 small businesses in operation.

Directory

Governor: ANATOLII IVANOVICH LISTISYN; Yaroslavskaya obl., 150000 Yarovslavl, Sovetskaya pl. 3; tel. (0852) 22-23-28; fax (0852) 22-34-25.

Chairman of the Regional Government: VLADIMIR ALEKSANDROVICH KOVALEV.

Chairman of the Regional Duma: SERGEI ALEKSEYEVICH VAKHRUKOV; tel. (0852) 30-39-36.

Permanent Representative of the President of the Russian Federation: IGOR AFANASIYEVICH ZARAMENSKII; tel. (0852) 22-01-05.

Head of Yaroslavl City Administration (Mayor): VIKTOR VLADIMIROVICH VOLONCHUNAS; Yaroslavskaya obl., 150000 Yaroslavl, ul. Andropova 6; tel. (0852) 30-46-41.

Federal Cities

Moscow

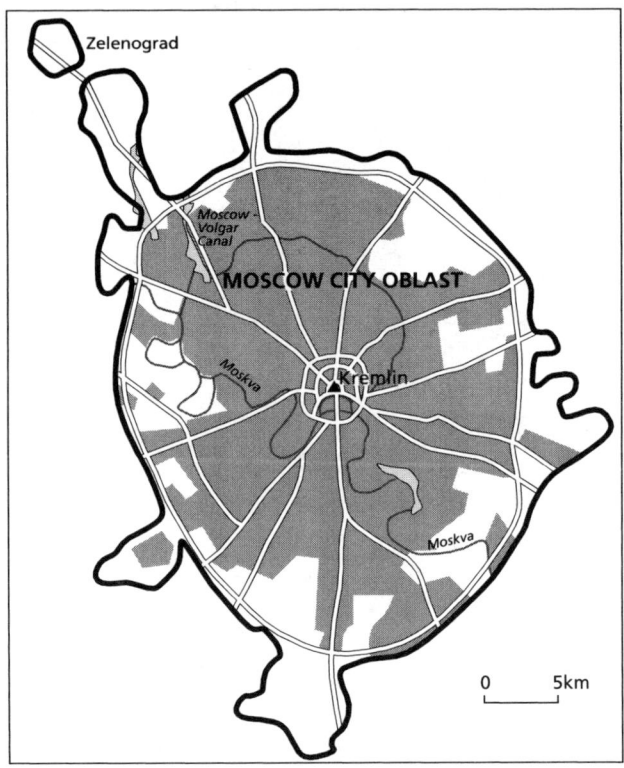

Moscow (Moskva) is located in the west of European Russia, on the River Moskva, which crosses the city from the north-west to the south-east. It is connected to the Volga river system by the Moscow–Volga Canal. Moscow is included in the Central Economic Area. The city's total area is 994 sq km (384 sq miles), and it consists of nine administrative districts and the town of Zelenograd. Moscow is the largest city in the Russian Federation and had an estimated total population of 8,664,000 at 1 January 1996; in 1992 its population had contracted by 292,500 and this trend continued (official estimates put the population at 8,600,000 by the beginning of 1998). In 1997 around 90.5% of the city's population were ethnic Russian, 2.4% were Ukrainians, 1.9% were Tatars and 1.5% were Jews.

History

Moscow city was founded in about 1147. In 1325 it became the seat of the Eastern Orthodox Metropolitan of Russia (subsequently the Patriarchate of the Russian

Orthodox Church) and the steadily expanding Muscovite state became the foundation for the Russian Empire. The centre of tsarist government was moved to St Petersburg in 1712, but Moscow was restored as the Russian capital, hence becoming the Soviet capital, in March 1918.

In the 1980s and 1990s, while reformists enjoyed considerable support in the city, there were also powerful forces of conservatism. On 12 June 1991 the first mayoral elections were held in the city. The Moscow Government, the centre of a new executive power structure, to be headed by the Mayor, was created in January 1992. On 4 October 1993 the Russian President, Boris Yeltsin, ordered the offices of the Moscow City Soviet to be closed. On 7 October the powers of the City Soviet were suspended by presidential decree. Elections to a new 35-member Municipal Duma were held on 12 December 1993. The Duma held its first session on 10 January 1994.

In February 1996 the Municipal Duma voted to hold a mayoral election simultaneously with the presidential election, scheduled for 16 June 1996. The reformist, generally pro-government incumbent, Yurii Luzhkov, was re-elected by a large majority (88.7%). Thereafter, however, Luzhkov began to distance himself from his reputation as a liberal and criticized central government. In September 1997 the international organization, Human Rights Watch, issued a report condemning the local administration's discrimination against non-Muscovites and accusing the Mayor of implementing tough measures to prevent citizens of other former Soviet republics from entering the city. In the same month Luzhkov opposed the federal Government over economic policy, opposing the latter's plans to increase utility costs and declaring himself in favour of state intervention in the economy. Such policies were popular, but the Mayor also created a considerable power base in the city: by the end of 1997 the Moscow City Government owned controlling stakes in a television station and a bank, in addition to a chain of convenience food stores and a network of petrol stations. Furthermore, the prefects in the city's administrative constituencies, rather than being elected, were appointed by the Mayor. The city council, however, maintained its liberal tradition—in municipal elections held in December 1997 the majority of seats were won by the Democratic Choice bloc.

The city's extravagant 850th anniversary celebrations, which were held in 1997 and alleged to have cost some US $60m., were widely seen to have been used by Luzhkov to further his political career. By 1998 Luzhkov, who was outspoken on national issues, was perceived by many to be a probable candidate for the federal presidency (an election was scheduled for 2000). He concluded a number of agreements designed to widen his support in the country (such as economic links with other regions) and, towards the end of the year, he founded a nationwide political movement, Fatherland, and revealed a 1999 city budget which concentrated on social spending.

Economy

In 1995 the city of Moscow's gross regional product amounted to 144,370,300m. roubles, equivalent to 16,611,700 roubles per head (the highest rate in the Russian Federation). There are nine railway stations in the city and 11 electrified radial lines. The metro system includes nine lines and 150 stations and extends for 244 km (152 miles). Its trolleybus and tram routes are 1,700 km long, its bus routes 5,700 km. The public-transport system carries around 6.5m. passengers per day. Moscow's waterways connect with the Baltic, White, Caspian and Black Seas and the Sea of Azov. There are also four airports on the city's territory.

Moscow's industry consists primarily of mechanical engineering, electro-technical metallurgy, production of chemicals, petroleum refining, the manufacture of building materials, light industry and food processing. Industry employed around 18.1% of the city's working population in 1995 (in contrast to the 0.3% engaged in agriculture) and generated 55,880,000m. roubles. The Moskvich Automobile Plant is one of the city's major companies, although at the end of 1997 it was producing just 3,000 cars per month, compared with its maximum capacity of 160,000, a situation that necessitated the restructuring of the plant's production. Services were also important to the territorial economy, with the city authorities having successfully consolidated its leading position within Russia during the reform period of the 1990s: in 1992–95 significant changes occurred in the structure of Moscow's economy—industrial production declined by 52%, while financial institutions, such as commercial banks, joint-stock companies and commodities and stock exchanges increased). By 1997 there were around 1,000 commercial banks in the city, although the financial crisis of August 1998 seemed likely to ensure a restructuring of the sector. As the Russian capital, the city was the site of a large number of government offices, as well as the centre for major business and financial companies. Tourism was another important service industry.

The economic problems of the 1990s were less accentuated in Moscow than in the rest of Russia—the economically active population grew from 4.7m. in 1992 to 5.2m. in 1995. There were some 27,900 (0.5%) registered unemployed in the city in 1995. Those in employment earned, on average, 1,804,000 roubles per month, one of the highest rates in the Federation. The 1995 budget showed a surplus of 106,600m. roubles, but the city finances, while undoubtedly healthy, are notoriously lacking in transparency. Capital investment in the city represents around one-10th of that in Russia as a whole. More than one-half of Russian enterprises and organizations involving foreign capital were situated in Moscow. Total foreign investment in the city amounted to over US $1,312m. in 1995. In September 1997 Moscow became the first city in Russia to enter the international capital market and place a Eurobonds issue. Local companies also flourished, in one of the few regions of Russia which could claim significant economic growth during the 1990s. At the beginning of 1996 there were 79,157 small companies registered in the city.

Directory

Mayor: YURII MIKHAILOVICH LUZHKOV; 103032 Moscow, ul. Tverskaya 13; tel. (095) 292-72-38.

Deputy Mayor: VALERII PAVLINOVICH SHANTSEV.

Speaker of the Municipal Duma: VIKTOR MIKHAILOVICH PLATONOV; 103051 Moscow, ul. Petrovka 22; tel. (095) 923-50-80.

Permanent Representative of the President of the Russian Federation: VLADIMIR FEDOROVICH KOMCHATKOV; 121205 Moscow, Kutuzovskii pr. 39; tel. (095) 249-33-41.

St Petersburg

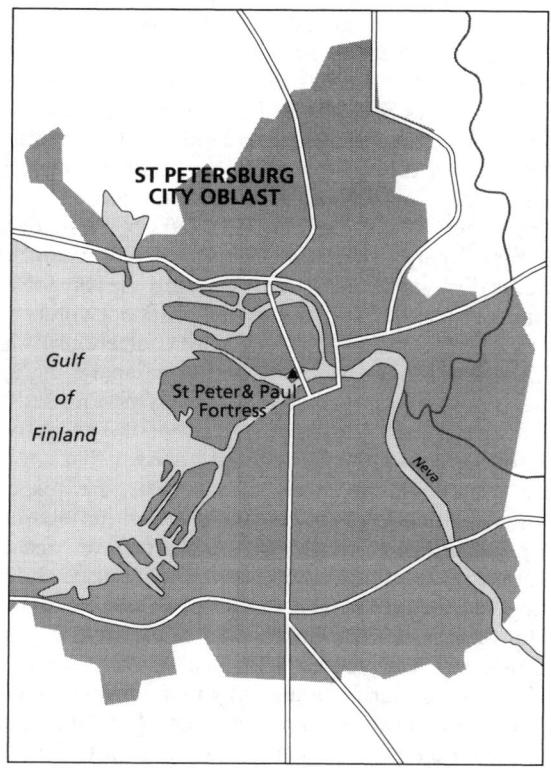

St Petersburg (Sankt Peterburg) is a seaport at the mouth of the River Neva, which debouches into the easternmost part of the Gulf of Finland (part of the Baltic Sea). St Petersburg is included in the North-Western Economic Area. The city's territory, a total of 42 islands in the Neva delta, occupies an area of 570 sq km (220 sq miles—making it the smallest of the Russia's federal subjects), of which its waterways comprise around 10%. There are more than 580 bridges in the city, including 20 drawbridges. The population of the city was an estimated 4,801,000 at 1 January 1996, making it Russia's second-largest city.

History

St Petersburg was founded by the Tsar, Peter I ('the Great'), in 1703 as a 'window on the West' and was the Russian capital from 1712 to 1918. At the beginning of the First World War, in 1914, the city was renamed Petrograd. Following the fall of the Tsar and the Bolshevik Revolution in 1917, the Russian capital was moved back to Moscow. In 1924 the city was renamed Leningrad. During the Second World War it was besieged by German troops for 870 days, between November 1941 and January 1944. In June 1991 the citizens of Leningrad voted to restore the old name of St Petersburg and their decision was effected in

October. On 24 September 1998 the federal President, Boris Yeltsin, approved the administrative merger of the city with Leningrad Oblast, although actual implementation required a number of other stages, including a referendum.

During the federal constitutional crisis of 1993 the city legislature variously opposed and complied with the demands of the Russian President, Boris Yeltsin. The Soviet was finally dissolved by presidential decree on 22 December. On 24 April 1996 the liberal Mayor of the city, Anatolii Sobchak, approved a draft treaty on the delimitation of powers between St Petersburg and the federal Government. Sobchak was defeated in a mayoral election held in May by Vladimir Yakovlev, who was also a liberal (or, certainly, backed by powerful business interests), but soon acquired a reputation for autocracy in government.

The city was one of just two constituent members of the Federation to give the reformist Yabloko bloc a majority in the December 1995 general election. A series of corruption scandals during the mid-1990s damaged support for Yabloko, because it was the dominant party, but also disillusioned potential voters (thus, a low level of participation in the December 1998 legislative elections was to the cost of Yabloko). In addition, the Mayor was powerful in campaigning against the movement. On 14 January 1998 the Legislative Assembly had passed the controversial City Charter, which greatly restricted the powers of the executive. Yakovlev not only challenged it in the courts, but sponsored his own 'list' of candidates in the legislative elections. His influence was enhanced by the resources of the city administration (which owned 38% of the main television station and controlled the leading newspaper). There were also allegations of undemocratic tactics, including intimidation and official harassment, being used in the controversial campaign preceding the elections. The murder of Galina Staravoitova, a federal deputy and a leader of Russia's Democratic Choice Party, in November shocked the political establishment and united reformist opinion for a time. It did not, however, prevent Yabloko suffering at the polls in the following month. The results of the elections gave the Governor's supporters control of the Legislative Assembly. In January 1999, in accordance with Yabloko's decision to become an opposition party in the city, the first deputy mayor (the Yabloko candidate who had withdrawn in favour of Yakovlev in the 1996 election) resigned his office.

Economy

In 1995 St Petersburg's gross regional product amounted to 47,011,600m. roubles, or 16,611,700 roubles per head (one of the highest levels in the Federation). All transport systems in the city have been privatized.

Industry in St Petersburg, which employed around 25.4% of its work-force in 1995 (compared to the 0.5% engaged in agriculture), consists mainly of mechanical engineering, ferrous and non-ferrous metallurgy, electricity generation, manufacture of chemicals and petrochemicals, rubber production, light manufacturing, the manufacture of building materials, food and timber processing and printing. Total industrial production in the city amounted to a value of 23,947,000m. roubles in 1995. The city is also an important centre for service industries, such as tourism, financial services and leisure activities. At the beginning of 1996 there were 117 commercial banks registered in the city, including 54 local banks. The city is an extremely important centre of trade: turnover from foreign trade in 1996 amounted to over US $1,000m. Around 30% of Russia's imports and 20% of its exports pass through the city.

At the end of 1996 the economically active population in St Petersburg amounted to 2.6m., of whom around 45,000 (1.7%) were officially registered as unemployed. The average wage in St Petersburg in August 1996 was 826,100 roubles—between four and five times higher than the national average. In 1995 foreign investment in St Petersburg amounted to just under US $155m. Despite its significance as a trading centre, by the beginning of 1999 St Petersburg was not a strong commercial capital—the number of Western companies it had attracted and the extent of its property development failed to rival those of Moscow. However, compared to other regions of the Federation, it enjoyed fairly sound public finances, a degree of prosperity and less pervasive organized crime.

Directory

Mayor (Governor and Premier of the City Government): VLADIMIR ANATOLI-YEVICH YAKOVLEV; 193060 Saint Petersburg, Smolnyi; tel. (812) 271-74-13; fax (812) 276-18-27.

Speaker of the Legislative Assembly: SERGEI MIRONOV (acting).

Permanent Representative of the President of the Russian Federation: SERGEI ALEKSEYEVICH TSYPLYAYEV; tel. (812) 319-93-54; fax (812) 310-43-54.

Autonomous Oblast

Jewish AO

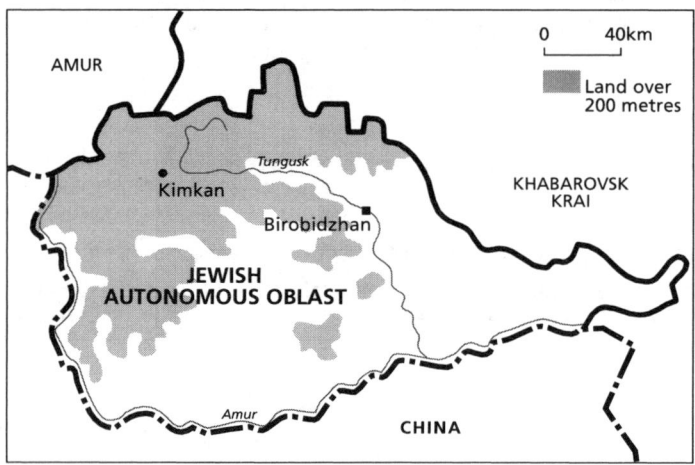

The Jewish Autonomous Oblast (Birobidzhan) is part of the Amur river basin, and is included in Russia's Far Eastern Economic Area. It is situated to the south-west of Khabarovsk Krai (of which it formed a part until 1991), on the international border with the People's Republic of China. There is a border with Amur Oblast in the north-west. Apart from the River Amur, which is frozen for around five months of the year, the region's major river is the Tungusk. Forest, which is particularly concentrated in the north-west, covers more than one-third of its territory. Around one-half is mountainous, with the south and east occupying the western edge of the Central Amur Lowlands. It occupies 36,000 sq km (13,900 sq miles) and has five administrative districts and two cities. The Jewish AO had an estimated population of 210,000 in January 1996 and a population density, therefore, of 5.8 per sq km. Around 67.3% of its population inhabited urban areas at this time. The census of 1989 found that ethnic Russians accounted for some 83.2% of the Autonomous Oblast's population and ethnic Jews for 4.2%. The regional capital is at Birobidzhan, which had an estimated population of 84,100 in January 1996.

History

The majority of Russian Jews came under Russian control following the Partitions of Poland between 1772–95. The Soviet regime established an autonomous Jewish province at Birobidzin in 1928, but it never became the centre of Soviet (or Russian) Jewry. It was renamed the Jewish Autonomous Oblast on 7 May 1934 and formed part of Khabarovsk Krai until 25 March 1991. In the early post-Soviet period the region remained a redoubt of Communist support. Despite the advice of the Russian President, Boris Yeltsin, at a session on 14 October 1993 the Regional Soviet announced that it would not disband itself. Subsequently, however, the council was replaced by a new body, the Legislative Assembly, elections to which confirmed Communist domination. A gubernatorial election held on 20 October 1996 was won by the incumbent. A wage crisis in the region in May 1998 resulted in a decree by the Governor, Nikolai Volkov, that the salaries of local-government officials be put towards repayment of wage arrears.

Economy

In 1995 the Jewish Autonomous Oblast's gross regional product stood at 1,188,900m. roubles, equivalent to 5,637,100 roubles per head. Birobidzhan is the region's main industrial centre. There are 530 km (330 miles) of railway track on the Autonomous Oblast's territory. By the late 1990s construction of a bridge across the Amur river, to provide road and rail links with the city of Khabarovsk was nearing completion. There are around 600 km of navigable waterways in the south of the Jewish AO.

Agriculture, which employed some 16.5% of the region's work-force in 1995, consists mainly of grain, soya-bean, vegetable and potato production, animal husbandry, bee-keeping, hunting and fishing. Total agricultural production in 1995 amounted to 374,400m. roubles. There are major deposits of coal, peat, iron ore, manganese, tin, gold, graphite, magnesite and zeolite. The main industries are mechanical engineering, the manufacture of building materials, wood-working, light manufacturing and food processing. Industry employed around 20.7% of the Autonomous Oblast's working population and generated a total of 536,000m. roubles in 1995. In the mid-1990s the region's foreign economic activity was largely concentrated in the Far East, including the People's Republic of China and Japan.

Its economically active population numbered 78,900 in 1995, of whom some 2,900 were registered unemployed. The average monthly wage in the Autonomous Oblast was 411,000 roubles at this time. At 1 July 1996 there were 79 enterprises with foreign partners and around 900 small businesses registered in the region.

Directory

Head of the Regional Administration: NIKOLAI MIKHAILOVICH VOLKOV; Yevreiskaya avtonomnaya obl., 682200 Birobidzhan, pr. 60-letiya SSSR 18; tel. (42622) 6-02-42; fax (42622) 4-07-25.

Chairman of the Legislative Assembly: STANISLAV VLADIMIROVICH VAVILOV.

Permanent Representative of the President of the Russian Federation: IOSIF DAVIDOVICH NEKHIN; tel. (42622) 6-98-92.

Head of Birobidzhan City Administration: VIKTOR VLADIMIROVICH BOLOTNOV; Yevreiskaya avtonomnaya obl., 682200 Birobidzhan, ul. Lenina 29; tel. (42622) 6-22-02; fax (42622) 4-04-93.

AUTONOMOUS OKRUGS (DISTRICTS)

Aga-Buryat AOk

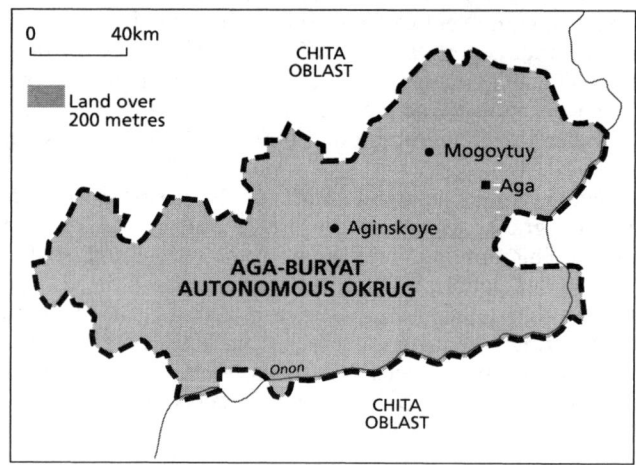

The Aga-Buryat Autonomous Okrug is situated in the south-east of Transbaikal, in the southern part of Chita Oblast. It forms part of the Eastern Siberian Economic Area. Its major rivers is the Onon, and about one-third of its territory is forested. Aga settlement is about 550 km (just under 350 miles) to the east of Ulan-Ude, the capital of Buryatiya (which lies to the west of Chita Oblast). The Autonomous Okrug contains varied terrain, ranging from desert to forest-steppe. The Aga-Buryat AOk occupies a total of 19,000 sq km (7,340 sq miles) and extends for about 250 km (155 miles) from south to north and 150 km from west to east. It has three administrative districts and four urban-type settlements (towns). Its climate is severe and annual precipitation is as little as 250 380 mm (about 100–150 inches) per year. Its population at 1 January 1996 was estimated at 79,000, of whom just 32.4% inhabited urban areas; the population density was, therefore, 4.2 per sq km. In 1989 ethnic Buryats were found to make up some 54.9% of the population, and ethnic Russians 40.8%. The Buryats inhabiting the district are Transbaikal Buryats, who are more closely related to their Mongol ancestors than their western counterparts, the Irkutsk Buryats. The Autonomous Okrug's administrative centre is at Aga, which had an estimated population of 9,300 in January 1996.

History

The Aga-Buryat-Mongol Autonomous Okrug was created on 26 September 1937, as part of Stalin's (Iosif Dzhugashvili) policy of dispersing the Buryat population, whom he perceived as a threat because of their ethnic and cultural links with the Mongolian People's Republic (Mongolia). Its formation occurred as part of the division of the Eastern Siberian Oblast into Chita and Irkutsk Oblasts (the former of which it became a part). It assumed its current name on 16 September 1958.

Under the Federation Treaty of March 1992, the Autonomous Okrug was recognized as one of the constituent units of the Russian Federation. The old Communist élite remained pre-eminent in the district, mainly represented by the Communist Party of the Russian Federation. The area attracted some notoriety in late 1997, when Iosif Kobzon, a popular singer frequently referred to as the 'Russian Frank Sinatra', beat four rival candidates in a by-election for an okrug seat in the federal State Duma; he won 84% of the votes cast. Kobzon was controversial because of the rumour of his close connections with organized crime both within Russia and in the USA.

Economy

The Autonomous Okrug's transport infrastructure is relatively unsophisticated— there are only 70 km of railway track and 890 km of roads, of which 866 km are paved. The economy of the Aga-Buryat Autonomous Okrug (much of the data for which is included in Chita Oblast) is based on agriculture, which consists mainly of animal husbandry (particularly sheep-rearing), fur-animal farming and grain production. Agricultural production amounted to a value of 190,800m. roubles in 1995. The territory is rich in reserves of wolfram (tungsten) and tantalum. Its main industries are non-ferrous metallurgy, ore mining, the manufacture of building materials and the processing of forestry and agricultural products. Industrial output was worth 314,000m. roubles in 1995. The district's main foreign trading partners are the People's Republic of China and Mongolia. In 1995 its foreign-trade turnover amounted to US $2.04m., of which exports (largely consisting of raw materials) comprised $1.77m. The transport, trade and services sectors were fully privatized by this time. The Aga-Buryat AOk is one of the most under-developed federal territories in terms of its health and social-security provision and educational establishments. There were some 700 registered unemployed in the territory in 1995. The 1995 district budget showed a deficit of 2,400m. roubles.

Directory

Head of the District Administration: BAIR BAYAS-KHALANOVICH ZHAMSUYEV; Chitinskaya obl., Aginskii Buryatskii a/o, 674460 pos. Aginskoye, ul. Bazara Rinchino 92; tel. (30239) 3-41-52; fax (30239) 3-49-59.

Chairman of the Duma: DASHI TSYDENOVICH DUGAROV.

Permanent Representative of the President of the Russian Federation: DASHI-DORZHI BUDAYEVICH BUDAYEV.

Head of the District Representation in Moscow: VLADIMIR DYMBRYLOVICH SHOIZHILZHAPOV; tel. (095) 203-95-09.

Chukchi AOk
(CHUKOTKA)

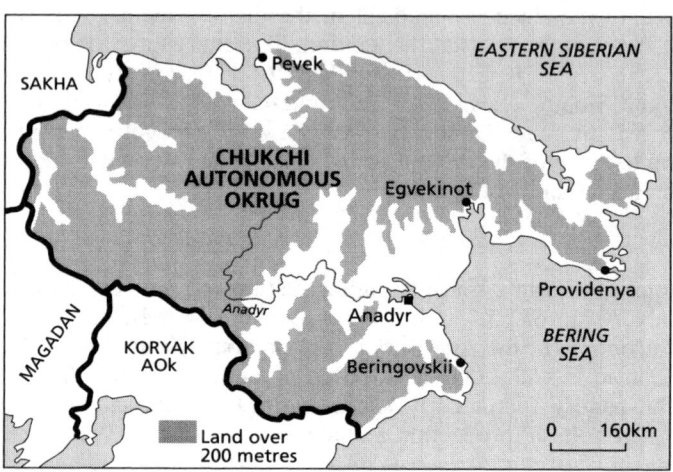

The Chukchi Autonomous Okrug (formerly known as the Chukot Autonomous Okrug) is situated on the Chukotka Peninsula and an adjacent section of the mainland. The district forms part of the Far Eastern Economic Area. It is the easternmost part of Russia and is washed by the Eastern Siberian Sea (Arctic Ocean) to the north and the Bering Sea to the south; the Anadyr Gulf, part of the Bering Sea, cuts into the territory from the south-east. The USA (Alaska) lies eastwards across the Bering Straits. The western end of the district borders the Republic of Sakha, to the west, and Magadan Oblast (of which Chukotka formed a part until 1992), to the south. Also to the south lies the Koryak AOk (part of Kamchatka Oblast). The district's major river is the Anadyr. The Chukchi AOk occupies an area of 737,700 sq km (284,830 sq miles), of which approximately one-half lies within the Arctic Circle, and is divided into eight administrative districts and three cities. Its climate is severe, with the average annual temperature ranging from −4.1°C to −14.0°C. The Autonomous Okrug is a sparsely populated area, with an estimated total of 91,000 inhabitants at 1 January 1996, and a population density of 0.1 per sq km. Approximately 70.1% of the territory's population inhabited urban areas at this time. Around 100,000 people were thought to have left the Autonomous Okrug between 1991 and 1996, reducing the population by about one-half. According to the census of 1989, ethnic Russians represented 66.1% of the region's total population, while only 7.3% were Chukchi. The Chukchi speak the Chukotic language as their native tongue, which belongs to the Paleo-Asiatic linguistic family. Until the 20th century the Chukchi (who call themselves the Lyg Oravetlyan, and are also known as the Luoravetlan, Chukcha and Chukot) could be subdivided into several distinct tribal groups. Traditionally they were also divided into two economic groups, the nomadic and semi-nomadic reindeer herders (the Chavchu or Chavchuven), and the coastal dwellers (known as the An

Kalyn). The district's administrative centre is at Anadyr, which had an estimated population of 13,200 in 1996.

History

Russian settlers first arrived in the territories inhabited by Chukchi tribes in the mid-17th century. Commercial traders, fur trappers and hunters subsequently established contact with the Chukchi and many were forcibly converted to Orthodox Christianity and enserfed. Economic co-operation continued to grow and reached its height in 1905, with the construction of the Trans-Siberian Railway. A Chukchi okrug was created as part of Magadan Oblast by the Soviet Government on 10 December 1930, as part of its policy to incorporate the peoples of the north of Russia into the social, political and economic body of the USSR. It later acquired autonomous status. Simultaneously, collectivization was introduced into the district, which encouraged the assimilation of the Chukchi into Russian life. Throughout the 1950s and 1960s eastern Siberia was rapidly industrialized, resulting in extensive migration of ethnic Russians to the area and a drastic reduction of the territory available to the Chukchi for herding reindeer. Many abandoned their traditional way of life to work in industry.

After 1985 the Chukchi, in common with the rest of the Soviet population, experienced more political freedom. On 31 March 1990 the Chukchi participated in the creation of the Association of the Peoples of the North. They also campaigned for the ratification of two international conventions which would affirm their right to the ownership and possession of the lands they traditionally inhabited. In the early 1990s the Chukchis began to demand real political autonomy: in February 1991 the legislature of the Chukchi AOk seceded from Magadan Oblast and declared the territory the Chukchi Soviet Autonomous Republic (the word 'Soviet' was dropped from the district's title following the disintegration of the USSR in December). This move failed to be recognized by the federal Government, although the district was acknowledged as a constituent member of the Federation by the Treaty of March 1992 and, subsequently, as free from the jurisdiction of Magadan Oblast.

Economy

Alone among the autonomous okrugs, Chukotka is no longer included in a larger territory and there is, therefore, fuller coverage of it in official statistics. In 1995 the Chukchi Autonomous Okrug's gross regional product amounted to 1,344,600m. roubles, equivalent to 14,138,700 roubles per head. Although relatively high, this level of regional wealth was highly dependent on federal transfers. The territory has no roads and very little infrastructure. Anadyr is one of the district's major ports, the others being Pevek, Providenya, Egvekinot and Beringovskii.

The Autonomous Okrug's agriculture sector, which employed some 8.3% of its work-force in 1995, consists mainly of fishing, animal husbandry (especially reindeer-breeding) and hunting. Total agricultural production in 1995 was worth 44,200m. roubles. In 1992 it was estimated that some 500,000 reindeers were raised in state-controlled breeding areas. In the early 1990s increasing demands were made by Chukchi activists for the privatization of reindeer herds, but the usefulness of state support was apparent in the winter of 1996/97, when the lives of some 30,000 reindeer were threatened after heavy rains were followed by freezing temperatures and blizzards, covering the grazing areas in a thick sheet of ice. The region contains reserves of coal and brown coal (lignite), petroleum and natural gas, as well as gold, tin, wolfram (tungsten), copper and other minerals. It is self-sufficient in energy, containing two coal-mines, six producers of electricity and one nuclear power-station. Its main industries are ore mining and food processing. Industry employed some 17.4% of the Autonomous Okrug's working population in 1995 and generated 701,000m. roubles.

Its economically active population numbered 45,500 in 1995, of whom some 2,500 (5.5%—a relatively high level) were officially registered as unemployed. Those in employment earned an average of 1,072,000m. roubles per month, but living costs were high (in common with the rest of the Russian north). The 1995 district government budget showed a large deficit, of 401,700m. roubles. In December 1998 the federal authorities claimed that the payment of wages in the district was, on average, just over seven months late—the worst record on payment arrears of any region of the Federation. At 1 January 1996 there were some 600 small businesses registered in the Autonomous Okrug; an extra-budgetary fund was created for the support and development of small business during 1996 and 1997.

Directory

Head of the District Administration (Governor): ALEKSANDR VIKTOROVICH NAZAROV; Chukotskii a/o, 686710 Anadyr, ul. Lenina 22; tel. (41361) 4-21-26; fax (41361) 4-29-19.

Chairman of the District Duma: VASILII NIKOLAYEVICH NAZARENKO.

Permanent Representative of the President of the Russian Federation: PAVEL MIKHAILOVICH VASHCHENKO; tel. (41361) 4-21-02.

Head of the District Representation in Moscow: MIKHAIL IVANOVICH VORONOV.

Head of Anadyr City Administration: VIKTOR ALEKSEYEVICH KHVAN; Chukotskii a/o, 686710 Anadyr, ul. Lenina 45; tel. (41361) 4-45-33; fax (41361) 4-22-16.

Evenk AOk

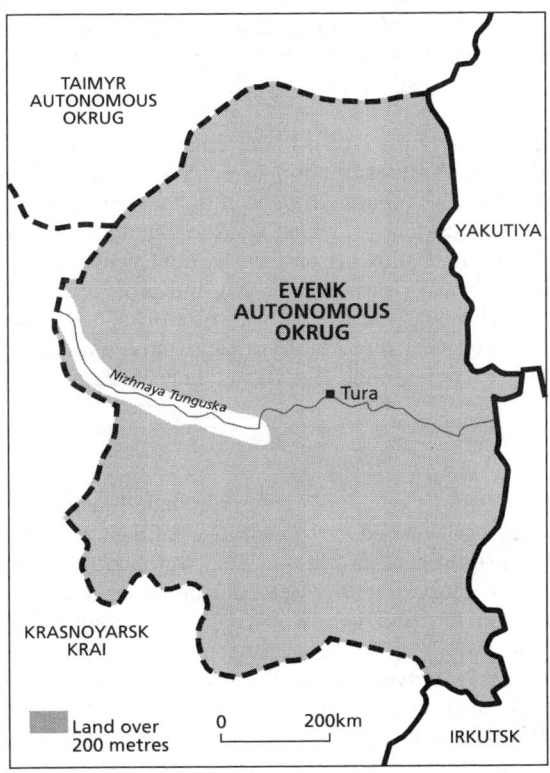

The Evenk Autonomous Okrug is a land-locked territory situated on the Central Siberian Plateau. It is part of the Eastern Siberian Economic Area. The district forms the central-eastern part of Krasnoyarsk Krai, with the core territories of the province lying to the west and south and the other autonomous okrug, the Taimyr (Dolgan-Nenets) AOk, to the north. It has numerous rivers, the largest being the Nizhnaya Tunguska and the Podkammenaya Tunguska, both tributaries of the Yenisei river. The Evenk district occupies a total area of 767,600 sq km (296,370 sq miles), of which almost three-quarters is forested, and comprises three administrative districts and one urban-type settlement (town). At 1 January 1996 the Autonomous Okrug's population was estimated at 20,000, of whom just 29.1% inhabited urban areas. Its population density, of 0.03 per sq km, was the lowest in the Federation. According to the 1989 census, ethnic Russians comprised some 67.5% of the district's population and ethnic Evenks 14.0%. The Evenks' native tongue is part of the Tungusic group of the Tungusic-Manuchu division of the Uralo-Altaic language family. The region's administrative centre is at Tura settlement.

History

The Evenks, who are thought to be descended from a mixture of Tungus and Yukagir culture, were first identified as an ethnic group in the 14th century. Their first contact with Russians occurred in the early 17th century, as Russian Cossacks and fur trappers advanced eastwards through Siberia. By the mid-1620s many Evenks were forced to pay fur taxes to the Russian state. The Evenks' right to land, pasture, and hunting and fishing preserves was officially guaranteed in 1919 by the Soviet Commissariat of Nationalities, but in 1929 forced collectivization of their economic activities was introduced. On 10 December 1930 the Evenk National Okrug was established and the first Congress of Evenk Soviets was convened.

Nationalist feeling among the Evenks later emerged as a result of environmental damage sustained from the construction of hydroelectric projects and extensive mineral development in the region. In the 1980s there were plans to build a dam across the Nizhnaya Tuguska river, which would have flooded much of the territory of the Autonomous Okrug. Following protests by the Evenks, and by the Association of the Peoples of the North (formed in 1990), the project was abandoned. In the post-Soviet period, following the forcible dissolution of the federal parliament in 1993, the District Soviet was replaced by a Legislative Assembly or Suglan. The speaker of the Suglan, Aleksandr Bokivkov, later became head of the district administration.

Economy

Much of the Evenk district's economic data is included in figures for Krasnoyarsk Krai. Despite its size and, indeed, its potential wealth, it remains an undeveloped and economically insignificant producer. The Autonomous Okrug's agriculture consists mainly of fishing, hunting, reindeer-breeding and fur farming. Total agricultural production in 1995 was worth 10,100m. roubles, the second-lowest such total for any Russian region. The estimated combined hydroelectric potential of the district's two major rivers is 81,300m. kWh. Its main industries otherwise are the production of petroleum, natural gas, graphite and Iceland spar, and food processing. In 1995, however, industry generated only 18,000m. roubles, the lowest such total for any federal territory. There were some 300 registered unemployed in that year. The 1995 budget showed a surplus of 7,500m. roubles. At 1 January 1997 there were 82 small businesses registered in the Autonomous Okrug.

Directory

Head of the District Administration: ALEKSANDR ALEKSANDROVICH BOKO-VIKOV; Krasnoyarksii krai, Evenkiiskii a/o, 663370 pos. Tura, ul. Sovetskaya 4; tel. (39113) 2-26-57; fax (39113) 2-26-55.

Chairman of the Legislative Assembly (Suglan): ANATOLII YEGOROVICH AMOSOV.

Permanent Representative of the President of the Russian Federation: VALERII KAZAKOV.

Head of the District Representation in Moscow: ANATOLII SAFRONOVICH SAFRONOV.

Khanty-Mansii AOk

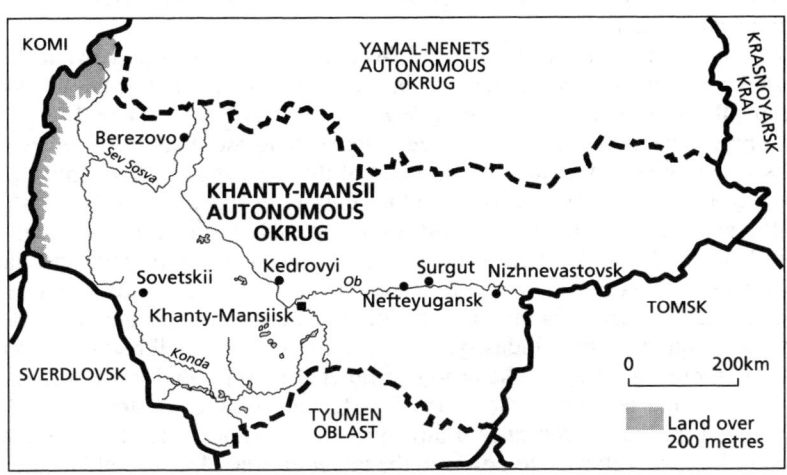

The Khanty-Mansii Autonomous Okrug is situated in the Western Siberian Plain and the Ob-Irtysh river basin. The district forms part of the Western Siberian Economic Area and lies within the territory of Tyumen Oblast. The other autonomous okrug within Tyumen Oblast, the Yamal-Nenets AOk, lies to the north, while to the south of the district's centre lies the region of Tyumen proper. Komi is in the west and Sverdlovsk in the south-west; to the south-east lies Tomsk and east Krasnoyarsk. Apart from the Ob and the Irtysh, the district's other major rivers are the Konda, the Sosva, the Vakh, the Agan and the Bolshoi Yugan. It has numerous lakes, and much of its territory is Arctic tundra (frozen steppe) and taiga (forested marshland). More than one-third of the territory of the Khanty-Mansii district is forested. It occupies a total of 523,100 sq km (201,970 sq miles) and measures about 900 km (560 miles) from south to north and 1,400 km from east to west. There are nine administrative districts in the Autonomous Okrug and 15 towns. Its estimated total of inhabitants was 1,331,000 at 1 January 1996, of whom as many as 91.4% lived in urban areas. The population density was 2.5 per sq km. Ethnic Khants and Mansis, collectively known as Ob-Ugrian peoples, are greatly outnumbered by ethnic Russians in the district: the census of 1989 found that some 66.3% of total inhabitants were Russians, 0.9% Khants and 0.5% Mansis. The Khanty and the Mansii languages are grouped together as an Ob-Ugrian sub-division of the Ugrian division of the Finno-Ugrian group. The Autonomous Okrug's administrative centre is at the town of Khanty-Mansiisk, which had an estimated 34,600 inhabitants at 1 January 1996. Other major cities in the Okrug are Surgut (266,300), Nizhnevartovsk (236,100), Nefteyugansk (96,800) and Kogalym (51,300).

History

The Khanty-Mansii region, known as the Yugra region in the 11th to 15th centuries, came under Russian control in the late 16th and early 17th centuries as Russian fur traders established themselves in western Siberia. Attempts were made to assimilate the Khants and Mansis into Russian culture, and many were forcibly converted to Orthodox Christianity. The territory was created on 10 December 1930, as the East Vogul (Ostyako-Vogulskii) National Autonomous Okrug (adopting its current name in 1940).

From about the time of the Second World War the district became heavily industrialized, causing widespread damage to fish catches and reindeer pastures. Consequently, during the period of *glasnost* (openness) in the late 1980s, many of the ethnic inhabitants of the area began to demand more cautious development policies which would guarantee the survival of the indigenous inhabitants and their cultures. In the mid-1990s the okrug authorities were concerned to establish local control over natural resources. In 1996 they appealed to the Constitutional Court against Tyumen Oblast's attempt to legislate for district petroleum and natural-gas reserves. This dispute partly reflected the domination of different interest groups in the two administrations—the district authorities favoured the federal Government and the energy industry, while the Communists still had strong support in Tyumen Oblast generally. The pro-government faction found most of its support in the urban centres, while the more disaffected rural areas tended to favour the extremist parties. Aleksandr Filipenko, the moderate head of the district administration, was returned to power in the gubernatorial election held in late 1996.

Economy

The Autonomous Okrug's economy (much of the data for which is included as part of Tyumen Oblast) is based on industry, particularly on petroleum extraction and refining. In 1996 it produced 5.0% of Russia's entire industrial output and 56.3% of its petroleum. Its main industrial centre is at the petroleum-producing town of Surgut. Its major river-port is at Nizhnevartovsk. There are 1,286 km of railway track in the district and 15,260 km of roads. Agriculture in the Khanty-Mansii AOk consists mainly of fishing, reindeer-breeding, fur farming, hunting and vegetable production. Total agricultural output in 1995 was worth 462,100m. roubles, while industrial production amounted to a value of 50,801,000m. roubles. Industry is based on the processing of agricultural and forestry products, and the extraction of petroleum and natural gas. Khanty-Mansiisk Oil Company (KMOC) was formed in the mid-1990s by the merger of Khanty-Mansiiskneftegazgeologiya (KMNNG)—a petroleum exploration company in possession of oilfields containing up to 3,000m. barrels of petroleum—and UPC (of Delaware, USA). KMOC is one of Russia's largest independent exploration companies. In 1995 there were some 16,900 registered unemployed in the district. The local budget in that year showed a deficit of 109,200m. roubles.

Directory

Governor: ALEKSANDR VASILIYEVICH FILIPENKO; Tyumenskaya obl., Khanty-Mansiiskii a/o, 626200 Khanty-Mansiisk, ul. Mira 5; tel. (34671) 3-20-27; fax (34671) 3-34-60.

Chairman of the District Duma: SERGEI SEMENOVICH SEBYANIN; tel. (34671) 3-06-00; fax (34671) 3-16-84.

Permanent Representative of the President of the Russian Federation: VLADIMIR MIKHAILOVICH KURIKOV; tel. (34671) 2-33-06.

Head of the District Representation in Moscow: VLADIMIR ALEKSEYEVICH KHARITON; tel. (095) 347-25-26.

Head of Khanty-Mansiisk City Administration: VLADIMIR GRIGORIYEVICH YAKOVLEV; Tyumenskaya obl., Khanty-Mansiisk a/o, 626200 Khanty-Mansiisk, ul. Dzerzhinskogo 6; tel. (34671) 3-23-80; fax (34671) 3-21-74.

Komi-Permyak AOk

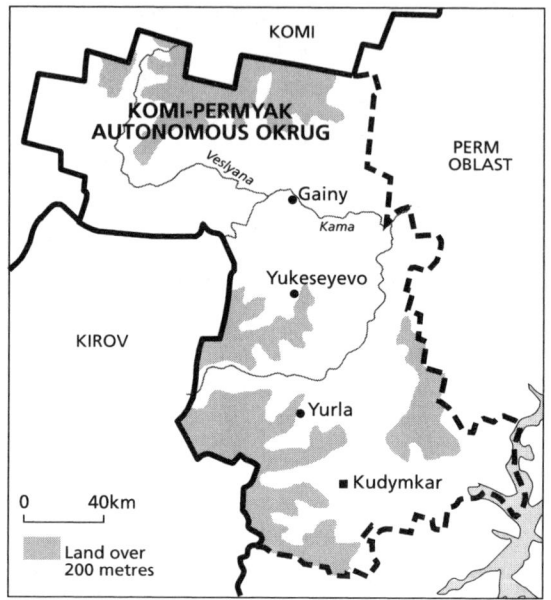

The Komi-Permyak Autonomous Okrug is situated in the Urals area on the upper reaches of the Kama river and forms the north-western part of Perm Oblast. The region is part of the Urals Economic Area. The other neighbouring federal territories are Komi to the north and north-west and Kirov to the west. A largely forested territory, it occupies an area of 32,900 sq km (12,700 sq miles) and comprises six administrative districts and one city. The region's population was estimated at 157,000 at 1 January 1996, of whom some 69.5% inhabited urban areas, and the population density was 4.0 per sq km. According to the 1989 census, of the district's total population, some 60.2% were Komi Permyak and 36.1% ethnic Russian. The Komi Permyaks speak two dialects of the Finnic division of the Uralo-Altaic linguistic family. The district's capital is at Kudymkar, which had an estimated population of 33,700 at 1 January 1996.

History

The Komi Permyaks became a group distinct from the Komis in around 500, when some Komi (Zyryans) migrated from the upper Kama river region to the Vychegda basin, while the Komi Permyaks remained. The Komi-Permyak Autonomous Okrug was established on 26 February 1925. The area frequently perceived the central authorities to be neglectful of their interests, and the harsh economic conditions of the mid-1990s doubtless contributed to the dissatisfaction that produced a significant level of support for the nationalist Liberal Democratic Party. In May 1996 the Autonomous Okrug's administration signed a treaty with the federal Government on the delimitation of powers between the two bodies. An August presidential decree permitted a gubernatorial election to be held in October–November; the post was retained by the incumbent, Nikolai Poluyanov.

Economy

Separate data on the Komi-Permyak Autonomous Okrug is difficult to obtain as it is usually included in the figures for Perm Oblast as a whole. The district's agriculture consists mainly of grain production, animal husbandry and hunting. Agricultural production amounted to a value of 333,900m. roubles in 1995. Its timber reserves are estimated at 322m. cu m. There are significant peat deposits and approximately 12.1m. metric tons of petroleum reserves. Its industry is based on the processing of forestry and agricultural products and light manufacturing; the sector generated 173,000m. roubles in 1995. There were some 5,700 registered unemployed in that year, while the district budget showed a deficit of 12,100m. roubles.

Directory

Head of the District Administration: NIKOLAI ANDREYEVICH POLUYANOV; Permskaya obl., Komi-Permyatskii a/o, 617240 Kudymkar, ul. 50 let Oktyabrya 30; tel. (34260) 2-09-93; fax (34260) 2-12-74.

Chairman of the Legislative Assembly: IVAN VASILIYEVICH CHETIN.

Permanent Representative of the President of the Russian Federation: VIKTOR VASILIYEVICH RYCHKOV; tel. (34260) 2-17-17.

Head of the District Representation in Moscow: ANDREI MIKHAILOVICH YABLOKOV; tel. (095) 202-37-82.

Head of Kudymkar City Administration: ALEKSANDR ALEKSEYEVICH KLIMOVICH; Permskaya obl., Komi-Permyatskii a/o, 617240 Kudymkar, ul. M. Gorkogo 3; tel. (34260) 2-00-47.

Koryak AOk

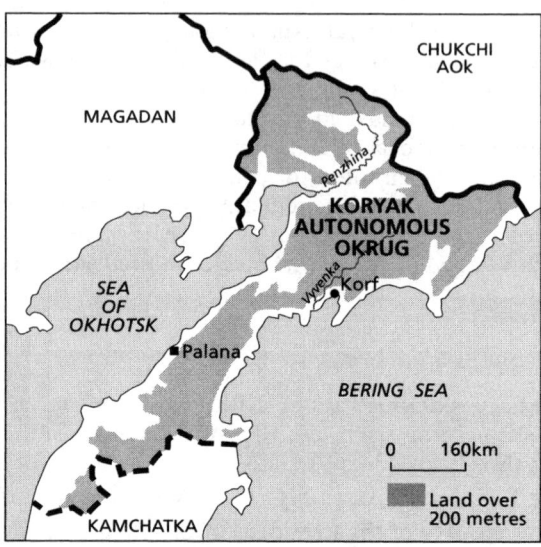

The Koryak Autonomous Okrug comprises the northern part of the Kamchatka Peninsula and the adjacent area of mainland. It forms part of the Far Eastern Economic Area and of Kamchatka Oblast. Its eastern coastline lies on the Bering Sea, and its western shores are washed by the Shelekhov Gulf (Sea of Okhotsk). South of the district lies the rest of Kamchatka Oblast. In the north it is bordered by the Chukchi AOk and Magadan Oblast, to the north and to the west, respectively. The Koryak AOk occupies 301,500 sq km (116,410 sq miles) and is divided, for administrative purposes, into four districts and two urban-type settlements (towns). At 1 January 1996 its estimated total population was 33,300 (of whom just 24.7% inhabited urban areas) and its population density, therefore, stood at 0.1 per sq km. Around one-third of its inhabitants are Koryaks, Chukchis, Evenks and Itelmens. The capital of the district is at Palana settlement.

History

The area was established as a territorial unit on 10 December 1930. Like the Chukchis, the Koryaks have always been divided into nomadic and semi-nomadic hunters and more sedentary coastal dwellers. They first encountered ethnic Russians in the 1640s, when Cossacks, commercial traders and fur trappers arrived in the district. The Soviet Government attempted to collectivize the Koryaks' economic activity, beginning with the fishing industry in 1929, and continuing with reindeer hunting in 1932, a move which was violently opposed by the Koryak community. After the Second World War large numbers of ethnic Russians moved to the area, which was becoming increasingly industrialized. The resultant threat to the Koryaks' traditional way of life, and the environmental deterioration, became a source of contention between the local community and the federal Government during the period of *glasnost* (openness) in the late 1980s. In the first years of independence, however, the local élite were sufficiently placated to be generally supportive of both the federal Government and, indeed, of the reformists. An independent candidate, Valentina Bronevich, was elected governor in late 1996, the only woman to head the administration of a territorial unit in the Russian Federation.

Economy

Most economic data on the Koryak Autonomous Okrug is included in the figures for Kamchatka Oblast, although certain indicators are available. Fishing is the most important economic activity in the district, contributing 60% of total industrial output. The Autonomous Okrug's agriculture consists mainly of reindeer-breeding, fur farming and hunting. Total agricultural output was worth 52,100m. roubles in 1995. The main industries are food processing, the production of electrical energy and the extraction of brown coal (lignite). Industry generated a total of 242,000m. roubles in 1995. At 1 January 1997, out of an economically active population of 17,800, around 1,600 (9.0%) were registered unemployed. The 1995 budget showed a small deficit, of 1,800m. roubles. By 1997 just under two-thirds of enterprises in the Koryak district had been privatized. However, it remained impoverished and dependent on federal subsidies; in December 1998 the Koryak AOk was reckoned to be the second-worst region in the Federation for the late payment of wages (on average, 6.6 months behind).

Directory

Governor: VALENTINA TADEYEVNA BRONEVICH; Kamchatskaya obl., Koryakskii a/o, 684620 pos. Palana; tel. 3-13-80; fax 3-13-70.

Chairman of the District Duma: VLADIMIR NIKOLAYEVICH MIZININ; tel. 3-10-30.

Permanent Representative of the President of the Russian Federation: ANDREI MIKHAILOVICH MESHALKIA; tel. 3-20-87.

Head of the District Representation in Moscow: STANISLAV STEPANOVICH NIKITIN; tel. (095) 932-25-49.

Head of Palana City Administration: VIKTOR GRIGORIYEVICH KORNEV; tel. 3-10-22.

Nenets AOk
('NENETS REPUBLIC')

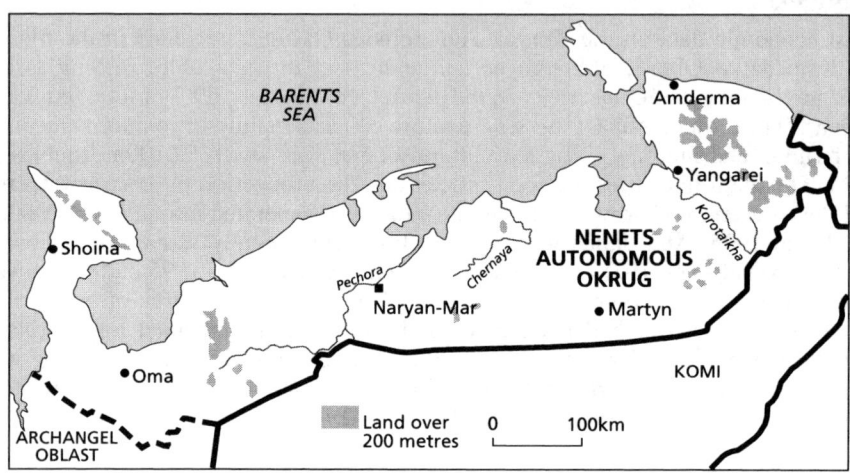

The Nenets Autonomous Okrug (the self-proclaimed Nenets Republic) is part of the Northern Economic Area and is situated in the north-east of European Russia. Its coastline lies, from west to east, on the White, Barents and Kara Seas, parts of the Arctic Ocean. The district is under the jurisdiction of Archangel (Arkhangelsk) Oblast and most of its territory lies within the Arctic Circle. Archangel proper lies to the south-west, but most of the Nenets border is with the Republic of Komi, which lies to the south. At its eastern extremity the district touches the Yamal-Nenets AOk (part of Tyumen Oblast). The major river is the Pechora, which drains into the Pechora Gulf of the Barents Sea just north of Naryan-Mar. The territory occupies an area of 176,700 sq km (68,200 sq miles) and extends some 300 km (190 miles) from south to north and 1,000 km from west to east. For administrative purposes it is divided into one city and two urban-type settlements (towns). At 1 January 1996 the estimated total population of the Nenets AOk was 48,000 and its population density was, therefore, 0.3 per sq km. Around 59.7% of the population inhabited urban areas at this time. At 1 January 1997 some 70.0% of the region's population were ethnic Russian, while 15.6% were Nenets and 9.5% Komi. The language spoken by the Nenets belongs to the Samoyedic group of Uralian languages, which is part of the Uralo-Altaic linguistic group. In 1997 a Norwegian anthropologist claimed to have discovered a forgotten tribe of nomads in the Autonomous Okrug, the Nentser, hitherto unrecognized by the Russian authorities. The Nentser inhabit a vast area south of the Novaya Zemlya islands and comprise around 200 reindeer herders. The district capital is at Naryan-Mar, the only city, which had an estimated population of 19,200 at 1 January 1996.

History

The Nenets were traditionally concerned with herding and breeding reindeer. A Samoyedic people, they are believed to have broken away from other Finno-Ugrian groups in around 3000 BC and migrated east where, in around 200 BC, they began to mix with Turkish-Altaic people. By the early 17th century their territory had come entirely under the control of the Muscovite state. The Russians established forts in the region, from which they collected fur tax. The Nenets Autonomous Okrug was formed on 15 July 1929. During the Soviet period, collectivization of the Nenets' economic activity, and the exploitation of petroleum and natural gas, which resulted in mass migration of ethnic Russians to the region, posed an increasing threat to the traditional way of life of the indigenous population and to the environment. In the early 1990s the Nenets organized public demonstrations against the federal Government's development projects.

On 11 March 1994 the Russian President, Boris Yeltsin, suspended a resolution by the District Administration ordering a referendum to be held on the territory of the Autonomous Okrug. Participants in the referendum were to vote on the status of the district within the Russian Federation. In spite of the President's move, however, the district maintained its style of the 'Nenets Republic'. A district Deputies' Assembly replaced the old legislature and election results in the mid-1990s indicated continued disaffection with federal policies—there was strong support for the party of Vladimir Zhirinovskii. These sentiments rendered the outcome of the December 1996 election to head the district administration uncertain; in the event it was won by an independent candidate, Vladimir Butov.

Economy

As part of Archangel Oblast, despite its claims, the 'Nenets Republic' is usually subsumed into the region's overall statistics, so few separate details are available. The Autonomous Okrug's major ports are Naryan-Mar and Amderma. Its agriculture consists mainly of reindeer-breeding (around two-thirds of its territory is reindeer pasture), fishing, hunting and fur farming. Agricultural production amounted to a value of 33,600m. roubles in 1995. There are substantial reserves of petroleum, natural gas and gas condensate. These have yet to be exploited, although Exxon Arkhangelsk Ltd, an affiliate of Exxon (of USA), in 1997 purchased a 50% stake in the development of oilfields in Timan-Pechora. The district's industry is based on the processing of forestry and agricultural products. Industrial output was worth 443,000m. roubles in 1995. There were some 2,100 registered unemployed in that year, while the Nenets government budget managed to record a surplus, albeit one of just 400m. roubles, largely dependent on federal transfers.

Directory

Head of the District Administration: VLADIMIR YAKOVLEVICH BUTOV; Arkhangelskaya obl., Nenetskii a/o, 164700 Naryan-Mar, ul. Smidovicha 20; tel. (81853) 2-22-69; fax (095) 253-51-00.

Chairman of the Deputies' Assembly: VYACHESLAV ALEKSEYEVICH VYUCHEISKII; Arkhangelskaya obl., Nenetskii a/o, 164700 Naryan-Mar, ul. Smidovicha 20; tel. (81853) 2-21-59; fax (095) 253-51-00.

Permanent Representative of the President of the Russian Federation: SERGEI ALEKSANDROVICH POPOV; tel. (81853) 2-28-64.

Head of the District Representation in Moscow: TATYANA ALEKSEYEVNA MALYSHEVA; tel. (095) 202-63-74.

Head of Naryan-Mar City Administration: GRIGORII BORISOVICH KOVALENKO; Arkhangelskaya obl., Nenetskii a/o, 164700 Naryan-Mar, ul. Lenina 12; tel. (81853) 2-21-53; fax (095) 253-51-00.

Taimyr (Dolgan-Nenets) AOk

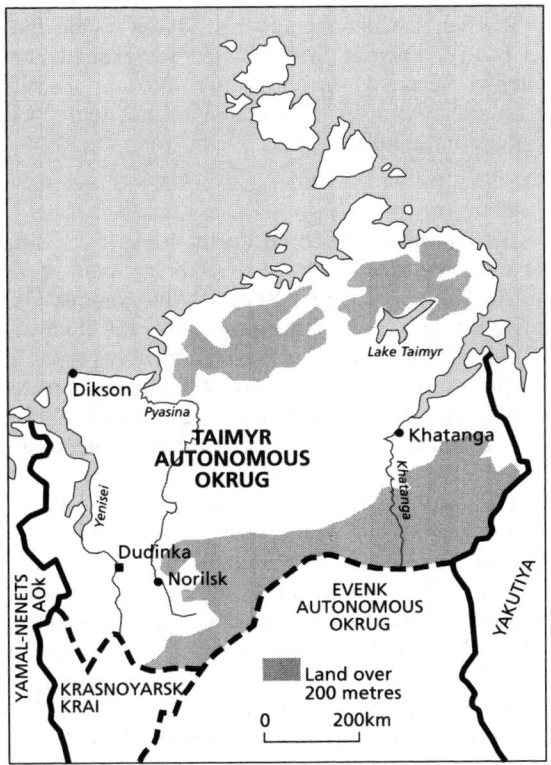

Taimyr (Dolgan-Nenets) Autonomous Okrug is situated on the Taimyr Peninsula, which abuts into the Arctic Ocean, separating the Kara and Laptev Seas. The district comprises the northern end of Krasnoyarsk Krai and, like its south-eastern neighbour, the Evenk AOk, is, therefore, part of the Eastern Siberian Economic Area. The Yamal-Nenets AOk, in Tyumen Oblast, lies to the west and the Republic of Sakha (Yakutiya) stretches eastwards. The Taimyr district's major rivers are the Yenisei (which drains into the Kara Sea in the west of the region), the Pyasina and the Khatanga. The district is mountainous in the south and in the extreme north and just under one-half of it is forested. It has numerous lakes, the largest being Lake Taimyr. The territory occupies a total area of 862,100 sq km (332,860 sq miles), which is divided into three administrative districts and one city. The climate in the Autonomous Okrug is severe, with snow for an average of 280 days per year. The Taimyr AOk had an estimated population of 47,000 at 1 January 1996. Its population density, therefore, was 0.05 per sq km, one of the lowest of any federal unit. Some 66.2% of the total population inhabited urban areas at that time. In 1989 some 67.1% of the district's inhabitants were ethnic Russians, 11.9% Nenets and 8.9% Dolgan. The Autonomous Okrug's administrative centre is at Dudinka, its only city, which had an estimated population of 30,000 in 1997.

History

The territory of the Taimyr district was first exploited by Russian settlers in the 17th century. An autonomous okrug was founded on 10 December 1930, as part of Krasnoyarsk Krai. In 1993, following Russian President Boris Yeltsin's forcible dissolution of the Russian parliament and his advice to the federal units, on 18 October 1993 the Taimyr District Soviet voted to disband itself and a District Duma was subsequently elected as the legislature. The administration was generally supportive of the federal regime of Boris Yeltsin, but there was also significant popular support for the nationalist Liberal Democratic Party.

Economy

As with most of the national territorial formations (excluding the republics), separate economic data are scarce, the district being part of Krasnoyarsk Krai. The major ports in the Taimyr (Dolgan-Nenets) Autonomous Okrug are Dudinka, Dikson and Khatanga. There is limited transport—only the Dudinka–Norilsk railway line (89 km, or 55 miles, long) operates throughout the year. The district's roads are concentrated in its more populous areas. Agricultural production, the lowest in the Federation, was valued at just 9,300m. roubles in 1995, mainly provided by fishing, animal husbandry (livestock- and reindeer-breeding) and fur-animal hunting. There are extensive mineral reserves, however, including those of petroleum and natural gas. The main industries are ore mining (coal, copper and nickel) and food processing. Total industrial production in 1995 amounted to a value of 37,000m. roubles—the Taimyr district is home to Norilsk Nikel, the world's largest producer of nickel, which accounted for some 20% of the world's, and 80% of Russia's, nickel output in the mid-1990s. The plant also produced 19% of the world's cobalt (70% of Russia's), 42% of the world's platinum (100% of Russia's) and 3% of the world's copper (40% of Russia's). Its activity, however, caused vast environmental damage to its surroundings, in the form of sulphur pollution. In 1995 there were some 1,100 registered unemployed in the region. The district administration budget for that year showed a surplus of 44,000m. roubles.

Directory

Head of the District Administration (Governor): GENNADII PAVLOVICH NEDELIN; Krasnoyarskii krai, Taimyrskii (Dolgano-Nenetskii) a/o, 663210 Dudinka, ul. Sovetskaya 35; tel. (39111) 2-53-74; fax (39111) 2-52-74.

Chairman of the District Duma: ALEKSANDR IVANOVICH ZABEIVOROTA; Krasnoyarskii krai, Taimyrskii (Dolgano-Nenetskii) a/o, 663210 Dudinka, ul. Sovetskaya 35; tel. (39111) 2-37-37; fax (39111) 2-12-30.

Permanent Representative of the President of the Russian Federation: VALERII KAZAKOV.

Head of the District Representation in Moscow: OLEG YEVGENIYEVICH MORGUNOV.

Head of Dudinka City Administration: SERGEI MATVEYEVICH MOSHKIN; Krasnoyarskii krai, Taimyrskii (Dolgano-Nenetskii) a/o, 663210 Dudinka, ul. Sovetskaya 35; tel. (39111) 2-13-30; fax (39111) 2-55-52.

Ust-Orda Buryat AOk

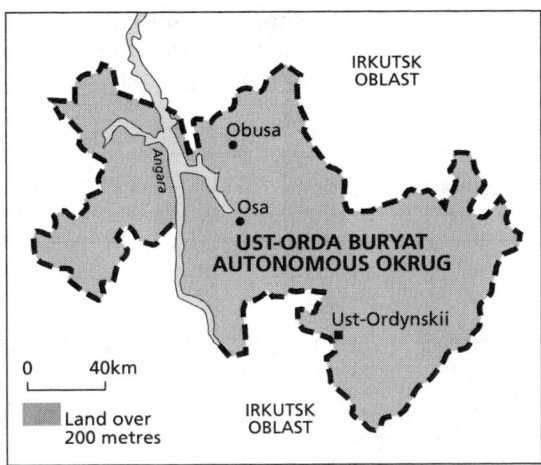

The Ust-Orda Buryat Autonomous Okrug is situated in the southern part of the Lena-Angara plateau. The district forms part of Irkutsk Oblast and, hence, the Eastern Siberian Economic Area. It lies to the north of Irkutsk city, west of Lake Baikal. Its major rivers are the Angara and its tributaries, the Osa, the Ida and the Kuda. Most of its terrain is forest-steppe. It occupies an area of 22,400 sq km (8,650 sq miles) and comprises six administrative districts. At 1 January 1996 the estimated population was 143,000 and the population density, therefore, stood at 6.4 per sq km. Of the total population, according to the 1989 census, some 56.5% were ethnic Russians and 36.3% were western or Irkutsk Buryats. The capital is at Ust-Ordynskii settlement.

History

The Buryat-Mongol Autonomous Soviet Socialist Republic (BMASSR), created in 1923, was restructured by Stalin (Iosif Dzhugashvili) on 26 September 1937. Anxious to discourage nationalism and links with Mongolia, Stalin had resolved to divide the Buryat peoples administratively. The Ust-Orda Buryat Autonomous Okrug, which represented the four western counties of the BMASSR, was established on the territory of Irkutsk Oblast. Essentially a conservative district, the Communists remained the most popular party in the Legislative Assembly (which replaced the District Soviet in 1994). However, the federal Government also had important local supporters. In May 1996 the federal President, Boris Yeltsin, signed an agreement with the Autonomous Okrug's administration on the delimitation of powers between the federal and district authorities. Later that year an independent candidate, Valerii Maleyev, was elected governor.

Economy

Statistical information for Irkutsk Oblast generally includes data on the autonomous district, so separate figures are limited. The district's agriculture consists mainly of grain production and animal husbandry. Total agricultural production in 1995 was worth 861,300m. roubles. Its main industries are the production of coal and gypsum, light manufacturing, the manufacture of building materials and the processing of agricultural and forestry products. Industry generated just 146,000m. roubles in 1995. In 1995 there were around 1,200 unemployed in the Ust-Orda Buryat Autonomous Okrug. There was a budgetary deficit in that year, of 4,300m. roubles. By 1997 just under two-thirds of the industrial sector had been privatized.

Directory

Head of the District Administration: VALERII GENNADIYEVICH MALEYEV; Irkutskaya obl., Ust-Ordynskii Buryatskii a/o, 666110 pos. Ust-Ordynskii, pl. Sovetov; tel. (39541) 2-10-62; fax (39541) 2-25-93.

Chairman of the District Duma: LEONID ALEKSANDROVICH KHUTANOV; tel. (39541) 2-16-87.

Permanent Representative of the President of the Russian Federation: VIKTOR BORISOVICH MODONOV; tel. (39541) 2-10-41.

Head of the District Representation in Moscow: OLEG BORISOVICH BATOROV; tel. (095) 202-89-39.

Head of Ust-Ordynsk City Administration: PETR PETROVICH USOV; Irkutskaya obl., Ust-Ordynskii Buryatskii a/o, 666110 pos. Ust-Ordynskii, ul. Baltakhinova 19; tel. (39541) 2-10-42.

Yamal-Nenets AOk

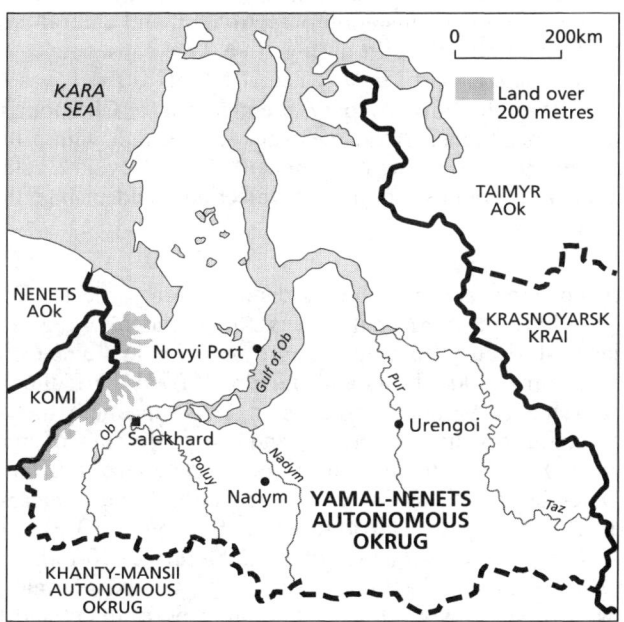

The Yamal-Nenets Autonomous Okrug is situated on the Western Siberian Plain on the lower reaches of the Ob river. It forms part of Tyumen Oblast and, therefore, the Western Siberian Economic Area. The territory lies on the Asian side of the Ural Mountains and has a deeply indented northern coastline, the western section, the Yamal Peninsula, being separated from the eastern section by the Ob bay. The rest of Tyumen Oblast, immediately the Khanty-Mansii Autonomous Okrug, lies to the south. To the west lie the Nenets AOk (part of Archangel Oblast) and the Republic of Komi, to the east Krasnoyarsk Krai (including the Taimyr AOk in the north-west). Apart from the Ob, the Yamal-Nenets district's major rivers are the Nadym, the Taz and the Pur. Around one-10th of its area is forested. The territory of the Yamal-Nenets AOk occupies 750,300 sq km (289,690 sq miles). It comprises seven administrative districts and seven cities. It had an estimated total population (at 1 January 1996) of 488,000 inhabitants. The population density of the region, therefore, was 0.7 per sq km. In 1998 ethnic Russians represented some 62.8% of the population, while Nenets represented just 6.7%. The district administrative centre is at Salekhard, which had an estimated population of 29,600 in January 1996. Its other major cities are Noyabrsk (95,500), Novyi Urengoi (90,000), Nadym (47,800) and Muravlenko (35,000).

History

The Nenets were traditionally a nomadic people, who were totally dominated by Russia from the early 17th century. The Yamal-Nenets Autonomous Okrug was formed on 10 December 1930. Environmental concerns provoked protests in the

1980s and 1990s, and prompted the local authorities (consisting of an administration and, from 1994, an elected Duma) to seek greater control over natural resources and their exploitation. The main dispute was with the central Tyumen Oblast authorities (more pro-Communist than the district's own), and the Autonomous Okrug's rejection of regional legislation on petroleum and natural-gas exploitation first reached the Constitutional Court during 1996. One consequence of this dispute was that the largest single party in the Yamal-Nenets district was Our Home is Russia, which is led by the former federal premier, Viktor Chernomyrdin. Furthermore, as in the Khanty-Mansii AOk, the other federal unit within the territory of Tyumen Oblast, the pro-government incumbent, Yurii Neyelov, retained his post as head of the district administration in the elections held in late 1996.

Economy

Few statistical indicators are available as distinct from those for Tyumen Oblast in general. Agriculture in the Yamal-Nenets Autonomous Okrug consists mainly of fishing, reindeer-breeding (reindeer pasture occupies just under one-third of its territory), fur farming and fur-animal hunting. Total agricultural production amounted to a value of 98,800m. roubles in 1995. Its main industries are the production of natural gas and petroleum, and the processing of agricultural and forestry products. In 1995 the industrial sector generated a total of 15,126m. roubles. The potential wealth of the district generated foreign interest. In January 1997 a loan of US $2,500m. to Gazprom was agreed by the Dresdner Bank group (of Germany), to support construction of a 4,200-km (2,610-mile) pipeline from the Autonomous Okrug to Frankfurt-an-der-Oder on the German border with Poland. This was to be the world's largest gas-transport project and was expected to start phased operation in 1998. In 1995 there were some 7,800 registered unemployed in the Autonomous Okrug, while the district government budget showed a deficit of 122,300m. roubles. District finances were sufficiently strong later in the decade, however, for the federal authorities to cite the Yamal-Nenets AOk as among the three regions with the least problem with wage arrears during 1998.

Directory

Governor: YURII VASILIYEVICH NEYELOV; Tyumenskaya obl., Yamalo-Nenetskii a/o, 626600 Salekhard, ul. Respubliki 72; tel. (34591) 4-46-02.

Chairman of the District Duma: ANDREI VIKTOROVICH ARTUKHOV.

Permanent Representative of the President of the Russian Federation: SERGEI LOMAKHIN; tel. (34591) 4-35-63.

Head of the District Representation in Moscow: NIKOLAI ARKADIYEVICH BORODULIN.

Head of Salekhard City Administration: OLEG VASILIYEVICH DEMCHENKO; Tyumenskaya obl., Yamalo-Nenetskii a/o, 626600 Salekhard, ul. Respubliki 72; tel. (34591) 4-51-35; fax (34591) 4-79-66.

KRASNOYARSK KRAI

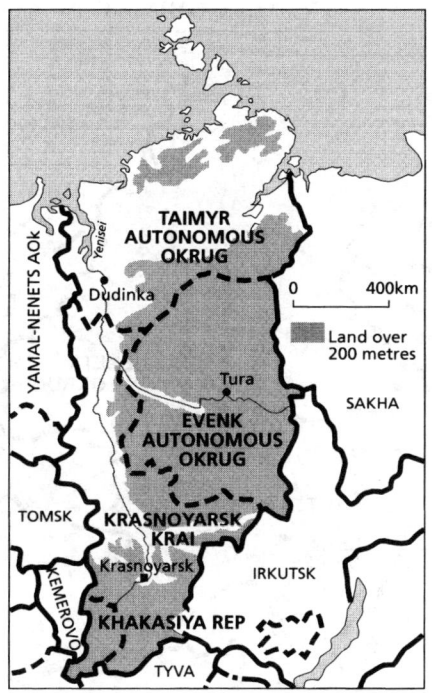

ARCHANGEL OBLAST

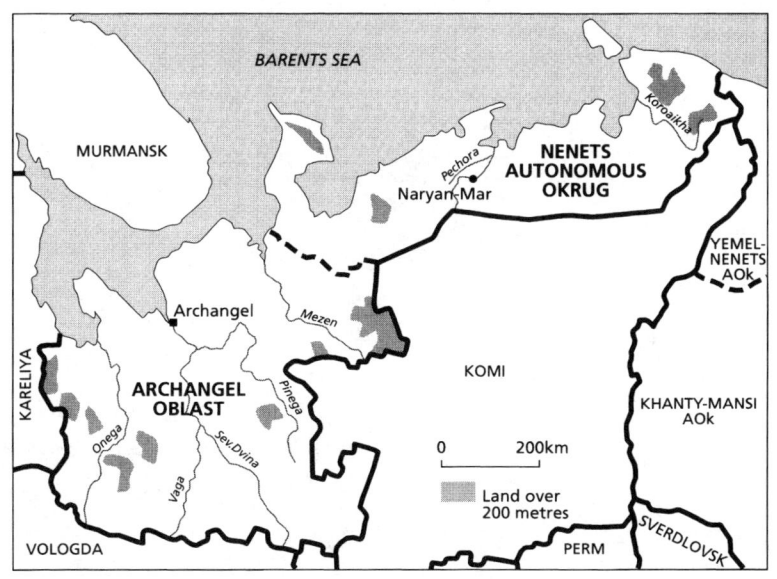

TYUMEN OBLAST

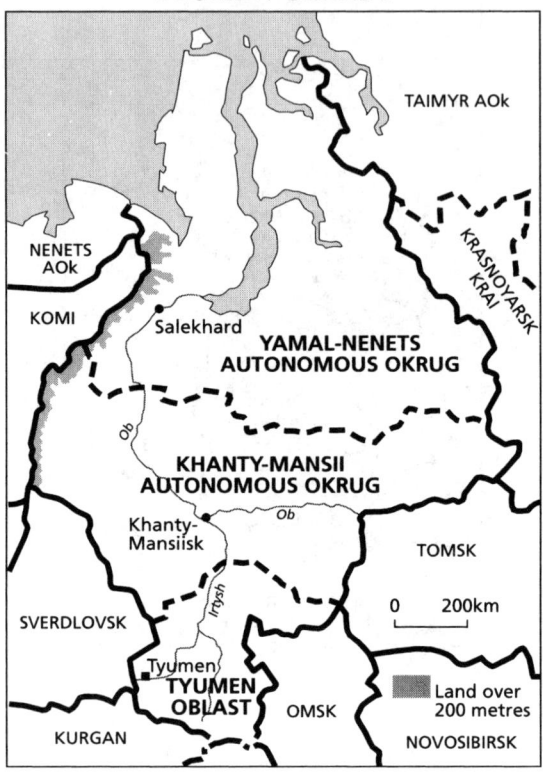

PART THREE
Indexes

Alphabetic List of Territories
(including a gazetteer of alternative names)

	Adygeya	see Krasnodar
	Aga-Buryat AOk	see Chita
	Alaniya	see North Osetiya
107	Altai	Krai
40	Altai (Republic)	Autonomous Republic
126	Amur	Oblast
129	Archangel	Oblast
270	Nenets AOk (Nenets Republic)	Autonomous Okrug
132	Astrakhan	Oblast
	Balkariya	see Kabardino-Balkariya
	Bashkiriya	see Bashkortostan
43	Bashkortostan	Autonomous Republic
135	Belgorod	Oblast
	Birobidzhan	see Khabarovsk (Jewish AO)
137	Bryansk	Oblast
47	Buryatiya	Autonomous Republic
	Chechen Republic	see Chechnya
	Chechen-Ingush ASSR	see Chechnya or Ingushetiya
50	Chechnya	Autonomous Republic
139	Chelyabinsk	Oblast
	Cherkessiya	see Stavropol (Karachayevo-Cherkessiya)
142	Chita	Oblast
256	Aga-Buryat AOk	Autonomous Okrug
	Chkalov	see Orenburg
258	Chukchi AOk	Autonomous Okrug
	Chukot (Chukotka) AOk	see Chukchi
54	Chuvashiya	Autonomous Republic
	Circassia (Cherkessiya)	see Stavropol (Karachayevo-Cherkessiya)
57	Dagestan	Autonomous Republic
	Dolgan-Nenets AOk	see Krasnoyarsk (Taimyr AOk)
	East Vogul AOk	see Tyumen (Khanty-Mansii AOk)
	Evenk AOk	see Krasnoyarsk
	Far Eastern Republic	see Chita Oblast, etc.
	Gorkii	see Nizhnii Novgorod
	Gorno-Altai AO	see Altai (Altai—Republic)
	Gorskaya People's Republic	see Kabardino-Balkariya, etc.
	Ichkeriya	see Chechnya
	Ingodinskoye Zirnove	see Chita
61	Ingushetiya	Autonomous Republic
145	Irkutsk	Oblast
275	Ust-Orda Buryat AOk	Autonomous Okrug
148	Ivanovo	Oblast
254	Jewish AO (Birobidzhan)	Autonomous Oblast
65	Kabardino-Balkariya	Autonomous Republic
	Kabardiya	see Kabardino-Balkariya
	Kalinin	see Tver
150	Kaliningrad	Oblast
68	Kalmykiya	Autonomous Republic
153	Kaluga	Oblast
155	Kamchatka	Oblast
268	Koryak AOk	Autonomous Okrug
	Karachayevo-Cherkessiya	see Stavropol
75	Kareliya (Karelia)	Autonomous Republic
	Kazakh ASSR	see Orenburg

INDEXES

	Kazan (Khanate)	see Astrakhan
158	Kemerovo	Oblast
110	Khabarovsk	Krai
	Jewish AO (to 1991)	see Jewish
	Khadzhi-Tarkhan	see Astrakhan
	Khakasiya	see Krasnoyarsk
	Khalmg-Tangch	see Kalmykiya
	Khanty-Mansii AOk	see Tyumen
161	Kirov (Vyatka)	Oblast
81	Komi	Autonomous Republic
	Komi-Permyak AOk	see Perm
	Königsberg	see Kaliningrad
	Koryak AOk	see Kamchatka
164	Kostroma	Oblast
113	Krasnodar	Krai
37	Adygeya	Autonomous Republic
116	Krasnoyarsk	Krai
261	Evenk AOk	Autonomous Okrug
78	Khakasiya	Autonomous Republic
273	Taimyr (Dolgan-Nenets) AOk	Autonomous Okrug
	Kuban	see Krasnodar
	Kuibyshev	see Samara
166	Kurgan	Oblast
	Kurile Islands	see Sakhalin
168	Kursk	Oblast
	Kuzbass	see Kemerovo
	Kyrgyz ASSR	see Orenburg
170	Leningrad	Oblast
	Leningrad City	see St Petersburg
172	Lipetsk	Oblast
174	Magadan	Oblast
	Chukot AOk (to 1992)	see Chukchi
84	Marii-El	Autonomous Republic
119	Maritime (Primorye)	Krai
	Middle Volga Oblast	see Samara
	Molotov	see Perm
87	Mordoviya	Autonomous Republic
176	Moscow	Oblast
248	Moscow City	Federal City
	Mountain People's Republic	see Kabardino-Balkariya, etc.
178	Murmansk	Oblast
	Nenets AOk/'Republic'	see Archangel
	Nizhegorod	see Nizhnii Novgorod
181	Nizhnii Novgorod	Oblast
	North Caucasus Krai	see Stavropol
90	North Osetiya (Alaniya)	Autonomous Republic
184	Novgorod	Oblast
	Novonikolayevsk	see Novosibirsk
187	Novosibirsk	Oblast
190	Omsk	Oblast
	Ordzhonikidze Krai	see Stavropol
193	Orel	Oblast
195	Orenburg	Oblast
	Ossetia (Osetiya)	see North Osetiya
	Ostyako-Vogulskii AOk	see Tyumen (Khanty-Mansii AOk)
197	Penza	Oblast
199	Perm	Oblast
266	Komi-Permyak AOk	Autonomous Okrug
	Petrograd	see St Petersburg
	Pihkva	see Pskov

284

	Primorye	*see* Maritime
201	Pskov	Oblast
	Romanov-na-Murmane	*see* Murmansk
203	Rostov	Oblast
206	Ryazan	Oblast
251	St Petersburg	Federal City
94	Sakha (Yakutiya)	Autonomous Republic
208	Sakhalin	Oblast
211	Samara	Oblast
	Sankt Peterburg	*see* St Petersburg
214	Saratov	Oblast
	Severnaya Osetiya	*see* North Osetiya
	Shcheglovsk	*see* Kemerovo
	Simbirsk	*see* Ulyanovsk
216	Smolensk	Oblast
	South-Eastern Oblast	*see* Stavropol
	Sredne-Volzhskaya Oblast.	*see* Samara
	Stalingrad	*see* Volgograd
123	Stavropol	Krai
72	Karachayevo-Cherkessiya	Autonomous Republic
218	Sverdlovsk	Oblast
	Taimyr AOk	*see* Krasnoyarsk
221	Tambov	Oblast
	Tannu-Tuva	*see* Tyva
98	Tatarstan	Autonomous Republic
223	Tomsk	Oblast
	Tsaritsyn	*see* Volgograd
225	Tula	Oblast
	Tuva	*see* Tyva
228	Tver	Oblast
231	Tyumen	Oblast
263	Khanty-Mansii AOk	Autonomous Okrug
277	Yamal-Nenets AOk	Autonomous Okrug
101	Tyva	Autonomous Republic
104	Udmurtiya	Autonomous Republic
234	Ulyanovsk	Oblast
	Ural Republic	*see* Sverdlovsk
	Ust-Orda Buryat AOk	*see* Irkutsk
236	Vladimir	Oblast
238	Volgograd	Oblast
241	Vologda	Oblast
243	Voronezh	Oblast
	Voroshilovsk	*see* Stavropol
	Votyak AO	*see* Udmurtiya
	Vyatka	*see* Kirov
	Yakutiya	*see* Sakha
	Yamal-Nenets AOk	*see* Tyumen
245	Yaroslavl	Oblast
	Yekaterinburg	*see* Sverdlovsk
	Yekaterinodar	*see* Krasnodar
	Yugra	*see* Tyumen (Khanty-Mansii AOk)

Economic Areas

Central
Bryansk Oblast	137
Ivanovo Oblast	148
Kaluga Oblast	153
Kostroma Oblast	164
Moscow City	248
Moscow Oblast	176
Orel Oblast	193
Ryazan Oblast	206
Smolensk Oblast	216
Tula Oblast	225
Tver Oblast	228
Vladimir Oblast	236
Yaroslavl Oblast	245

Central Chernozem
Belgorod Oblast	135
Kursk Oblast	168
Lipetsk Oblast	172
Tambov Oblast	221
Voronezh Oblast	243

Eastern Siberia
Buryatiya (Republic)	47
Chita Oblast	142
Aga-Buryat AOk	256
Irkutsk Oblast	145
Ust-Orda Buryat AOk	275
Krasnoyarsk Krai	116
Evenk AOk	261
Khakasiya (Republic)	78
Taimyr (Dolgan-Nenets) AOk	273
Tyva (Republic)	101

Far East
Amur Oblast	126
Chukchi AOk	258
Jewish (Birobidzhan) AO	254
Kamchatka Oblast	155
Koryak AOk	268
Khabarovsk Krai	110
Magadan Oblast	174
Maritime (Primorye) Krai	119
Sakha (Yakutiya) (Republic)	94
Sakhalin Oblast	208

North Caucasus
Chechnya (Republic)	50
Dagestan (Republic)	57
Ingushetiya (Republic)	61
Kabardino-Balkariya (Republic)	65
Krasnodar Krai	113
Adygeya (Republic)	37
North Osetiya (Republic)	90
Rostov Oblast	203
Stavropol Krai	123
Karachayevo-Cherkessiya (Republic)	72

North
Archangel Oblast	129
Nenets AOk	270
Kareliya (Republic)	75
Komi (Republic)	81
Murmansk Oblast	178
Vologda Oblast	241

North-West
Leningrad Oblast	170
Novgorod Oblast	184
Pskov Oblast	201
St Petersburg Federal City	251
and (usually) Kaliningrad Oblast	150

Urals
Bashkortostan (Republic)	43
Chelyabinsk Oblast	139
Kurgan Oblast	166
Orenburg Oblast	195
Perm Oblast	199
Komi-Permyak AOk	266
Sverdlovsk Oblast	218
Udmurtiya (Republic)	104

Volga
Astrakhan Oblast	132
Kalmykiya (Republic)	68
Penza Oblast	197
Samara Oblast	211
Saratov Oblast	214
Tatarstan (Republic)	98
Ulyanovsk Oblast	234
Volgograd Oblast	238

Volga-Vyatka
Chuvashiya (Republic)	54
Kirov (Vyatka) Oblast	161
Marii-El (Republic)	84
Mordoviya (Republic)	87
Nizhnii Novgorod Oblast	181

Western Siberia
Altai Krai	107
Altai (Republic)	40
Kemerovo Oblast	158
Novosibirsk Oblast	187
Omsk Oblast	190
Tomsk Oblast	223
Tyumen Oblast	231
Khanty-Mansii AOk	263
Yamal-Nenets AOk	277

EASTERN EUROPE AND THE COMMONWEALTH OF INDEPENDENT STATES 1999

This award winning reference work accurately and impartially records the very latest economic, political and social developments in this rapidly changing part of the world

- Over 1,000 pages of meticulously researched information
- Individual chapters on the 27 countries that now make up the region
- Analytical commentary from more than 30 specialists
- Comprehensive statistical and directory information

CONTENTS
A series of introductory essays by leading experts in the field of East European affairs, cover key issues and offer a unique overall perspective on the area.
Topics covered include: A Political Perspective on Eastern Europe; Economies of Eastern Europe and of the Former USSR; Economic Transition and the Environment; Religion in the Region; The Former Yugoslavia after Dayton; The Politics of Energy in the Caspian Region and The Russian Rouble Crisis.

Individual country chapters provide:
Geographical profile; chronology; historical, political and economic sections with essays written by specialist contributors; a statistical section covering area and population, agriculture, forestry, fishing, mining, industry, finance, external trade, transport, tourism, communications media and education; a directory section with invaluable information on the constitution, government, diplomatic representation, judicial systems, religion, trade and industry, major companies, transport, tourism, energy, culture, education, social welfare, environment, defence and a select bibliography.

Political Profiles of the Region:
Details of more than 260 leading personalities in the political arena.

What the press said about previous editions
"A mine of statistical information of many kinds, geographical, demographic and economic, it also contains penetrating articles on the history, politics and economy of each of the 27 states concerned, written by specialist contributors." - *Russia Express*

"The amount of information in this book is impressive and could answer a multiplicity of enquiries." - *Reference Reviews*

Eastern Europe and the Commonwealth of Independent States is part of the Europa *Regional Surveys of the World* Series. Other titles in the series include: *The Far East and Australasia; Africa South of the Sahara; The Middle East and North Africa; South America, Central America and the Caribbean; The USA and Canada;* and *Western Europe*.

For further details or a complete list of titles contact Alison Weldon
Europa Publications Ltd., 18 Bedford Square, London WC1B 3JN
Tel: + 44 171 580 8236 Fax: + 44 171 580 3919
E-mail: sales@europapublications.co.uk
www.europapublications.co.uk

OTHER EUROPA TITLES

The Europa Directory of International Organizations

- A new extensive one-volume guide to international organizations around the world
- Over 1,700 international and regional organizations, details their activities, membership, representation, finance, publications, affiliated organizations and lists full directory information
- Defines the changing role of international organizations in today's world
- Includes a chronology charting the major events in the history of the leading organizations and extracts from significant international documents

1 85743 068 9

The European Union Encyclopedia and Directory 1999

- Provides the very latest information on the European Union
- Charts the Union's development from its creation through to the the Treaty of Amsterdam to present day policies and activities
- Includes an A-Z section, introductory articles, a statistical section and an extensive directory, including details of all major European Union institutes and their official bodies
- Details MEPs, their political groups and national parties, members of major committees, Directorates-General and other Commission bodies

1 85743 056 5

Western Europe 2000

- Political and economic information on more than 30 Western European countries and territories
- Includes articles, statistics, directory material and maps
- Contributions from acknowledged experts
- Country surveys include details of geography, recent history and the economy
- Statistics on finance, industry, agriculture, trade, population, education, transport and tourism
- Indispensable for anyone interested in European affairs

1 85743 066 2

The World of Learning 1999

- Forty-ninth edition of a reference book classic
- The definitive guide to higher education world-wide, over 2,000 large-format pages
- Details over 25,000 universities, colleges, schools of art and music
- Names over 150,000 staff and officials
- Details more than 400 international organizations concerned with education
- Fully revised and updated to reflect new developments in the academic sphere
- Exceptional as a world-wide academic mailing list
- Fully indexed for easy reference

1 85743 049 2

The International Who's Who
2000 - Also available in CD-ROM

- Special Millennium Edition of this reference book classic
- A biographical A-Z of our most gifted and influential contemporaries from around the globe
- From heads of state, politicians, and diplomats to the eminent and successful in business, finance, science, technology, literature, film, sport and the performing arts
- Nearly 20,000 detailed biographies
- Entries include: nationality, date and place of birth, education, marital and family details, past career, awards and publications, leisure interests, current address and telephone numbers

1 85743 050 6

The Europa World Year Book 1999

- Unique reference survey of every country in the world
- A large-format two volume work
- Nearly 4,000 pages of the most current information available
- Each country chapter includes an introductory survey, economic and demographic statistics and a wide-ranging directory of essential names and addresses
- Lists over 1,650 international organizations with principal officials and publications
- Invaluable to anyone dealing with overseas markets

1 85743 051 4 (two volume set)

For further details or a complete list of titles contact Alison Weldon
Europa Publications Ltd., 18 Bedford Square, London WC1B 3JN
Tel: + 44 171 580 8236 Fax: + 44 171 580 3919
E-mail: sales@europapublications.co.uk
www.europapublications.co.uk